*Suggestology and Outlines of Suggestopedy*

# PSYCHIC STUDIES

Editor: Stanley Krippner, Ph.D.

WAKING DREAMS   Mary M. Watkins
SUGGESTOLOGY AND OUTLINES OF
SUGGESTOPEDY   Georgi Lozanov
LIVING YOGA   Swami Satchidananda

Other volumes in preparation

# Suggestology and Outlines of Suggestopedy

*Georgi Lozanov*

Translated by
*Marjorie Hall-Pozharlieva and Krassimira Pashmakova*

AN INTER∫ACE BOOK

An INTERFACE book, published by Gordon and Breach, New York

*Copyright* © *1978 Dr. Georgi Lozanov, SUGGESTOLOGIA*

Gordon and Breach Science Publishers Ltd.
42 William IV Street
London WC2 4DE

Gordon and Breach Science Publishers Inc.
One Park Avenue
New York NY10016

Gordon & Breach
7-9 rue Emile Dubois
75014 Paris

*Library of Congress Cataloging in Publication Data*

Lozanov, Georgi
Suggestology and outlines of suggestopedy

(Psychic studies)
First ed. published in 1971 under title: Sugestologiia.
"An Interface book"
Bibliography: p.
1. Mental suggestion. 2. Learning, Psychology of.

I. Title.
BF1156.S8L6813   1977      153.1'52      76-28639
ISBN 0-677-30940-6

This edition is a revised and updated translation of G. Lozanov's book
*Suggestology*, published in 1971, "Nauka i Izkustvi", Sofia, Bulgaria.

# Introduction to the Series

American history is basically a saga of people concerned with external voyages. At first the exploration, exploitation, and settlement of a new continent occupied their attention. This was followed by the development of industrial empires at home and the assertion of diplomatic power overseas. Then came the most distant venture of all – the probes into outer space.

In recent years, a small but growing number of Americans has placed a high priority on internal events and inner growth. Some individuals view this in terms of a spiritual quest while others consider it a voyage of self-discovery or a search for personal fulfilment.

The roads taken to attain these goals vary. Of current appeal are the quick and hazardous openings offered by LSD, the explosive encounters found in sensitivity training, the deep probes provided in Jungian psychotherapy, and the creative routes implicit in development of artistic and scientific creativity. Awareness of Eastern wisdom has helped facilitate the process of many seekers. Yoga, Zen, and the Oriental disciplines are all alternatives to consider, either in their original form or in the synthesis offered by many contemporary scholars.

A synthesis with the external world is offered by research workers in psychoenergetics, psychotronics, and parapsychology who seek to explain the relationship among consciousness, energy, and matter.

A Reformation of Consciousness may well evolve as, for the first time in its history, the entire gamut of human hopes, aspirations, and teachings are available for us to grasp and to incorporate. Our series is a part of this reformation and should shed light upon the road taken by many curious travelers.

Stanley Krippner

*Humanistic Psychology Institute*
*San Francisco, California*

SUGGESTOLOGY is the science of the art of liberating and stimulating the personality both under guidance and alone.
SUGGESTOPEDY is suggestology applied in the process of instruction.

# Contents

# Chapter 1

## Introduction

No one is entitled to deny a science that is unknown to him.

Suggestology, the science of suggestion, and its concomitant penetration into pedagogy, suggestopedy, is a newly developing science.[1] Some of its aspects are being experimented with in various universities and institutes around the world, but the concept of "suggestion" has not yet been fully explained or specified. What is its nature? What are its possibilities? Is the term "suggestion" to be used only in *belles-lettres,* deserving no place in strictly scientific literature? Or is suggestion perhaps to be classified as a kind of hypnosis, a very light type of hypnosis?

Numerous and conflicting questions of this type have been asked by specialists and nonspecialists alike. The answers have often been as conflicting as the questions. It was in the author's country (Bulgaria) that suggestology was chosen as the basic research subject of one of its institutes—the Suggestology Research Institute. This has

---

[1] The particle "suggesto" is related to the Latin verb suggero, suggessi, suggestum, to get under or suggest. The particle "paedy" (pedy) is related to pedagogy and thus is connected with matters of teaching, learning and education. Hence "suggestopedy" denotes education and instruction in which the laws and principles of suggestion are taken into account. Uncontrolled and insufficiently understood suggestion occurs in any form of education, and in any communicative act in general but organized, purposeful suggestion is given absolute prominence in the practice of suggestopedy. However it is necessary to point out that we understand and research the problem of suggestion not in the sense of limiting, constraining, conditioning and manipulating but in the sense of the English meaning of the word "suggestion": to offer, to propose—i.e. to offer the personality a wide choice as Nature does. This extension of the personality's freedom to choose is realized through the organized utilization of the paraconscious contents of the mind which give shape and "volumeness" to the integral conscious—unconscious communicative process and may create a disposition favorable for tapping the reserve capacities of the personality.

made it possible to organize research work quickly, rationally, and to generalize what has been done in world research in suggestology, comparing it with our own experimental results.

Above all, our research has been directed toward the role and significance of suggestion in the process of teaching and learning. There are always favorite teachers whose lessons are easy to remember and easy to understand and in whose classes the discipline is always good. There are also teachers who are just the opposite—whose lessons are difficult to remember and to understand, and who encounter disciplinary problems. Usually both types of teachers are equally familiar with the basic requirements of pedagogy and the different teaching methods. Why then are there differences in results? It is quite obvious that there exists a psychological technique—often not comprehended by the teachers themselves—that helps them to hold the attention of their students. Because of its intimate nature, this technique still remains outside the scope of pedagogy.

Teachers exert an influence on the students not only with what they say, but also with the intonation of their voices, their smiles, gestures, clothes, movements and their whole attitude toward the pupils.

Suggestology could teach the physician not only how to talk with his patients, but the inner approach he must take to gain their confidence. Unfortunately, for general medical practitioners as well as for psychiatrists, the various methods of suggestion remain hidden in a haze of mystic uncertainty. When a press announcement about some interesting and almost miraculous result of suggestion is published, it tends to provoke dogmatic reactions rather than constructive scientific discussion. The scientific facade is dropped, and there is usually a summary rejection of the information without any check on the validity of the facts. The result is rejected by people with no experience in or knowledge of the literature on the subject. The grounds are simply, "this is impossible". It is even more unfortunate when specialists in related fields of science draw conclusions based on psychotherapeutic knowledge of the late nineteenth century.

Modern experimental suggestology has shown that suggestion and hypnosis are not found in rough quantitative relationships as was previously thought. In fact, recent research has shown that hypnosis itself is a special condition outwardly resembling sleep. This aspect of it requires further investigation and it is, therefore, wrong to confuse the nature, fundamental laws, and patterns of the broad psychological concept of suggestion as a communicative factor with the narrow clinical concept of hypnosis as a kind of state, sleeplike altered state of consciousness.

Recent studies have quite definitely proved that suggestion is one of the main factors in the most suitable psychotherapeutic methods for the treatment of neurosis. However the curative effect of psychotherapeutic methods on neurosis made many physicians, at first, underrate the gravity and significance of functional disorders which some tended to consider errors of diagnosis, even "imaginary complaints". This resulted in a nonpsychotherapeutic and, therefore, nonmedical and nonhumane approach by some physicians toward patients suffering from neurosis.

Simultaneously, the notion that psychotherapy can actually have a curative effect—but only on imaginary complaints—gained ground. This was the sole "concession" that conventionally minded physicians made to psychotherapy.

But both in Bulgaria and abroad there have been many cases of favorable therapeutic effect, not only with neuroses but also in some somatic ailments of psychotraumatic genesis. It was further proved that not only can such somatic ailments be improved or cured by suggestion in a waking state, but so could a number of internal, skin and other diseases, none of which have a psychotraumatic genesis. Conservatively minded scientists are silent on this point, simply ignoring the significance of these facts and thus retarding further experimentation and possible use in wider practice.

Suggestology also has its place in art; it could show the actor how to win the audience, the writer how to touch the heart of the reader; the musician how to inspire the listener. In sport, suggestology could show the athlete how to rally his energy and use it at the most strenuous moment to achieve victory. Suggestology has its place in advertising and commerce, too. In fact, there is no sector of public life where suggestology could not be useful.

It can be expected that, with further development, suggestology will elucidate the effect music and the other arts have on different people at given times and in given situations. This will reveal prospects for a better understanding of works of art and for better selection of the effects of the arts. The paraconscious (more or less unconscious) suggestive effect will be sought not only in the arts but in every communicative process. Thus, one day, neither blind chance nor ignorance or malice will be able to cause any negative effect on personal and social life.

Such uses, however, are merely vague formulations and wishes. They are most often considered a matter of the "sensitivity" of the physician, businessman, teacher, sportsman, actor and writer, the friend, parent, husband, wife and child. Today, suggestology is researching the most intimate and subtle psychological mechanisms. Scientific explanations for them are being found and they can thus be put to practical applications. Use of these mechanisms in a pure form frequently leads to surprising results, which for centuries have been interpreted as miracles or supernatural phenomena.

Primitive man dumbfounded before lightning; the Indian fakir on his bed of nails, the children's crusades; Don Quixote not only under the pen of Cervantes but also in real life attacking windmills; whole nations in a state of psychical drunkenness, forgetting logic, facts and morals; the physician who with a few words makes the patient rise from his bed—all these and many other written or unwritten pages in the history of life are, perhaps, to a considerable degree manifestations of suggestion. Suggestion has served many shrines on the altars of many religious, philosophical, and scientific systems and finally it has found its place in science.

Suggestology investigates primarily the ordinary and the more or less known forms of suggestion, relying on authority, infantilization,[1] the arts, double planeness,[1] motivation, setup and expectation—on the whole everything that creates "volumeness" through the paraconscious mind contents. At its present stage of development, suggestology makes use of and elaborates mainly on the emotional and peripheral subsensory mechanisms which are also elements of the factors of suggestion already mentioned. Its subjects are also the classic subsensory or subliminal reactions when the absolute physical qualities of the stimuli are the dominant ones. The experimental trend in suggestology is expanding, and there is good reason to believe that this will lead to considerable theoretical generalizations as well as practical results.

Subsensory (or subliminal) reactions, if provoked by a specific system, can affect the ability to memorize despite the fact that the subjects do not realize their existence. It has been shown in a number of experiments that subsensory reactions can affect man's intellectual activity, his mood and perceptions.

Suggestology, however, does not research only these types of unconscious and unrealized reactions, but also the still insufficiently studied nonspecific subsensory reactions, such as, for example, dermooptical sensitivity. Of interest in this respect is the capacity of the central nervous system to perceive directly, through still unknown receptory fields, the changes in the electromagnetic field in various frequency bands when information interrelations arise. Some authors connect this type of nonspecific subsensory reaction with the so-called extrasensory perceptions studied in parapsychology. These reactions are in some way related to the biological teleinformation of animals. These kinds of phenomena in man, however, are too often placed in the realm of mystical conceptions. Thus, some scientists and materialist philosophers, contrary to their own evolutionist ideas, have rejected the possibility of the existence of these phenomena in human beings. They have failed to reply to mysticism with science's strongest argument—the facts of experimentation—and instead have descended to the level of, "I don't believe it". But disbelieving is believing with a negative sign.

The problems which parapsychology is attempting to set apart in a separate branch of science are still devoid of practical significance. On the other hand, suggestology has taken root most firmly in medical practice, where the ordinary clinical type of suggestion is a basic tool in psychotherapy. In addition, the properly planned use of suggestion, in its broad meaning as a universal phenomenon of unconscious and unrealized (paraconscious) interrelations, is entering pedagogical practice as suggestopedy. Of course, prior to the suggestopedic period suggestion was more or less used spontaneously and intuitively by some teachers, just as in the pre-scientific, pre-psychotherapeutic period of the organized application of suggestion in medicine, it was used by a great many physicians.

Suggestopedy started purely as a psychological experiment aimed at increasing memory capacities in the educational process. This experiment, however, opened the way for a new trend in pedagogical practice. Suggestopedy gradually developed into a method for experimental study of suggestion itself, to determine its basic components, specific features and laws. At the same time, suggestopedy made it possible to penetrate deeper into the paraconscious psychical activity with which the realization of suggestion is directly connected. Bearing in mind that suggestopedy is applied only in a normal waking state, it is an indication of the great value of the experimental results toward the explanation of a number of aspects of unconscious psychical activity under ordinary conditions—without hypnosis and without sleep. Simultaneously, suggestopedy has created conditions in which problems in the means of suggestion, especially the important problem of the dialectical unity of the desuggestive—suggestive process and of getting into pitch with the antisuggestive barriers can be solved.

Suggestopedy, as an experimental method of suggestology, has revealed new laws and patterns of human memory. And, moreover, it has not ended with only experimental results or theoretical generalizations, but has quickly found application in practice. On the basis of research into suggestive supermemory, a number of new methods of teaching have been, and are still being, elaborated. This is quite understandable in view of the fact that the methods used, so far, have had to be in agreement with what was considered to be the capacity of man's creative reasoning and memorizing abilities. Now it can be seen that the newly revealed possibilities, especially of the human memory, open up fresh prospects for teaching.

In the process of teaching and learning, besides the problem of understanding the material given in a lesson, there is that of memorizing and automating it. All instruction and training becomes pointless if the new knowledge, habits and skills are not memorized and automated so that they can be used as a basis for further study.

The present-day rapid development of science and technology, as well as the continuous growth of cultural, economic and political relations between nations, have confronted humanity with exceptional difficulties in the assimilation of useful and necessary information. No way has yet been found to solve the problems in overcoming language barriers and of accelerated assimilation of scientific and technological achievements by either the traditional or modern methods of teaching. A new approach to the process of teaching and learning is, therefore, required if the world is to meet the needs of today and tomorrow. But the question immediately arises of whether we can count on a new methodological approach to save the situation and whether, in the long run, everything is not brought down to man's "limited abilities". If this is assumed to be true, it would doom the rapid development to a standstill in the not-so-distant future because of humanity's supposed psychological and physiological inability to catch up, and still less to stimulate its own further progress.

Fortunately we have no justification in taking such a pessimistic view. Some anatomical and physiological research has shown that in all probability man uses only four percent of the brain's capacities. The other 96 per cent are unactivated potentials. This theory is supported by convincing data obtained in a number of phenomenal cases, as well as in experimental psychological studies on the potential capacities of the paraconscious psychical sphere. We should not neglect the significance of the results already obtained from experiments with hypnosis. It is important to note, however, that some of these results have been obtained only by suggestion in an ordinary waking state, without resorting to hypnosis. Unusual phenomena in psychotherapeutic practice also bear testimony to the rich potential capacities of man.

Last, but not least, by way of argument for the yet untapped capacities of the human being, are the practices in ancient and modern times of various occult and mystical schools and movements. The best-known of these are the achievements of the yogis. For them hypermnesia was necessary to be able to preserve popular experience for coming generations at the then low level of science and technology and, above all, in the absence of literacy at that time.

The Brahmans used to select their most gifted students and, from their earliest age, subject them to special training to develop their memory. It was necessary to learn the vast and ancient Brahman teaching by heart. The *Rig-Veda,* for example, which is the oldest of the four *Vedas* and the oldest known work of Indo-European literature, contains 1017 hymns composed of 10,550 verses, a total of 153,826 words. And if we add the other three *Vedas,* the Upanishads, the Ramayana, the Mahabharata with the Bhagavad-Gita, the Yoga-Sutra, Vinaya-Pitaka, Abhidamma-Pitaka and others, there is an enormous body of literature which they had to know by heart. There were among the yogis certain disciples, known as Stotrayas, whose sole occupation was to memorize these scriptures. Thus should all the ancient books of India be destroyed, the entire literature could be restored from memory if but one of these Stotrayas remained alive.

For instance, Harvey Day (1960) reported that the Indian Audhani, who lived until recently in Bombay, India, knew the Vedas by heart and could repeat 1000 phrases from memory after hearing or reading them only once. He could remember any poem in any language after hearing it once.

In Bombay, in March 1967, a yogi named Shaa, a lawyer by profession, demonstrated for us his hypermnestic abilities for figures and objects. After reading an 18-digit figure only once, he was able to repeat it backwards and in mixed order. He was also able to recognize and memorize about ten objects which were given him to touch for a moment behind his back. He developed these abilities after

*Figure 1* The yogi Shaa demonstrates his hypermnestic abilities for figures and objects—Bombay, Santa Cruz.

three years of intensive yoga exercises (Figure 1).

The Maoris also have a considerable and ancient culture. Because of their lack of literacy and fear that their scriptures might be destroyed, they were formerly trained to memorize everything in accordance with the methods of the Brahmans. When a delegation visited New Zealand, the Maori Chief Kaumatana, for three days on end, recited the history of his tribes over 45 generations (a period covering more than 1000 years) without using any notes.

Individual cases of astonishing hypermnesia are known in other countries as well as in Bulgaria. Quite often this hypermnesia is connected with automatic performance of complicated mathematical operations. For example, K.M., who was recently examined at the Suggestology Research Institute, multiplied 5 pairs of figures, namely

28 × 424, 53 × 541, 23 × 344, 63 × 256 and 27 × 473, in 16.86 seconds. It took the operator of the electronic calculator (ELKA) 28 seconds to multiply these figures. K.M. was also able to add 5 multi-digits (265 + 3864 + 5342 + 75, 412 + 384, 651) in 5.55 seconds, which included the time required to write down the answer. It took the operator 20 seconds to do the same on the calculator. K.M. does not find such computations tiring but rather pleasing to do (Figure 2).

The nature of the yoga hypermnesia mechanism and that of spontaneous hypermnesia have still not been fully elucidated. Psychotherapy put forward the results of hypnotic experiments as a way to the understanding of hypermnesia. Investigations have shown, however, that hypermnestic results are not obtained consistently in hypnosis. Many researchers even find a recession of memorization abilities during hypnosis. Our experiments have shown that the hypermnestic phenomenon during hypnosis depends primarily on suggestions which the experimenter conveys, either consciously or unconsciously, to the subject. This holds good mainly for long-term memory.

Proceeding from such observations and experiments, we reached the conclusion that hypermnesia is the result mainly of a suggestive or autosuggestive setup directed toward the memory potential. And this means that it can be obtained not only in a state of hypnosis but also in a normal waking state, since suggestion is an unceasing universal phenomenon in human psychical activity.

It is important to note once again that if the use of its mechanisms is well organized, suggestion can reveal not only the reserves of memory but many other possibilities as well. Suggestopedic research has shown, for example, that intellectual processes can be activated by creating a suggestive setup of accelerated formation of speech habits and skill in a student's training. When the suggestive setup was introduced in algebra, geometry and physics courses it became clear that the reasoning power was considerably improved, and an attentive attitude was created in the students toward the respective lesson. In this setup man's creative abilities in general were enhanced.

As a universal form of communication and inner re-adaptation related mainly to paraconscious psychical activity and containing the informative and algorhythmical-re-programming aspects activating man's mental and emotional potentials the desuggestive-suggestive, liberating-stimulating mechanisms have proved to be of exceptional importance for understanding the activity of the individual. There is

*Figure 2 a, b.* KM demonstrates extraordinary quickness in solving problems due to his hypermnestic abilities for figures and high automation of brain processes.

insufficient scientific explanation of these very complicated spheres of human psychology, that "territory" that has been ceded to mysticism and speculative dogmatism. It is quite natural that in reclaiming this territory, the natural owner—experimental science—should meet with great counterreactions involving specialists misinformed in this sphere, though otherwise clear-thinking.

We do not doubt that we too have made errors. But through our own experience we have become firmly convinced that there is no error about the main point—the right to existence of the science of suggestology and its newest branch, suggestopedy. We are far from saying that we can supply the ultimate answers to all the problems. We have only taken one of the possible roads to revealing a small part of man's possibilities.

# Chapter 2

# The Beginning

We have been in a position to observe suggestive hypermnesia for long-term memory since the early years of our psychotherapeutic work. Some of the results of our experiments with the suggestive hypermnesia we encountered most often in experiments with hypnosis, were published in 1955:

In the experiments we observed the recalling of things which are generally not retained in the mind of a normal person, things of which he is not conscious, but which do exist and exercise an effect.

It is amazing to realize that while the mind is selectively pinning the attention to the phenomenon that is interesting at the moment, it does not fail to notice quite insignificant and irrelevant things, especially if they are frequently encountered, such as the number of steps climbed every day or the number of glass panes in the window of the study. The possibility of a considerable increase in memory by suggestion alone in a normal waking state was observed very clearly in one of our patients treated in 1955. He was an arc-welder who attended evening high-school classes. He looked very tired when he visited the psychotherapy consultation room for his regular therapeutic session late one afternoon, and complained that he had to go to school in a couple of hours without having had time to memorize a Russian poem that he had been given to learn by heart. So suggestions for raising his general tonus, especially for refreshing his memory, were added to the therapeutic suggestion for his principal ailment. He left the room buoyant and in excellent spirits. The next day he said in a very excited way:

What did you do? It was a miracle. I was asked to recite the poem, so I tried and to my surprise I recited the whole of it without a mistake. I had heard it only once when we had the lesson.

This experiment was later repeated with other people who had to take difficult examinations. In carrying out the individual experiments to improve memory by suggestion in a normal waking state, we became convinced that this method gave better results than training people in a hypnotic state. This gave us grounds for mentioning "suggested hypermnesia in which unsuspected past perceptions are recollected" in a publication in 1963, and in another joint publication with A. Atanassov in 1964, for writing: "There can be no doubt that suggestive hypermnesia does exist".

## FIRST GROUP EXPERIMENTS WITH SUGGESTIVE HYPERMNESIA

Conditions for experiments to improve memorization by creating a pleasant suggestive atmosphere in groups already formed to study foreign languages were provided only in 1964, in the Department of Psychiatry of the Postgraduate Medical Institute (ISUL). From these experiments we obtained the expected high memorization results and the Pedagogy Research Institute was informed of them. The Board of the Institute then took a decision to begin experimenting immediately under their supervision. All this, however, has its own history.

## SUGGESTOPEDY RESEARCH GROUP

The stages of suggestopedy are of significance not only for suggestopedy itself but also for the development of suggestology, because suggestopedy is not only a trend in pedagogy but an experimental method for suggestology as well. Suggestive hypermnesia is the decisive phenomenon which has spurred on the development of suggestology.

In the summer of 1965, a research group was formed at the Pedagogy Research Institute[1] for the study of problems arising in teaching foreign languages by the suggestopedic system. It took the research group very little time to get organized. In November, of the same year, experimental suggestopedic French and English courses began.

There were 75 students divided up into 6 groups, 3 experimental

---

[1] The Group was set up under a joint ordinance No. 2541, of 26 June 1965, issued by the Minister of National Education and Minister of Public Health and Social Welfare.

and 3 control groups. Each lecturer taught two groups—an experimental and a control group, one after the other the same evening. The experimental groups started immediately with the suggestopedic system, but the control groups, although they studied the same material, were taught by conventional methods. The aim was to see if during the course of the experiment the control groups would keep up with the experimental ones, and the point at which the control groups' further instruction would become impossible because of the accumulation of unassimilated material. At that point the control groups were to become experimental ones. The control groups were not informed of the aims and nature of the experiment, and were told to make every effort to memorize everything they were taught.

Although the quantity of the material was considerable and it was impossible to learn it by any of the conventional methods even if repeated continuously during the day, in order to ensure there was no cheating in the experiment, the students were selected and the courses organized under the following extremely unfavorable conditions.

1) Almost all the students were selected mainly among people who worked and lived at some distance from their place of work, thus leaving little or no free time to learn their lessons outside the courses.

2) Almost all the students were beginners, starting the new language from scratch, with the alphabet.

3) They had only a smattering of other foreign languages, and many had given up learning any foreign language at all because of boredom.

4) The lessons were given every day after work in three academic periods, two being used for revision of the former lesson and the giving of the new lesson, and one for the suggestopedic session. Such a program leaves no free time for homework and if the material is not learned during the lesson, the result is an accumulation of unassimilated material.

5) Most of the students were over 30 years of age.

6) Nearly half the students had nervous complaints at the beginning of the course.

7) The students were told that if they were absent from the course more than once they would have to drop out of it, because they would not be able to keep up with the material. This requirement, of course, deprived them of a certain amount of entertainment outside their work and their courses.

The students in this first large scale experiment, which was observed by a special commission, were grouped according to various factors (see Table 1).

The students in the control groups did not know the nature of the experiment and were surprised by the great volume of material they were given. They decided to show what they could do and not to get behind in learning the material. A competitive atmosphere was thus created. By the eighth day, however, it became impossible for them to keep up with the groups which were taught by suggestive methods. They were visibly tired, on the verge of a nervous breakdown, and protested insistently against the unbearable burden of the program. At the same time the experimental groups were advancing rapidly, they were in excellent spirits, and learned the material without feeling any strain. A short time before the control groups refused to go on with the course, written tests were given to check the amount of material memorized (see Table 2). The experimental and the control groups showed a difference of 21.5 percent in the amount of memorized words. This difference evaluated by $T$-criterion ($T=2.54$) proves significant.

The tests showed the learning peak the control groups reached after which they were unable to learn any new material. Then the control groups began to be trained by the suggestopedic system. They had a feeling of relief immediately when the lessons were given to them in the same way as the experimental groups. After being given desuggestive-suggestive training, the control groups caught up and attained the same level as the experimental ones. Near the end of the course a number of the nervous complaints (headache, insomnia, depression, irritability) which some students had at the start, disappeared.

Under these exceptionally difficult conditions with evening instruction after a full day's work, 60 people completed their courses. All students filled in special questionnaires, both at the beginning and at the end of the course, which supplied the data for Table 1.

The other 15 students, mainly for official reasons (business trips) or for personal reasons (emergency absences for two or three sessions

*TABLE 1   Numbers of Students According to Various Groupings*

| Education | Occupation | Sex | Age groups | Previous training in the language | Knowledge of other languages | Special training | Conditions of health | Free time to study |
|---|---|---|---|---|---|---|---|---|
| High school 22 | Engineers 26 | Men 34 | 19 – 29 17 | Yes: | Yes: | *In the arts:* Fine arts 6 | Past neurosis cases 5 | Sufficient 2 |
| Further Education 53 | Economists 16 | Women 41 | 30 – 39 40 | Little 8 | Little 27 | Literature 10 | Individual nervous complaints before course 30 | Very little 10 |
| | Pharmacists 4 | | Over 40 18 | In high school 9 | Fair 23 | Music 11 | | None 63 |
| | Technicians 5 | | | No 58 | Spoken 12 | *In science* Physics & Mathematics 25 | No complaints 40 | |
| | Bookkeepers 4 | | | | No: 13 | Natural sciences 6 | | |
| | Lawyers 3 | | | | Abandoned learning foreign language because of boredom 21 | Philology 5 | Curative effect from course 17 | |
| | Architects 2 | | | | | Social sciences 8 | | |
| | Students 2 | | | | | None 4 | | |
| | Other occupations 13 | | | | | | | |

TABLE 2    Results of the First Written Tests

| Type of group | Experimental | | | Control | | |
|---|---|---|---|---|---|---|
| Group Index | Ia | IIa | IIIb | Ib | IIb | IIIa |
| No of students in group | 11 | 11 | 14 | 12 | 10 | 13 |
| Percentage of words learned by group | 92.0 | 93.6 | 94.7 | 80.6 | 80.0 | 58.2 |
| Mean percentage | 93.6 ± 5.68 | | | 72.1 ± 14.8 | | |

[a] guaranteed probability 0.95

with subsequent inability to cope with the accumulated material) were unable to complete the course. Only three did not complete the course because of loss of confidence in their own abilities. Practically all those who were hesitant at the beginning—and there were one or two such persons in each group—were able to overcome this feeling of uncertainty and the majority of them became excellent students. Many of those who were absent for a few days because of business trips tried to rejoin the groups but in most cases this proved impossible as they were unable to catch up.

In three groups the new words and phrases were given before the lessons. In this way the new lesson for the day was a kind of review. The percentage of memorization was the same as in the other groups.

In three of the groups the new material was given only in the first, active part of the sessions (omitting the usual second relaxed part). It has been noticed in some previous experiments that memory functions have already begun to intensify in the active part of the sessions. Due to associating, coding and symbolization, the effect of the second part of the session is shifted forward and accumulated over and above the "pure" effect of the first part of the session. It should be noted, however, that the students preferred to have the passive (relaxed) session since then their rest was more profound and what they memorized was more lasting.

Judging from the students' written tests on most of the material, the results were excellent (Tables 3, 4, 5). Their marks were high both in the sessions with more than 100 words and in those with less (Table 6).

In about 20 days the groups in English covered C.E. Eckersley's Book 1, and the groups in French, Mauget's first volume. This is a

TABLE 3    *Results of French Written Tests: Groups 1a and 1b*

| 0400 | | 17 Nov. | 25 Nov. | 29 Nov. | 1 Dec. | 4 Dec. |
|---|---|---|---|---|---|---|
| | | On 100 of the first 500 words % | On 100 of the second 500 words % | 100 words of the first 1000 from Bulg. into French % | Translation of summing up text | Answers to 50 questions on entire material % |
| 1a | H.B. | 100 | 100 | 98 | Excellent 6 | 100 |
| | L.T. | 100 | 99 | 100 | Excellent 6 | 100 |
| | B.G. | 99 | 99 | 92 | Excellent 6 | 100 |
| | P.G. | 100 | 99 | 99 | Excellent 6 | 100 |
| | H.I. | 100 | 100 | 100 | Excellent 6 | 100 |
| | M.P. | 100 | 100 | 100 | Excellent 6 | 100 |
| | B.V. | 100 | 100 | 100 | Excellent 6 | 100 |
| | Z.M. | 100 | 100 | 98 | Excellent 6 | 100 |
| | L.S. | 100 | 99 | 95 | Excellent 6 | 100 |
| | B.D. | 96 | 99 | 97 | Excellent 6 | 100 |
| | Average for the group | 99.5 | 99.5 | 97.5 | Excellent 6 | 100 |
| 1b | TG. | (Absent) | 60 | 90 | (Absent) | 50 |
| | B.B. | 100 | 100 | 100 | Excellent 6 | 100 |
| | S.G. | 98 | 92 | 90 | Excellent 6 | 100 |
| | E.R. | 100 | 99 | 100 | Excellent 6 | 100 |
| | A.D. | 84 | 94 | 60 | Excellent 6 | 100 |
| | L.K. | 100 | 100 | 96 | Excellent 6 | 100 |
| | A.M. | 96 | 98 | 97 | Excellent 6 | 100 |
| | S.M. | 100 | 100 | 100 | Excellent 6 | 100 |
| | B.P. | 99 | 100 | 99 | Excellent 6 | 100 |
| | N.P. | 100 | (Absent) | 97 | Excellent 6 | 100 |
| | Average for the group | 97.4 | 93.7 | 92.9 | Excellent 6 | 95 |

TABLE 4    Results of the French Written Tests: Groups IIa and IIb

|  |  | 17 Nov. | 25 Nov. | 29 Nov. | 1 Dec. | 4 Dec. |
|---|---|---|---|---|---|---|
|  |  | On 100 of the first 500 words % | On 100 of the second 500 words % | 100 words of the first 1000 from Bulg. into French | Translation of summing up text | Answers to 50 questions on entire material |
| IIa | A.K. | 100 | 100 | 100 | Excellent 6 | 100 |
|  | V.M. | 100 | 100 | 99 | Excellent 6 | 100 |
|  | B.B. | 100 | 100 | 99 | Excellent 6 | 100 |
|  | V.G. | 100 | 100 | 100 | Excellent 6 | 100 |
|  | N.B. | 98 | 98 | 99 | Excellent 5+ | 100 |
|  | M.B. | 99 | 99 | 99 | Very good 5 | 100 |
|  | P.A. | 100 | 100 | 100 | Excellent 6 | 100 |
|  | S.A. | 100 | 100 | 99 | Excellent 6 | 100 |
|  | N.B. | 100 | 100 | 100 | Excellent 5.5 | 100 |
|  | Average for the group | 99.7 | 99.7 | 99.4 | Excellent  5.72 | 100 |
| IIb | A.I. | 98 | 92 | (Absent) | (Absent) | — |
|  | B.D. | 96 | 95 | 96 | Excellent 5.5 | 100 |
|  | V.V. | 96 | 86 | 93 | Very good 5-- | 100 |
|  | V.Y. | 100 | 100 | 100 | Excellent 6 | 100 |
|  | T.F. | 97 | 100 | 100 | Excellent 6 | 100 |
|  | K.I. | 96 | 99 | 100 | Excellent 6 | 100 |
|  | M.L. | 100 | 96 | 97 | Excellent | 100 |
|  | N.R. | 97 | 97 | (Absent) | (Absent) | (Absent) |
|  | N.N. | 100 | 100 | 100 | Excellent 6 | 100 |
|  | T.G. | 100 | 100 | 100 | Excellent 6 | 100 |
|  | T.I. | 100 | 100 | 100 | Excellent 6 | 100 |
|  | Average for the group | 98.2 | 96.8 | 98.4 | Excellent (5.83) | 100 |

TABLE 5   *Results of English Written Tests: Groups IIIb and IIIa*

| IIIb | 18 November<br>100 words of the<br>first 500 | 24 November<br>Answers to 50 questions<br>of the enitre material |
|---|---|---|
| D.D. | 88 | 87 |
| N.P. | 95 | 94 |
| V.C. | 89 | 96 |
| S.D. | 83 | 88 |
| M.O. | 89 | 81 |
| N.K. | 98 | 100 |
| M.S. | 99 | 99 |
| T.S. | 98 | 98 |
| S.S. | 94 | 97 |
| K.D. | 99 | 100 |
| Average for the group | $93.2 \pm 15.94$ | $94.0 \pm 15.03$ |

| IIIa | 27 November | |
|---|---|---|
| B.B. | 98 | (Absent) |
| G.D. | 100 | 100 |
| D.B. | 99 | 97 |
| E.K. | 99 | 100 |
| L.V. | 100 | 99 |
| M.S. | 98 | 96 |
| R.D. | 96 | 96 |
| Average for the group | $98.6 \pm 10.56$ | $98.0 \pm 12.0$ |

considerable amount of material, especially when it is taken into account that the groups had only two normal academic hours a day and one hour a day for a suggestopedic session. It must also be stressed that their duties outside the courses were considerable. Not only the students but also the teachers were overburdened with work at this time. They came directly from regular work to teach in these evening courses and remained with them till 11.00 p.m. One of the main reasons the students were able to stand up to this was that the sessions offered them relaxation, rest and recreation.

During the courses the percentage of memorized words and phrases did not seem to fluctuate with the amount of material given in the lesson: small and large numbers of words were equally well memorized. That is why we decided to experiment with the memori-

TABLE 6 Results of Written Tests of Memorized Words Given in Sessions Comprising (1) Less than 100 Words, (2) 100 Words, (3) More than 100 Words, and (4) Words Given Only in Active Sessions

| Ia | 30 Nov. 100 words given on 19 Nov. % | 1 Dec. 70 words given on 24 Nov. % |
|---|---|---|
| H.B. | 100 | 100 |
| D.T. | 100 | 99 |
| V.G. | 99 | 97 |
| V.G. | 100 | (Absent) |
| H.I. | 98 | 100 |
| I.P. | 100 | 100 |
| V.V. | 99 | 100 |
| Z.M. | 78 | 100 |
| H.S. | 96 | 100 |
| V.D. | 97 | 99 |
| Average | 96.7 | 99.4 |

| IIa | 29 Nov. 135 words from 2 sessions only active % | 1 Dec. 110 words % | 2 Dec. 60 words % |
|---|---|---|---|
| A.E. | 100 | 100 | 100 |
| V.M. | 92 | 100 | 100 |
| V.V. | 100 | 100 | 100 |
| V.P. | 100 | 100 | 100 |
| I.V. | 100 | 100 | 100 |
| M.B. | 100 | 100 | 100 |
| N.I. | 100 | 100 | 100 |
| R.A. | 100 | 100 | 100 |
| S.A. | 100 | 100 | 100 |
| — | — | — | — |
| Average | 99.1 | 100 | 100 |

| Ib | 30 Nov. 150 words given on 20 Nov. % | 1 Dec. 80 words given on 24 Nov. % | 1 Dec. 70 words with active session on 26 Nov. % |
|---|---|---|---|
| T.G. | (Absent) | (Absent) | (Absent) |
| V.V. | 100 | 100 | 100 |
| S.G. | 87 | 98 | 93 |
| E.R. | 98 | 99 | 100 |
| A.D. | 92 | 95 | 89 |
| L.K. | 97 | 99 | 99 |
| A.M. | 97 | 97 | 100 |
| S.M. | 100 | 99 | 100 |
| B.P. | 99 | 98 | 100 |
| N.P. | 95 | 99 | 99 |
| Average | 96.1 | 98.2 | 97.8 |

zation of the meanings of 500 new words. Two groups of volunteers (one of 6 and the other of 7 students) were given 16 lessons in one day from Mauget, Vol. II, a total of 500 words. The new 500 words were given in one three-hour session with a 15-minute break in the middle. The written check was carried out in the following way: in the first group half the new words, in mixed order, were tested immediately the next day, leaving no time for the students to study them. The other half of the words were examined three days later. Both tests proved that there was no difference in the degree to which the words were known. The check of the second group also took place the next day, but of all the words at one. The meanings of all 500 words had been memorized by the students, irrespective of whether they had attended the whole session or only the active part of it (Table 7).

TABLE 7    *Words Memorized When Given in One Session of 500 New French Words and Phrases (The written test includes all the 500 words, given in the session)*

| Name | Age | Sex | % of correct answers |
|------|-----|-----|----------------------|
| | | *Group A* | |
| A.M. | 37 | m. | 100 |
| S.M. | 26 | f. | 100 |
| H.B. | 39 | m. | 100 |
| Z.M. | 40 | f. | 100 |
| H.I. | 28 | f. | 100 |
| N.P. | 31 | m. | 99 |
| Average | 33.5 | | 99.8 |
| | | *Group B* | |
| N.S. | 43 | m. | 100 |
| D.S. | 34 | f. | 100 |
| V.P. | 30 | f. | 100 |
| F.S. | 36 | f. | 98 |
| V.Y. | 34 | m. | 96 |
| R.A. | 25 | f. | 100 |
| Average | 33.7 | | 99.0 |

Some of the students attending the course said that the more words they were given the better they remembered them. The last two large sessions provided corroboration for our assumption that even 1000 or more words can be easily memorized. Thus, the problem of memorization of new words and phrases, as well as the problem of memorization in general, seemed to be on the way to be solved.

The experimental work with the six groups of students taught by suggestopedic methods was conducted, supervised and documented by the Suggestopedy Research Group. At the end of the courses, the Research Group and the Board of the Pedagogy Research Institute with the Ministry of National Education summoned a general meeting of all the students who had taken the courses for a frank conversation and an exchange of views on the suggestopedic method of teaching.

## THE SUGGESTOPEDY RESEARCH GROUP'S REPORT OF THE RESULTS OF THE LARGE-SCALE EXPERIMENT

The Research Group prepared a detailed Report for the Scientific Council of the Pedagogy Research Institute and the Ministers of National Education and Public Health and Social Welfare. What follows is the most important part of this document.

I.   In accordance with Ordinance 2541, June 26, 1965, of the two Ministries, the Research Group, set up at the Pedagogy Research Institute with the Ministry of National Education, and supervised by Prof. E. Sharankov, Head of Department of Psychiatry of the Postgraduate Medical Institute (ISUL), began its work of research into Dr. Georgi Lozanov's system of teaching and learning foreign languages, called suggestopedy, on July 6th, 1965.

The preparatory work of the Pedagogy Research Institute was to find suitable premises and adequate equipment, while that of Dr. G. Lozanov (G.L.) and the teachers was to select students for the groups and to arrange the programmes.

Provisions were also made for members of the Research Group to observe the experimental work of each teacher and the work of each experimental and control group.

II.   At the beginning of November, Dr. G.L. and the three teachers began giving their suggestopedic lessons in three quiet rooms, on different floors of the Moskva Hotel on Triaditsa Street. The Board of the Pedagogy Research Institute, duly ensured the necessary funds and created favorable conditions for the normal running of the courses. Six training groups were formed: three experimental (by suggestopedic methods) and three control (by conventional methods). Each group comprised of 10—12 students, mainly beginners. Classes were held for 30 days on every working day from 5.00 to 8.00 p.m. for some groups, and from 8.00 to 11.00 p.m. for the others. Each lesson lasted for three academic hours (one academic hour = 45 min.).

The lessons themselves, for both the experimental and control groups, were documented to the greatest possible extent and observed in various aspects: the teaching approach to the lesson, the degree of assimilation, the condition and the spirits of the students at all times during classes, and the achievements in the different groups. The classes were attended by members of the Research Group.

III.   The work of the Research Group was guided by the following considerations:

1) We found no scientific, theoretical and experimental data on teaching and learning by suggestion in a waking state in the available Bulgarian and foreign literature dealing with educational problems. In it the problems on memory and memorization are elucidated in many other different aspects: historical, medical, pedagogical, microbiochemical, etc. New methods of teaching also vary: learning in sleep (hypnopedy), learning in sleep and hypnosis (hypno-hypnosopedy), all day "immersion" of a single student who is subjected to verbal "bombardments" throughout the day by three instructors working in shifts, etc.

However, in this literature there is no mention of any kind of teaching and learning by a method which could be considered similar in theoretical formation and in practical application to suggestopedy. After examining all the available pertinent literature, the Research Group was of the opinion that the suggestopedic methods proposed and applied by Dr. G.L. were unique, unknown elsewhere and unstudied anywhere.

2) The Research Group found that whatever method of accelerated teaching had been used, the theoretical motivation and, above all, the practical results had met with varying receptions and were in part disputed as to their ultimate value. Some were regarded with scepticism because of the possible risk to the health of the student.

3) The suggestopedic methods of Dr. G.L. raised new problems both theoretical and practical which some research group would have to examine and compare with all other related methods of teaching.

IV.   The Research Group's direct observation and the experimental data the members collected were eloquent.

1) The enthusiasm and devotion of the lecturers, who put in six extra hours with the evening experimental courses after a full day's work and family obligations were exceptional.

2) The enthusiasm of the students, all of whom had to overcome many obstaclas in order to attend classes regularly, was impressive.

3) The objective methods we used were: (a) Questionnaires filled in by each student at the beginning and the end of the course; (b) Many written tests were given and these provided a clear picture of the number of words taught and learned, 50–150 in one lesson, and in some cases up to 500; (c) Some tape recordings and films were made of each group and these showed the general atmosphere and manner of teaching; (d) Electroencephalograms of two students

were made before the session, in the active session, in the passive session and after the session.

The following are the electroencephalographic data which established an indisputable waking state: (a) Activation (desynchronization) in the active part of the session, (b) No essential changes during the passive part of the session; (c) Absence of any indication of a state of sleep throughout the entire session.

4) The suggestopedic session consists of an active and a passive part. During the active part the teacher reads the unfamiliar words and phrases three times (with their Bulgarian translation), using a special kind of intonation. The students listen intently and follow the words and phrases on a printed program.

During the passive part the students lay aside the program and relax in a "passive" state of distraction without concentrating their attention on anything in particular. The words and phrases are read again with special intonation by the teacher.

5) The state of relaxation and "passivity" is not sleep, nor is it hypnosis. This is proved not only by the EEG data but also by the following: (a) The students declare that they have not been asleep and fully recollect the whole session, (b) If in some sessions a student begins to breathe more deeply as in sleep (which seldom happens) the teacher immediately approaches him and gives him a light touch so that he does not fall asleep. In some cases students will have made a sign before the teacher gets to them to show they are not asleep; (c) In some cases students have had other engagements before the session was over and have had to leave it. They have always remembered to do so and this has never involved any special effort; (d) Whenever the teacher has put a new or already familiar word deliberately into the text being given, the students have always noticed it and have said they have done so; (e) Whenever the teacher has deliberately omitted some of the words in the text he has always been corrected by the students; (f) The students have always noticed who has come in or gone out of the room during the session.

6) The 60 students who remained in the course until the end showed that they had been able to learn an average of 80 new words every day besides grammar, spelling and pronunciation. Moreover, all this material was acquired only during the two academic hours of teaching and revision, and the one hour's suggestopedic session for the memorization of the new program. There was no time for homework. In some sessions, up to 150 new words were memorized, and in two extraordinary sessions 500 new words were given and learned. There are indications that many more new words could be memorized in one day.

Many of the students assured us that the teaching and learning did not tire them, that in fact they felt rested, and some of their neurotic complaints were cured.

V. The following are the verbatim thoughts of some of the students and of the three teachers at the meeting of the members of the course and the Research Group on the termination of the course.

*A. Students;*

1) A.K., a student in Group 2:

Our dream of easy and quick learning became a reality. We can now take part in an elementary conversation.

2) R.A., a student in Group 2:

This method is simply miraculous and I must go on with the course at any cost. I simply could not believe that I had learned so much. My husband is learning French in another course by another method. He is given at the most 40 words a week. He tries to learn them but when I examine him at the end, he does not know the words well.

3) E.K., a student in Group 3:

I began the course with great fear and hesitation as I suffer from acute neurosis accompanied by headache, nausea and other disorders. After the fourth session I began to take an active and successful part in the work without my noticing it. Although I am very busy all the time, I am at work and have three children at home, I suddenly found that I had lost my feeling of tiredness and my headache. My husband attended a 7 months' course, and after he had been learning the foreign language for 2 or 3 months, and I had been learning in my course for only 10 or 12 days, he was surprised when he examined me to see how many of my 70 words I knew. In his course they learned no more than 25 words a day, and with strenuous training at that, sometimes even until 1.00 a.m. But I, with only 10 or 12 day's' learning, was able to read his textbook and understand the sense though I did come across unfamiliar words. I had no time to do homework as he had, because of my three children. My neurosis reappeared a few days after I had finished taking the course. Actually I rested during the courses and it seems that is the reason that I felt all right.

4) N.K., a student in Group 3:

This course was very pleasant and very useful. If I compare the old ways of teaching and learning languages with the present new method, I see that all the advantages are on the side of suggestopedy. The essential thing is to achieve that state, the marvellous state of relaxation, which is not so easy and requires a certain amount of practice, to free the mind of strain and everything that inhibits it and to have one's body relaxed in an easy position. In such a state one is actually like a piece of blotting paper. It was really strange: even on our way home we began examining each other and somehow we already knew the words. The method consists in achieving this psychological and physical relaxation.

5) L.T., a student in Group 1:

I entered the course in a state of depression that affected my work and my entire life. In the course not only did my neurotic state disappear, but while gaining a knowledge of the language I became able to free my mind of worries.

*B. Teachers:*

1) Ivanka D., a teacher in French, pointed out that suggestopedy for her was an historical discovery.

For years in our profession no such event as this discovery has been known, i.e. in a month's time to be able to give students a basic knowledge of a foreign language. Before our experimentation, it was impossible to think that, in a month's time, students could memorize 2000 words and use these words in discussing written subjects based on 50 questions. The easiness with which the language was taught, the creation of the right atmosphere and the self-confidence that was inspired in the students were truly astonishing, facilitating, as they did, not only the learning of the language patterns but also the ability to think freely in the foreign language. In the courses, the words sprang readily to the students' minds as if speaking their own language, and from then on it was only a matter of the creative study of the foreign language. In the above experimental groups the emphasis was on the possibility of memorizing large numbers of words in a short time. For this reason very little time was given to grammar. Now that word memorization is no longer a problem, we can deal more easily with grammar, revision and consolidation of knowledge. For a whole year at the university I was in charge of a course being taught by the old, conventional methods for students who do not read philology, and for whom a foreign language is a second speciality. The students in the experimental groups acquired far greater mastery of the foreign language than did those taught in my university courses by the conventional methods. In the experimental groups our aim was not just the spelling, but in spelling we had a great success, too.

2) Yolanta G., a teacher in French:

Up till now we have known only theoretically that the capabilities of human memory are inexhaustible and possibly unlimited. Today we have seen that in practice it is possible to memorize 500, 1000 and even 2000 words if only there is someone able to give such lessons. Moreover, we should not restrict ourselves to using this method only for learning foreign languages. Any other subject can be taught in this same way. And grammar, too! The efficiency of the intellectual work done by our students went up in some cases by 2500 percent in comparison with that of students taught in the conventional manner.

VI. General Discussion of the Research Group's Findings.

1) Suggestopedy shows the possibility of suggestive memory increase in a waking state. This underlies the suggestopedic method.

2) As seen from the results obtained in the experimental groups, memorization in learning by the suggestopedic method seems to be accelerated 25 times over that in learning by conventional methods. This means the efficiency of intellectual work could be considerably raised—hence the great saving in time of this method.

3) Any time of the day or night is suitable for suggestopedic lessons.

4) The method requires a very quiet place for the lessons, one with a pleasant atmosphere. This makes it possible for every student to relax.

5) Lessons can be either very short or very long, depending on the time, desire and age or occupational requirements.

6) It can be said, on the basis of the experiments in memorizing 50 to 500 words in one session, that even more than this can be achieved.

7) The degree of memorization of suggestopedically learned words varies from 96 to 100 percent. The same is true of the two experiments with 500 words each.

8) The number of students can vary: (a) the nature of the session makes it possible to teach large groups of students as in group psychotherapy; (b) but the additional work done on the material given in the session makes it necessary that some limit should be put on the number of attendant students.

9) The suggestopedic method can be used in teaching all kinds of groups: (a) nonworking people whose time can be devoted entirely to learning the language; (b) students of all ages in their regular daily or weekly curricula; (c) working people in their free time.

10) A comparison of the data on the experimental (taught by suggestopedic methods) and the control groups (taught by conventional methods) proves unequivocally the superiority of the suggestopedic teaching. The numerous written tests gave a clear picture of the very unsatisfactory state of the knowledge of the students in the control groups and their complete helplessness after the first few days of the experiment.

About a week after the course began, the control groups were switched over to the suggestopedic method and managed, even with the burden of having to learn the words they had missed, to catch up with the experimental groups and complete the course.

11) In a number of cases, suggestion in a waking state when used for teaching purposes had a wonderfully therapeutic effect. People who were overtired or suffering from such neurotic complaints as hypersthenic, hyposthenic, hypochondriac, hypodepressive, intrusive and neurovegetative ailments, spoke gratefully of the disappearance of all disorders of this kind. In two or three persons, the disorders showed a tendency to recur a few days after the completion of the course but in milder forms than before.

VII. The Research Group's Proposal for Further Work:

1) Experimentation in the teaching of languages by the suggestopedic method should continue, because the data so far collected had revealed many valuable aspects of it. However, it did not completely answer all the questions as to its positive and negative effects from the pedagogical point of view and from that of health.

2) The creation of the necessary conditions and, if possible, the setting up of a suggestopedic center were not only desirable but also necessary in order to deal with suggestopedy teaching problems both theoretically and practically.

3) In founding such a suggestopedic center the following fundamental scientific and organizational tasks should be specially noted: (a) profound theoretical and practical research into suggestopedic teaching should be undertaken; (b) there should be methodological supervision and control of future teaching by the suggestopedic method; (c) permanent premises should be provided with the necessary furnishings and equipment.

4) It was necessary that experiments should be carried out with new groups, or more specifically: (a) some of the students who had taken the beginners' course should continue in one for advanced students: (b) a class of university or high school students should be formed; (c) a group should be formed in a holiday home where the students would not be engaged in work.

5) The application of the suggestopedic method for memorizing material in other sectors of science and life should be discussed. Consideration should be given to introducing it in mathematics, history, geography, the natural sciences, medicine, production, and in general wherever a large amount of difficult material has to be memorized.

6) Considering the remedial effect on a number of neurotics who had taken the suggestopedic foreign language course, it would be useful to include university and high school students suffering from neurosis in the suggestopedic experimental study groups. This would facilitate the introduction of suggestopedy later on as a therapeutic means in rest homes and sanitariums.

7) In consideration of the possibility of using the suggestopedic method to learn and memorize languages and other sciences, in some of the experiments which were to follow, Dr. G.L. should not be present. The lessons should be given by some of the present lecturers.

8) Finally, it would be necessary to forbid any arbitrary use of the suggestopedic teaching method by persons who had not been trained and had not worked under the supervision of Dr. G.L.

The above were the main points taken from a report drawn up on the basis of the oral and written recommendations of the members of the Research Group.

## SUGGESTOPEDY SECTION AND THE FIRST EXPERIMENT IN MEMORIZING THE MEANINGS OF 1000 FOREIGN WORDS IN ONE SESSION

Taking into consideration the exceptional results obtained during experimental teaching by the suggestopedic method, as well as the recommendations of the Research Group which observed and controlled the experiment, the Scientific Council of the Research Institute of Pedagogy with the Ministry of National Education suggested that the two Ministries should set up a Suggestopedy Research Section with the following tasks:

a) to carry out scientific research in the field of suggestopedy and related fields of applied psychology;

b) to organize various experimental and study courses in which languages and other subjects in different branches of the sciences, arts and technology would be taught by the suggestopedic method;

c) to train teachers to use the suggestopedic method according to the requirements of scientific research work, and to supervise the application of the suggestopedic method.

The new Suggestopedy Section was set up at the T. Samodumov Pedagogy Institute, and its activities increased rapidly. Experiments continued with new groups. At the same time as the specification of the suggestopedic method was made, experiments were carried out to elucidate certain aspects of suggestion in general, as well as to determine the limits of human memory. This resulted in the first experiment with the memorization of the meaning of 1000 new French words in one session.

The experiment was carried out by I. Dimitrova, a lecturer at Sofia University. The group consisted of 15 members of both sexes, aged between 22 and 60 and with different occupations. No preliminary selection of the members of the course was made. It was decided that in one of the courses the entire new vocabulary should be given in one day's session and the other 10 days should be used to elaborate grammar and to exercise habits of speech. To have witnessed the eagerness and excitement of both students and lecturers was to understand the feeling of responsibility with which this experiment was launched. One thousand words in one session of one working day were planned (the day before was used for preliminary preparation for giving the words). The thought of 1000 words in one session was disturbing at that time. Many members of the course did not believe anything would come of it. They even suggested that the experiment should be given up.

Nevertheless, the experiment took place The day before it began, each student crossed out all the words he knew or those whose meaning he could guess from a long list of foreign words. After these deletions there remained about 1000 unknown words, expressions and phrases on the list of each student.

The following was the final result of the written tests on the 1000 words given to each student in one study session:

A.K. – aged 53, a physician at the Government Hospital. 100%
B.P. – aged 26, a planner at the Rare Metals Enterprise. 98%
B.G. – aged 38, an architect at the Chamber of Commerce. 97%
V.M. – aged 46, an adviser to the Ministry of Education. 98%
V.M. – aged 36, a chemical engineer at the Research and Design Institute of the Electrical Industry. 100%
V.V. – aged 22, a protocol secretary at Pharmachim. 100%
G.D. – aged 60, chief engineer at the Science and Technical Progress State Committee. 96%
L.T. – aged 25, a judge. 100%
P.V. – aged 48, a senior research associate at the Pedagogy Institute. 100%
R.V. – aged 40, a chemical engineer at the Higher Institute of Mining Geology. 90%
R.T. – aged 41, an employee at the Pedagogy Institute. 100%
R.D. – aged 42, an employee at the Pedagogy Institute. 100%
H.I. – aged 29, an accountant at Sofia Airport. 100%
H.B. – aged 40, an employee at the Transport-Machinery State Economic Association. 94%
Y.K. – aged 42, an engineer at the Science and Technical Progress State Committee. 98%

Average number of memorized words = 98.08%±7.39%

Consequently, the average memorization of the given 1000 words was 98.08 percent. Thus, we can assume with $p=0.95$ that this figure will not fall below 90.69 percent under the same conditions.

## SUGGESTOLOGY RESEARCH CENTER

As the work of the suggestopedy section of the Pedagogy Research Institute grew, some of its research went beyond the scope of this Institute. Since a number of people were involved in the experiment the results could not be kept secret. The cultural public of Bulgaria became interested. Interest was also shown for suggestopedy in other countries. Our success attracted due attention and conditions were created for our further research work. On October 6th, 1966, the first Suggestology Research Center started its independent life. This Center was charged with the tasks of carrying out research into the psychology and physiology of suggestion, of developing the suggestopedic system of teaching and learning, and of investigating other fields related to paraconscious mental activity. These were the beginnings which have produced fruitful results.

# Chapter 3

## Man and His Environment

Suggestology has as its object of research the human personality in all its rich variety and its complex interrelations with the environment. Suggestology pays the greatest attention to those perceptions unnoticed by man, or of which he is insufficiently conscious or even completely unconscious. This is an enormous world of interrelations so far neglected by science as being insignificant, or on the contrary, given exaggerated importance by some scientists who interpret it as concealed fatality with aggressive and destructive tendencies.

More and more significance is being attached to very weak signals for understanding the specificities of the personality's reactions. An ever greater number of laboratories are allotting funds for experimental research in this area. D.D. Fedotov (1968) oriented himself to ". . . cases of weak signals where the signal itself can be regarded as subsensory or extrasensory". Research into subsensory stimuli is of general interest for the clarification of the specificities of perception "on a low level" about which T. Pavlov wrote:

It is the task of specialized scientific research to discover and examine in greater detail all those forms and degrees of "reverberation in general" which bear the nature of consciousness (of psychic) only in its higher forms and degrees. In all its lower forms and degrees reverberation is unconscious, and, as such, it is before consciousness, up to it and under it without this signifying that it is no reverberation and has no significance for orientation in the environment and its effect on it.

(1947: p. 53)

The human individual as a psychosomatic entity is a product of the natural and social environment. It is impossible to regard the individual outside his environment, the social environment where he grows up and develops. The biological heritage is moulded, directed and rebuilt under the conditions of the social environment.

The individual as in Freudian psychoanalytic theory (1921, 1923, 1925-a, 1925-b, 1926, 1930-a, 1931) is difficult to accept. Man, according to this theory, resembles a helpless plaything in the grip of dominating inferior instincts of which the sex instinct and the propensity for death and destruction are foremost. If egotistic pleasure and destructive instincts guided the behavior of each individual, there would be no human society. People would in fact be just a pack of wolves that would devour each other when there was no other prey. History, as well as everyday life, is filled with examples testifying to exactly the opposite. The fact that there is human society, is because there is human heroism, human goodness and moral principles. Of course, the "law of the jungle" often makes a breach in social life. But the mere fact that these are individual breakthroughs with which society copes, shows that the Freudian understanding of dominating and destructive instinctual activity does not reflect the reality. This kind of activity does exist but does not always dominate. To formulate and oppularize a general theory of the human personality based on the ordinary sexual urge and some psychopaths' urge for death and destruction is  from the suggestological point of view, absolutely unacceptable. These concepts which are upheld by prominent scientists and argued with the seemingly logical facts of psychopathology and crime detection, are nothing but discouraging mass suggestion to the average man unfamiliar with scientific thinking and for young people whose moral restraint is still unstable.

The ideas of those who broke away from Freud in principle remained in the same position. C. Jung (1921, 1926, 1928, 1943) in the elaboration of his ideas about the conscious and the unconscious, and A. Adler (1912, 1924, 1927) in his *Individual Psychology,* did not fully understand the role and significance of the social factor. In the neo-Freudians, such as E. Fromm (1947), this can be seen still more clearly. Many other authors, in spite of their deep reasoning and detailed research, have defined the human personality without taking the social links and the specific human consciousness into consideration.[1]

Modern existential writers (K. Jaspers, 1948; L. Binswagner, 1951; V. Frankl, 1956) also regard the personality dissociated from the important influence of the environment. Existentialism brings the idea of existence to the fore, implying that the unconscious internal

---

[1] Such empirical definitions have, for example, been given by G. Allport (1937, 1950) W. Stern (1911, 1922, 1935, 1954), E. Kretschmer (1931, 1956), and others.

life of the individual is somehow independent of the objective world.

Personalism (Wistern, 1922), holism (J. Smuts, 1926), gestalt (W. Kohler, 1930; K. Koffka, 1925; M. Wertheimer, 1925), and authors who uphold various ideas about the layer structure of the personality (J. Schultz, 1930, 1935, 1954, 1958, 1964; L. Klages, 1926; K. Kahn, 1928; E. Braun, 1928) treat it as more or less dissociated from its environment.

The unity in the structure of the personality built up in continuous interrelations with the environment, especially with the social environment, has been emphasized by many authors.[1]

These conceptions were based on the physiological trend developed by I.M. Sechenov (1947, 1952), and I.P. Pavlov (1948, 1951-52, 1954-57). According to Sechenov, all activities of the organism are determined by the environment. The same reflex principles underlie both neurophysiology and psychology. These principles were further developed by I.P. Pavlov. His teaching on conditioned reflexes raised the problem of the signal role of external stimuli. Hence the dependence of reactions on the past experience of the organism. The nervous system was not likened to an automation since one and the same stimuli could cause different reactions, depending on the individual experience of each person. This was already a form of prediction, of forestalling the changes in the environment on the basis of the past experience of the personality.

The principle of the conditioned reflex which brings about the connection between organism and environment, between personality and environment, as well as the teaching on the higher nervous activity, acquires a new meaning in the light of later physiological research.

Many investigations[2] have given us better insight into the cortico-subcortical connections and their unity in the formation of the regulating mechanisms for maintaining equilibrium between organism and environment. A study has been made of the polysynaptic route from the receptors to the cerebral cortex passing through the

---

[1] A.G. Kovalev (1968), A.G. Kovalev and V.N. Myassishtev (1957), V.S. Merlin (1959), V.N. Myassishtev (1926, 1930, 1939, 1960, 1960-a), S.L. Rubinstein (1947, 1957, 1959) *et al.*

[2] G. Moruzzi and H. Megoun (1949), H. Megoun (1961), G. Moruzzi (1964), F. Bremer (1935, 1937), F. Bremer and Z. Terzuollo (1953, 1954), M. Rheinberger and H. Jasper (1937), M.A. Zherebtsov (1939, 1940), M.I. Shaibel and A.B. Shaibel (1958), G.F. Rossi and A. Zanchetti (1960), and others have done important work.

reticular formation and activating the cerebral cortex in the presence of receptor excitation. The descending effect of the central sectors of the nervous system on the work of the analyzers to their ultimate receptory function has also been established.

At the same time, the development of the modern exact sciences—the theory of associations, cybernetics, etc.—has directed the attention of physiologists to measuring the quantity of information penetrating into the receptors from the outside world. Questions have been raised on the penetrating capacity of the analyzer as a channel for communication with regard to the association between the signal transmitted along the nerve fiber and the information carried, and also the coded information in the nerve fiber. But it has been seen that the information carried by the different signals varied in accordance depending on whether it was related to something which had already been communicated or to a little expected event which was to occur. Less is expected from the given signal the larger the quantity of information. Thus, the processes of prognosis based on the past experience of the organism have begun to be studied in modern physiology in a new manner.

In analyzing the role of the conditioned reflex, in modern physiology new conceptions arose which allow for the necessity of elaborating the question of feedback during the process of the purposive action itself. Feedback enables the organism to correct, stop or continue an action which has already begun. At the same time, physiologists reached the conclusion that an apparatus containing information on the expected result of the action must exist in the structure of the reflex. In this manner, information about the process of carrying out the action is compared with information on the expected result. The action itself is subject to correction, stopped or continued on the basis of past experience. The particular form, created by the excitement of foreseeing the results of the activity which is compared with the information coming from the feedback, requires the acceptance of the idea of the closed circuit of the reflex are as a working hypothesis. Such a tendency to coordinate the reflex theory with the achievements of cybernetics (hence the term feedback) can be found in the theory about the action acceptor and sanctioning afferentation[1] of P.K. Anokhin (1957—1962), in the physiology of activity of N.A. Bernstein (1946, 1962-a), as well as in the ideas of M.I. Grashchenkov (1966), G.Y.

---

[1] These terms are closely related to the concept of the feedback.

Belitsky (1957, 1966), and others.

These are attempts at a physiological explanation of the activities of the organism. Activity is guided by plan, assignement, current information, past experience, etc. All this is possible, provided the brain possesses an apparatus for foreseeing the results of actions which have not yet been carried out. Past experience would, of course, lie at the basis of such an apparatus. But prognosis cannot be absolute. The prognostication apparatus would be of the nature of a probabilities analysis. Of the possible foreseen results, the most probable one is selected. Such ideas about the physiological mechanisms participating in the active operations do not contradict the principle of determination. The ultimate result of the action is determined by the incoming information and the past experience of the organism.

The physiological mechanisms for maintaining the organism's equilibrium with nature and the social environment for forming the indestructible link between the individual and his social community, most often occur below the threshold of the conscious. Man is not aware of the course and nature of these regulating and balancing physiological mechanisms. Frequently, the ultimate psychological result of these mechanisms also escapes our consciousness. In this respect, the research carried out by the school of D.N. Uznadze was of particular interest. The activity of the individual, according to Uznadze, does not take place only in the form of a simple "stimulus-response" connection. The preliminary "setup" of the individual, built on past experience, is also of significance. The setup is created in the course of experience but remains below the level of conscious reflective mechanisms. F.V. Bassin (1963) found that Uznadze's ideas.

.... provide us with a concept disclosing the very nature of the "unconscious".

(p. 470)[1]

Uznadze emphasized that the setup is a state which is unconscious, but at the same time there is no experimental evidence ruling out the formation of a setup in a conscious state as well. Bassin also emphasized this thought. At the same time he found that the concept of setup is in fact very close to

---

[1] A.S. Prangishvilli (1967), Z.I. Hodzhava (1961, 1964), E.A. Gersamiya (1960) I.T. Bzhalava (1966), B.I. Hachapuridze (1966), T.A. Ratanova (1962), E.D. Kozheradze (1960), and others have elaborated on various aspects of Uznadze's concepts on the role, significance and peculiarities of the setup.

what P.K. Anokhin tried to introduce as early as 1956, speaking of the excitations of an anticipating type, i.e., of nervous activity anticipating events which have not yet occurred and preparing the organism's response to these forthcoming objective effects. Close to this circle of concepts are some of the ideas put forward recently as a result of N.A. Bernstein's analysis of motor activity and a number of the opinions expressed about the intentional "anticipating" activity of the central nervous system . . .

(p. 466)

This complex of physiological mechanisms should, however, be examined with a comprehensive phylogenetic and ontogenetic approach. From the interaction between the hereditary and congenital qualities of the individual and the characteristic features of the social and natural environment both the health of the individual and his education and development are built up. In actual fact the environment is not always able to prevail over certain qualities of the personality. For example, the environment cannot change temperament to such an extent as to basically alter its reaction under particular conditions. But the environment can often shape the personality sufficiently to make it possible for the individual to put his capabilities to the most valuable use, or, on the other hand, the environment can have such a bad effect that the individual's capabilities are suppressed and extinguished.

We remain largely unconscious of environmental effects—very often because of the fact that they are our natural continuous environment which seldom shows changes of great amplitude. For example, air waves are not usually felt until they become sufficiently strong to excite the receptors on the surface of the body. On the other hand, there are effects the receptors of which have not yet been established, such as the electromagnetic field.[1]

A number of questions connected with the interrelations of man and nature are not only still unanswered, but they have not yet

---

[1] The experiments of F.P. Petrov (1935, 1952), Y. Kholodov (1958, 1963-a, 1963-b, 1964, 1965-a, 1966-a, 1966-b, 1966-c), Y. Kholodov, S.N. Lukyanova and R.A. Chizhenkova (1967), G.F. Plekhanov (1965), G.F. Plekhanov and V.V. Veduyishkina (1966), H. Lisman and K. Mashin (1963), A.N. Malakhov, *et al.* (1963), G.A. Amineev and M.I. Sirkin (1965), A.G. Subotta (1958) and others have shown that the electromagnetic field affects both conditioned and non-conditioned reflex activity. In addition, there are indications of an effect on isolated organs and nerves. We can, therefore, agree in principle with A.S. Presman (1968) that the ability to generate and perceive the electromagnetic field of various frequency bands is an indication of the existence of information interrelation with the aid of the electromagnetic field. As some of the experiments have shown, in man this information interralation occurs unconsciously.

been raised. Any bold generalization with respect to these questions would ultimately be a temporary hypothesis formulated at a given stage.

Of special psychological significance are the formative effects of the social environment on the individual. The relations between the personality and the social environment are most often realized through the mechanisms of suggestion.

The enormous role played by suggestion in public life has been pointed out by a number of authors.[1] Social environment with its prestige, its requirements for the individual member of society, and its generally accepted concepts and tastes imposes subordination on the individual. The social environment exercises a suggestive influence on the individual in an unconscious manner--not only through fear of the power of the collective or through blind subordination, but often the individual accepts suggestions in the absence of any fear or subordination—suggestions which are in harmony with the generally accepted social norms and views. Since the very beginnings of man's existence, society has exercised a powerful and sometimes insurmountable influence over the individual.

The force of social suggestion, developed to the point of mass morbidity, can be seen with particular clarity in "psychic epidemics". There occur "political epidemics" when a society or a nation, gripped by the suggestive effect of an idea harmful to the interests of humanity, can fanatically perpetrate brutal mass outrages which are in radical contrast to the culture of the time. Religious psychic epidemics also occur. Psychic epidemics may originate outside the sphere of political life. They may appear outside religious movements. All psychic epidemics, however, are nurtured by the mental attitude of the given society, the community in which they originate. Old beliefs were expressed in mystic poetry in a number of national legends and sagas, and often assisted in inducing mass psychosis. In some cases, the legends have a purely national character and, in others, they have acquired international significance.

One such legend is that of Ahasuerus, the Wandering Jew, which was narrated all over Europe at the end of the sixteenth century. It tells how an untidy old man with a long, white beard was seen near Brussels. His name was Isaac Laacdem. His age, he said, was 1600 years. His story was that he had taken an active part in the crucifi-

---

[1] V.M. Bekhterev (1908, 1923), B. Sidis (1902), N.V. Kraininsky (1900), V.S. Yakovenko (1911), A.I. Sikorsky (1893), D. Garvalov (1937), E. Sharankov (1947) and others.

xion of Christ, for which he was damned to walk day and night non-stŏp until Doomsday. Some force was constantly pushing him on. 'I cannot stay here", said Isaac, "I must go. I suffer more when I stop somewhere". The Wandering Jew was known by different names in different countries. He was "encountered" in different places at different times. He was seen in Britain, France, Italy, Hungary, Persia, Spain, Poland, Russia, Lithuania, Sweden, Denmark, Scotland and other lands. In each country he spoke the respective native tongue. Two ambassadors saw him in Madrid, in 1575, and some people saw him in Vienna, in 1953. It was alleged that he had also been seen in Russia and even in the Court of Louis XIV.

Of course, legends have not always assumed the nature of psychic epidemics in the morbid sense of the word. Legends in which the people expressed their hope of liberation from foreign bondage and suffering were told in different historical epochs in Bulgaria and had a positive mass effect. The legend of Krali Marko, who defeated the Turks and liberated the people, was embodied in poetic images which warmed the hearts of the people.

Many kinds of psychic epidemics have occurred in all parts of the world. In Russia, during the reign of Catherine II, there was a case of a dog with rabies in Voronezh County. Soon after, 58 men and 41 women had paroxysms of hydrophobia, headache, fear, a desire to run away, salivation and even complex psychoses. In the end all got well except those who had actually been bitten. Epidemics of suicides are not unknown and there have also been epidemics of murder, looting and free love.

The environmental effect is especially strong on young people. No matter how eloquent or strong words may be or how effectively they are "supported" by regulations, norms and the law, they cannot suggest and induce a lasting desire for the cultivation of sensible habits, or give rise to the urge to search for an enlightened outlook if they are not backed up by personal example and a stable social environment. Only in this way can the suggestions which come by word of mouth from leaders, teachers, educators and others be gradually transformed into convictions, consolidated under the effect of the suggestions of the harmonious social environment. But when the environment is not salubrious, when there are conditions which can cause mental disorders, psychic epidemics may appear.

Besides being one of the decisive factors in forming the personality, the suggestive effect of the social environment also plays an important role in psychotherapeutic treatment. This was seen as early as the 1830's by V.F. Sabler, who not only removed the fetters from mental patients, but also tried to create conditions for them to enjoy a collective life, recreation, etc. S.S. Korsakov (1901, 1954) also attributed great importance to the group psychotherapeutic effect. Group psychotherapy is not satisfied with merely creating a calm atmosphere and organizing entertainment; it also organizes a system that will have an active psychological effect on the individual with a view to his rapid restoration and integration. The therapeutic effect of group psychotherapy shows very clearly the dominant role of the social environment in the general building up and balancing of the personality. The impact of the concentrated social effects in group psychotherapy has been noticed by a number of psychotherapists.[1] The views of A.P. Slobodyanik (1966) are very similar to those of A.S. Makarenko (1940), according to whom the individual develops and finds meaning in life in his complex inter-relations with the collective.

Group psychotherapy is applied not only in the treatment of neurosis but also in that of patients with various somatic ailments. Thus, as early as 1906, J.H. Pratt (1945) was treating tuberculosis patients by means of group psychotherapy.[2] M.S. Lebedinsky (1959) found that group psychotherapy could be used in the treatment of

---

[1] It was recommended by V.M. Bekhterev for treating alcoholics. N.V. Ivanov (1958), M.G. Itkin (1936), E.G. Breus, V.V. Plavinska and A.B. Besmen (1968), V.M. Palamarchuck (1968), M.U. Moushlovina (1968) *et al.* recommended the application of group psychotherapy on a wide scale in dispensary treatment. A number of authors K.I. Platonov (1957, 1966), I.Z. Velvovsky (1966-a, 1966-b), V.N. Myassishtev (1966), M.S. Lebedinsky (1966, V.Y. Tkachenko (1966) N.V. Ivanov (1966), M.E. Teleshevska (1966), A.L. Groisman (1966), K.M. Dubrovsky (1966), V.M. Panteleev (1966), and I.A. Sherman (1966)— have pointed out the significance of group psychotherapy in sanatorium and resort establishments.

[2] L.C. March (1931) gathered together groups of up to 500 patients. He thought that hospitals for neurotics should be more like schools than hospitals because ". . . the neurotic is not a patient, but a student who has been given a poor mark in the great subject (discipline) called civilization. Not treatment but reeducation '. J.W. Klapman (1946) is a great adherent of group bibliotherapy. M. Prados (1951) uses visual methods—pictorial images, films, etc. Recently, I.Z. Velvovsky and M.E. Markov (1968) proposed to develop a new trend in psychotherapy--videopsychotherapy, in which pictorial images are projected not only liminally but also subliminally. In their films, H.E. Rubin and E. Hatz (1946) use abstract colour combinations, accompanied with soft music. There is another technique, too—"the question box". Each patient writes his question on a sheet of paper anonymously and drops it into the box. The psychotherapist answers each question without knowing whose question it is.

patients with tuberculosis, hypertension and neurosis. He reported good results from group psychotherapy in treating patients with agoraphobia with whom he used to go for walks in groups. I.Z. Velvovsky, *et al.* (1950, 1958, 1967-a, 1967-b) point out the importance of the influence of the group and of the role played by the collective psychoprophylactically and psychohygienically. Group psychotherapy has recently been gaining ground rapidly in a number of countries. In the West it is developing mainly under the influence of the sociometric and psychodramatic conceptions of G.L. Moreno (1958) and along the lines of the psychoanalytic trend in modern psychosomatic medicine.[1] The pantomime group psychotherapy of O. Horetzky is a variation of the psychodrama, no matter how much its author would like to ascribe greater independence to it. The psychosomatic trend in group psychotherapy was clearly evinced at the 16th International Congress of Applied Psychology in Amsterdam, in 1968, and was, of course, emphasized at the International Psychomatic Week in Rome, in 1967. While E. Enke-Ferschland put forward proposals for group diagnostical research in the psychosomatic clinic, a number of other authors expounded concepts on how to obtain favorable results from a psychosomatically organized approach to the patient.[2]

In the light of suggestological concepts, the modern experimental trends of psychology, social psychology, physiology and psychotherapy create conditions for giving better argumented meaning to the connection between the individual and the environment. This is especially true of group psychotherapy, where the maximum use is made of the purposively arranged corrective and therapeutic effects of the communication links existing between individuals. In some

---

[1] This was clearly seen at the 4th International Congress of Group Psychotherapy in Vienna, in 1968, as well as in the papers of the International Congress of Psychodrama in Prague and Vienna, 1968. With particular clearness of purpose this trend was further developed by a number of authors in the USA, France, the Federal German Republic, Holland, Italy, and Switzerland: P.B. Schneider, C.Van Ende Boas, C.L. Van Blaaderen-Stock, G. Derbolovsky, D.T. Allen, L.T. Moreno, R.C. Cohn, A. Starr, A. Schutzenberger-Ancelin, E. Knepler, J G. Rojas Bermudes, A.B. Brind and N. Brind, D.G. Elefteery, P. Bour, R.M. Leal, F Bassaglia, A.B. Brind, I.A. Caruso, B. Danilovich, U. Derbolovsky, V. Dolezal and M Hauzner, L.E. Graubard, Straub, H.O. Weiss and R.V. Zaslov.

[2] A. Cirrincione; G. Tatarelli; P.J. O'Connor; A. Guerra and A. Cirrincione; C. Bertone, G. Leone and L. Pacilli; C. Bertone and L. Pacilli; F. Miraglia; E. de Winter, E. Jokl, G. Calderaro; J.F. Hombravella; B.J. Cratty; M. Damasiewicz, St. Grochmal and A. Pachalski; L. Ancona; F. Antonelli; A. Marino, and others.

aspects psychotherapy is converted from a therapeutic approach into an experimental method.

Adherents of the various psychotherapeutic schools are prone to infighting and very often avoid experimenting with those psychotherapeutic methods of which they happen to disapprove. Each one reports only the remedial results of his own methods. Some authors reject group psychotherapy because of the inconveniences involved in individualizing the approach to each patient. In its turn, individual psychotherapy is rejected because in using it, it is impossible to make use of the social effect on the individual. This dispute has arisen, however, because people have not penetrated into the essence of the phenomena. In actual fact, in individual psychotherapy the social influence is felt through public opinion and contacts with other patients before the one in question enters the psychotherapist's consultation room. The individual effect in group psychotherapy is brought about by the conversation which the patient has with the physician, and by the fact that each patient "takes" from the group what is required to bring him out of his particular state.

There are similar disputes between the champions of the three methods: abreaction and analysis; suggestion in a waking state or hypnosis; and conviction and re-education. The adherents of the abreaction and psychoanalysis methods do not realize that many suggestive elements can be detected at the basis of their methods. For example, conversations between the patient and the psychotherapist with great social prestige; preliminary meetings with patients who have been cured by this physician; the atmosphere of quietness, peace, and confidence in the analytical conversations and the abreaction procedures; the certainty with which the physician assures the patient that he will be cured by his method, and the physician's explanation that abreacted experiences or realized complexes are of therapeutic value.

Those who adhere to methods of suggestion in a waking state or hypnosis fail to notice how some of the patients spontaneously abreact their complexes and psychotraumatic experiences during their sessions. They do not see how their suggestions fuse with the methods of conviction and reeducation.

The champions of the conviction and reeducation methods in their turn do not realize that their own prestige and the whole atmosphere of the conversation with the patient play a suggestive role. If the therapeutic talks with patients are carefully examined, elements of discrete abreaction can be detected in them.

The psychotherapist with prestige, regardless of whether or not he is aware of and understands his role, is a universal suggestive placebo for the patients, a convincing example of a correct philosophical attitude toward life, and a soothing confessor all at the same time. On the basis of this conception of a uniform therapeutic mechanism determining the effect of the majority of the psychotherapeutic methods (1968), was developed the so-called *integral psychotherapy* (1967), in which the best use is made of many of the present psychotherapeutic methods.

*Figure 3*    A moment in a session of integral psychotherapy.

In integral psychotherapy the patients are in groups of 40 to 100 people (Figure 3). Patients with all types of neurosis, urticaria, bronchial asthma, neurodermatitis, hypertension of a neurogenic type, allergies, ulcers in the digestive system, etc., are treated. In integral psychotherapy the following is adhered to:

1) Preliminary suggestive preparation of patients while waiting to

enter the consultation room by meeting people who have already
been cured of the same ailments;

2) A brief conversation between the psychotherapist and each
patient before the latter joins the group. In the conversation each
patient's difficulties and psychotraumatic experiences are analyzed
individually.

3) A strict individual approach to each patient during group
therapeutic sessions. The first step in this approach is taken in the
preliminary talk or in the time of the group suggestion with
additional individual suggestion whispered in the ear of the patient.

4) Free abreaction at the time of the group session for those
patients who feel the need for it. The abreaction is controlled by the
physician to avoid it taking on dramatic proportions which would
traumatize the rest of the patients in the group.

5) A combination of suggestion and reeducation to change the
patient's outlook on life. Assistance is given to the patient to enable
him to rise above the petty everyday involvement in the vicious circle
of micropsychotraumata caused by the conditions of the daily
round.

6) Psychoprophylactic training to enable patients to cope more
easily with psychotraumatic situations that might arise in the future.

The first meeting between the physician and the patient is in the
presence of the group but at a small table, a little to one side, where
a quiet conversation takes place. After this, the new patient joins the
group and the physician gives a short psychotherapeutic lecture. The
lecture is reeducative and suggestive in nature. During the lecture, or
after it, individual patients tell the group how after the first or
second session they felt a marked improvement. Sometimes the
group is given a demonstration of the power of suggestion and autosuggestion and the capacities of the human mind. This reinforces the
physician's lecture and strengthens his arguments. After this the
patients are asked to relax in their easy chairs and listen to the voice
of the physician. A brief suggestive-autosuggestive session now takes
place. Individual patients may reach the state of hypnosis, and if they
have given their consent, their hypnosis may be demonstrated to the

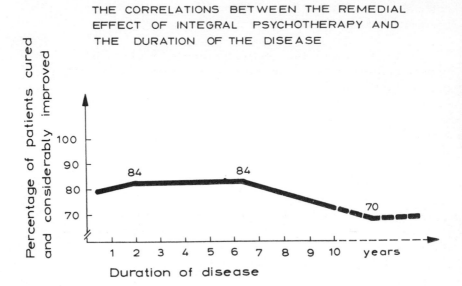

THE CORRELATIONS BETWEEN THE REMEDIAL
EFFECT OF INTEGRAL PSYCHOTHERAPY AND
THE DURATION OF THE DISEASE

*Figure 4*   The correlations between the remedial effect of integral psychotherapy and
the duration of the disease.

group. During this suggestive-autosuggestive session most of the
patients are fully awake and calm, a few are in a state of hypnosis and
some patients abreact psychotraumatic experiences spontaneously.
Finally, after a few invigorating suggestive formulae, they leave in
good spirits. The therapeutic session lasts from 30 to 50 minutes.

Integral group psychotherapy organized in this way is directed
toward bringing about a transformation of the morbid setup into a
healthy one by guiding and utilizing attitude, motivation and
expectancy. That the best use is made of the desuggestive-suggestive
factors in this process depends on the psychotherapist's professional
experience.

The results we obtained from integral psychotherapy, in 1965,
were the following: of the 351 patients treated, 267 (76 percent)
were either cured or considerably improved. It should be emphasized
that these 351 were specially selected as chronic cases of patients
who had been treated with all other medicamental, physiothera-
peutic and psychotherapeutic methods without success. Many of
these patients had been unable to work for months and years.

These results were obtained on an average after four or five
sessions. In some cases there was an unexpected and immediate

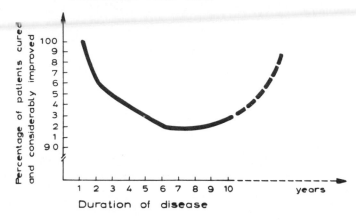

THE CORRELATIONS BETWEEN THE
STABILITY OF THE REMEDIAL EFFECT
OF INTEGRAL PSYCHOTHERAPY AND
THE DURATION OF THE DISEASE
CATAMNESIS - ONE YEAR

*Figure 5*  The correlations between the stability of the remedial effect of integral psychotherapy and the duration of the disease. Catamnesis — one year.

therapeutic effect in the first few sessions, but in others it was necessary to have a score or more.

Since assessments of therapeutic effect are often doubted on the assumption that psychotherapists introduce many subjective elements into them, an effort has been made to give an objective assessment and, at the same time, the catamnestic condition of the patients has been traced.

To enable us to do this, letter questionnaires were sent to all the patients treated in Bulgaria.

The results are shown in Table 8, based on the 233 replies received (See Table 8 and Figures 4 and 5).

It was of interest to know not only how the patients felt immediately after the treatment, but also after they had returned to the environment familiar to them and to the conditions which had been psychotraumatic for them. There was no possibility of actively interfering in lives and changing their living and working conditions because they were living in different places all over the country, and it was impossible to study the conditions under which each one lived. The system, however, provided for the mental readjustment of the patients so they could cope without changing the living and working

TABLE 8    *Written Data Obtained from Patients Who Underwent Treatment with*
*Intergral Psychotherapy*

| Duration of disease prior to integral psychotherapy treatment | Up to 1 year | From 1—3 years | From 3—10 years | Over 10 years | Total |
|---|---|---|---|---|---|
| Patients | 31 | 58 | 93 | 51 | 233 |
| Patients not treated with other means prior to integral psychotherapy | 11 (36%) | 12 (21%) | 15 (17%) | 6 (12%) | 44 (18%) |
| Recovered by integral psychotherapy | 24 (80%) | 49 (84%) | 79 (84%) | 36 (70%) | 188 (80%) |
| Patients who continued to be well after 1 year | 24 (100% ±7.86) | 47 (95.9% ±5.66) | 73 (92.4% ±5.96) | 36 (100%) ±7.86) | 181 (96.3% ±2.76) |

TABLE 9    *Assessment of the Results of Integral Psychotherapy in 1965, by the*
*Physician in Charge and the Patients*

| Indicators according to: | Patients treated | Cured or considerably improved | |
|---|---|---|---|
| *Physician* Immediately after treatment | 351 | *In numbers* 267 | % 76 |
| *The patients:* a) immediately after treatment | 233 | 188 | 80 |
| b) 1 year after treatment | 233 | 181 | 77 |

conditions. The results obtained from this delayed check can be seen
in Tables 8 and 9.

In the answers to the questionnaire most of the patients said that
they were able to cope more easily with their difficulties, and that
psychological trauma had ceased to have any effect on their health.

The conclusions that could be drawn from the answers to the questionnaire are not only of practical importance, they also give backing to the concept of a uniform suggestive therapeutic mechanism in most psychotherapeutic methods. The therapeutic and invigorating effect of the environment comes not only from psychotherapeutic procedures and methods, but also from the arrangement of the environment and regime around the patient. Thus, the concept of a remedial-preventive regime is formed in the spirit of modern neurism. It comprises the manner in which the therapeutic procedure is started, the behavior of the medical staff toward the patient, the relations between individual patients, the arrangement of the rooms, the decor, in fact, everything with which the patient is in contact. If the social and natural environments are able to cause an illness, they should also be able to cure and reeducate. It is, however, impossible to apply all the requirements for good organization of the curative-preventive regime without a profound theoretical and practical knowledge of the principles of psychotherapy. It requires a profound knowledge of the patient's typological features, character, interests and goals, as well as a knowledge of all the difficulties he encounters in life. The psychotherapist should also be familiar with the features of the social environment, the nature of its contradictions, and its effect on the individual in order to use the available possibilities for arranging the environment so that it has a therapeutic effect on the individual.[1]

D.G. Oppenheim (1954) determined the requirements for a correctly organized remedial regime as follows: (1) Elimination of the mental stress connected with the disease and the forthcoming treatment; (2) Elimination of pain caused by therapeutic manipulations (incisions, injections, etc.); (3) Establishment of a regime of rest combined with movement; (4) The creation of mutual confidence and unity between the medical staff and the patient; (5) Elimination of negative effect stimuli, auditory, visual or olfactory; (6) The prolongation of physiological sleep; (7) Regular meals, (8) Constructive companionship with the hospital staff.

---

[1]M.Y Mudrov (1820), C.A. Zakharine (1909), S.P. Betkin (1952), S.S. Korsakov (1901), and others examined the problem of the interrelations between organism and environment, recognizing the leading role of the environment in the formation and development of the organism, as well as in the origination of diseases and their treatment. I.M. Sechenov (1947) wrote that the term environment must be included in the definition of organism, because it affects the organism and without it, the organism cannot exist.

A remedial-preventive regime organized in such a way is not only a matter of culture and upbringing, but also a strict scientific requirement.[1]

Environmental factors are also of decisive importance in upbringing. The environment suggests habits, conduct, and attitudes to both the growing generation and to adults. L.N. Tolstoy (1934) wrote that people learn and are educated only by suggestion, which comes into the mind in two ways: consciously and unconsciously. A.S. Makarenko (1940) attached great significance to the suggestive effect which the group has on the individual.

Emphasis on the significance of the social environment for the formation of the individual in no way signifies that the individual and the influence which he, in his turn, has on the collective are neglected. B. D. Parigin (1968) was absolutely correct in writing:

The neglect of the psychic content of the individual turns him into a personified social function, into a "unit", a "bolt ' in an impersonal social mechanism.

(p. 123)

In actual fact, socialization, the build up of the human personality through and for society, begins from the very first days of life. As an illustration of this, one can study the cases of children who were brought up among wild animals. R.C. Cohn (1968) cites an example of two Indian girls, Kamala and Amala, who were found in the lair of a wolf, in 1920. The former was eight years old and the latter a year and a half. Both looked like human beings, but their behavior was that of wolves. Amala died soon after being found. Kamala learned some 30 words and would obey a few simple orders, sometimes imitating a normal child, but normalization of her mental development and satisfactory adaptation to human society were never achieved. She died in 1929. The cases of animal-reared children, as far as their authenticity can be guaranteed, have illustrative rather than demonstrative value because a number of questions in connection with them have not been convincingly

---

[1] The important role played by environmental factors both in falling ill and in recovering, has been pointed out by a great many number of authors: A. Baruk (1958), V.A. Gilyarovski (1954), S. Danadjiev (1935), D. Daskalov (1947), O.V. Kerbikov (1955), Lubotskaya-Rosetts (1957), V. Makedonski (1957), N. Muller-Hegemann (1957), A.M. Svyadosht (1955), T.P. Simson (1958) G.E. Suhareva (1959), J. Fischer (1959), H. Hristozov (1959-a, 1959-b, 1960) E. Sharankov (1961, 1963), N. Schipkovensky (1956), and many others.

answered. For example, it is not clear whether the considerably delayed and incomplete development of these children in human society is not due to biolgoical causes, whether it is not a case of oligophreny which may also be based on some anatomical impairment of the central nervous system.

As has been emphasized, the individual cannot be studied only through his socially conditioned development. Indeed, according to I.S. Vigotsky (1937, 1956) the interpsychic, interpersonal social processes are the foundations for the development of the intrapsychic, inner processes, and P.C. Cohn (1968) added:

. . . the "external" (in respect of a given individual) and his "internal" nature prove to be bonded both genetically and functionally

(p. 8)

Social influence is, however, a complex result of interpersonal relations. Research will clarify many aspects not only of social psychology, but also of social suggestology as far as social interrelations are built insufficiently consciously or completely unconsciously on the basis of suggestive associations.[1]

The pattern of interpersonal relations would become more complex if not only the psychological interrelations but also some bio-energetic factors, into which research is only just starting, were taken into consideration. For example, still unclarified is the effect of the electromagnetic field on the physiological and psychological state of the individual, although research work is being carried out in this sphere. But there are grounds to believe that weak energetic fields also arise in the activities of the individuals, irrespective of the well-known psychological forms of informational interrelation. A.S. Pressman (1967), proceeding from observations of earlier phylogenic stages and experiments with them, thinks that radiated biochemical fields possess information value for other individuals as it is in the case of the distant interrelations in the attraction of the opposite sex, the coordination of simultaneous movements in birds and fish and the coordination of activities in social insects. He finds that in the case of man there are indirect experimental data showing the existence of electromagnetic interrelations between persons in

---

[1] The sociometric methods of G.L. Moreno (1958, 1968) offer possibilities for experimental development in this respect. The rational aspects of these methods of revealing the intimate structure in the different teaching and educational teams have been utilized by Y.L. Kolominskiy (1963, 1965), Y.L. Kolominskiy and A.I. Rozov (1962), M Andreev (1966, 1967), and others.

. . . on the one hand, the capabilities of the human organism to receive an HF-field with very small intensity in the order of $10^{-4}$ v/m (Plekhanov, 1965) and, on the other, the generation of SHF-field.

(Gasky, 1960), (p. 347)[1]

Psychological and sociological problems are the leading ones in the suggestive interrelations of individual and environment. These interrelations are suggestive in so far as they are more or less unconscious. P.M. Jacobson (1969) also included behavior motives in the unconscious interrelations. Motivation is far from being conscious all the time. Uznadze (1966) linked motivation with the setup theory. He wrote that parallel to the vital physical needs there are others which have nothing in common with the vital ones. These are the intellectual, moral and aesthetic ones. For some people the vital needs are of greater significance, but for others, their higher needs determine their way of life. Thus, every man has his own special set-up which determines the manifestation of various motivation trends in his activity. A.N. Leontiev (1959) found that

. . . the formation of the human personality finds psychological expression in the development of its motivation sphere

(p. 432)

Motivation is of considerable significance in the suggestive interaction between individual and environment. It is, however, connected with attitude and expectancy in an indivisible complex. As a result of a number of experiments, T.X. Barber, N.P. Spanos and G.F. Chaves (1974) conclude

---

[1] The extent to which these weak bioenergetic fields would be of significance to other individuals in the communication process is not yet clear, but any research along these lines is worthwhile. Thus, for example, P.I. Gulyaev, *et al.* (1968-a, 1968-b) recorded from a distance an electromagnetic field around a man and from its characteristics assessed the functional state of the individual organs. G.A. Servaev, *et al.* (1969-a, 1969-b, 1969-c) employed a new type of transducer to record some telebioenergetic process characteristics around the organism, which they linked with the specific functional organization and mental strain of the individual. At the Suggestology Research Institute, a similar transducer was used to record from a distance certain changes in the electromagnetic field around the head in connection with mental activity. There is still no convincing evidence that these telebioenergetic fluctuations are received by people in the near vicinity, but such a possibility cannot be ruled out. In such a case, questions will arise about their information values and mental reflection.

that the subject's responsiveness to test suggestions is in part mediated by his attitude, motivation and expectancy

(p. 129)

In our opinion, these mental (psychological) mediators are, on the one hand, the expression of the setup and, on the other, they influence its dynamic changes. The suggestive factors in the communicative process mould, direct and make use of these psychological mediators in the process of building up a more or less suggestively directed unconscious setup, i.e., a setup to plus or minus reserves.

These suggestive factors, which exist in the ordinary communicative process, are considerably intensified in some specific forms of the communicative process, such as education, treatment of the sick, contacts with art, etc. Suggestive communicativeness is of special significance in art because of art's powerful influence and great popularity.

In all this variety of suggestive interrelations between man and his environment, suggestology must seek to define more accurately when and which stimuli are positive for a given person, and when and which are negative. Only then, if society ever does find the strength and power to define them, will the development of the personality be organized on constructive, scientific bases.

The suggestive interaction between individual and environment is related to conformity but should not be confused with it. Because of ambiguity in the terminology, certain suggestive events are ascribed to conformity and vice versa, there is a danger that suggestive interrelations will be debased to conformity. Conformity and suggestivity may in some cases be combined, and it is necessary that the intimate mechanisms and manifestations of the one or the other phenomenon be clearly differentiated. While in suggestive interaction there is bilateral influence with the dominance of the social environment, in conformity there is adaptation, a retreat by the individual because of group pressure. In the extreme stages of conformity there is a loss of independence, of the individualism of the personality. The conformity behavior may be only external, as in cases when the individual is subordinated to the standards and requirements of the group –but preserves his inner freedom. Thus, for example, the individual may accept a fashion only not to differ in this from what has been accepted by the collective, without being internally convinced of its usefulness. Inner conformity is rather more complicated, for the individual may change his behavior and concepts under the impact of the group, not because of convincing arguments and not because of the mechanisms of the unconscious suggestive association, but from fear of isolation or from lack of sufficient criticism. A particularly clear example of conformity is described in Hans Christian Anderson's story *The Emperor's New Clothes.* Conformity can possess positive educational significance. It should, in any case, be distinguished from suggestive interrelations. To determine the difference, profound psychological research is necessary. In many experiments carried out to measure conformity, suggestive mechanisms creep in and these are not always accounted for. S.E. Ash's experiments (1956) were interesting. He distributed two white sheets of paper to groups of 7 to 9 people. On one sheet was one line, and on the other, three lines of different length. One of the three lines was equal in length to the control line on the first sheet. Each person had to identify the equal line. The difference in length was so significant that in the control test with each person alone each one gave the correct answer. The quintessence of this experiment lay in the fact that in the group test to identify the equal line, with the exception of one person, all were led astray and gave the wrong answer. The one exception had to give his answer last, or last but one. Of the 123 persons tested, each of whom gave 12 answers, 37 percent gave wrong answers, i.e., in concurrence with group opinion. In the enquiry held after each experiment, people said that the opinion of the majority was very important to them and that it was about their own perceptions that they had a feeling of uncertainty and not about those of the majority. Those who did not yield to group influence confessed that in withstanding it they had experienced an unpleasant feeling of uneasiness. Some had feared that they had failed to understand something, that they might prove to be wrong or to show some sort of inferiority. They said it was much more pleasant when they agreed with the others.

Conformity depends on many factors such as the character of the group, the difficulty of the task, the characteristics of the individual, etc. Unlike conformity, suggestive interrelations have nothing in common with oppression and submission. They are an expression of the natural unconscious interrelations between individual and environment. It can be expected that with future research into conformity, some phenomena will be dropped from the conformist category and will be explained in the light of the general theory of suggestion. The differentiation of conformity and suggestivity will also enrich psychotherapy, which is closely associated with the concept of personality, B.M. Segal, *et al.* (1969) find that such factors as intensification of suggestivity, group conformism, imitation of "leaders", etc., play a therapeutic role in the psychotherapeutic group. The individual environment relations stand out with particular clarity in group psychotherapy where the actuating role of the environment in the course of the therapeutic process is manifested. While the effect of conformity results only in adaptation, suggestivity ensures the activation of reserves of the individual.

# Chapter 4

# Towards a General Theory of Suggestion

The first serious obstacle encountered by any author examining the problem of suggestion is to define the concept of suggestion. Every definition is already an expression of a theory. Suggestion, like many other phenomena, was first observed in life and only then investigated and consciously used. But the practical application of suggestion is still very unorganized, with scanty knowledge of its objective inherent laws. Considering the complexity of the phenomenon, very little experimental research has been carried out. The incompleteness of the experimental material available and suitable for comprehensive theoretical conclusions, and the influence of various philosophical currents, result in unilateral and biased definitions of suggestion.

A.M. Weitzenhoffer (1953), A. Forel (1925), and others consider suggestion to be ideas connected with belief in something or conviction of something, ideas which are actually realized in the moment of their origination. H. Bernheim (1892), W. Hilger (1928, and others regard suggestion as a form of ideomotor action. W. Wundt (1892, 1894), L. Lowenfeld (1922), and L. Lefevre (1903) define suggestion as an idea in which limited associative activity exists. In general, those defining suggestion by one kind of concept or another are inclined to reduce the mechanisms of suggestion to the mechanism of self suggestion, that is, they explain suggestion as autosuggestion. Suggestion, according to them, evokes ideas which are afterward realized by autosuggestion within the framework of consciousness. In particular, C. Baudouin (1922) distinguishes two phases in suggestion: (1) An idea imposed by person making the suggestion on the recipient, and (2) the transformation of this idea in the recipient and the realization of the suggestion through the mechanisms of autosuggestion. Baudouin considers that the first phase, the imposing of an outside idea on the recipient, is not important for suggestion. He states that the second phase, the transformation and realization of an already accepted idea, is decisive in defining the conception of suggestion and in understanding its mechanisms. Baudouin calls the first phase "perception" and the second "the ideoreflex process", and maintains that the ideoreflex process contains the basic mechanisms of suggestion. Suggestion, he says, is not perception plus the ideoreflex process: it is contained only in the ideoreflex process. The same mechanism also underlies autosuggestion. In autosuggestion there is also the perception of an idea, although it originates within the individual, and it is then followed by the realization of this idea through the ideoreflex process. Both in autosuggestion and suggestion, Baudouin considers the decisive factor is the ideoreflex process itself, while perception has no significance for the realization either of suggestion or autosuggestion.

To explain suggestion as a mechanism of autosuggestion does not help in solving the problem: it merely displaces the center of this problem's gravity to one of the links in the desuggestive—suggestive process. It is quite natural that, insofar as the suggestive effect is realized in a particular individual, it is of certain significance to him and brings about complicated internal processes, which are paraconscious. But simply because the processes develop within the person, is insufficient grounds for the suggestive to be reduced to the autosuggestive. One cannot explain suggestive effects only on the basis of automatic realization of ideas, because there are a number of situations in which there is no knowledge of the psychic process taking place and, therefore, no attitude of belief can be expected in the suggestively affected person. As an example, in some subsensory reactions the stimulus is perceived, but for the individual the end effect of the reaction occurs "in an unknown way". Such "unknown way" reactions are an exceptionally frequent phenomenon in desuggestive-suggestive interrelations. Therefore one can speak about suggestion and autosuggestion as conditional only as regards the origin of the stimulus, whether the suggestive factor originates within or without the individual. The subsequent complex and unconscious mechanisms are probably identical in both cases of origination. The problem, however, becomes more complicated in trying to understand what is meant by "within or without a person". A number of subliminal sensations from the consititutional sphere which affect the psyche, mood and thinking, appear to be "without", in so far as, the central nucleus of the individual is concerned, although they are in fact essential elements of the inner milieu of the individual. Conversely, a number of stimuli which seem to be "within" could originate in stimuli from "without" and be imperceptible at the present level of research in this sphere.

For B. Stokvis (1955), suggestion is a deliberate and unforeseen form of affective resonance. According to B. Sidis (1902), P. Janet (1909, 1911, 1925, 1925/28), W.D. Furneaux (1956), and others, suggestion is in a broad sense compulsion of the will and suppression of criticism. According to the psychoanalytic ideas of S. Freud (1921, 1923, 1925-b, 1926, 1930-a, 1931), S. Ferenzi, and other psychoanalysts, suggestion is a form of transference or creation of subordination in the child—father pattern. J. Schultz (1930) defines suggestion as an immediate intrusion or excitation of mental content or processes which are realized without any critical, rational or affective cooperation on the part of the person involved in the experiment. V.M. Bekhterev (1908, 1923) defines suggestion as a grafting of psychic states in the recipient without the participation of his will (attention) and often without any clear awareness of the suggestion on his part. K.I. Platonov (1930-a, 1939, 1957) added that the perception of psychic states occurs without criticism. According to E. Kretschmer (1947), suggestion enters without argument, directly through stimuli. I.P. Pavlov defined suggestion from a mainly physiological point of view as

concentrated excitation at a particular point or region of the large hemispheres. . . an excitation obtaining a predominant illicit and insurmountable significance . . . In a weak low tonus of the cortex it (excitation), being concentrated, is accompanied by strong negative induction which isolates it from all necessary side influences.

(1951—1952)

He describes the response to suggestion as "the most simplified and most typical conditioned reflex in man".

Suggestion has been defined in one way or another by many scientists. These different definitions are based not only on clinical considerations but on different physiological, psychological and philosophical concepts. This fact shows how wide is the scope and significance of the problem but, at the same time, hinders the orientation of research into the intrinsic nature of the phenomenon.

## SUGGESTION AND CONVICTION

Suggestion is usually the counterpart to conviction. While conviction is built on a base of logical argument, on recoding consciousness and concentration of attention, suggestion originates as a direct link between the unconscious mental activity and the environment where no recoding of consciousness occurs, no logical arguments are tolerated and no concentration of attention is required. Analysis of these complicated mental phenomena shows that each of the terms needs clarification in order to avoid the vulgarization of the concept of suggestion.

In the first place, when speaking of recoding in the consciousness, it should always be borne in mind that every process of conviction carries also an innumerable quantity of signals which enter directly into the unconscious mental activity along with the conscious recoding. This paraconscious stream of information, by way of intuitive, emotional and subsensory paths, creates conditions for control and feedback on various functional levels. The paraconscious control during conscious activity has an unnoticed effect on motives and decisions. On the other hand, when we say that in suggestion— just the opposite to conviction—there is a direct connection between unconscious (paraconscious) mental activity and the environment, this does not mean there may not also exist information in the conscious activity of the individual.

Logical arguments, motivation in forming a specific attitude, decision, etc., should also not be understood schematically as criteria for either participation of suggestive reactivity or not. If the psychology of motivation is analyzed, it will be seen that it exerts an effect not only in accordance with the laws of logic but it can have an effect by suggestive channels. This is realized in the manner of the presentation of the motivation: the accompanying suggestive elements from the second plane of the communication which engage the non-specific mental reactivity. Here one may also refer to the authority of the source of motivation. However, the logical presentation of arguments can have its own suggestive effect. An idea that is well presented may in itself be suggestive: the authority of logic, of the well-expressed thought, these have an enormous additional suggestive power. It must be borne in mind that the most effective logical, rational and conscious activity is based on numerous unconscious and automated details, codes and elements. The suggestive interrelations created by the inevitable participation of the emotional sphere with its suggestive potential, the unconscious automated details, codes and elements, do create to some degree possibilities for additional suggestive interrelations.

Analysis of the concentration of attention in conviction and suggestion also shows complex associations. It is true that in conviction attention is concentrated, but to what extent behavioral concentration corresponds to actual inner concentration has not yet been established experimentally. The opposite is true of the concentration of attention in suggestion. It is true that in a considerable part of the suggestive mechanism attention seems to be passive. This is the reason it is termed "pseudopassiveness" in our suggestopedic setup. Behavioral passiveness of attention with considerable internal activity is characteristic of the suggestive setup. However, although this activity is unconscious, very often processes with much higher efficiency than the ordinary occur, releasing reserve possibilities.

In every rational, logical activity suggestive factors may exert their influence through the following unconscious channels:

1) emotional background;
2) peripheral perceptions,
3) automated details, codes and elements;
4) associating, symbolization and coding on the basis of which authority is most often built,
5) previous suggestive setup, attitudes, motivation and expectancy.

All this shows how complicated and how practically impossible it is to isolate a purely rational and a purely suggestive communicativeness.

## SUGGESTION AND SUGGESTIBILITY

It is usually believed that suggestive readiness is different in different persons at different moments. This varying readiness for the perception and realization of suggestions is called suggestibility. It should be emphasized, however, that research work on suggestibility so far has been one-sided and that no complete idea has been formed about its characteristic features and possibilities.

Earlier researchers regarded suggestibility as closely connected with neurotic diseases, particularly hysteria. This belief is still held by a number of clinicians who lack experimental psychological experience with suggestibility in healthy, normal individuals.[1]

Experimental research work on healthy people has shown that suggestibility is a general human phenomenon. Every person possesses a certain degree of expressed suggestibility, which is a variable quantity. At different times the same person can have quite different degrees of suggestibility.

A great number of different tests have been proposed for measuring the degree of expressed clinical suggestibility. These tests, when used for clinical purposes to measure the suggestibility of persons undergoing psychotherapy, have a certain practical importance. Under clinical conditions, however, a number of additional suggestive factors, which may be of decisive importance for the degree of the reaction, are most often missed. The role of the examining psychotherapist with his authority and ability to create suggestive contact is sometimes overlooked although it is important who carries out the tests and how they are conducted.

If the requirements for absolute suggestive pureness are observed, each of these methods would provide a possibility for research into suggestion in a great variety of psychological aspects. For example, by means of the inclined or swinging body test, C.L. Hull (1933) studied several types of suggestive reactions. Unknown to the subject he connected his body to a rotating drum to record his movements. The kymogram obtained showed the suggestive processes which originate along the mechanism of unconscious imitation. If an unsuspecting subject watches forward or backward leaning movements of another person, he begins unconsciously to repeat these movements, and they are registered on the kymograph. The subject has no idea he is making the movements. In other variations of the experiment, the same movements are registered but only when the subject

---

[1] P. Janet (1907) maintained that suggestion is a very rare phenomenon existing only in hysteria and that suggestibility was the most important symptom in hysteria. J.E. Babinsky and J. Froment (1918) thought that abnormal suggestibility was the most significant symptom of the hysterical individual. H. Bernheim (1887), and the Nancy School, in general, maintained that everyone is suggestible under given conditions and that suggestibility is not a symptom of morbidity. Nevertheless, they did not reject the view that intensified suggestibility was observed in hysteria. Suggestibility as a leading symptom in hysteria was accepted by many later authors, such as McDougal (1911), L.F. Schaffer (1936), J.B. Morgan (1936), L. Hirschlaff (1919), L. Satow (1923), V.E. Fischer (1937), and E. Bleuler (1924).

imagines very clearly that he is falling forward or backward, or when he whispers quietly that he is falling, or when he listens to a tape recording inviting him to fall forward or backward. In another variation of the experiment, the suggestion of falling is made by the experimenter himself.[1]

F. Aveling and H. Hargreaves (1921–22), C.L. Hull (1933), and others would call suggestions where the experimenter takes a direct part in the suggestive formulations, prestige suggestions, to distinguish them from the nonprestige ones. They originated in A. Binet's progressive lines and progressive weights tests (1900), which were later modified by W. Brown (1916), G. Williams (1930), and others. In these tests the subject is given 15 irritants which are so arranged that the first five gradually increase in length or in weight, creating the expectation that the following ten will continue to do so. These ten, however, are all the same in length or in weight. The subjects usually report that the following lines are longer or the weights are heavier. The measurement of suggestibility is calculated by the number of lines which are indicated as longer or of objects indicated as heavier, but which are in reality equal in length or equal in weight.

Hull (1933) thinks that prestige suggestions differ from nonprestige suggestions in their internal mechanisms. The most essential difference, according to him, is the relation of the one or the other form of suggestibility to hypnosis. While prestige suggestibility increases during hypnosis, it seems that the nonprestige does not increase.

## Primary and secondary suggestibility

A number of other authors have also tried to introduce some kind of system into the interpretation of the various manifestations of suggestibility. The greatest popularity is enjoyed by the suggestibility classification proposed by H.J. Eysenck (1943, 1945, 1947), and W.D. Furneaux (1945, 1946, 1956). They consider that a single mechanism cannot explain suggestibility which is measured by conventional tests. At least two factors and perhaps more are involved. The main factor determining the so-called "primary suggestibility"

---

[1] Such experiments have been carried out by a number of researchers—J.V. Berreman and E.R. Hilgard (1936), H.J. Eysenck and W.D. Furneaux (1945) *et al.* These experiments make possible the quantitative measurement of suggestibility by the degree of deflection of the body as a result of the suggested movement.

is related to direct verbal suggestions for specific muscle movements without the active volitional participation of the subject. The second factor, which determines "secondary suggestibility", has been formulated rather more hazily and is related to "indirectness" and "credulity". Secondary suggestibility is manifested in cases of suggestion of a particular perception when there is no real basis for it. Primary suggestibility is most often tested by the body-inclining tests and secondary suggestibility by the ink-blot and the lines and weights tests.

Primary and secondary suggestibility are not very clearly distinguished and are still the subject of discussions. Experimental research in both areas is still continuing.

## a) *Primary suggestibility*

L.R. Wolberg (1948), A.M. Weitzenhoffer (1953), K.V. Stukat (1958) and others have grouped the numerous existing concepts of primary suggestibility into physiological, dissociative, ideomotor, conditioned reactions and Freudian.

According to the physiological theories, which originate from R. Heidenhein (1906), the foundation of suggestibility lies in the inhibition of the ganglionic cells of the brain. B. Sidis (1902) accepted functional dissociation between the nervous cells as the physiological basis of suggestibility.

Those who hold the dissociation theories consider suggestibility to be an expression of the activity of a second subconscious ego which also exists in the normal waking state of the consciousness. These theories originated from C.T. Burnett (1925), P. Janet (1925/28), and others. Janet, the most prominent representative of the dissociation theories, refers suggestion to the group of automatisms. In his view, suggestion is something alien of which the individual is not aware. Janet emphasizes the significance of speech for the origination of suggested reactions.

The adherents of the concepts of ideomotor and conditioned reflex mechanisms of primary suggestibility firmly back up the idea of the connection between speech and action, because they believe the connection is decisive in giving rise to suggestion. W. James (1890) wrote that any idea of movement awakens, to a certain extent, the actual movement which is its object. A.L. Thorndike (1919) criticized the ideomotor action concept, maintaining that ideas do not cause action by themselves but only by way of habits and instincts. The research of E. Jacobson (1930, 1938), G.L. Freeman (1931), and others showed that there exists latent muscular tension which aspires to participate in imaginary movement connected with the respective concepts during the time of intellectual activation. It was established in the electromyographic investigations of L.N. Gould (1948, 1949) that verbal hallucinations are most often accompanied by hyperactivity of the vocal musculature. In some cases, this hyperactivity was so strong that it resulted in subvocal speech which could be heard through a stethoscope and a sensitive microphone. A.A. Smith, R.B. Malmo and C. Shagass (1954), and H. Wallerstein (1954) detected an increase of the electric activity of specific muscular groups during concentrated listening to texts and conversation, and they ascribed this to the attention and activity necessary to understand the verbal material. The research of F.V. Bassin and E.S. Bein (1957) led to the conclusion that electromyographic reactions are a necessary link in the mechanism of articulation. L.A. Novikova's experiments (1955), with deaf children trained in oral and dactylic speech, established an intensification of electric activity both in the muscles of the tongue and in those of the arm when the children are given mental tasks. K. Faaborg-Andersen (1957) established appreciable activation of the speech musculature in silent reading. E. Kurka (1959, 1961) carried out spectrographic research, which showed that the strain on the musculature of the speech and voice in soundless verbal activity are specific. He registered the spectrum of the sounding of control tones which are emitted before and after work which is accompanied with continuous internal speech. Such work, for example, is done by typists and compositors. He established that in the spectrum of sounding of control tones, changes occur due to fatigue of the vocal musculature in performing work connected with internal speech. The latent locomotor reactions which are recorded electromyographically are also affected by vegetative and reticular activation, but their specificity, nevertheless, makes it possible to penetrate into the language of the ideomotor actions. A great amount of experimental research into these reactions were carried out by A.N. Sokolov (1968) who studied internal speech.

Research into the participation of internal speech in the process of short term memorization of words in Bulgarian and foreign languages was also carried out at the Suggestology Research Center. It proved that the more difficult and unknown the words, the more difficult their memorization and the greater the participation of

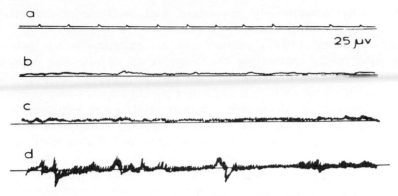

*Figure 6* EMG of lower lip of subject P.B.
a: Time count, 1 sec.  b: At rest.  c: In experiment to memorize 15 words of the mother tongue.  d: In experiment to memorize 15 words of the Hindi language.

internal speech in the process of memorization (Figure 6).

All the research studies are directly related to problems of ideo-motor actions which, according to many authors, underlie primary suggestibility.

This view is maintained by C.L. Hull (1933), M.B. Arnold (1946), H.J. Eysenck (1947), and A.M. Weitzenhoffer (1953). For the first time this kind of suggestibility was measured objectively by Chevreul (1954) with his pendulum. In this test, the subject holds a string to the end of which a weight is tied. He must try to keep the weight above a straight line drawn on the table. The experimenter tells him that the pendulum will start swinging along the line. The degree of suggestibility in the subject is judged from the number of swings and the degree of deflection.

Primary suggestibility is often measured by the "inclining body". In this test it is suggested to the subject that his body is inclining forward or backward. The deviation from the initial position is measured by an instrument. The degree of deviation determines the degree of suggestibility.

Another often used test is the suggested giving and releasing of the hand. With his eyes closed, the subject holds a rubber balloon in his hands. The experimenter tells him several times to start squeezing the balloon hard. In the second variation of this test, the subject is asked to squeeze the balloon as hard as he can and, at the same time, it is suggested to him that he is no longer able to hold the balloon in his hands. Suggestibility in both cases is measured by the pressure on the balloon. In general, any movement can be transformed into a primary suggestibility test.

H.J. Eysenck (1947) carried out an experiment for primary suggestibility by instructing the subjects to oppose the expected ideomotor movement. Thus, he was able to separate the pure ideo-motor action from volitional and other psychological components.

The concept of ideomotor reaction needs some explanation. It can be regarded as a readiness action for possible subsequent develop-ment of a conditioned reflex. It is evident from I.P. Pavlov's teaching that ideomotor actions are built on the basis of past experience and Ideomotor actions are outwardly built on the basis of past experience. For instance, the ideomotor action for the word "motherland" will be different with different nationalities and will depend on the language which the person learned to speak during early childhood. Thus, in a Frenchman the word "motherland" would cause ideomotor movements in certain groups of muscles, in an Englishman in other groups of muscles, and in the Bulgarian in still other groups—all depending on the pronunciation of the word in the respective language. It is obvious that these ideomotor movements connected with speech are built ontogenetically in the life experience because, the same ideomotor movements as the Frenchman has can be caused, for example, in the Bulgarian if he grows up in France, and vice versa, if the Frenchman grows up in Bulgaria. These are conditioned associa-tions which are built up from early childhood and are constantly reinforced during a person's life.

Those who uphold the concept of the idcomotor nature of sugges-tion proceeding from ideomotor actions extend the concept of suggestion, considering that the same principle is also valid for suggestively caused sensations, illusions and all the other reactions of the individual.

L. Welch (1947) interprets suggestibility, both under ordinary conditions and under hypnosis, as being the result of a conditioned reflex process which originates in the procedure of suggestion itself. The classical method of hypnotizing can be taken as an example: the physician who induces the hypnosis tells the patient to look intently at a bright object. At the same time, he tells him that his eyes will become tired. Since straining the eyes will inevitably result in fatigue, the physician's words that the eyes will get tired in fact represent a conditioned stimulus which is supported by the unconditionally arriving eye fatigue. Thus, in this first phase of hypnosis, the sugges-tion that the "eyes are tired" is supported by the actual fatigue of eye strain. In the second phase, the physician tells the patient that his eyes will begin to blink and will finally close. But this is, in fact, also the natural reaction of the eyes to the fatigue of continuously staring at something. The physician's words, however, anticipate the natural reaction and begin to play the role of conditioned stimulus, of a signal for an unconditionally arriving reaction. When, finally, the physician suggests to the patient that he is going to feel relaxed and sleepy and is going to fall asleep, conditions have already been created to attain this state without these words. The calm quiet atmosphere, the soft monotonous voice of the experimenter, the relaxed position of the patient, all predispose the patient to fall asleep. In this way, words precede nonconditioned reactions, acquire the value of signals, and begin to have a suggestive effect.

## b) Secondary suggestibility

Considerably fewer hypotheses have been put forward to explain secondary suggestibility. It is believed that it is comprised of more varied and complicated phenomena than primary suggestibility.

The best known are A. Binet's (1900) secondary suggestibility tests for graded lines and weights which have already been mentioned. However, olfactory stimuli can also be used. The subject is given several bottles of liquids with different odors and asked to identify them. Then bottles of water are given and the person is asked again to do the same. The identification of the odor in this case is demonstrative of the degree of suggestibility in the subject.

When visual instead of olfactory stimuli are used only very pale colors are shown for recognition. Then plain white sheets are shown as misleading tests. With auditory stimuli, the tests are made with very low sounds and the misleading ones with periods in which there is no sound whatsoever.

Rather different are the tests in which the memory and imagination participate. For example, the person is shown a picture after which a number of misleading questions are posed. The answers to these questions are used to calculate the extent of suggestibility in the subject. Similar also are the ink-blot tests. The subject is asked whether he can see certain suggested but not existing colored spots in an ink-blot. Depending on the number of spots he alleges he has seen is judged a subject's suggestibility.

H.J. Eysenck (1947) indicated the above-mentioned tests as typical of secondary suggestibility. The majority of researchers, however, give a much wider definition to the concept of secondary suggestibility. Binet (1900) points out the following more important mechanisms of secondary suggestibility: (1) subordination to outside influence, (2) tendency toward imitation; (3) influence of a preconceived idea, (4) expectant attention. K.G. Stukat (1958) unites the first and second mechanisms, pointed out by Binet, into one, "the need felt by the individual to submit" and the third and fourth again into one, "the mechanism of expectation". W. McDougall (1908) believed that each human being has "instincts" of self-assertion and submission which are the most important prerequisites for suggestibility. According to him, the presence of a person whom one considers to be inferior to oneself, gives rise to a self-assertive impulse. Such an impulse signifies a considerable drop in suggestibility. But in the presence of a person who creates an impression of superiority of any kind, there arises an impulse, a tendency to subordination which places one in a state subordinate and receptive to that person. The impression of strength and superiority can be in many directions: with respect to physical strength, social position, intellectual level, or work skills.[1]

The role of cognitive factors and even the belief that suggestion in secondary suggestibility is a purely rational process are pointed out in the investigations of K. Duncker (1938), R.W. Berenda (1950), S.E. Ash (1948, 1952), and others. They criticize the view that social relations are the result of suggestive effects, resulting in automatic reactions. This would signify that man in his social environment is not critical, and is completely subordinate to the authority dominating in the environment and is in constant interaction with the environment. In fact, it cannot exist without its environment. But this does not mean that the individuals act as one in a somnambulistic phase of hypnosis. Ash even purports to show that when the individual yields to the influence of a certain authority, this is not due to automatic subordination but to the acceptance of the situation and to seeing it in a new and more rational light. The same thought expressed by persons with various degrees of authority sounds different and is

---

[1] Muzaffer Sherif (1936) writes about the complexity of the connections of the suggestive stimulus, especially in a group situation. R.E. Coffin (1941) points out that during the preparatory period for ordinary experiments with secondary suggestibility, conditions for establishing the preliminary setup are created. It can be accepted that this setup is experimentally prepared (created) behavior. The subjects' answers in the course of the experiment depend on this preliminary preparedness. It contains a number of cognitive factors in itself.

understood differently not only because of the suggestive effect
of the authority, but also because the authoritative person introduces
his own nuance to what he has said. Thus, Ash considers that the
reaction to the same thought in different ways, according to whether
it has been expressed by a person of higher or lower authority,
depends on a new cognitive property implied in the thought—a
cognitive property depending on the authority of the person who
uttered it. Ash says the influence of the authoritative person is not so
much by way of automatic subordination but rather by the rational—
cognitive elements which a thought can acquire when expressed by a
person with considerable authority.

D. Krech and R. Crutchfield (1948) accept Ash's view, but do not
think that it is always so. In some cases suggestion by the
mechanisms of authority is realized because of a person's tendency
toward consent and subordination. In such cases, suggestion is first
accepted, and then the cognitive qualities of what is suggested are
changed subjectively.

J. Das, R. Rath and R.S. Das (1955) carried out experiments in
which the subjects had to arrange excerpts from poems in the order
of their value, without knowing the authors of the poetry. They had
to arrange the same excerpts according to their value a second time,
but this time they were told the authors of the poems. From the
results it was evident that the authority of the authors had a significant influence on their judgment and understanding of the merits
of the given excerpts.[1]

K.G. Stukat (1958) finds that secondary suggestibility is greater
in individuals whose position requires greater subordination. His
experiments also appear to indicate that younger people are more
suggestible than adults, women more than men, and neurotics more
than healthy individuals. He concludes that secondary suggestibility
is determined by a number of subjective factors originating mainly
in the need for subordination and expectation. Thus, research into
secondary suggestibility approaches psychological research—through
which it has been established that cognitive functions are

---

[1] The effect of the preliminary reinforcement of suggestibility has been
studied by H.K. Kelman (1950), B. Mausner (1954), F. Samelson (1957) *et al.*
The very varied data and the insufficient preliminary research work that has
been done on the typological characteristics of individuals makes it impossible
to draw comprehensive and uniform conclusions. Nevertheless, interesting results
from preliminary individual research and subsequent experimenting in groups
have been obtained.

determined, to a large extent, by the functional state of the individual, as well as by a number of other psychological factors, such as needs, past experience, frame of mind, etc. This can also be seen in the experiments of F. Barlett (1932), L. Carmichael, H. Hogan and A. Walter (1932), and others.[1]

In some experiments, the subjects are shown the individual features of a given object after which a study is made of their power of perception and assessment. In experiments carried out by J. Bruner and G. Goodman (1947), ten-year-old children had to determine the size of coins of different values. It was found that the children tended to overestimate all coins that were shown that the children tended to overestimate all coins that were shown and that this overestimation increased with the increase in the face value of the coins. However, the results were quite different when the coins were made of cardboard. In these experiments, as well as in those of L. Carter and K. Schooler (1949), the overestimation of the coins was greater when the assessment had to be made from memory. It was likewise observed that children from poor families tended to overestimate the coins more than did children from well-to-do families. W. Ashley, R. Herper and R. Runyon (1951), in an interesting variation of this experiment, hypnotized the subject and suggested to one group that they were rich, and to another that they were poor. These investigations showed that under the suggestion of being poor the subjects overestimated the coins all the time, and under the suggestion of being rich they regularly underestimated them.[2]

The experiments of McGinnies (1948) on the influence of emotionally saturated words on perception are also related to secondary suggestibility. With a tachistoscope he presented a number of loaded words, such as "rape", "prostitute" and "penis", and also a number of neutral words. The exposure time was gradually

---

[1] A considerable amount of experimental work has been done on the various aspects of the functional determinants. For instance, R.H. Sanford (1936), R. Levine, I. Chein and G. Murphy (1942), G. Geilchrist and L. Nesberg (1952) *et al.* have studied the effect of hunger on the perception of indistinct figures. The subjects, when hungry, give answers connected with food more often than they do when they are not.

[2] In experiments carried out by L. Postman, J. Bruner and McGinnies (1948), words were shown in a tachistoscope at various speeds. The words of a higher value for the subjects were discovered more quickly than the words of a lower value.

increased. At the beginning, the word was under the threshold of recognition. The gradual increase of exposure time led to a moment when correct identification of the words became possible. The loaded words required a longer exposure time than did the neutral words and caused a much stronger cutaneous galvanic reaction before recognition.

That the mechanisms of suggestibility have not yet been clarified can be seen in the fact that there are different concepts of primary and secondary suggestibility. There are authors, such as Eysenck (1947), who are inclined to accept the existence of even tertiary suggestibility. Eysenck attributes the ideomotor actions to primary suggestibility, indirect suggestion to secondary suggestibility, and prestige suggestions (suggestions arising out of the influence of society or authority in general) to tertiary suggestibility. As a typical example of tertiary suggestibility he pointed out an experiment he carried out with a group of schoolchildren. He gave them question-naires and they had to give written answers to questions about their views on various subjects. In a few days' time he asked them to answer the same questions but this time he told them in advance the views of whole groups of people or of prominent authorities on the same questions. According to the extent of deviation from the original answers, conclusions were drawn as to the degree of tertiary suggestibility of the subjects.[1]

A number of authors differentiate between suggestibility in a state of hypnosis and suggestibility in a waking state under normal conditions. A.G. Hammer, F.J. Evans and M. Bartlett (1963), F.J. Evans (1967), and others accept the concept that suggestibility in a normal waking state and suggestibility in a state of hypnosis are essentially different. At the same time they reject the division of suggestibility into primary and secondary. Evans (1967) thinks that the psychometric properties of the suggestibility measuring tests are better known than the phenomena which they measure. The attempts to classify suggestibility into primary and secondary is given no convincing support from the results of the research work in this sphere.[2]

---

[1] Such a trend toward splitting the mechanisms of suggestion can lead to concepts of quaternary suggestibility, quintuple suggestibility, etc. So far, however, there are insufficient data from experimentation on this sphere to warrant such a division of the different forms of suggestion.

[2] F.V. Grimes (1948) carried out experiments with 233 children from 8 to 15 years of age. He gave them 16 suggestibility tests in a group atmosphere, but he

## PSYCHOLOGY AND PHYSIOLOGY OF SUGGESTION

Suggestion is being applied in psychotherapeutic practice in an organized scientific way before all its characteristic features have been explained through experimentation and before a comprehensive theory has been built up. In therapeutic practice, as well as in a few experimental studies, some of the characteristic features and possibilities of suggestion have already been outlined. However, its organized introduction into teaching through the suggestopedic system of education has made it possible to get more knowledge of suggestion itself as a phenomenon of everyday relations between individuals.

To understand the qualities of suggestion, it is necessary to examine the following: (a) the features, characteristic of suggestive phenomena, which determine their control of the functional reserves of the brain; (b) conscious and unconscious mental activity; (c) the phase encirclement, (d) nonspecific mental reactivity; (e) antisuggestive barriers; and (f) the means of suggestive connections.

In our experimental research into *suggestion,* we reached the conclusion that the process is not only a *direct incoming information stream* (with algorithmical and reprogramming functions) but, simultaneously, a developing *desuggestive–suggestive process* in which the *functional reserves of the brain* can be revealed and utilized. Therefore, *suggestion is a regulator of activity and functional organization on a more specific level.*

To understand the qualities of suggestion, it is necessary first to examine some of its aspects, conditions and characteristic features.

### Characteristic features of the suggestive phenomena

In order to develop the functional reserves of the brain, suggestive phenomena must possess features distinguishing them from "ordinary" nonsuggestive mental phenomena. Analysis of psycho-

---

failed to obtain the interrelations he had expected in his hypothesis of primary and secondary suggestibility. A.L. Benton and A. Bandura (1953), in most of their experiments, did not find essential interrelations and data on the expected factors of primary and secondary suggestibility in tests of suggestibility in 50 students. J.D. Duke (1964) investigated 91 persons, aged 34 to 72, but did not obtain any positive evidence of secondary suggestibility factors. G.A. Schichko (1969) proposed five suggestibility investigation tests without discussing the problem of the form in which they would be carried out.

therapeutic practice and the results of experimental suggestology and suggestopedy show that suggestive phenomena possess a number of distinctive features. The most important ones, those which deserve special examination, are: *directness, automation, speed, plasticity, precision* and *economy*

*Directness.* The term "directness" means that the suggestive connection mechanism is making use of more direct paths than those normally used to penetrate into the mental sphere; critical—logical discussion and recoding are not relied on but rather some emotive, automatical and intuitive mechanisms. In suggestion, the flow of information goes directly into the functional areas of the unconscious or the insufficiently conscious (paraconscious) mental activity. The consciousness only marks the ultimate results or some key stage moments.

*Automation* is another essential feature of the suggestive pheno-menon: conditions are created for speedy and very often sudden automation. Automation can easily comprise not only motor actions but also mental activities including memorization of an enormous amount of material. Thus, for example, it has been accepted that normally a student can learn the meaning of 30 to 50 foreign words in a day. Experiments with the suggestopedic system showed that students could memorize on an average 95 percent of the meaning of 1200 unfamiliar foreign words in a day. As has already been mentioned automation is easily brought about by suggestion directed to a number of motor actions. The quick curing of neurotic hyperkinesis or akinesis in only one session is based on this possibility.

The *speed* and *plasticity* of suggestive realization is likewise regularly observed in psychotherapeutic practice and in the suggesto-pedic pedagogical process. When the suggestopedic system of teaching and learning is used, memorization and the assimilation of study material is characterized by a speed several times greater than the ordinary and a possibility for the plastic use of the material learned.

The *precision* of suggestive results is due mainly to the general mechanism. This mechanism is related not only to the motor reactions but also to mental activity. Speed and precision of reactions can be seen in suggestive experiments with vegetative and biochemical functions of the organism. We noticed this both in our experiments with vegetative alterations (1955), and in our joint bio-chemical experiments with M. Markov and P. Kirchev (1962). The greater precision of mental operations is of particular significance for suggestopedic pedagogical practice.

The *economy* of suggestive phenomena is mainly the result of directness, automation, speed and precision. Economy should be understood mainly as economy of energy. It is well known that suggestive activities are accompanied by the minimum loss of energy. One of the basic paradoxical phenomena in suggestopedy is hyper-memorization with no fatigue and even the effect of rest. The absence of fatigue in suggestive activities has been established not only by the subjective state of the students who took part in the experiment but by objective indicators as well.

## Conscious and paraconscious mental activity

Many of the definitions of suggestion refer its mechanisms to the more or less unconscious.[1] These definitions of it are mainly the psychological ones emphasizing the absence of criticism, or the lack of attention and even cloudy consciousness, as the basic requirements for the realization of suggestion and as the basic characteristic feature. Without having fully explored the possibilities of the most essential features of suggestion, these definitions are, nevertheless, closest to the core of the matter.

In 1963, we expounded our view that the enormous role played by the unconscious mental activity cannot be denied, emphasizing that:

---

[1] We are introducing the term "paraconscious" in order to unite all "more or less unconscious" contents and processing of the mind. They comprise the unconscious setups of D.N. Uznadze which are close to the actions of inertia and the secondary automated actions. The term "para-consciousness" covers the deep instinctive tendencies which S. Freud and I.P. Pavlov interpret in two different ways. The term paraconscious also covers: all automatic or secondary automated activities; unconscious automated elements in the field of conscious mental activity; subsensory (subliminal) stimuli; peripheral (marginal) perceptions; most of the emotional stimuli; intuitive creativity; the second plane of the communicative process; a considerable part of the processed information in the process of conditioning, associating, coding and symbolizing; and a number of unconscious interrelations which have informational, algorhythmical and reprogramming effects on the personality.

The whole mental content and mental processes, designated under the term "paraconsciousness" have a number of common characteristic features. Sugges-tology utilizes a part of them, the paraconsciousness being considered as always indivisibly bound up with consciousness, constantly in mergence and refluence with the consciousness. Here and there we shall use "unconscious" as a synonym for paraconscious in the meaning of "more or less unconscious".

There are many facts known from life, from clinical practice, from hypnosis and from physiological experiments, indicating that understanding of the extra-conscious mental activity is of importance in understanding the human being in health and in sickness.

(p. 49)

Those denying the concept of the dominant instinctive—atavistic tendencies which constitute the unconscious and hence direct all human activity, have, in certain cases, ignored and even completely rejected the possibility of the existence of extraconscious mental activity. However, removal of the inconsistent biopsychic content from the concept of unconsciousness should under no circumstances signify the rejection of the concept of unconsciousness itself. Arguments can be adduced which make us bring up the question of the actual existence of the extraconscious mental activity. Without knowing these extraconscious mental mechanisms, it is impossible to reach a comprehensive and true understanding of the human personality and to build up a theory of suggestion.

## Paraconscious mental activity during sleep

There are indications of belief in the existence of paraconscious mental activity during natural sleep in the religions of ancient times. Of course, the empiric experience of humanity at that time found explanations which corresponded to the level of knowledge and beliefs of a given culture at a given time. The idea that certain intellectual activities occur in sleep still continues today. This idea is backed up to a great extent by the personal experience of many people, as well as by many curious reports about considerable creative achievements in science and the arts. For example, D. Mendeleev completed his work on the periodic table of the chemical elements during a dream. A. Kekule von Stradonitz solved the problem of the structure of the benzene nucleus in his sleep; and S.T. Coleridge envisioned Kubla Khan while drugged by a medicinal potion, and then wrote his poem.

The creative paraconscious mental processes during sleep can be controlled; this knowledge has been employed since antiquity both in healing and teaching. In modern psychotherapeutic practice, there are methods to bring about a therapeutic effect by suggestion during sleep. The therapeutic effect is noted the following day, most often with the patient unable to remember the procedure. In certain cases of marked negativism this method may prove a salutary one.

Control of some of the paraconscious mental processes during sleep has been revived in the procedures of modern hypnopedic methods.[1] The question arises, however, as to what extent this sleep is normal sleep, and to what degree it is transformed into hypnosis. This question will be discussed later.

Modern electrophysiological research has shown that the forms of cerebral activity observed in clear consciousness preserve to some extent their characteristic features from lowered levels of wakefulness to profound sleep. Since ancient times, attempts have been made to explain the invariably occurring condition of sleep and its power to restore the strength of the organism.

The natural sciences launched the first scientific explanations about sleep. C.V. Economo (1929) emphasized that some of the first attempts at a scientific explanation of sleep were made by Maussot, Claude Bernard, Nathanson, and others who explained this state as due to changes in the cerebral blood circulation. Contradictions appeared, however: some of the authors attributed sleep to cerebral hyperaemia and others to cerebral anemia. There were four variations of the theory of cerebral hyperaemia: (1) higher intracranial pressure, (2) passive hyperaemia, (3) active hyperaemia, and (4) partial hyperaemia.

Also quite widespread were the theories which explained the onset of sleep as the accumulation of a special "substance of fatigue" in the blood. These physiological autointoxication theories indicated

---

[1] The research of H. Gernsback (1911, 1962, 1967), Z.N. Finey (1967), A.M. Svyadosht (1962, 1965), L.N. Bliznichenko (1966), I. Balkhaashov (1965), B. Zukhar (1967, 1968), I.P. Pushkina (1967), V.P. Zukhar *et al.* (1965), I.P. Pushkina and V.P. Zukhar (1967), N.P. Zavalova, V.P. Zukhar, Y.A. Petrov (1964), V.N. Kulikov (1964-a, 1964-b), V.A. Artemov (1967), E.L. Leon (1967), E.M. Sirovskiy (1967), Y.A. Maksimov (1967), A.S. Segal (1967), J. Genevay (1959-a, 1959-b), J. Pichon (1960), G. Stocker (1967), and others revealed the possibility of receiving information during sleep. They found that this information could later be put to practical use. A. Haller (1772), E. Darwin (1801), J. Muller (1940), J.E. Purkinje (1846) *et al.* adhered to the concept of higher intracranial pressure and hyperaemia, while W. Hammond (1880), A. Henoque (1881), I. Tarchanoff (1894), G. Bunge (1901) *et al.* held opposite views: they attributed the cause and nature of sleep to cerebral anaemia. Because of these contradictory opinions, E. Bertin, C. Richet (1898) *et al* doubted the effect of cerebral blood circulation as the origination of sleep. Nervous mechanisms were sought to explain the rapidity of the change of the translucency of cerebral blood vessels. Brown-Sequard (1889) observed that anaemia of the cortex occurred with hyperaemia of the brain stem.

various substances as being the cause of sleep. C.V. Economo (1929) examined them, discussing the experiments of Legendre and Pieron, who held dogs in a state of wakefulness by keeping them running on a rotating drum from 5 to 22 days. After this they isolated special substances, "hypnotoxins" from their blood and their brains which, when introduced into the circulation and liquor systems of waking animals, brought on a state of sleep. However, the explanation of these authors is not convincing as there is no absolute parallel between fatigue and sleep. Sometimes one falls asleep without being tired, and often one stays awake although one is very tired. Also, recorded observations of Siamese twins with common blood circulation (about whom I. Gall, 1901; and W. Washide, 1904, wrote; and on whom P.K. Anokhin, 1958, dwelt later on) show that quite often one of the twins can sleep while the other remains awake. The "hypnotoxins" of Legendre and Pieron are evidently toxic decomposition products, the result of extreme fatigue which does not occur under normal physiological conditions. It is possible that these substances have an autointoxicating effect on the brain, leading to a state similar to narcosis. It is quite natural that because of their toxicity they will have an effect on other animals, too. This, however, does not permit us to treat the sleep-like state originating in this way as identical with normal, physiological sleep. Since these experiments, a great deal of research work has been done in attempts to explain what causes sleep.[1]

---

[1] Some authors maintain that of decisive importance in the onset of sleep are the changes in the functions of the endocrine glands and their effect on the vegetative nervous system. L. Stern (1937) examines Salmon's conception associating the inhibiting effect exercised by the posterior section of the pituitary gland on the sympathetic centers in the basis of the third ventricle with the function of sleep. A. Brissemoret and A. Joanin (1911), and H. Marchand (1921) discussed the role played by cholestrol, E. Devaux (1910), R. Dubois (1901, 1909), E. Rosenbaum (1892) *et al.* dwelt on the osmotic hypotheses and on the intercellular bloating of neuralgia; P. Kronthal (1907), H. Zwaardemaker (1908) *et al.* find that congenital cellular and nervous mechanisms explain the periodicity of sleep; in the biological approach of H. Foster (1900, 1901), M. Nicard (1904) *et al.* greater attention is given to the sense of sleep and its phylogenesis. Attempts have been made to explain sleep by changes in the ionic equilibrium of the body. L. Stern (1937) attributes the reduced excitability of the nerve centers to the increased concentration of calcium ions and the decreased concentration of potassium ions and explains the changes in the composition of the liquor by changes in the hemocerebral barrier caused by the endocrine glands.

L. Mauthner (1890), O. Vogt (1895), E. Berger and L. Loewy (1898), L.

The hypotheses on the nature and mechanisms of sleep do not account for everything which has been said on this matter, but they show how easily certain phenomena can be accepted as causes of sleep when it has not been proved that they may be only its results. Many vegetative, endocrine and humoral alterations occur in the body during sleep, but this does not mean that the functions of the brain, associated with one of its most important states, i.e., sleep, are subordinate to them or to centers lying in the subcortex.

I.P. Pavlov came upon the problem of sleep accidentally when, in a number of experiments, the animals fell asleep and hindered him in getting on with his work. The sleep originating during the experiment intrigued him and became one of the subjects of his research. In 1910, the first publication on the problems of sleep was made by two of his students, O.S. Solomonov and A.A. Shishlo (1910). Pavlov found that sleepiness and sleep develop when the process of inhibition begins to take the upper hand in the incessant interaction between excitation and inhibition, and flows along the cortex and its lower "storeys".

Pavlov regards the nature of sleep as a reduction of the external activity of the nerve cells and considerable activation of the internal constructive processes. The energy reserves, which have been destroyed during the functioning of the cell "outside" at the time when the process of excitation has been mainly brought about, are restored during sleep. Then the diffuse process of inhibition diverts the activity of the cells "inward", and the assimilation processes are increased. It is clear that sleep is a necessary phase of the nervous system. This is the reason it inheres in each cell and can start diffusing from the most tired functional cerebral regions which have been the most exhausted from active functions "outward". The cortical cell, phylogenically the youngest and functionally the most reactive, is most vulnerable and prone to fatigue, and for this

---

Oppenheimer (1902), R. Dubois (1901), A. Cartaz (1901), F. Veronese (1910), E. Tromner (1910), and L. Haskovec (1911) seek the center of sleep, localizing it mainly in the mesodiencephalic region. Recent authors, accepting a center of sleep, base their views mainly on Economo (1929), and W.R. Hess (1948, 1949). In somnolent encephalitis, Economo discovered alterations in the posterior wall of the third ventricle and in the gray matter around aqueductus Silvii, on the basis of which he concluded that the change from a waking state to one of sleep must be regulated there. Hess provoked sleep in cats by isolated stimulation with weak electric current in the region below the third ventricle between commissura anterior and nucleus ruber. V. Demole (1927) injected calcium bichloride into the infundibulum and also provoked sleep.

reason it is the first to fall into a state of inhibition.

Sleep can be provoked by a conditioned reflex by associating it with an indifferent stimulus, as in the formation of an ordinary conditioned reflex. I.P. Pavlov examines the case of the de-afferented dog of A.D. Speransky and V.S. Galkina, and connects it with Schrumpel's patient who maintained contact with the world by means of only one eye and one ear. There is also the question of the two types of sleep: passive sleep, due to the disappearance of the numerous stimuli which usually enter the large hemispheres, and active sleep, resulting from the diffusion of a process of inhibition which can be regarded as an active process and not as a state of inactivity.

The question arises as to whether the nervous system does not go through three different states: a state of excitation, a state of inhibition and some indifferent state where both are absent? Pavlov stated that life is a constant flux between destruction and restoration so that a neutral state would be actually difficult to comprehend. He emphasized that sleep in de-afferented animals is also active. In them, the tonus is reduced and the process of excitation weakens, facilitating the diffusion of the generating process of inhibition. The possibility that this sleep is based on inhibition proceeding from the remaining receptors, which are subjected to continuous monotonous stimuli, cannot be excluded.

Pavlov also considers that de-afferentation in respect to internal stimuli explains the sleep in lethargic encephalitis. He is inclined to explain sleep in dogs, whose large hemispheres have been removed, by inhibition which begins directly in the cells of the lower formations, instead of their cortices which have been taken out.

In regard to sleep caused by stimulation of the hypothalamus, he is of the opinion that the faradic current used by Hess may stimulate not the centers but the routes. It may, through its monotony, cause a purely reflectory sleep such as is brought about by any slight rhythmical stimulus.

P.K. Anokhin (1958), G.N. Sorokhtin (1961), and others do not find sufficient justification for accepting Pavlov's concept that sleep is an active process of diffused inhibition. These doubts have been vindicated by modern electrophysiological research. L.P. Latash (1968) wrote that

. . . facts obtained in research work in the last few years have proved unexpected to a considerable degree, as they plainly contradict many stable concepts about the nature of cerebral processes connected with these states, and make it necessary to reassess certain general principles connected with the organization of the cerebral functions.

(p. 8)

And Bassin (1968-a) writing about the "very profound changes now taking place in ideas about the mechanisms of sleep", concluded,

In the whole incompleteness of these changes, the two general ideas emphasized by us above (the inadequacy of the concepts about a diffuse-sleep cortical inhibition and the stress that is put on the complex interactions of the functionally differentiated cerebral systems) are obviously receiving more and more corroboration every year from the results of experimental work.

(p. 181)

Much experimental material has been accumulated since the first electrophysiological research into the reticular formation and into the role it plays in the mechanisms of sleep. In order to get a better idea of the complexity of the problem, it is necessary to recall the exciting research which roused a great deal of discussion and led to a more profound understanding of the neurophysiological mechanisms of sleep.

F. Bremer (1935, 1937) proceeds from the working hypothesis that the sleep of mammals is due to functional de-afferentation of the hemispheres. In experiments with isolated cat brain, involving high fission of the stem on the level between the bridge and the mesencephalon and preserving the blood supply from the vertebral and carotid arteries, the EEG shows the pattern of typical normal sleep. When an incision is made into the cerebral stem of the bulbo-spinal boundary, no essential changes occur in the alertness and sleep of the preparation.

This has led to the conclusion that impulses conducted along ascending routes raise the tonus of the cortex and create the state of alertness. This is the reason that the cerebrum, isolated on the level of the upper cervical vertebrae, is sleeping, but can be easily awakened by light, sound and smell stimuli. The isolation of these stimuli in anatomical or functional de-afferentation, however, results in sleep. In experimental work it has been found that absolute de-afferentation of the cortex results in complete and irreversible sleep of the cortical centers, ending in the death of the animal in a few days. The sleep is assessed by the EEG.

The EEG during sleep is characterized by slow waves of high

voltage. It is thought that there is synchronization of the potentials from more than one structure. The impulses of the various receptors, if they reach the cerebrum cortex as they do in a waking state, cause desynchronization, which is expressed in faster waves and lower potentials. Usually, this reaction also coincides with changes in the behavior of the animal, which begins to move and gradually takes on the appearance of being awake.

G. Moruzzi and H. Megaun (1949), using a spontaneously sleeping or narcoticized preparation of an isolated cat brain, introduced thin electrodes into the reticular formation. As soon as they stimulated the reticular formation with weak current, the EEG changed from slow high voltage waves to the rapid lower voltage waves, which characterized the waking state of the preparation. From these experiments it can be concluded that the stimulation of the reticular formation with electric current results in awakening the sleeping brain. To find an answer to the question of whether the stimulation of the reticular formation spreads to other formations of the stem, i.e., the specific afferent system in the lemnisci, other experiments were carried out. The lemnisci in the stem were destroyed in advance and then the reticular formation was stimulated. The reaction of awakening again appeared on the EEG. Therefore, the stimulation not of the specific afferent system but of the reticular formation changed the electrical activity and the behavior of the preparation. Reverse experiments, with preliminary destruction of the reticular formation, have confirmed the correctness of this concept. In these experiments, the preparation continued its sleep.

The electroencephalographic research showed that in the stimulation of any exteroceptive field two types of electrical responses are recorded in the cerebral cortex. A primary potential which has a brief latent period is led off from the projectional region of the respective exteroceptive field. The so-called secondary potential, which has a longer latent period, is led off, along with it, from the rest of the cerebral cortex. This is the reason that it has been generally accepted that there are two afferent systems. One is the familiar system which conducts the sensory stimuli to the cortex. Travelling along it, the stimulus moves with great speed and only reaches the respective projectional field. This is the *specific system.* There is also a separate *non-specific system,* the routes of which have so far been inaccurately defined. The stimulus travels slower, and reaches not only the respective projectional field, but also all the rest of the cortex.

Thus, for example, M.A. Zhrebtsov (1939, 1940) showed that vestibular stimuli can cause the awakening of a dormant cortex even when the projectional zone of the vestibular analyzer in the cortex has been separated. A. Rheinberger and H. Jasper (1937) found that the awakening of the cortex does not necessarily begin from the projectional zone of the stimulated analyzer but spreads concentrically.

G. Nastev and R. Koinov (1961) wrote that the data given in literature on the existence both of an ascending activating system and of a descending inhibiting system serve as confirmation of Pavlov's teaching that there are no regions in the nervous sytem for the production of excitation, inhibition, wakefulness or sleep: these are two forms in which the same material structure is manifested.

Effects of the cortex on the reticular formation have also been discovered. F. Bremer and C. Terzuolo (1953, 1954) observed the same bilateral diffuse desynchronization as usually occurs in the stimulation of the reticular formation in the stimulation of certain regions of the cerebral cortex of a dormant cat preparation. Subsequent research work made it possible to determine the cortical regions where desynchronization reactions can be obtained in stimulation.

C.F. Rossi and A. Zanchetti (1960) believe that cortico-reticular impulses can be conducted directly by the collaterals of the basic cortico-spinal fibers like the collaterals of the ascending nonspecific system of the reticular formation. The results of the research carried out by R.S. Cajal (1909–1911), and later by M.E. Scheibel and A.B. Scheibel (1958), gave convincing support to this possibility.

Since the early publications of F. Bremer (1935, 1937), G. Moruzzi and H. Megaun (1949), M. Rheinberger and H. Jasper (1937), P.K. Anokhin (1949, 1957-b), and many others, the problem of scientifically explaining sleep has become very much more complicated. It has been · found that both synchronizing and desynchronizing impulses can be obtained from various levels of the nervous system. G. Berlucchi *et al.* (1965), G. Moruzzi (1964), S. Narikashvilli (1965), A. Zanchetti (1965) and others pointed out the presence of synchronizing structures in the caudal sections of the stem of the brain. M. Bonvallet and P. Dell (1965) described yet another bulbular synchronizing area. M. Monnier *et al.* (1968), J. Schlag and F. Chaillet (1963) showed that desynchronization of the EEG and behavioral activation arise in high frequency stimulation of the nonspecific nuclei of the thalamus, while in low

frequency stimulation synchronization of the EEG arises with manifestations of behavioral sleep. According to Monnier *et al.* (1960),
the two thalamic systems interact with the same cortical regions,
but they can be differentiated pharmacologically, i.e., they are
heterogeneous in their chemical structure. Research carried out by
Monnier *et al.* (1963), S. Narikashvilli (1965), E. Favale *et al.* (1961),
G. Rossi (1962), and Penalosa-Rojaz (1964) showed that the
frequency of the stimuli is of decisive importance in bringing about
a synchronizing or desynchronizing effect at all levels of the reticular
formation, from the medulla oblongata to the cortex. Regardless of
where it is applied, high frequency stimulation causes the reaction
of awakening and low frequency, the reaction of falling asleep. In
this diffusion of the mechanisms, the separate centers show only
increased reactivity, an enhanced readiness to react to applied
stimuli. In some places, this readiness is of a mainly synchronizing
nature and in others, mainly desynchronizing.

N. Buchwald *et al.* (1961) reported that low frequency rhythmic
stimuli in the head of nucleus caudatus cause synchronization and
behavioral inhibition, and high frequency stimuli result in an activation in the EEG and the behavior. This indicates that nuclear structures which are not included in the nonspecific formations of the
brain stem and the thalamus, also participate in the system of regulation of the waking–sleeping states.

C. Clement and M. Sterman (1963), R. Hernandez-Peon (1965)
described a hypogenous zone in the basal sections of the frontal lobe
which, so far as is known, is the only brain structure which in every
stimulating impulse frequency results in synchronization of the
EEG and behavioral sleep.

O. Pompeiano and J. Swett (1962), and A. Roitbak (1962)
showed in their research work that low frequency stimulation of
many afferent cutaneous nerves results in synchronization of the
EEG and behavioral sleep. High frequency stimulation results in an
EEG activation reaction.

If, to the whole of this complicated picture, we add the results
of the research carried out by P. Anokhin (1962-b, 1963), T.
Tokizane (1965), C. Fangel and B. Kaada (1960), A. Roitbak and
S. Buthuzi (1968), R. Naquet *et al.* (1965), and V. Eddy and D.
Lendsley (1959) it becomes clear how intricate is the structure of
the multisectional system for the maintenance of the different levels
of the waking state under different life conditions. On the harmonious coordination of this entire apparatus depends the regular func-

tioning of those nerve mechanisms, which ensure a considerable part of the material substratum of many of the unconscious mental processes.

Before neurophysiological research along these lines had been concluded, reports appeared in the relevant scientific literature showing that the matter was even more complicated. The mechanisms for maintaining the different levels of wakefulness would have to be examined in a different light, namely in connection with the so-called "paradoxical" sleep, "activated" sleep, "rapid eye movements" (REM) sleep, etc. It is still too early to foresee the consequences of this research along new lines, but undoubtedly they will be of particular significance.

F. Azernsky and N. Kleitman (1953) published the results of their EEG investigations of healthy adults during natural night-time sleep. They found that rapid movements of the eyeball (REM) occurred four or five times during one night's sleep, and were accompanied by an accelerated pulse and accelerated breathing. These periods occurred every one or two hours, the first occurring one or one and a half hours after falling asleep. They were of varying duration, lasting from 6 to 53 minutes. They found that if the subjects were awakened during a REM period, 74 percent of them said that they had been dreaming. If awakened outside the REM periods, the subjects very seldom said they had been dreaming. Research along these lines was carried a step further by W. Dement and N. Kleitman (1957-a, 1957-b), N. Kleitman (1961) and others who found that in the REM period there appeared changes in the EEG similar to those of activation during the waking state. The REM cycles and EEG activation were repeated five or six times during the night, and their duration increased with the approach of morning. In these experiments 80 percent of those awakened during the period of activation were dreaming. All this led to the conclusion that sleep in this stage is lighter and more superficial, despite the fact that in this same stage the sonic awakening threshold is simultaneously raised.

A similar stage of sleep was observed in animals by W. Dement (1958). The combination of low voltage rapid EEG activity (similar to the reaction of awakening), REM and abrupt muscular relaxation with the sensory threshold of awakening considerably raised, furnished grounds for considering that the REM stage is not a superficial sleep but a paradoxical sleep, i.e., sleep in which there is dissociation between EEC readings and behavior. This kind of sleep was observed for the first time in the atropine and physostygmine paradox, hence, its name.

The research work carried out by many experts has thrown a great deal of light on different aspects of paradoxical sleep.[1] For example, in Jouvet's laboratories it was shown that "slow" sleep and "rapid" sleep are related to different brain formations: the slow to the telencephalon and the rapid to the rhombencephalon. The reduction in behavior activity, the rise of the awakening threshold, the delay in the heart rhythm and breathing during rapid sleep made these researchers come to the conclusion that it was a sounder sleep related to smaller brain structures, or "archeosleep". They defined slow sleep as "neosleep". However, K. Lissak *et al.* (1961) found in their experiments that if high frequency mesencephalous reticular-formation stimulation is used with subliminal intensity to awaken a test animal, then rapid sleep can be obtained. This effect suggested that rapid sleep reflects a state of shallower sleep due to the intensification of the activity of the reticular activating system. On the other hand, apart from vegetative evidence of the intensification of sleep during rapid sleep, research into the spinal motor apparatus has shown that sleep is intensified during this phase. F. Baldissera and M. Mancia (1965), K. Kubota *et al.* (1965) and others demonstrated in their experiments with animals, and R. Hodes and W. Dement (1964) and J. Paillard (1965) with people, that the moderate and selective inhibition of the spinal apparatus in slow sleep increases very considerably and becomes generalized in the transition to rapid sleep. E. Kantzov (1965) discovered that the cerebral blood circulation is intensified from 30 to 50 percent in the transition from slow to rapid sleep. He attributed this to active vasodilatation resulting from an increase in cerebral metabolism. He also reported a transitory rise in blood pressure which he attributed to dreams occurring at the moment. K. Bulow (1965) did not consider pulmonary ventilation and $CO_2$ sensitivity in rapid sleep as proof of the correctness of the view that it is sounder than slow sleep. D. Hawkins *et al.* (1962) reported an increase in electrocutaneous resistance in rapid sleep.

---

[1] M. Jouvet (1961, 1962, 1965), M. Jouvet and D. Jouvet (1963), M. Jouvet *et al.* (1965), K. Lissak *et al.* (1961), A. Rechtschaffen and E. Wolpert (1964), A. Rechtschaffen *et al.* (1963-a, 1963-b), A. Rechtschaffen and P. Verdone (1964), A. Rechtschaffen and L. Maron (1964), A. Rechtschaffen and D. Foulkes (1965), D. Foulkes and A. Rechtschaffen (1964), G. Redding *et al.* (1964), K. Bulow (1965), H. Caspers (1965), F. Motokizawa and B. Fujimori (1964), D. Hawkins *et al.* (1962), and F. Snyder (1963).

Many authors are inclined to consider rapid sleep as a state of a particular kind, one which has a special functional purpose. F. Snyder (1963) even believed rapid sleep to be a third state, differing from sleeping and waking. Confirmation of these assessments has been provided by research into the selective exclusion of rapid sleep, into dreams occurring in it and into the phylo- and ontogenesis of rapid sleep, and by microelectrode investigations of individual neurones in rapid and slow sleep.

In many experiments the subjects were allowed to sleep only while there was evidence of slow sleep. At the appearance of rapid sleep they were immediately awakened. In the investigations of W. Dement (1965), R. Berger (1961), L. Oswald (1962), B. Schwartz (1962) and others, the transition was assessed by EEG activation and the reduction of electric activity in the front cervical muscles, REM, etc. The control group was awakened several times during rapid sleep. H. Agnew *et al.* (1974), W. Dement (1965), and F. Snyder (1963) found that cutting out rapid sleep results in its becoming more frequent during the rest of the night and in the following nights. This is at the expense of slow sleep, and also results in raising the threshold of awakening in the time of rapid sleep. W. Dement (1965) showed that if such experiments continued for more than 7 nights in succession, it could result in mental disturbance. As the time spent in a waking state also increases with the increase in the frequency and duration of rapid sleep, W. Dement (1965), in some of the experiments, did not awaken the subjects during rapid sleep, but excluded this phase pharmacologically. Through the experiments of A. Rechtschaffen and L. Maron (1964), it was established that amphetamines almost completely eliminate the REM phase. At about the same time, G. Rossi (1962), L. Oswald *et al.* (1963) reported that barbiturates also suppress the REM periods. The paradoxical effects of these two opposite (as far as maintaining of the waking state is concerned) pharmacological substances is emphasized by the opposite effects they have on the reticular formation. In the experiments of P. Bradley (1963), G. Hiebel *et al.* (1944), A. Rothballer (1957), Van Meter and G. Ayala, it was found that amphetamines stimulate the activating functions of the reticular formation. It was emphasized in the experiments of J. French (1953), A. Arduini and M. Arduini (1954) that the barbiturates have an inhibiting effect on the reticular formation. The pharmacologically excluded rapid sleep produced the same results by waking the person during the transition to the rapid sleep phase. The psychic disturbances developed later, however, about a fortnight after the subject had been deprived of rapid sleep. Similar results were obtained by M. Jouvet *et al.* (1962, 1965) in experiments with animals: they found that continuous deprivation of paradoxical sleep is fatal. These data show that paradoxical sleep is related to vitally important functions of the cerebral system.

Doubt was cast on the initial hypothesis that the elimination of rapid sleep is connected with the elimination of dreams and, hence, the harmful consequences, because it was observed there was dreaming during slow sleep. The hypothesis that rapid sleep originates because of the accumulation of an unspecified toxic substance during the waking state, a substance which was supposed to decompose during that phase, also proved untenable. It was inexplicable how paradoxical sleep could increase in the morning hours and not in the initial period, when a great accumulation of this hypothetical toxic substance might have been expected.

The presence of rapid sleep in the newly born and the evidence of A. Rechtschaffen *et al.* (1963-a), showing that dreams occur during slow sleep, also threw doubt on the hypothesis conjecturing the absolute association of activated sleep and dreams. Of course, the conservation of dreams in the memory for a certain period after the termination of rapid sleep must also be taken into account. There is also evidence suggesting that the REM are connected with dreams which are in progress. REM are identical with eye movements made to examine objects in a waking state. By the nature of the eye movements in sleep, one can even get a rough idea of the image which is being dreamed. W. Dement (1965) found this coincidence in 80 percent of his subjects. It is also interesting that no REM has been observed in blind adults in the time of their activated sleep.

The contradictory data about the significance of REM brings us back to Dement and Kleitman (1957-a) who found that EEG activation is a more reliable criterion for the onset of dreams than the observation of REM. Our research into eye movements during sleep has confirmed this, we have observed eye motor activity during natural and hypnotic sleep. We made a more profound study of an eye phenomenon which refutes E. Hering's law (1868) of simultaneous uniform binocular transference of motor impulses both in a waking state and in sleep. According to this law, it is impossible under normal or clinical conditions for human eyes to move independently of each other, even for a moment. Research showed, however, that in sleep there is quite a clear deviation from Hering's law. This has consequences for the specialists' view on the anatomy of simultaneous eye movements, the physiology of eye movements, clinical practice, the theory of sleep, particularly the association between rapid movement of the eyes and dreaming and, hence, unconscious information processing. Experimental research was carried out into the eye motor movements of 240 healthy sleeping subjects who were divided up into groups as follows: 40 of up to one year of age, 60 of one to three years of age, 100 of three to seven years of age, 35 of seven to fourteen years of age, and 5 of over eighteen years of age.

The following methods were employed: the experimenter stood without making any sound by the bedside of those falling asleep and softly touched the upper part of their eyelids. If there was no reaction, the experimenter carefully raised both eyelids at the same time. It is possible to keep a sleeper's eyes open in this manner without disturbing him and on waking he remembers nothing about it. Some people sleep with only half-closed eyes. This made it possible to carry out our experiment with subjects of this type without even touching them and under completely natural conditions.

Our experiment established the following facts: in all children under two years of age, the eyes move most often in an unassociated manner and slowly in the time of sleep. Each eye moves on its own, independently and in all directions, including an upward one. Sometimes the movements stop for a time and then continue in the same manner. In children under two years of age the association of the eye movements is observed very rarely. In most cases, the movement which starts in one eye seems to entrain the other eye, which begins to follow suit in its movement only with a delay, moving slower as various transitionary positions of strabismus appear. We called this form of unassociated movement "entraining movement". When the subjects are older the unassociated movements gradually decrease but do not disappear completely. The eyeballs of adults, when the lids are raised, are sometimes turned upwards and immobile. Most often they move in an associated manner and gradually move upwards. Sometimes brief unassociated movements occur (Figure 7).

In the presence of eye movements, the waking threshold is higher than in the absence of eye movements, but it is still higher on the appearance of unassociated eye movements.

The results of this research was published in the *Journal of Neuropathology and Psychiatry,* Moscow, 1959. In 1965, A. Rechtschaffen and D. Foulkes reported analogical observations in an article in *Perceptual and Motor Skills,* Vol. 20, 1149—1160.

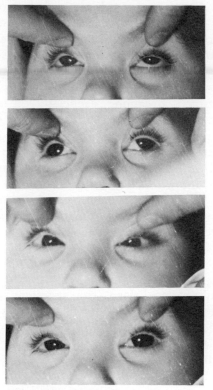

*Figure 7a*     Movements of the eyeballs in a child during sleep.

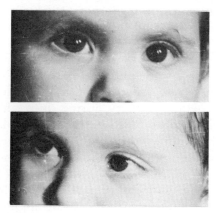

*Figure 7b*     The eyeballs of the same child (one year and 3 months of age) when looking forward and aside—in a waking state.

Because they do not comply with Hering's law of binocular vision, the unassociated movements of the eyeball during sleep cast doubt on the concept that the eye movements follow the form of the image of the dream. However, the phenomenon of unassociated eye movement does not preclude the occurrence of dreams at the same moment. It only casts doubt on the motor participation of the eyeballs while a person is dreaming, especially on the coordination of the eye movements with the visual outlines of the dream.

Unassociated movements of the eyes are frequent in early age. As the child gets older the movements become more and more connected, until in adults unassociated movements are observed considerably less frequently. As the unassociated eye movements are a part of the rapid eye movement phase, it is interesting to note that the ontogenesis of these movements coincides with a number of later observations of the ontogenesis of rapid sleep. Thus, for example, H. Roffwag *et al.* (1963), J.M. Valatx *et al.* (1964), I. Gohblit (1960), G. Meier and R. Berger (1965) and others found that rapid sleep is the first to originate in the ontogenesis and initially is the only form of sleep. The first signs of slow sleep appear a few weeks after birth and, gradually, in the years after this the proper interrelations between the two phases of sleep are established.

Research into the activity of single neurons in a waking state and in sleep brought quite interesting and, to a certain extent, unexpected results. For example, in the microelectrode investigations of the individual neurons during sleep carried out by P. Huttenlocher (1961-a, 1961-b), E. Evarts (1963, 1964, 1965), and in the investigations of single neurons by H. Jasper (1961), M. Verzeano (1961), F.F. Strumwasser (1958) and others, it was found that the concept of sleep as a diffused inhibition of the cortical neurons would have to be re-examined and specified at a new level. Even evidence of quantitative predominence of the inhibition process was not obtained. Instead of this, these researchers got the impression that there was a reorganization of neuron activity during sleep, the activity of some neurons being inhibited and of others intensified. The same results were also obtained in the investigation of slow sleep and, thus, it was difficult to make them fit into the former concept of sleep as a diffused inhibition. I. Volpert's experiment (1966), explaining dreams as incomplete and partial sleep which has remained as a phylogenically rudimentary heritage, is not applicable as an explanation of the rapid sleep phase. Taking into consideration the many experiments which have been carried out with selective elimination of this phase and the origination of psychic disorders in people and even death in animals as a result, one cannot but recognize the biological necessity of paradoxical sleep. And as most of the experimental data back up the concept that paradoxical sleep is most often accompanied by dreams, it is clear that the question of the usefulness of dreams will again come to the fore, this time with no need for psychoanalytical speculative interpretations.[1]

Bassin (1968-a) wrote,

Until the grave clinical consequences of selective inhibition of the rapid sleep phase are given a concrete biochemical explanation, we shall have to accept the possibility of dreams, as a psychic phenomenon, having a certain usefulness. And if this idea of usefulness is accepted, a very profound analysis would be necessary to see whether it is compatible with the idea of dreams as logically purely accidental, psychologically absolutely uncontrollable and only physiologically determinable reanimation of traces, i.e., with the idea which is fundamental in the hypothesis of fragmentation.

(p. 333)

Bassin's conclusion in summing up the results of modern neurophysiological research is a corroboration of the concept of the unconscious forms of the higher nervous activity playing a decisive role in the materialization of the principal internal mechanisms of suggestion. He sums up his understanding of the unconscious processing of information in the following passage:

On the basis of numerous observations speaking of the preservation by the sleeping brain of its capability to receive and analyze information in some forms and on the basis of the many special vegetative changes accompanying rapid sleep, it can be assumed that not only do the electrophysiological manifestations or somnolent states of the mind reverberate the basic and vitally important metabolic activity of the nervous tissue, but also that some of their components are related to the unconscious processing of information.

(pp. 188 and 189)

---

[1] Even Volpert (1966), no matter how he tried to reduce the importance of dreaming and connect it with the phylogenetic past, had to admit the following:

Dreaming has, nevertheless, some importance in that it reproduces in a natural or symbolic form the impressions or the conscious or unconscious experiences we have had during the day. Calm dreams are also of a certain biological significance as a factor of fixation of the inhibition of the "nucleus" of the dominant; the enlivening of its peripheral inessential elements by the rules of induction causes an inhibition of the essential elements constituting the "nucleus" of the dominant.

(p. 159)

The division of sleep into "slow" and "rapid" does not eliminate the problem of the various degrees of sleep, assessed on the basis of electroencephalographic evidence. While H. Davis *et al.* (1938) determined five degrees of sleep, other authors accept different variations in grading the profoundness of sleep. Thus, P. Passouant (1950) proposed three states of sleep by merging the first two states into one and the last two also into one; P. Spielberg (1955) described four stages of sleep; H. Blake *et al.* (1939) put forward a proposal whereby the second of Davis' phases should be called "zero". There was relatively widespread acceptance of the classification proposed by Dement and Kleitman (1957-a), who considered there were four stages, with REM included in the first one. In respect to the EEG characteristic of the first stage of sleep, there is quite a number of differences that are made still more complicated by the necessity of finding a place for rapid sleep in these phases. The research work of F. Gibbs and E. Gibbs (1941), W.R. Hess (1964), B. Roth (1961), H. Fischgold and B. Schwartz (1961), P. Gulyaev (1955) and others showed the great variety of EEG in the first phases of sleep and the difficulties encountered in making a strict identification of them. The paraconscious mental activity expended in these stages is still the object of research, all the more so because from this point of view the investigations of paradoxical sleep and slow sleep have not yet been completed. At the present stage one can only accept the fact that there are many indications of complex, but more or less unconscious, mental activity during normal sleep.

*Paraconscious mental activity in a normal waking state*

Paraconscious mental activity forms an unsuspected and large part of our activity in a normal waking state. V. Matveev (1967) points out 10 types of unconscious mental processes. Apart from posthypnotic suggestions, hypnopedy, dreams and natural somnambulism, he also emphasized: (1) the unconscious reverberation of the stimuli subliminal by their intensity (changes in atmospheric pressure, causing changes in cardiovascular reactions, vague anxiety, origination of dreams with given content, etc.); (2) the unconscious reverberation of stimuli subliminal by their duration (visual stimuli with a speed of under 1/25 second causing unconscious reactions in the form of suggested actions or influencing decisions in a situation of struggle between motives); (3) nonspecific sensations which are received unconsciously by the various receptors (the phenomenon of skin

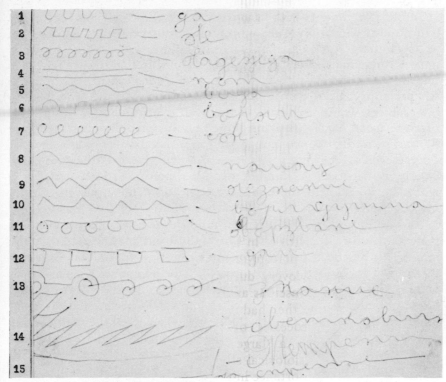

*Figure 8* Symbolic alphabet unconsciously created by subject N in his automatic writing.
1: yes. 2: no. 3: hope. 4: road. 5: water. 6: give back. 7: dream. 8: help. 9:ignorance. 10: (illegible). 11: tying together. 12: give. 13: knowledge. 14: quick as lightning. 15: (illegible).

sight which Leontiev (1959) refers to as atavistic subsensory reactions), (4) the unconscious reverberation of the properties of the objects (things) which biologically and socially are nonessential in a given moment to the subject (the uneven pavement for pedestrians engaged in a dispute, the type (print) of letters in a book which fascinates the reader); (5) ideomotor movements and a considerable number of habits and customary mannerisms.

The phenomenon of automatic writing, which has been described by A. Muhl (1930, 1956), G.G. Heyer (1959), and C.L. Tuckey (1921) could be used as one of the methods to study paraconscious mental activity and to reveal its nature. In experiments with automatic writing, part of the subject's life experiences, preserved in the paraconscious sphere, are tapped.

In our experiments with automatic writing, the subjects very often had no idea what they were writing and read what they had written as something quite unfamiliar. In some cases the subjects' handwriting changed or their writing was not in their native language but in other languages which they had studied. Furthermore, the writing materialized with great ease. Sometimes in the same session one subject would write in several styles. Automatic writing most often revealed some side of the unconscious mental activity (Figure 8), and proved to be subject to training. The absence of any signs of fatigue even after lengthy and intensive periods of writing was particularly noticeable. A number of other methods—free association method, Rorschach method, etc.—can also be used in similar investigations.

An enormous amount of information enters the central nervous system by way of receptors, more or less outside the scope of the mind. This has been proved in some hypnotic experiments in which the subject recounted perceptions which he had never been aware of before. Until their recovery during hypnosis, these perceptions had been subliminal, unconscious and unknown. Experimental research, however, showed that they had nonetheless affected the mental state and physiological processes of the personality. Such subliminal perceptions comprise a large part of the general suggestive background. The physiological study of the general suggestive background is of great importance in understanding the physiological and psychological mechanisms of the behavior of the individual.[1] M. Rosenzweig and L. Postman (1958) found that with a specific noise background, subliminal words were more easily perceived when they were longer or when they had greater frequency of usage in the language. F.H. Goldberg and H. Fiss (1959) obtained better

---

[1] The subsensory reactions observed by G. Gershuny (1947, 1951), the presensory reactions—by A. Pshonik (1952), the first signal system reactions—by A. Ivanov-Smolensky (1950, 1951, 1952), and others threw light on a number of physiological aspects of subliminal stimuli. Here F. Bassin (1958) refers to EEG changes, skin biopotentials, etc., caused by speech stimuli under the hearing threshold (Mazzumotto and Chzan Tsuli), the conditioned reflectory reactions to light stimuli in cases of hysterical amaurosis (Bogavut and Obolenska), A.K. Williams (1938), W.E. Vinacke (1942), and H.E. King, C. Landis and I. Zubin (1944) examined subliminal visual perceptions under different conditions of illumination. I. Goldiamond (1954, 1959, 1962, 1964) considers that the role of the subliminal stimuli is much smaller than is usually thought; the weaker the stimulus is (the farther it is from the threshold), the weaker its effect on the personality.

identification of the subliminal stimulus when some individual elements of it were perceived in a conscious manner. E. Kostandov (1967) measured responses to subliminal stimuli by the cutaneous— galvanic reaction, the desynchronization of cortical potentials, respiration reaction and the vessel structure in the plethysmogram. He discovered changes in the thresholds in photostimulation and in the pharmacodynamic effects. He thought that

in the elaboration of a nonspecific subsensory reflex such a lowering of the thresholds of bioelectrical or vegetative components of the orientation reflex could imitate the formation of a temporary connection.

(p. 641)

According to him, this was somewhat different from many reports about the actually built subsensory conditioned reflexes. Kostandov also reported differences in the threshold level in the perception of both emotionally saturated and neutral words. The emotional words in their subliminal effect may cause bioelectrical and vegetative reactions. A. Yus and K. Yus (1967) carried out research into the perception thresholds and the elements of "the unconscious" when conditioned reflexes were being worked out. They found that in some cases both a conditioned irritant and conditioned reaction could remain unrealized, while in other cases some of the elements were realized. At the same time, they found that subsensory stimuli had not only an effect on various vegetative reactions but also on the subject's consciousness in the form, for example, of a desire to perform a given motion.

In our experiments with the subliminal presentation of words in an unknown foreign language (Hindi), we connected the subliminal with research into memory.

This research showed that the subliminal or subsensory presentation of material increased the probability of its memorization very considerably. However, experimental postulations were necessary to bring us closer to the possibility of applying subsensory methods in practice.

Subsensory support was tested by us in clinical practice, too. In our psychotherapeutic system we included a number of subsensory elements. And, in 1963, we worked out a psychotherapeutic method for subliminal suggestion. We called it the "whispering method". We were looking for a shortcut to paraconscious mental activity. The method was found to be useful with extremely critical patients with hypertrophied antisuggestive barriers who did not yield easily to ordinary methods of suggestion.

When the whispering method is employed, the therapeutic suggestions are presented quietly in a whisper, under the threshold of conscious hearing by the patient. Careful attention must be paid to finding the optimal loudness and intonation of the whispering which ensures the overcoming of the antisuggestive barriers.

It could be argued that the therapeutic effect in cases of this kind is due not to the subliminal speech but to the autosuggestion, which may emanate when a "special" therapeutic session is conducted by a physician who has been able to win the confidence of the patient. The conception that autosuggestion plays some part in the suggestive sessions can be taken into consideration in every type of therapeutic session, including medicament treatment and other kinds of treatment. Autosuggestion is not always favorable; sometimes it hinders the therapeutic process. It is possible that in some particular cases autosuggestion acts favorably on the therapeutic effect of suggestion. However, the results of using the whispering method in treating a number of patients serve to confirm our opinion that the role of autosuggestion in this case is not a leading one. In treating many patients we obtained exactly those concrete effects which we were suggesting. And when it is taken into consideration that in some cases the suggestions were strictly specific and not known in advance, it is clear that there was little probability that the effect of the specific suggestion would coincide with the effect of autosuggestion.

There is one category of stimuli which in their absolute intensity should belong to the sensory, but which under specific conditions remain unconscious. This occurs most often when the attention is attracted by some stimuli while other stimuli remain on the "periphery" of the attention. This type of unconscious stimuli are called marginal subsensory stimuli. They are subsensory not in their absolute intensity but in their topicality in the given moment. They are realized either in the peripheral reception fields of the sense organs or in the central zones as automated details unmarked by attention. Peripheral subsensory stimuli play an important role in all interhuman relations.

These are perceptions which do not fall within the focus of the consciousness owing to its limited volume. The reception fields, however, are considerably wider than the scope of the conscious perceptions. The peripheral perceptions are non-conscious perceptions and therefore they are different from incidental learning and nonvolitional memory. However sometimes such a difference is difficult to make. This peripheral information from the unconscious stimuli without and within the focused field of the consciousness can be not only relevant, but also irrelevant to the direction of the attention and the content of the consciousness at that moment. Having once entered the brain, there is a delay before it floats up in the consciousness or it has an effect on the unconscious motives in decision making. Our studies have shown that this peripheral unconscious information rests at the basis of long-term memory. The following is one of the characteristic experimental patterns.

The experiment was carried out with a group of students (182 subjects over the age of 25) in a course studying a foreign language by the suggestopedic method. For one minute they were shown a board with 10 unknown foreign words in the respective language. (To be sure that they were not familiar with the words, they were given a preliminary test with 50 unknown foreign words, including the 10 words on the board.) Over the 10 words and a translation of them in the native language, there was a headline in small letters and this was also translated into the native tongue. It read: "Will you please memorize the following 10 words". All this shows that the students had to memorize the meaning of the 10 new foreign words. Not, of course, the words in the headline.

Immediately after being shown the board (for one minute), the students were given the same list of 50 unknown foreign words with the instruction: "Underline the words given on the board for memorizing". The same test work was given on the 2nd, 3rd, 4th, 5th and 10th day, without repeating the showing of the board. The results can be seen in Figure 9.

An analysis of the data shows that in the immediate check on the first day, the main information—"words from the board"—was 52.9 percent. On the second day it dropped to 37.3 percent and, with slight fluctuations, was retained at this level up to the tenth day. The difference between the results of the immediate check the first day and each successive day is statistically significant ($p < 0.01$). This curve comes close to Ebbinghaus' normal curve of forgetting.

The curve of the peripheral perceptions—"words of the headline" —is somewhat different. Whereas in the immediate check on the first day the students' unconscious recollection was 2.5 percent. On the following days it increased and on the 10th day reached a figure that was five times greater than on the first day—13.8 percent. The difference between the immediate check on the first day and each

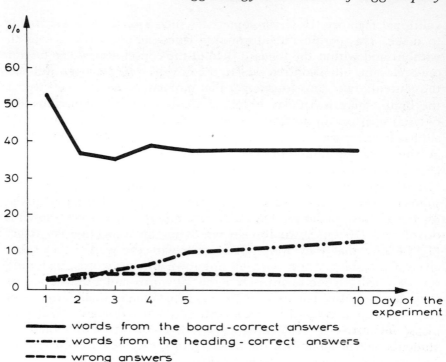

*Figure 9*

successive day was of growing statistical significance (on the fourth day—$p<0.05$, the fifth day—$p<0.05$ and the tenth day—$p<0.01$). This curve is different from Ebbinghaus' curve of forgetting and may be called "curve of recollection".

The curve of the incorrect words, which did not correspond either to the words of the main information or the words of the peripheral perception, is different from the first two curves. In the immediate check on the first day the incorrect words were 2.6 percent and there was a slight increase on each of the following days, until on the 10th day the percentage had approximately doubled and was 4.8. The analysis of the three types of curves show different regularities of recollection.

The results obtained in another mass experiment with a group of 533 subjects (10 to 15 year-old pupils) were a confirmation of the principal conclusions drawn from the above-mentioned experiment, although showing certain slight deviations. With the pupils the experiment was carried out in the same way: they were given slips of paper with the names of 10 towns in Bulgaria written on them.

Some of the towns were underlined with a barely visible colored line. Each pupil was given a slip with the names of towns that were not repeated in the slips of his fellow pupils so that he could not be influenced by them. In three minutes the pupils had to memorize the names of the towns written on the slips. Then they were immediately given sheets of paper on which the names of 180 Bulgarian towns were written. After this they were instructed to underline in a matter of three minutes the 10 towns they had had on their slips of paper. Along with the list of the 180 towns they were given another slip of paper on which the following two questions were written: "Were there any underlined names of towns, and if there were, in what color were they underlined?" The checks took place on the 1st, 3rd, 5th, 10th, 15th, 20th, 30th and 60th day. The results are given in Figure 10.

Here the curve of the words memorized also dropped abruptly in the second check, in a way similar to Ebbinghaus's curve of forgetting. Owing to the specificity of the experiment, it remained so until the sixtieth day. The difference between the first and each successive day was statistically significant ($p < 0.01$).

The curves of the peripheral perceptions of the first order and those of the second order, in the same way as in other experiments with peripheral perceptions, did not drop but rose. In this way they remained "curves of recollection". As their initial level as early as the immediate check on the first day was very high, 96 and 89 percent, the increase in recollection could not be more markedly expressed.

The incorrect words here again had approximately doubled by the 10th day, remaining at about this level up to the 60th day.

The characteristic curve of peripheral perceptions—"curve of recollection" —was obtained in many other experiments and in some cases even more markedly expressed. This has led to the ever more frequent utilization of peripheral perceptions as a suggestive factor in the teaching process, in combination with the other paraconscious factors.

It is necessary to point out that the experimental study of the paraconscious factors shows their importance for the personality as a whole, not only for the memory. Memory registration is only a more convenient means of understanding and interpreting the results.

A. Leontiev (1959) also thinks that skin sensitivity to light stimuli is one of the subliminal orientation reactions. Research is still being carried out into the intimate physiological mechanisms of this pheno-

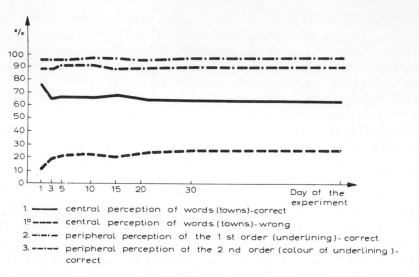

1. ——— central perception of words (towns)-correct
1ᵃ ---- central perception of words (towns)-wrong
2. —··— peripheral perception of the 1 st order (underlining)-correct
3. —··— peripheral perception of the 2 nd order (colour of underlining)-correct

*Figure 10*

menon but, as it is a matter of perception through a specific receptor which most often remains below the threshold of consciousness, for the time being it seems more correct to refer skin--optical sensitivity to the subsensory reactions.

Cutaneous—optical sensitivity has been investigated by N.B. Poznanskaya, I. Nikitsky, K. Kolodnaya and T. Shakhnazaryan (1937), as well as by Poznanskaya (1938), and Leontiev (1959) who studied the possibility of making a conditioned reflex of light stimuli affecting the skin of the hand.

These experiments show that subliminally the skin perceives light stimuli. And taking into consideration the possibility of changing the threshold or even of connecting the vague sense with their correct meanings, it will be clear that this process of decoding conceals some form of conscious cutaneous—optical sensitivity.

Persons with high cutaneous—optical sensitivity have also been known in the past. At the end of the nineteenth century, A. Hovrin (1898) described a patient of his who probably had skin hyperesthesia for nonspecific stimuli.

There has been a particular growth in our knowledge of cutaneous—optical sensitivity since 1962, when Roza Kuleshova made her appearance. The first investigations of Kuleshova were made by I. Goldberg (1963, 1965). Later, experiments brought confirmation of the results he obtained and also established the fact that there is comparatively well expressed skin-optical sensitivity in some normal, healthy persons, as well as in the blind. It was also shown that it is possible to develop this sensitivity in some people. The results of this experimental research were published in scientific reports to which many well-known research institutes lent their authority.[1]

Strictly organized research work was carried out by M. Bongard and M. Smirnov (1965) of the Institute of Biophysics and the Problems of Information Transmission Institute with the Academy of

These experiments refuted the hypothesis that Kuleshova, if unable to peer under the bandage or recognize the object by the touch of it, guesses what it is by chance or takes advantage of the unintentional prompting of the experimenters. The colors of some of the radiations presented were not known to the experimenters before Kuleshova gave her answers . . and what is most important in the assessment of the whole phenomenon under research in conditions excluding any possibility of peeking, the subject was able to perceive the light with her fingers.

(p. ?)

The first of this research work was concentrated mainly in the Sverdlovsk State Pedagogical Institute which also published a collection of experimental materials, in 1968. Teams of psychologists, physiologists and physicists took part in the investigations.[2] The summing up of the experimental data, according to some researchers, showed that in many respects cutaneous photoreception is subject to the laws of normal vision.

F.E. Chetin and A.S. Novomeisky (1968) noted the following major laws which are identical for skin photoreception and the eyesight: (a) mixing colours; (b) chromatic and light contrast; (c) Purkinje's phenomena; (d) the constancy of the perception of colors

---

[1] Y. Fishelev and S. Dobronravov (1965), A. Novomeisky (1963-a, 1963-b, 1963-c, 1963-d, 1963-e, 1965), S. Dobronravov (1963), M. Leites and P. Kazmislov (1963), S. Dobronravov and Y. Fishelev (1963), M. Kozhevnikov (1965), N. Sudakov (1965), D. Gilev (1965), N. Kolesnikov, V. Filimonov, V. Belousov (1965), and others published the results of their own experiments and analyses.

[2] Experimental research into cutaneous-optical sensitivy were also carried out by A.S. Novomeisky, V.A. Bikard, A.S. Novomeisky and V.I. Yakovlev, A.N. Demeneva and A.M. Kochigina, I.M. Goldberg, S.N. Dobronravov, N. Ivanov and M. Zakharov, I.A. Krupnov, A.S. Novomeisky and V.A. Bikard, and others. Because of their particular nature, these experiments deserve to be repeated and extended until the most important points in them are elucidated.

and graphic forms; (e) optic perspective; (f) optic illusions; and (g) adaptation to light and dark.

Through some of the experimental research into cutaneous–optical sensitivity, it was found that this sensitivity could materialize in media which are not transparent to the eyesight. At the same time, attempts were made to explain these data by infra-red radiation generated in room temperature by the color stimuli and perceived by the skin. If future experimentation proves that this explanation is true, it is likely that some of the experimental evidence of the so-called extrasensory perception will approach the evidence of the subliminal stimuli experiments. The problems of extrasensory perception are related to suggestology insofar as the phenomena of suggestology are realized in the paraconscious mental activity.[1]

In recent years there has been a great deal of theoretical generalization in the studies of dozens of authors.[2] In addition to the research, experiments have been carried out and they seem to explain the so-called extrasensory perceptions in their physiological aspects. I.P. Pavlov wrote:

.. In some cases when ordinary conscious activity undergoes changes the differentiating ability becomes sharper. In the peculiar state of so-called clairvoyance,

---

[1]M. Shakhnovich (1965), D. Biryukov (1965), A. Kitaigorodski (1967), O. Prokop (1957, 1962), G. Zverents (1956), V. Gubish (1961), H. Hall (1968), E. Hansel (1966), R. Tocquet (1952), and others wrote against these facts and were even against further research in this field. It should not be forgotten, however, that theoretical considerations can always be invalidated if they are not based on experimental or clinical experience. The phenomena of extrasensory perception are historically related to clinical practice. They were observed as early as in Mesmer's session (529). Later, they were observed in the hypnotism work of E. Azam (1887), A. Liebault (1889), P. Janet (1886, 1935), Richet (1888, 1923), and others. At the beginning of the 20th century, they were described by S. Freud (1922, 1938, 1948) and psychoanalysts W. Steckel (1921), H. Deutsch (1926), D. Burlingham (1935), J. Hollos (1933), G. Roheim (1932), M. Peerbolte (1937), J. Eisenbud (1948, 1949), J. Ehrewald (1948), E. Servadio (1938), N. Fodor (1947), G. Pederson-Krag (1947), and others. Of the Russian and Soviet scientists, V.M. Bekhterev (1920), N. Krainski (1900), N. Kotik (1908), V. Sreznevsky (1927), A.G. Ivanov-Smolensky (1920), L.L. Vasilev (1959, 1962, 1963), V. Kazhinski (1962), and L. Kogan (1966) have published the results of their research in this field.

[2]J.B. Rhine, L.E. Rhine, G. Murphy, G. Schmeidler, S. Soal, J. Pratt, R. Thouless, W. Tenhaef, R.K. Rao, B. Kanthamini, K. Chari, M. Ryzl, M. Humphrey, K. Osis, G. Estabrooks, J. Jepson, R. Chauvin, G. Freeman, W. Cox, H. Forwald, L. Casler, J. Fahler, J. Grella, P. Sailaja.

this ability comes to infinitesimal subtlety.

(*Complete Collected Works*, v. V, 1925, p. 520)

K. Zaimov (1963) is inclined to explain presentiment as signals from the material world entering the central nervous system subliminally. The Leningrad philosopher, B. Tugarinov (1964), is indignant at any attempt to exploit Marxism and Marxist philosophy as a means of maintaining scientific and technical conservatism in this field of investigations. The Bulgarian philosopher, T. Pavlov (1957, 1952), in the third edition of his *Theory of Reverberation* wrote:

It is theoretically logically admissible that those born deaf and blind can develop their abilities of sense in their fingers, forehead, lips, etc., to such an extent that, although not seeing colors and not hearing noises, are still able somehow to distinguish them, i.e., they can still get their bearings (although in an extremely weak and limited manner) in light and sound phenomena and react to them in their own way. Something very similar was observed in Helen Keller, who was blind and deaf from birth, and in other defective subjects (as well as in others who were nondefective but who had exceptionally sensitive perceptions). . .

And in the fourth edition we read:

The correctly apprehended nonpsychological and nonlogical theory of reverberation would reveal to scientific psychology grandiose perspectives not only in the fields of the so-called normal psychic manifestations but also in those of the morbid ones, as well as in those of sleep, suggestion, social imitation, hypnotism, telepathy, etc.

(p. 379)

In the *Philosophical Encyclopaedia*, published by the Institute of Philosophy of the USSR Academy of Sciences, we read:

In recent years the methods of biophysics, electrophysiology, radioelectronics, etc., have begun to be applied in parapsychology. In spite of the disputable nature of the problems raised by parapsychology, it would hardly be right to treat this field of psychological research as at variance with philosophical materialism merely because parapsychology admits the existence of still unknown forms of sensory ability and, consequently, the possibility of expanding the means of cognitive activity, which in the long run, according to the representatives of the natural science trend in parapsychology, through their nature, pass into the sphere of sensory cognition.

(p. 213)

In spite of being hotly debated, these problems will be solved only by laboratory research work. No matter what generalizations are made on the basis of experimental results, they are related to paraconscious mental activity and their further elucidation will be of importance to general suggestology.

Paraconscious mental activity in a normal waking state does not refer only to subsensory and extrasensory stimuli: it is the basis of a number of our activities. Paraconscious mental activity is not only connected with the activity of perception. It also includes inclinations, affection, aspirations and the whole disposition of the personality. These continue to exist even after they cease to be centered in the attention. According to Bassin (1968-a), they continue to exist in the form of a setup in Uznadze's sense. They are manifested in the specific selectivity of reaction, and direct voluntary and involuntary actions.

An enormous number of automated actions fall within the sphere of paraconscious mental activity. It is usually considered that actions passing first through the consciousness phase, gradually become automated then sink into the paraconscious to reappear only when needed and always under the same strictly determined motor or mental formula. The especially important property of automated actions to change dynamically in accordance with specific conditions is not seen. Yet this property does visually demonstrate the important part that paraconscious mental activity plays in the control and regulation of automated activities. In a sudden fall, for example, within a second the falling person carries out an exceptional number of actions, which proceed from a desire to protect some part of the body or perhaps some object that is being carried. This protective adjustment of automated actions, in compliance with the needs of the moment, goes to prove their great plasticity. The unconscious mental activity, adjusting and controlling these actions, has much greater speed and accuracy than it would have if all these motor acts had had to become conscious, acquire a "sense" and then be directed. The abbreviated formulae of thinking, the ready concepts to which we are accustomed, the motor acts and many other activities are achieved thanks only to automation and to pushing a large part of the intermediate stages into the spheres of unconscious mental activity. The entire conscious activity is built up of unconscious components.

As already mentioned, the automation can be disturbed by illness (1963-a). Then its importance for the normal course of all vital activities can be seen very vividly. De-automation occurs quite often in serious forms of psychasthenia where the abbreviated motor formulae are again as they were at the time of their original formation; the patient is forced to reprocess everything that formerly occurred outside the field of the conscious. The treatment of these illnesses requires great patience on the part of the physician.

The morbid de-automation of the patient L., for example, was fully developed. He fell ill during puberty and had constantly to reprocess the process of writing in his mind. Every letter he wrote had to be carefully written, the letters had to form syllables and the syllables words, with great consideration given to every little stroke. The occupation of his mind with a process which normally at his age was already automated prevented him from grasping the sense of what he was writing. This tormented him and he was unable to cope with it by the efforts of his own will. De-automation progressed, and gradually included both drawing and reading. He had to sit looking at a single page of a textbook for whole days, read the words syllable by syllable, study the written form of each character, analyze all this, etc. The de-automation in the next few years took over his movements, too. Every impulse to walk, speak or play was accompanied by a counter-impulse. In this way, all automatic motor activities "entered" his mind again. A great effort was required to make any comprehensive movement; every step for him became an exercise in walking. The automation of thinking also disappeared to a considerable extent. His entire activity was impeded. Obsessions of experience and actions, also de-automated, began to originate on this background and this further intensified his general de-automation. The vegetative nervous system preserved its unconscious automated activity. Although he was very gifted and was able to delve with great detail into the mechanisms of his traumatic experiences, both mental and physical work became practically impossible for him.

In some normal cases, however, part of the automated activity can be volitionally extended again in the mind without unpleasant experiences. Not all automated actions can be arranged in the consciousness. Many of them remain in the microintervals of time and escape conscious autoanalysis. Study of the laws and features of automatic actions is one of the essential paths for research work on unconscious mental activity, and hence on suggestive mechanisms.

The automation of many mental processes is a basic prerequisite for the development of the individual. Under ordinary conditions this process goes unnoticed. In some people, however, it can be observed in a very marked manner. In these people one can clearly see that the automation of some functions ensures that they are speedily performed with a minimum number of errors, and with little fatigue or loss of energy. This fact alone offers considerable theoretical and practical advantages for research along this line. One can investigate problems concerning paraconscious mental activity and do experimental research on suggestion as a direct path to the reserve capacities of the human mind by the rapid automation of different processes.

In the Suggestology Research Institute laboratory, research was carried out in connection with 48-year-old K.M., a physically and mentally sound man who was an accountant by profession. Since early childhood, he had had a special liking for figures. As a child it seemed he had learned the multiplication tables in one attempt without having to make any effort. In his professional activity and outside it, he was constantly engaged in doing arithmetic. He was able to do computing work with extraordinary rapidity and accuracy and without experiencing any fatigue or boredom.

Psychological and physiological investigations were made of K.M. It was found that his memory volume in respect to letters and words did not deviate from the normal, nor did his I.Q. tests show any considerable deviations. But the investigations revealed that he had a much greater volume of memory for numerical figures. He multiplied fractions from memory with great ease, reduced large numbers into simple factors and performed other arithmetical operations. In adding he could sum up two columns of figures simultaneously. In multiplication he simplified the operation by multiplying simpler figures or even numbers, simultaneously performing the respective operations of the first order (adding or subtracting). K.M.'s mode of work presupposes the automation of a great part of the arithmetical operations in selective hypermnesia for numerical figures. The combination of these two elements satisfactorily explains the results he achieved.

To make a comparative assessment of K.M.'s speed in his computing operations, he was asked to solve the standard arithmetical problems (which are sometimes given to suggestopedic groups to solve during research work with them), for example, one like the following:

$$9 \times 99 - 589 - 302 \times 100 = ?$$

In five minutes, K.M. solved 60 problems, 57 correctly and 3 incorrectly. In the same time, the control groups solved an average of 5.5 problems of which only 3.5 were correct. Thus it was seen that

K.M. could solve arithmetical problems 11 times more quickly than the control groups. The best result achieved in any control group was 10 problems in 3 minutes. In solving arithmetical problems K.M.'s errors amounted to 5 percent, while those of the control groups amounted, on an average, to 36 percent (or seven times more errors than K M.).

According to evidence obtained from a proof-reading test, the mental working ability of K.M. after two hours of computing did not deteriorate, but even showed a tendency toward improvement.

From the numerous analyses of the time intervals of EEG waves made at rest and during the solution of problems, it was discovered that the mental burden of arithmetical operations in K.M. resulted only in insignificant changes in the percentage distribution of the alpha, beta, theta and delta waves (Table 10 and Figure 11). Under the same conditions (solving mathematical problems mentally in five minutes), the control subjects showed a considerable increase of beta waves and a reduction of alpha and theta waves (Figure 12).

These investigations showed the importance of unconscious mental activity in increasing the volume, accuracy and speed of mental operations.

The phenomena of suggestion in a waking state represent a large part of the varied unconscious or insufficiently conscious activities. So far, suggestion has found the largest practical application in medicine.

At first, medical psychotherapeutic practice made use of the experience of folk suggestive procedures, the healing effects of which had been attributed to supernatural powers. In different nations these beliefs took different forms. Some of them acquired quite well organized philosophical rationalizations which, in some cases, have survived to this day.

Yoga is one example. Interest in the teaching and practice of the yogis of India has increased greatly in many countries in recent years. In this system use of paraconscious mental activity is manifested, and is achieved by using the mechanisms of suggestion. Many of the former yoga "miracles" have today been understood scientifically and have even found practical application in modern psychotherapy. For example, the yogis can cause various changes in their vegetative (autonomic) functions. Among other things, they can change the rate of their pulse, increase the resistance of their tissues to injuries, attain considerable effects painlessly and bring about a loss of sensitivity. In some cases quite incredible and unacceptable achievements (from the scientific point of view) have been and continue to be ascribed to them. Much of the yoga phenomena, until recently denied, have now been explained scientifically and can be realized under ordinary experimental conditions. The so-called Hatha Yoga is the most widespread in the European countries at present. This is a system of yoga in which devotees engage mainly in doing special physical exercises that have been practised for centuries.

In all yoga schools, including Hatha Yoga, special attention is paid to spiritual purity and self-discipline. Mental concentration, combined with their own peculiar forms of self-relaxation, creates conditions for switching on the autosuggestive mechanisms and activating the unconscious mental activity. According to the yogis, mental enlightenment can be attained through: abstention (yama), culture (niyama), posture and exercise (asana), breath control (pranayama), shutting down feelings and senses (pratyahara), concentration (dharana), contemplation (dhiyana) and divine meditation (samadhi). All these sides of yoga are to be found in Hatha Yoga, but it is the position (asana) which is most important. Yoga practices are subject to systematic experimental research before being recommended for extensive use *under* present-day conditions. First it is necessary to investigate the physical exercises, but under no circumstances should the psychological aspect be neglected. Not only from the purely psychological point of view does yoga manifest many aspects of para-conscious mental activity in revealing the reserve capacity of the brain, but also many of the results of the yoga physical exercises would be unthinkable without the concomitant spiritual setup. For the time being, the research into yoga is being directed mostly toward the possibilities of Hatha Yoga. The present results of this research show that some of the yoga exercises actually result in relaxation. The external passiveness, however, is accompanied in the majority of the yoga exercises with activation of the nervous, cardiovascular, muscular and other systems. In the Suggestology Research Institute, some of these characteristic features were observed in a study (together with P. Balevski) of the EEG and pulse changes of six people doing yoga exercises. The investigations were carried out telemetrically. Besides taking a recording of the EEG and the pulse, an interval analysis of the EEG waves was made with an ART-1000 Analyzer. Each exercise continued one minute with the exception of the savasana (self-relaxation) exercise which continued from 5 to 16 minutes. Blood pressure changes were also studied in three of the subjects. The following exercises were included in our investigation: lotus,

TABLE 10    *Percentage Distribution of the Various EEG Waves of K.M. in State*
*of Rest and in Solving Problems Mentally*

| EEG waves | State of rest | In solving problems |
|-----------|---------------|---------------------|
| Alpha     | 35%           | 34%                 |
| Beta      | 58%           | 59%                 |
| Theta     | 7%            | 7%                  |
| Delta     | 0             | 0                   |

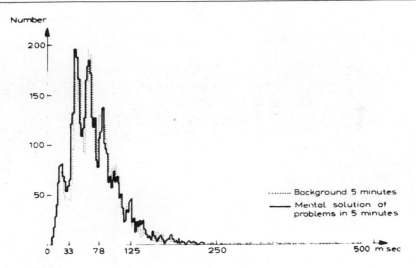

*Figure 11*    Interperiod analysis of the EEG waves of the subject K.M.

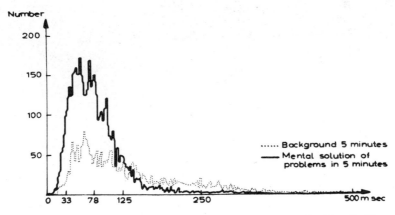

*Figure 12*    Interperiod analysis of the EEG waves of the control subject B. Ch.

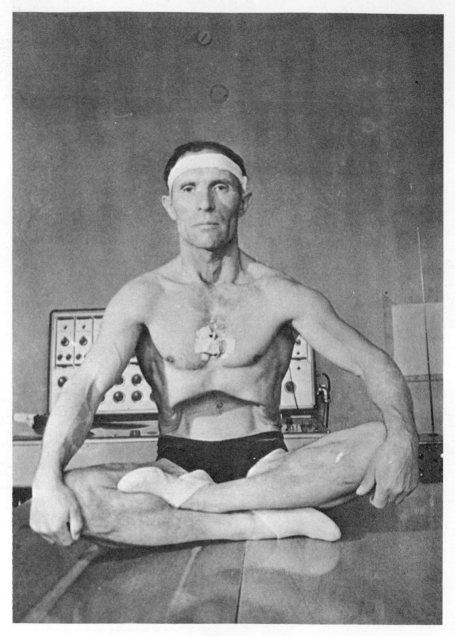

*Figure 13*    Telemetric investigation of the EEG and ECG of the subject F.M. during
yoga exercises.

*Figure 14*    The Bulgarian yogi L. doing a yoga leap with the back.

candle, yoga-mudra, throne position, pashi-montana, fish, crooked position, raven, turning, tortoise, double sirasana, plow and various breathing exercises (Figures 13 and 14).

Analysis of the data showed that in the exercises, (with the exception of the savasana and some breathing exercises) the pulses of the subjects were from 8 to 88 percent quicker than they had been before the exercises began—the accelerated rate depending on individual characteristics and the difficulty of the exercise (Table 11). With the help of breathing exercises, some of the subjects demonstrated voluntary delay or acceleration of the pulse. F.M., for example, delayed his pulse to 51 beats per minute, after which he accelerated it to 140 beats per minute. At the end of the savasana exercise, pulses were delayed by 14 to 21 percent compared with the initial data. In spite of this general tendency toward a delay in the pulse during self-relaxation, there was also a certain fluctuation in the frequency of the pulse as can be seen in the curves in Figure 15.

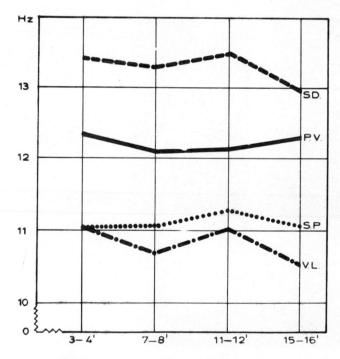

*Figure 15*  Dynamics of the average frequency of the brain bioelectric activity of four subjects while doing the Savasana exercise.

TABLE 11   *Changes in Pulse in Doing Yoga Exercises*

| Exercises | Subjects | | | | | |
| --- | --- | --- | --- | --- | --- | --- |
| | F.M. | S.D. | P.V. | S.P. | V.L. | I.V. |
| Pulse in state of repose | 72 | 88 | 75 | 75 | 64 | 62 |
| Lotus | 120 | 119 | 84 | 87 | 78 | 66 |
| Yoga-mudra | 114 | 115 | 96 | 129 | 71 | 78 |
| Candle | 118 | 105 | 98 | 107 | 78 | 75 |
| Turning | 128 | 116 | 96 | 116 | 74 | — |
| Fish | 117 | 113 | 93 | 104 | 99 | 96 |
| Plow | — | 108 | 93 | 105 | 69 | 69 |
| Crooked position | 138 | 138 | — | — | 111 | |

TABLE 12   *EEG, Pulse and Blood Pressure Changes of Subject S.D. in Doing Different Yoga Exercises*

| Exercise | EEG indicators | | | Average EEG frequency (Hz) | Pulse (beats per min.) | Blood pressure (mm mercury) |
| --- | --- | --- | --- | --- | --- | --- |
| | Alpha | Beta | Theta | | | |
| Lotus position | 26 | 55 | 19 | 11.23 | 119 | 150/95 |
| Candle | 20 | 55 | 25 | 11.45 | 105 | 130/85 |
| Yoga-mudra | 23 | 65 | 12 | 12.50 | 115 | 140/95 |
| Pashimontana | 24 | 66 | 10 | 12.89 | 108 | 145/95 |
| Philosoph. pos. | 17 | 77 | 6 | 14.35 | 118 | 150/90 |
| Double sirasana | 17 | 76 | 7 | 14.85 | 121 | 140/80 |
| Turning | 19 | 77 | 4 | 14.99 | 116 | 150/95 |
| Throne pos. | 17 | 80 | 3 | 15.16 | 138 | 160/100 |
| Crooked pos. | 14 | 79 | 7 | 15.30 | 138 | 160/90 |
| Fish | 15 | 81 | 4 | 15.48 | 113 | 150/100 |
| Raven | 10 | 86 | 4 | 16.67 | 149 | 165/100 |
| Savasana 3—4 | 25 | 69 | 6 | 13.42 | 84 | 130/90 |
| Savasana 7—8 | 26 | 67 | 7 | 13.31 | 78 | — |
| Savasana 11—12 | 27 | 67 | 6 | 13.49 | 75 | — |
| Savasana 15—16 | 27 | 66 | 7 | 13.15 | 74 | 125/85 |

According to the difficulty of the exercise and the individual features of the subject's organism, the maximum blood pressure increased by 10 to 35 divisions of a mercury column. The changes in the minimum blood pressure varied. In the candle position the blood pressure remained unchanged, and in savasana it dropped several units in comparison with the initial data. Volitional change of blood pressure was demonstrated by F.M., who made his blood pressure rise from 135/95 to 160/115mm. mercury column.

Yoga exercises affect the EEG wave distribution and the mean frequency of the cerebral bioelectrical activity. As can be seen in Table 12, there were considerable changes in the cerebral bioelectrical activity of subject S.D. in the different yoga exercises. It was found that while the more difficult exercises such as raven, crooked position, tortoise, plow, turning, considerably accelerate the cerebral activity, the lotus, candle, yoga mudra, pashimontana, and savasana exercises charge the cerebral cells only very slightly or even calm them. The individual features of the subject—age, training, the manner of performance and other factors—showed that they were of significance. In the subject S.D., doing the exercises resulted in a considerable loading of the nervous and cardiovascular systems (Tables 11 and 12). In P.V., these exercises brought less marked alterations in the EEG (Figure 16). The changes noted in the cerebral bioelectrical activity of the subjects while doing the exercise savasana are illustrated in Figure 17. In the cerebral bioelectrical activity, as in the pulse, it was found that there were periods of slight acceleration or reduction of activity on a background of general composure. While doing the yoga exercises, the changes in the cardiovascular indicators and in the cerebral bioelectrical activity were not always parallel in our subjects. (Table 12).

These investigations showed that, in spite of the apparent passiveness of the yoga exercises, some of them considerably burden the cardiovascular, nervous and muscular systems while others, especially the savasana, have a calming effect. The savasana exercise, when developed in a psychotherapeutic system such as autogenic training, can be of significance as a starting point for discovering the possibilities of paraconscious mental activity.

The unconscious factors are used especially well in suggestion for anaesthesia or at least for reducing the feeling of pain. But, in many cases, the anaesthetizing effect of suggestion is not taken into account as it makes its way, unnoticed, into the patient—therapist interrelations when the necessary suggestive sterility and suggestive therapeutic activity exist. The anaesthetic effect of suggestion is most widely applied in the painless childbirth method elaborated by I.S. Velvovski (1950, 1958). In actual fact, in this method as in any corrective and therapeutic suggestive method, there is first of all desuggestion of concepts accumulated for years about the necessity and inevitability of suffering the pangs of childbirth. In this method reliance is placed mainly upon the pedagogical approach without

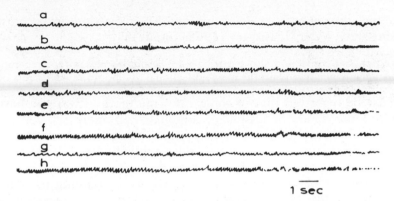

*Figure 16*  EEG bipolar recordings (from left PO) of the subject P.V. doing yoga
exercise with closed eyes (telemetric recording).
a: Background activity.  b: Padmasana.  c: Badriasana.  d: Pashchimontana.
e: Matsyasana.  f: Ardha-Matsyendrasana.  g: Sarvangasana.  h: Savasana.

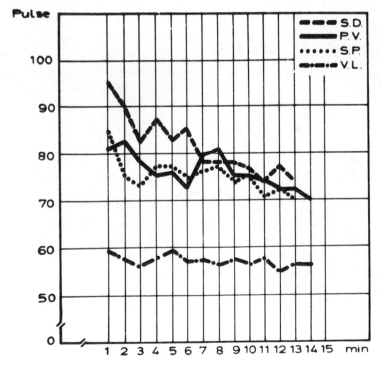

*Figure 17*  Dynamics of the pulse rates of four subjects while doing the Savasana
exercise.

rejecting the inevitable participation of suggestion in a normal waking state. V.N. Myasishtev (1968) found that

Suggestion and conviction also participate to various degrees in the preparation, but . . . that conviction plays the main educational psychoprophylactic role . . .

It must be regretted that in some cases the method was too hastily put into the hands of unskilled, although extremely self-confident persons. This resulted in its great promise being brought to nothing. However, in places where the method is applied with skill and understanding, much success has been achieved.

The role of paraconscious mental activity in tapping the reserve capacities of the brain can also be seen in suggestive anaesthesia in surgical intervention. No logical, rational and conscious expectancy could result in the deep anaesthetizing and bloodless effect known in clinical practice. Sceptics often deny the pain-killing effect of suggestion in small surgical interventions, alleging that "there was simply no time to feel any pain". Many authors concede that the painless effect can be attained but only under hypnosis. L. Shertok (1965), for example, gave as evidence an unsuccessful anaesthetizing attempt by T.X. Barber:

An experiment of this kind was the subject of a heart-rending picture presented by French television in a transmission, in February, 1963: the patient, prepared in advance but not hypnotized, was subjected to an operation (appendectomy) and gave expression to great pain.

(p. 45)

We undertook a lengthier surgical intervention in which the anaesthetizing was by suggestion in a normal waking state (Figure 18).

In 1965, a teacher, M.K., aged 50, who was acquainted with some of our cases of anaesthetization by suggestion in a normal waking state, proposed that he should be operated on in the same manner for a long-standing hernia condition. He feared heart complications if he were given an ordinary anaesthetic. He had been treated for a neurotic disease at the end of 1964 and the beginning of 1965. While waiting in the reception room, he had the opportunity to talk to patients on whom minor surgical operations had been performed. These operations were rendered painless by the suggestion method in a waking state. This encouraged him to propose that he should be operated on in the same way. It was decided that he should remain awake during the entire operation, completely conscious and, therefore, able to supply precise information about his sensations. This

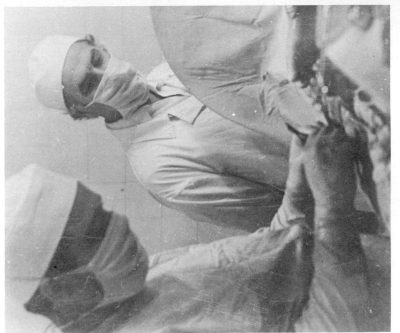

*Figure 18 a, b, c.* Documentary action stills of the surgical intervention in which the anaesthetizing was by suggestion in a normal waking state.

kind of control has a considerable advantage over operations under hypnosis. It permits not only a safer operation, but creates conditions under which the dynamics of suggestive anaesthetization can be observed in the various stages of the operation.

Twenty days before the operation, the patient was psychologically prepared by having "suggestive" conversations. We talked about how painless it would be, about the minimal loss of blood and the shortening of the postoperative period which was due to the operation being performed in this way. He was fully aware that he would not be operated on under ordinary anaesthetics or standard hypnotic treatment.

He was hospitalized for surgical treatment on 23 August, 1965. The diagnosis was: hernia inguinalis indirecta dextra, about the size of a child's head and descending to the scrotum. The hernia had appeared in October, 1962. From April, 1963, up to his operation it had been constantly supported by a bandage.

He was taken to the operating theatre and laid on the table. The surrounding conditions were the same as those under which any operation is performed, and it was explained to him that this was part of the preliminary preparations for his operation. Then it was suggested that he would feel no pain nor would there be any bleeding in the right abdominal region. Surgeons Dr. Ivan Kalupov and Dr. V. Tanev made numerous needle punctures in that region with needle No. 1.5 cm long, in the skin, the subcutaneous area and the aponeuroses of the muscles. The patient felt no pain and there was no bleeding.

A control test was made by puncturing the skin with a single superficial pricking in the same place but on the left side of the abdominal region. There had been no suggestion that this area would be touched and the result was that the patient reacted saying he felt a sharp shooting pain.

It was decided that there was a sufficient degree of painlessness achieved on the right side to permit the operation taking place the following day. The lack of pain felt by the patient had been achieved with suggestion applied in a waking state and not by use of an anaesthetic. Preparations were made for a local novocaine anaesthesis to be ready in case pain was felt.

This preliminary check and the inferences that could be drawn from it were described in a statement. The statement was signed by the medical personnel who were present and by the patient himself. The operation was performed on August 24th.

The following is the official report of the operation (with decursus and catamnesis):

The patient was in high spirits. Spent the night peacefully. Slept well. Had enema. Prepared for the operation. Looking forward to it with satisfaction, fully aware that herniotomy will be carried out with suggestive anaesthesia, without hypnosis and medication.

9.00 a.m. The patient lay calmly in the operating theatre. From 9.00 a.m. to the end of the operation (9.50 a.m.), Dr. Georgi Lozanov maintained local suggestive anaesthesia by speech contact. At the time of the operation, the patient also talked to the other people in the operating theatre. He answered adequately and was fully conscious. At every moment it was explained what was being done to him.

After a thorough cleaning of the region of the hernia, a preliminary check for pain was made by scratching the skin with a scalpel. The patient did not react. A typical skin incision for herniotomy (12 cm in length) was made in the right loin. The subcutaneous region and the aponeurosis of musculus obliquas abdominis externus was cut layer by layer and hemostatically. The bleeding was the same as that in operations performed with novocain-adrenalin anaesthesia. The preparation of the hernial bag bluntly and hemostatically began. It was the size of a man's fist. The funiculus spermaticus and the testicle with the epididimis were closely adherent to it.

When the operation reached the testicle, pain appeared. This made it necessary to stop the operation for a minute during which time the patient was subjected to additional suggestion. The operation of the sac continued and its preparation was finished. The sac was then opened and many small intestinal folds were found in it. They were reposed and the sac was ligated in its base by needle. The sac was resected. Pain again appeared at the time of resection but much weaker than before. The reinforcement of the front wall and the canalis inguinalis began. In the stitching of the ligamentum inguinale and the periosta of the tuberculum pubicum, the patient felt severe pain. In order to avoid traumatization of the patient and for the purpose of supplementary suggestion after the "placebo" mechanisms, it was decided to administer about 12 cub. cm 0.5% novocaine under the ligamentum inguinale in the region of the tuberculum pubicum. The plastic surgery was carried out according to Martinov's method. The abdonimal wall was restored painlessly layer by layer with the patient in high spirits. Dry sterile bandaging was applied.

Psychological status in the course of the operation: during the operation the patient was clearly conscious oriented, critical. He talked to everyone present. When the pain appeared in the second half of the operation, a marked fluctuation was noticed in the suggestive effect and this fluctuation was intensified or weakened on several occasions. Nevertheless, the condition of the patient was suggestively controllable. The small amount of novocaine, which was administered in the second half of the operation, was also for a suggestive purpose. During all the rest of the time, no fluctuation was noticed in the suggestive effect until the appearance of the above-mentioned painful sensations. At the end of the operation the patient was in high spirits, smiled and said that he felt excellent: "As if I had not been operated on".

The post-operative period passed without pain and with the patient invariably in high spirits. In his conversation he often repeated that he felt as though he had not been operated on.

On the day of the operation, at about 4.00 p.m., his temperature was 38°C, but by 8.00 p.m. the same day it dropped to 37.4°C. The following day it went down to 37°C. After a slight fluctuation the following day when it went up to 37.2°C, his temperature until the end of his hospitalization (1 September) remained within the normal range—under 37°C.

The operation was performed on 24 August, and the stitches were removed on 28 August—leaving only two supporting sutures which were removed the next day. The wound was in an excellent condition, well adapted, and healing per primam. The convalescent process was proceeding rapidly. The sutures could have been removed on the same day as the stitches.

When examined on the seventh day after his discharge, he was found to be in excellent condition and without any complaints. At a scientific medical discussion three months after his operation, the patient declared that if he had to face another operation he would choose to be operated on by us by the same methods. Check-ups five and ten years after the operation showed he bore no visible operative cicatrix.

Conclusions:

1) It can be considered that this operation performed with suggestion in a waking state was successful, because in the course of 50 minutes pain appeared only for about two minutes and in places where pain also appears when an ordinary anaesthetic is administered to the patient. What is more, these places were not the object of the preliminary suggestive anaesthesia. During the whole of the other 48 minutes, the patient talked calmly with all who were attending the operation.

2) The post-operative period was absolutely painless and the convalescent process was accelerated.

3) The operation proved that suggestion in a waking state in a surgical operation is equal in power to suggestion under hypnosis.

A documentary film was made of the operation which was reported at the International Psychosomatic Congress in Rome, in September, 1967.

Suggestion in a normal waking state can activate the reserve capacities of the paraconscious mental activity in a number of other directions as well. Most of the phenomena obtained by suggestion under hypnosis have also been obtained by suggestion without hypnosis. Vegetative, endocrine, trophic and other intimate physiological and biochemical processes, for example, can be changed by suggestion in a normal waking state. An interesting phenomenon was the suggestively obtained and afterward suggestively removed difference in the size of the pupils of the eyes of the subject I (Figure 19). Suggestive methods in a waking state for the treatment of various diseases are also built up on the basis of these possibilities. These methods quite obviously do not work through conscious and logical conception and planning, but through the engagement of the unconscious mental activity.

An interesting use of suggestion is in the treatment of many diseases with somatic symptoms, for example, gastroduodenal ulcers. The following is a description of one case.

One such patient of particular interest was D.M., who was treated in 1958. His case was demonstrated at the Scientific Association of Psychiatrists and Neurologists in Sofia on 21 April, 1960, and described in 1963. He came for treatment

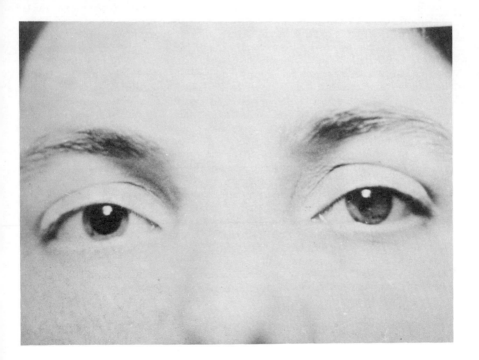

*Figure 19* Difference in the size of the pupils of patient I's eyes brought about by suggestion in a waking state.

in May, 1958 when he was 52. He had already taken 6 months' sick leave, and the question of his retiring on a pension because of illness was already being raised. In the spring of 1938, it was discovered that he had a duodenal ulcer. From that time until he came to consult us, he had had x-ray confirmation of his ulcer on numerous occasions. Except for several breaks of not more than one month's duration, his complaint had been in evidence all the time. He had had to adhere to a strict diet for 20 years. Practically every night of those 20 years he had been awakened by severe pain in the stomach, heartburn, belching, etc. He had had regular and systematic treatment, but there had been no improvement in his health. In November, 1957, he was admitted to the surgical ward as an emergency case with suspicion of ulcer perforation. He was not operated on. Then on several occasions he had melaena and haematemisis. In December, 1957, an x-ray examination established "cascade stomach", hypertrophic gastroduodenitis and ulcus duodeni (niche) on the back part of the bulbus, the size of a wheat grain. Frequent examinations and tests were necessary in connection with the melaena. There was suspicion of malignant ulcer degeneration. The patient felt giddiness, vertigo and faintness, could not walk without somebody helping him and a walking stick. On 27 April 1958, he was again admitted to the surgical ward as an emergency case with suspicion of ulcer perforation but, at his own request, was discharged without an operation. He lost more than 20 kilograms in weight. After a six months sick leave and with retirement looming in the near future, the patient came to us. He had emphasized cahexia and severe mental asthenia. He was given his first suggestive session immediately and without hypnosis. After carefully considering the matter, we decided to stop all dieting immediately. On leaving his first session he said he felt better, in fact very well. He went home without a walking stick and without the support of his relatives. Three days later he came again. He declared that he was feeling very well. He had started to eat some kinds of food, but still did not dare start on an ordinary diet. The only thing now that troubled him was his sleep which was disturbed. He had a second suggestive session in a waking state. Six days later he came for the third and last therapeutic session. He was already eating everything and had absolutely no complaints. He had even tried to go for short walks outside the town. In a catamnestic examination on 3 March, 1959, nearly a year later, he reported that he had absolutely no complaints. He adhered to no special diet, had gained about 20 kilograms in weight, and went hiking regularly alone. The x-ray report stated "Oblique evidence of past ulcus duodeni. No niche evident". Observed catamnestically on 16 December 1961—no complaints. He reported that the Golden Order of Labour had been conferred on him and added jokingly, "Instead of a pension for sickness '. In 1969, after more than 10 years, he was still feeling very well and working, and had no need of the psychotherapeutic physician.

Suggestion in a normal waking state also has a favorable effect on allergic ailments.

Of the many allergic patients who were helped in this way was the 36-year-old G.N., whose case was also demonstrated at the Scientific Association of Psychiatrists and Neurologists in Sofia. For four months he had suffered from insistent urticaria. The allergen was most probably in the dust of the factory where he worked. He had had treatment with synopen pyribenzamin, novocaine, cortancyl insulin with glucose, bromium and other preparations with no effect. In November and December, 1959, he was treated in an internal-disease ward of one of the city hospitals and discharged with the dignosis: urticaria, oedema angioneuroticum quincke. There was no improvement. We started immediate therapeutic-suggestive sessions, employing primarily the method of indirect suggestion and the method of curative reactions. We stopped all dieting the first day, and gradually discontinued the antihistamine treatment which he had been receiving until then. The patient recovered and returned to the same working environment without any drugs or dieting. Fifteen years later, G.N. had shown no relapse.

In treating skin diseases, quite often a favorable effect can be achieved through the suggestive engagement of paraconscious mental activity in a normal waking state. We obtained very good results in treating some skin diseases.

Of the cases demonstrated at the Scientific Association of Psychiatrists and Neurologists in Sofia, the case of T.D. was clear proof of this procedure. She came for treatment in 1958. She suffered from lichen ruber planus and was treated at the inpatient ward of the Skin and V.D. Dispensary. There she had a biopsy which confirmed the diagnosis. She was discharged with improvement, but this was followed by a relapse. From the first suggestive session with us she showed improvement, and in subsequent sessions she steadily improved. The numerous patches of rash all over her body disappeared. The pigmentation left by the rash also disappeared. In 1975, 15 years later, her condition was still regarded as "completely cured".

A number of organic diseases are also, within certain limits, affected suggestively.

An illustration of this is the case of patient D.P., who in January 1957, was 41, and had suffered from a severe form of diabetes insipidus for 15 years. She drank enormous quantities of water, urinating abundantly—up to 45 litres of urine a day. When in the streets she used to carry two bottles of water to be able to quench her thirst. In the period from 1949 to 1956, she had been treated repeatedly and continuously. Tests and observation always brought confirmation of the diagnosis: diabetes insipidus. Besides having been treated with sedatives, she had also undergone treatment with sleep therapy, had a hypophysis graft, pituglandol etc. Hospitalized in 1955, she underwent hypophysis gland implantation, but experienced no lasting improvement.

On January 8, 1957, the patient came for psychotherapeutic treatment to us. For two months systematic complex suggestive effects were conducted with her. Her thirst ceased, the diuresis dropped to the boundaries of the normal in its higher values, the specific gravity of the urine was raised from 1000 to 1005—1006. She became more cheerful. She stopped dieting at the beginning of the treatment and she gained weight. Twelve years later she showed no relapse.

Paraconscious mental activity has also been engaged in many physiological experiments in which suggestion has taken part voluntarily or involuntarily in the form of instructions or self-instructions. Attitude, motivation, expectancy, authority and many other psychological factors create a suitable atmosphere for suggestive access to the reserve capacities of unconscious mental activity. A. Egorov and B. Yakovets (1965) reported experimental results of research into the fatigue curve. They showed that it did not depend only on the duration of work, nor on the characteristic features of the subject's nervous system. Through verbal explanations they obtained one and the same type of fatigue curve in all the subjects. Psychologically they explained these results as a change in the subjects' attitude toward the work they were doing. A man's working capacity and his tolerance for fatigue should also be deduced from the psychological factors which may result in a high working capacity. When these psychological factors acquire a considerable degree of suggestiveness they engage the unconscious mental activity to the maximum and make good use of its reserve capacities. Many experiments have shown that verbal instructions can change the course of the conditioned reactions by accelerating the establishment of conditioned relations, inhibiting the established connections, regulating the course of differentiation, etc. Such verbal instructions often acquire a suggestive nature and engage the unconscious mental activity. How great or small the effect is depends on the extent of the suggestion implied consciously or unconsciously. Thus, for example, G. Shichko (1955, 1959) managed to work out conditioned reflexes by verbal instructions, and discovered that success in the elaboration and extinguishing of reflexes depends to a large extent on the attitude of the subject to the information received.[1]

E. Boiko (1957), and V. Chouprikova (1967) emphasized the significance of the spoken word in changing the excitation in the central nervous system. These controlling impulses have so far been

---

[1] The verbal instructive and, to a considerable extent, the suggestive effect on experimental results were noted in experiments on the cardiovascular system carried out by J. Notterman, W. Schoenfeld and P. Bersch (1952), and others; in the skin galvanic reaction experiments of S. Cook and R. Harris (1937), R. Silverman (1960), W. Grings and R. Lockhart (1963), and others; in the work on blinking conditioned reflexes of E. Hilgard. R. Campbell and W. Sears (1938), McAllister, Dorothy McAllister, and others; in the sensory conditioned reflex studies of A. Bogoslovski (1936), and in a great deal of other physiological research work.

insufficiently accounted for in the assessment of experimental results. They can enter into the subject as self-instructions too. Since the power of verbal instructions depends on a number of psychological factors such as confidence, authority, etc., there can be no doubt that they possess considerable suggestive value and contact paraconscious mental activity.

The experimental studies of the setup in Uznadze's sense are directly related to paraconscious mental activity. The setup is the mediator in the reaction, determining its strength and direction. It depends on a number of factors such as biological needs, attitude, motivation, expectancy, past experience, etc. For example, how a person reacts to food as a stimulus all depends on whether he is hungry or sated. Uznadze's classical example with heavy objects can serve to illustrate this further. If in one hand a person holds a heavy ball and in the other a light one, and then two equally heavy balls are given to him, the hand that previously held the lighter ball will feel the weight to be heavier. All this happens quite unconsciously. According to the Uznadze school, the setup is completely unconscious, directing the course of reactions. Thus, the research into the setup becomes research also into unconscious mental activity.

Research into the setup has prevailed against the behavioral principle of "stimulus-response" and, in general, against Descartes' understanding of the reflectory principle, affirming the complexity of the internal organization of the personality. Suggestion is the direct road to the setup. It creates and utilizes setups which can free and activate the reserve capacities of the human being. Uznadze (1966), relating suggestion to the setup, wrote:

And so the mechanism of the setup obviously underlies suggestion; otherwise it would be impossible to give a satisfactory explanation of suggestion. Fortunately there are also factual grounds in favor of this supposition.[1]

It is necessary to add that the setup is often mixed up with attitude, motivation, expectancies, interests and needs. These also take part in the realization of the desuggestive—suggestive communicative process as mediators. The setup, however, is considered by us to be an essential part of this process because of the fact that it always remains paraconscious. When this paraconscious inner function-

---

[1] The role of verbal suggestion as a factor in orienting the setup has also been pointed out by I. Bzhalava (1966), F.V. Bassin, and others.

al organization of personality is directed to the activation of the human potentials, we have a typical example of the suggestive organizing and utilizing of paraconscious mental activity. That the setup, on an unconscious level, is in a constant interrelationship with all the other mediators in the personality structure is another matter. It is exactly because of this that the setup is often mixed up with motivation, expectancies and other mediators.

Suggestion, through paraconscious mental activity, operates with the setup and with the paraconscious aspects of the personality's attitudes, motivation, expectancies, interests and needs. The better the means of suggestion are oriented to the paraconscious aspects of these mediators, the greater can be one's expectation of a considerable effect. Otherwise, they play the role of logicalized mediators with which the inevitable additional suggestive effect appears. This is due mainly to the authority of their logical soundness and orderliness (harmony).

We shall make an attempt to define these concepts.

Setup: the inner, paraconscious functional organization of readiness for a certain type of activity.

Attitude: one's conception of the value of a given phenomenon, a conception built up in one's experience of life.

Motivation: the augmented desire or lack of desire to achieve or live through something.

Expectancy: the belief that something is really about to be achieved or lived through.

Interests: the direction of the personality's search for self-realization.

Needs: things vitally important to a person.

An analysis of the above-mentioned mediators shows that a considerable number of them remain in people as insufficiently conscious impulses and aspirations.

The final effect of skillfully directed desuggestive—suggestive interrelations depends both on the complex combination of each of these factors in their conscious—paraconscious unity, and on the basic structure of the personality with its emotional—volitional and intellectual—mnestic qualities. The means employed in these desuggestive—suggestive interrelations must be adapted as much as possible to the characteristic features of the paraconscious aspects of the previously mentioned factors.

*Paraconscious mental activity during hypnosis*

Many of the possibilities of suggestion were observed first in subjects under hypnosis. This is one of the main reasons for the later
fusion of one concept with the other.[1]

If we make a historical survey of hypnosis, we see that it has been
known since ancient times. It was thought to be a special type of sleep
in which the person under hypnosis could communicate with the
supernatural. In ancient times, it was also used for therapeutic
purposes.

In ancient Greece, hypnosis found considerable application. Special
rituals—the taking of a pleasant bath, the burning of incense, the
chanting of long prayers or the offering of solemn sacrifices—often
preceded hypnosis. In ancient Egypt, those who were to be hypnotized were made to keep staring at glistening objects on which
various signs were written. Later, in Egypt, the hypnotists employed
the so-called "passi" method—the method of stroking the skin of the
subject whose eyes were covered, and other similar manipulations.
Hypnosis was known to the ancient Hebrews as a state in which one
is neither asleep nor awake, but in which one can answer questions
while the soul is absent. The ancient Indians attained great mastery
in hypnosis. It is well known that Indian fakirs could demonstrate
various hypnotic phenomena.

The Druids fell into a state of hypnosis by concentrating on the
rustling of trees and the gurgling of brooks. The ancient oracles,
priests, shamans and dervishes employed various techniques to bring
about a state of hypnosis, and the religious rites in many primitive
tribes resulted in mass hypnosis. The possibility of making people
fall asleep by using incantation and by touching them was known to
Roman writers.

In the Middle Ages, the absence of any knowledge of hypnosis
made various miraculous and mystical explanations of the phenomenon seem plausible. Thus, for example, the psychogenous anaesthesia and haemostasis, which is quite often achieved by suggestion
under hypnosis, was accepted as a proof of contact with evil powers.
A person who was thought to have such contact was accused of
witchcraft, and then they were pricked with long sharp iron rods
until a place was found on his or her body where no pain was felt and

---

[1] Some of the earlier authors, D. Grasset (1904), and others, confused the
two concepts.

there was no bleeding. This place was called the Devil's Seal. According to statistics, the Devil's Seal was found on the bodies of more than nine million people, from the fourteenth through the seventeenth century, and they were burnt alive as witches.

The concepts of Paracelsus, van Helmond, Maxwell, Fludd, and others influenced F.A. Mesmer's magnetic-fluid theory. He called the many hypnotic and hypnosuggestive phenomena he obtained "life magnetism". Mesmer's concepts on life magnetism made a great stir, but they were not accepted by the academic scientists of the time.

Many prominent scientists rejected hypnotism. H. Helmholz considered it to be a kind of conjuring. Even at the end of the nineteenth century, it required courage on the part of R. Heidenhein to begin scientific research into questions of hypnosis in his laboratory.

The English surgeon, J. Braid, rejected Mesmer's magnetic-fluid theory, and showed that a state of hypnosis can be attained by the continuous concentration of one's attention on a shiny object. At this time they ceased to call the special behavioral somnolent state created under such conditions "life magnetism" and renamed it hypnosis (from the Greek word "hypnos"—sleep).

Progress in the scientific elaboration of hypnotism began at the end of the nineteenth century when the French psychiatrists J. Charcot and H. Bernheim formed two great schools, one in Paris and the other in Nancy. Charcot and his assistants, who used hypnotism in treating hysterical patients, maintained that hypnosis was a pathological phenomenon, while Bernheim was of the opinion that hypnosis was artificially evoked sleep and that all normal healthy persons could be subjected to it.

A large number of works on various aspects of hypnosis were published during the century-long struggle for the acceptance of hypnosis as a scientific problem. Many have also been published in recent years since the research work in this field has been consolidated and extended.[1] V. Danilevsky, in his experiments with animals, showed that hypnosis can be brought about not only with verbal suggestion but also with various stimuli. This gave him grounds to reject the concept of the Nancy school that it can be induced only verbally.

A.A. Tokarsky (1887, 1891) opposed both Bernheim's suggestive hypothesis and Charcot's pathological hypothesis as explanations of

---

[1] The beginning of psychoanalysis is also connected with the use of hypnosis in the practice of J. Breuer and S. Freud (1909).

hypnosis. He stood for the reflexological conception of hypnosis as a normal phenomenon in human life. It was in the early 1880s that Tokarsky read his first course of lectures on hypnology.[1]

The history of hypnosis and psychotherapy, in general, goes back many centuries in Bulgaria.

Kliment of Ohrid, who lived in the second half of the ninth century, John of Rila, who lived in the tenth century, and others healed the infirm, cured the crippled and drove out the "evil spirit" by what was alleged to be magic. The founder of the Bogomil movement, who lived in Bulgaria at the end of the tenth century and the beginning of the eleventh, not only created an early mass movement foreshadowing the European Renaissance, but also cured the infirm in ways that the Church attributed to the "powers of darkness".

A few years before Bulgaria's liberation from five centuries of Ottoman bondage, in 1878, V. Beron published his *Natural History* (1870), in which he made an attempt to examine the problem of "animal magnetism in people, historically and scientifically". After this a number of authors wrote scientific studies on hypnosis and psychotherapy.

*Concepts of hypnosis.* If we set aside the magnetic-fluid hypothesis (as well as many others of the prescientific period), we can sum up the numerous ideas about the nature of hypnosis and divide them up in three main groups of hypotheses: pathological, physiological and psychological.

As we have already mentioned, the main exponent of the *pathological* hypothesis was Charcot (1882, 1888, 1889). He developed this theory based on his own experience with patients affected with hysteria.

*Physiological hypotheses* to explain hypnosis were devised from the moment it was scientifically defined. Braid (1884) looked for the physiological basis of the new psychological phenomenon in the changing composition of blood due to the disruption of the heart beat and respiratory balance.

After Braid various attempts to find a physiological explanation for hypnosis were made. J. Jeo (1884) assumed that in hypnosis a state of partial and local

---

[1] The significance of hypnosis in medical practice was underlined in many of the works of P.P. Podyapolsky (1903, 1904, 1909, 1913, 1915, 1926, 1927-a, 1927-b, 1929), V.M. Bekhterev (1892, 1893, 1898, 1911), and others. They maintained that hypnosis is a special state of modified natural sleep and not a pathological phenomenon as J. Charcot alleged. K.I. Platonov (1915, 1925-b, 1925-c, 1925-d, 1926-a, 1926-b, 1930-a, 1930-b, 1930-c, 1939, 1952-a, 1952-b, 1957) elaborated the problem of therapeutic and experimental hypnoses in their interrelations.

anaemia occurred in some regions of the cerebral cortex. E. Berillons (1874) maintained that the activity of the dominating hemisphere could be inhibited under hypnosis, and a stimulus different in type and strength could be directed to each of the hemispheres.

The attempts to find a physiological explanation of hypnosis have been given convincing experimental basis in I.P. Pavlov's teaching.

The conception of hypnosis as a special type of sleep should not, however, be associated only with the name of I.P. Pavlov. The phenomenological identification of hypnosis with ordinary sleep is so marked that Braid saw this external likeness and thence coined the name of hypnosis. Liebault, Bernheim, Lowenfeld, and others emphasized the similarity between hypnosis and ordinary sleep without being able to get out of the circle of their psychological concepts. Bekhterev also pointed out that hypnosis is a uniquely modified natural sleep.

While elaborating on the problem of sleep, Pavlov also carried out research into the physiological mechanisms of hypnosis. He thought hypnosis and normal sleep had the same physiological foundation—the diffusing process of inhibition. He showed that in dogs a hypnotic condition can be induced in a conditioned manner, and in this hypnotic condition dissociation of the secretory and motor reactions originates. B.N. Birman (1925) later induced conditioned sleep, keeping one waking region. He elaborated a reflex to the "do" tone with 256 vibrations per second and inhibition of the reflex by the other 22 tones. When he presented the inhibiting tones he induced sleep, while the "do" tone woke the animal. In this way, sleep with the existence of a waking region during it, was induced experimentally. Birman was of the opinion that the experimentally induced partial sleep was mechanically similar to the state of hypnosis in man. The principle of the "waking point", however, should be used only very carefully as a basis for reasoning in connection with "rapport" in human hypnosis. While the activation of the waking region in ordinary sleep in men and in animals results only in waking, the rapport relationship permits the performance of the most complicated mental activity without coming out of the hypnotic state. It is a known fact that hypnosis can easily change into ordinary sleep with a loss of rapport and that ordinary sleep can be transformed into hypnosis by establishing rapport. In some cases, too, behavioral assessment can apparently be proved by electroencephalographic methods. In the transition from hypnosis to ordinary sleep, as the research carried out by A. Marenina (1954) and others have shown, the synchronization of potentials increases and delta waves appear.

Many researchers have made EEG investigations of hypnosis. However, the results they have obtained are contradictory. A common feature, however, of all the EEG investigations[1] has been the absence of EEG changes typical of sleep. Data evincing general relaxation and very initial states of sleep have been marked only in some of the investigations. The brain biocurrent recordings under hypnosis are closer to a waking state than to sleep. Thus, it can be assumed that hypnosis differs from ordinary sleep in three basic ways: psychological, clinical and electrophysiological. The psychological criteria comprise the features of rapport under hypnosis. It has been emphasized that these are not identical with the features of the "waking point" during sleep. The clinical criteria comprise the diverse symptoms manifested in hypnotized persons which are not observed in ordinary sleep. The electrophysiological criterion shows differences in EEG during sleep and during hypnosis. Here we should bear in mind, however, that these differences should be reconsidered if we are to compare EEG under hypnosis with EEG in paradoxical sleep. Recent research into sleep has shown that many of its physiological aspects, such as paradoxical sleep, were unknown until recently. This means that we cannot compare one unknown phenomenon with another unknown one. Therefore, there are still not sufficient grounds either to accept or reject the physiological hypothesis that sleep mechanisms are similar to hypnotic mechanisms.

Of the *psychological hypotheses,* Bernheim's suggestive hypothesis (1881, 1910) has played the most important role. He believed that hypnosis is a state of elevated suggestibility achieved by suggestion. According to him, hypnotic sleep in no way differs from ordinary sleep. The difference is only that the hypnotized person falls asleep with the thought of the person who puts him to sleep. He rejected the existence of hypnosis independent of suggestibility. But in his ideas there is a measure of inaccuracy which makes it impossible to accept them fully. L. Shertok (1965) wrote in connection with this:

In reply to objections that his ideas were inspired by a love of paradox and that suggestibility is nothing but hypnotism in a waking state, Bernheim said still more categorically—"It would be more precise to say hypnotism is suggestion in a state of sleep". Here the ambiguity is evident, and it becomes still more

---

[1] A.L. Loomis, E.N. Harvey and G. Hobart (1936), G. Marinesco, O. Sager and A. Kreindler (1937), H. Lundhol and H. Loewenbach (1942), W.L. Ford and G.I Iaeger (1948), W. Barker and S. Bergwin (1949), H. Blake and R.W. Gerard (1937), M.P. Nevsky (1958), M.H. Starobinetz (1967), A.A. Genkin and E.F. Mordvinov (1969), P. London, J.E. Hart and M.P. Leibovitz (1968), V. Raikov (1969), and others.

obvious when we know that Bernheim added: "Besides this, as I have already stated, sleep should be incomplete."

J. Braid (1884). L. Liebault (1889), and L. Lowenfeld (1903, 1922, 1927) also refer to hypnosis as a psychological state of sleep and attempt to give some physiological interpretations of it.

The psychoanalytical hypothesis of hypnosis proceeds from the instinctive—libidinous experience of the hypnotized and the hypnotizer.

In the dissociative psychological hypothesis, expounded by P. Janet (1909, 1911, 1925, 1925—28), and B. Sidis (1902), points are sought in the lack of memory of some actions carried out under hypnosis to substantiate it.

The modern cognitive—behavioral viewpoint of T.X. Barber *et al.* (1974) has an advantage over other views, mainly because it is based on Barber's own well organized experimental experience. In accordance with it:

. . . the concept of hypnotic trance and related concepts—hypnotized, hypnosis and hypnotic state—are not only unnecessary but also misleading in explaining the phenomena.

This viewpoint in many respects comes close to our own conception of the possibility of obtaining all hypnotic phenomena by means of suggestion alone in a normal waking state. Some of the clinical and experimental results that have been obtained oblige us to reconsider the rejection of the fact that a specific "state" of the mind may also be induced by means of suggestion, too.

This is especially important now that attention has begun to be paid again to the great variety of altered states of consciousness, to which several congresses have recently been devoted.

Many hypnotic phenomena have demonstrated the existence and significance of paraconscious mental activity in a very clear way. Among these phenomena are not only the ordinary activities which are conscious and realized in a waking state and paraconscious and unrealized under hypnosis. They, by themselves, prove the reality of the unconscious mental activity and make it imperative that greater experimental interest is shown in it and its law-governed working. And here must be mentioned the unusual possibility of purposely changing under hypnosis many intimate biochemical, endocrine, trophic and other physiological processes, as well as various elements of the mental activity of the human being.

Control of the most complicated physiological processes can be profoundly affected under hypnosis. This psychogenic effect is achieved, of course, not by way of conscious logical and critical conviction, but through the mechanisms of paraconscious mental activity—no matter that sometimes it may seem, at first glance, that there is an indisputable conscious component. Interesting, in this respect, are the painless surgical operations performed under hypnosis.[1] J. Braid (1883), at the same time as he introduced the name "hypnosis", proposed that it should be used for painless amputations. Now thousands of operations have been performed under hypnosis. Furthermore, investigation has shown that the pain is not inhibited by conscious will power because very often the vegetative reactions accompanying it are absent. Research work in this sphere began as early as 1902, when V. Bekhterev and V. Narbut found that besides the absence of pain, in spite of strong stimulation of pain, there were no changes in the pulse and breathing.[2] I. Petrov (1968) showed that the stimulation of pain in some hypnotized subjects does not cause the so-called pathic mydriasis. These phenomena lead us to think that changes in sensitivity under hypnosis are not of a simulative nature: the physiological mechanisms of this anaesthesia are related to paraconscious mental activity.

The significance of paraconscious mental activity in the control of the organism was also seen in hypnotic experiments carried out to investigate the psychogenic changes in the functions of the vegetative nervous system, the metabolic processes and the trophics. Conscious critical and logical thinking could hardly play any part in these experiments.[3]

---

[1] P. Podyapolsky (1915, 1926), A. Nikolaev (1924, 1930), K.I. Platonov and I.Z. Velvovsky (1924), K.I. Platonov (1925-a, 1957), V. Bakhtiarov (1930, 1933,), A.V. Dick (1927), L. Amfiteatrov (1936), V.N. Konstantinov (1937), V. Zdravomislov (1930, 1958), V.A. Vashenyuk (1950), I. Petrov (1963), P. Petrov *et al.* (1963-a, 1963-b, 1964, 1965, 1966), G. Yankov *et al.* (1965-a, 1965-b, 1965-c), D. Traikov and S. Pashovski (1967), K.M. Kalitkin (1965), H. Lundholm (1928), V.E. Rozhnov (1954), F. Patrie (1937), L. Shaw (1949), J.W. Heron and M. Abramson (1956), A.R. MacCay (1936), A.Moss (1956), T. Burgess (1952, 1956), A. Chakurov *et al.* (1966), C. Tuckey (1921), and many others.

[2] These data were also confirmed by K.I. Platonov (1957), A.P. Slobodnyak (1966) in different experimental variants.

[3] A. Slobodnyak (1966), M. Lowy (1918), P. Astruck (1922), F. Deutsch and E. Kauf (1923), H. Cramer and E. Wittkower (1930), W. Bier (1930), E. Jennes

We found (1955) that in some people the pulse is decelerated under hypnosis, and in others accelerated. In two persons, however, it was found that the degree of pulse deceleration or acceleration corresponded to the suggested deepness of hypnotic sleep. The same relation was observed between the soundness of sleep and changes in blood pressure. Although blood pressure drops in some cases and rises in others, our research showed that it usually changes in accordance with the deepness of the hypnotic sleep. Since this graded deepness of sleep is induced by suggestive speech and the hypnotized person cannot give a conscious account of it, it is clear that it is effected outside the scope of conscious mental processes.

In other joint research work with V. Bakalska and I. Petrov (1957), we found that both the latent period of the motor reaction and the association period of the associative experiment were lengthened under hypnosis, the prolongation depending on the profoundness of the suggested sleep.

In hypnotic experiments with suggestions to investigate the

---

and C. Wible (1937), B. Stokvis (1938), H. Kleinsorge and G. Klumbies (1949), and P. Reiter (1956) showed that the rate of the pulse can change under hypnosis. G. Heyer (1921), O. Langheinrich (1922), R. Heilig and H. Hoff (1925-a), A. Luckhard and R. Johnston (1924), and M.L. Linetskiy (1967), observed a change in the secretion of the stomach acid. E. Wittkower (1928) found a change in bile secretion. F. Delhaugne and K. Hansen (1927) observed a change in the gastric and duodenal secretion in suggested feeding with various foods. R. Heilig and H. Hoff (1925-a) found changes in renal functions, and H. Marx (1926) in suggested drinking under hypnosis, observed an increase of urine with a reduction of its specific gravity. H. Marcus and E. Sahlgren (1925) in suggestion under hypnosis, reduced the reaction of the pharmacodynamic test with adrenaline and atropine. F. Glaser (1924), A.A. Tapilsky (1928), P.P. Istomin and P.Y. Galperin (1925), and others obtained alimentary leucocytosis by suggestion; and E. Wittkower (1929) obtained affective leucocytosis. A. Gigon (1926) reduced the blood sugar. F. Graser (1924), H. Kretschmer and R. Kruger (1927), Shazilo and N. Abramov (1928), and others changed the calcium level in blood serum to a moderate amount. H. Gessler and K. Hansen (1927), and P. Reiter (1956) affected the basic metabolism, M. Levine (1930) obtained differences in skin resistance, I.M. Korotkin, T.V. Pleshkova and M.M. Suslova (1968) changed the hearing thresholds in 14 out of 16 subjects; K.I. Platonov (1956) achieved a number of changes in the trophics and in the sugar metabolism; P.I. Bull (1958), V. E. Rozhnov (1954), M.S. Lebedinsky (1959), K.I. Platonov (1957), and many others made use of the possibility of achieving physiological and biochemical changes under hypnosis in clinical practice. The hypno-suggestive effect on skin trophics in a number of skin diseases, practised by A. Kartamishev (1936), M. Zheltakov (1958), I. Zhukov (1958), and others give a clear idea of this.

differences in the profoundness of sleep and to measure the latent period and the quality of the reactions, we came upon a phenomenon of spontaneous reproduction of schizophrenic symptoms which was not due to any verbal or involuntarily implied suggestion. When the hypnosis had deepened considerably the subject suddenly began to react at almost equal intervals of about 0.8 sec. without any stimulus being presented. The rhythmical movements repeated exactly the pattern of movements with which the subject usually reacted to the stimulus (red light). The thumb of the subject's right hand with which she had been pressing the key of a telegraph apparatus rhythmically contracted and loosened. These movements continued for about 20 minutes, after which the subject obviously went to sleep. She did not respond to the questions of the physician who had induced the hypnosis and was controlling it. In order to restore verbal rapport the suggestion "you should sleep lighter" was presented.

In some of the experiments with this subject the rhythmical movements spread from the thumb of the right hand to the right or left leg and to the lips, or the subject made movements with the same rhythm only with her lips. While the subject was making these rhythmical movements, she did not answer any questions in spite of the persistent suggestions that were presented to her proposing that she should give an answer. At the same time, however, suggestions changing the profundity of the hypnotic inhibition process had an effect on her.

Both in the first experiment and in those that followed, the rhythmical movements appeared when the latent period of motor reaction reached values of 1.30 sec. to about 2 sec.

These data showed that rhythmical movements appear at a given profundity of the hypnosis. In one of the experiments, when the subject began making rhythmical movements, we conditioned this hypnotic profundity in the following way: "This depth of sleep is called 'X'. Whenever I say 'you go to sleep to X degree' you will go to sleep to this depth". (It is necessary to point out that never in the subject's presence, whether she was hypnotized or not, did we even hint that she made rhythmical movements and that we were interested in them.) After this experiment the suggestion "you go to sleep to 'X' degree" always evoked the immediate appearance of rhythmical movements. We varied the experiments with the "X" degree" sleep in the following ways:

1) While the subject (in the "X degree" depth of hypnosis) was making the rhythmical movements, the suggestion was put forward: "You should now sleep lighter and lighter". The rhythm gradually became slower and the pressing of the thumb on the key grew weaker till the rhythmical movements stopped altogether. At the same moment as they stopped another suggestion was made, "now you should sleep deeper and deeper". Slow and, at the beginning, weak rhythmical movements appeared which gradually became quicker and more vigorous till the usual "X" degree rhythm was reached (0.8 sec.). If we started in the reverse order, i.e., from "X degree" to a deeper sleep and then to a lighter sleep, the same results were obtained. Sometimes the restoration of the rhythmical movements was not completely achieved. Once we observed only unconnected attempts to resume the rhythmical movements and in another experiment—rhythmical fascicular tremors of the two ante-brachii appeared. After suggestions to go into lighter and lighter sleep, the rhythmical movements ceased and the subject responded to the stimuli with a latent period of motor reaction of about 1.60 sec. When the rhythmical movements ceased, on a suggestion to go into deeper sleep, the latent period of motor reaction was about 3 or 4 seconds.

2) Association records were taken in "X degree". In this degree of hypnotic sleep no association replies appeared. The latent period was infinite even when the word-stimulus was presented several times.

The subject did not respond to words-stimuli given by the hypnotizer either. Sometimes, when the rhythmical movements became slower or were already disappearing, the subject responded with chaotic associations and repeated some of them many times. Sometimes, when the rhythm was slow or disappearing, the word-stimulus or the tapping on the table (a precursory stimulus) again provoked the already disappearing movements.

3) An attempt was made to carry on a conversation between the hypnotizer and the hypnotized subject in the "X degree" of sleep. No answers were given to questions repeated once or twice. Sometimes, showing a close similarity to the association records, when the question was asked the rhythmical movements, which had already ceased, would appear again. In the following experiments, when the question was being repeated persistently, the subject made

an attempt to answer and this led to a break in the rhythm of the movements. When the question had been repeated 25—30 times the subject answered by reproducing the question many times verbigerated echolalia) or repeated some words many times. In most cases, the word had no connection whatsoever with the question. Only on two occasions did the many-times-repeated word correspond to the question and this was accompanied by a change in the rhythm of the thumb movements. The subject's speech was also rhythmical. The two rhythms coincided. On the suggestion of lighter and lighter sleep as well as on the suggestion of deeper and deeper sleep, the subject began to give sensible answers after the rhythmical movements had disappeared. The following is one of the recordings of the subject's behaviour in "X degree" depth of hypnosis.

The experiment began at 12.10 p.m. The subject was asked questions at different levels of hypnotic inhibition. The subject's answers were adequate. When the latent period of reaction was shorter the answers were quicker, and more abrupt; when the latent period of reaction was longer, they were slower, drawled out, spoken in a low voice and vague. For example, to the question, "What is the weather like today?", the answer was, "The weather is cloudy". In the "X-degree" the subject tapped lightly with the thumb on her right hand and the heel of her right foot. To the same question: "What is the weather like?" she gave no answer. The question was repeated 12 times with different intonations of the voice and in different degrees of loudness. The subject answered vaguely "Sun!" and at the same time the rhythm of the hand movement became slower and almost stopped. It was again suggested to the subject: "You sleep in 'X-degree' ". As a result the subject began to tap rhythmically with the thumb of her right hand and her right heel. To the question: "What is the weather like now?" she did not answer but accelerated the tapping. The question was repeated 25 times. The subject made an attempt to say something which was incomprehensible and the rhythmical movements came to a stop. Slow rhythmical movements of the lips appeared. To the question: "What?" (10 times), she answered in a low voice: "Sun, sun, sun. . ." (repeating the words many times for about three or four minutes). While uttering the word "sun" the subject began to tap with her thumb. The rhythm of the subject's speech and the rhythm of the movement of her thumb was one and the same. When she was asked the question "Where do you want to go? Tell us!" the rhythm changed and she did not answer. The question was repeated many times. The subject continued tapping rhythmically with her thumb and heel. Another question was asked: "Did you see D. yesterday?" (D. is her brother). The question was repeated 12 times. The subject did not answer but only repeated "Sun . . .". Another question was asked: "How is D.?" The question was repeated 25 times and from time to time the persistent repeating of the question was accompanied by a gentle tapping on the subject's shoulder to elicit an answer. However, the subject repeated only: "Sun, sun, sun . . .".

On the suggestion of "You sleep a little lighter", the subject ceased repeating "Sun" and the rhythm of the movements became slower. "You sleep still lighter" and the question: "Did you see D.?" (many times repeated) elicited the answer: "Yes, I did." While the subject was giving the answer the rhythmical movements ceased and then began again. Then to the question: "How is D.?", the subject did not answer the question but repeated it word for word using the same intonation. On the suggestion: "You sleep still lighter", the rhythmical movements ceased. And now to the question: "Have you seen D.?" she answered, "Yes, I have". The question: "When?" brought the answer: "On Sunday", and the question "How is he?", the answer: "Very well, very well, very well . . ."

On the suggestion: "You sleep a little deeper", slow rhythmical movements appeared. The question: "Did you see D.?" brought no answer but the repetition of "Did you see D.?" (many times). After the suggestion: "You sleep still deeper", the subject's movements became more vigorous and their rhythm quicker. The question: "Did you see D?" elicited the answer: "Sun, sun, sun . . ."

A deeper and deeper sleep was suggested until the rhythmical movements stopped altogether. The subject was obviously in a deep sleep. The question: "Did you see D.?" brought no answer. The question was repeated many times but no answer was given to it. Then the suggestion was made that she should wake.

The repetitions of movements and words, which were not suggested in any way to this subject under hypnosis, resembled the repetitive phenomena which are well-known in the psychoneurological practice. perseverations, stereotypes, verbigerations, echolalias, palilalias, etc.

A. Boströem pointed out that in cases of schizophrenia the stereotypes are most often not verbally manifested.

A certain measure of antagonism most probably exists between thought and movement within the framework of the norm. In a normal state, when two centers are excited simultaneously, the activity of the one is inhibited by the activity of the other, but to a considerably lesser degree. The degree of this inhibition most probably depends on the general tonus of the cortex.

It is pointed out in the literature dealing with this question that repetitive phenomena have been observed in fatigue, somnolence, exhaustion, hypnosis, i.e., in states which represent different degrees of inhibition of the cortex. Our experiments (1) confirmed the fact that the tendency to repetition is a symptom of inhibited cortex, and (2) showed that on increasing the profundity of the inhibition process this tendency increases, reaching clear manifestation at a given profundity, and after which the increase in the profundity of the inhibition process leads to a decrease of the repetitive tendency.

In our experiments with latent period of reaction of 0.40 sec.

to 1.30 sec., 2, 3, 4, or 5 responses to one stimulus were observed. In the experiments with latent period of reaction of 1.30 to 2 or 3 sec., the rhythmical movements described above, were observed. In states of very deep inhibition, in experiments with a mean latent period of about 7.00 sec., no rhythmical movements were observed. Consequently, rhythmical movements appear at a given profundity of inhibition, one which is optimal for them.

These experimental data show various characteristic features of the paraconscious processes. But they could be interpreted also as a manifestation of certain mechanisms of the schizophrenic symptoms—a manifestation spontaneously modelled in the hypnotic experiment. These data also give grounds to suppose that in the presence of such symptoms the remedial effect will be less markedly manifested if it is directed only to the symptoms and much more effective if it is directed to the general state of the central nervous system.

The hypnosuggestive activation of the paraconscious mental activity can be seen with particular clarity in hypnosis experiments which try to change the whole personality or some separate mental functions. So far the greatest amount of experimental material has been collected on the still controversial problem of age regression. Personality regression, the return to earlier age and functional states, is a frequent phenomenon in clinical practice. Sometimes, it is only vaguely observed in the form of slight puerilism or as an intellectual reversion to concrete visual thinking, typical of the earlier age transitions. Regression is seen most clearly in the developed ecmnestic syndrome. It occurs both in psychogenous and organic diseases.

The ecmnestic syndrome can be observed very clearly in a suggested age regression under hypnosis. Kraft-Ebbing (1927), Lowenfeld (1901), Platonov (1957), V. Danilevsky (1924), F. Mayorov (1950), F. Mayorov and M. Suslova (1952), M. Suslova (1951), B. Stokvis (1955), and E.R. Hilgard (1965) carried out research into the question of whether the changes in the behavior, speech, handwriting and attitude toward the world in the time of the suggested younger age of a subject made them correspond to what they actually were when the respective subject was that age. Some rather special methods have been employed.[1] P. Young (1925, 1940, 1941), using test methods, investigated the intelligence at suggested younger ages of subjects and then made the same subjects simulate a younger age level in a waking state. He came to the conclusion that intelligence did not respond to the regressive age, and that regression to an age under six is impossible. In his experiments with adults, the demonstration of a child's age without hypnosis gave results closer to the demonstrated age than in hypnotic regression. M. Orne arrived at similar conclusions (1951). T. Sarbin (1950), however, repeated Young's experiments and found that Young had not paid sufficient attention to the fact that the deepness of hypnosis may be of importance for the results. He found that intellectual regression under hypnosis is more convincing than simulated regression in a waking state. R. True (1949), in an experiment with age regression in 40 men and 10 women, asked them on what day of the week had some memorable event occurred at a suggested age. The answers he received were amazingly correct. Thus, for example, at the suggested age of 10, 93 percent of their answers were correct, at the suggested age of 7, 82 percent, and at the suggested age of 4, 69 percent. Before and after the hypnosis, when the subjects were asked the same questions, only a small percent of their answers were correct.

L. Wolberg (1948) obtained regression down to the age of one year. L. Gidro-Frank and M. Bowerbuch (1948) found the appearance of the Babinsky Reflex in suggested regression down to the age of 7 months. R. True and C. Stephenson (1951, 1952) also observed a reversal of the reflex of the soles of the feet in hypnotic regression to the age of one month. In experiments with 12 persons, E. McCranie and H.B. Crasilnech (1955) found that only the volitionally controlled conditioned reflexes disappeared after the suggestion of age regression. L. Le Cron (1956), and K. Platonov (1957) reported spontaneously appearing pathological conditions in suggesting an age when the subjects had actually suffered from these pathological conditions at that age. Clearly observed in the spontaneous occurrence of special symptoms was the significance of specific hypnotic depth measured by some vegetative indicators or the magnitude of the reaction and the association time.

I. Watkins and B. Showalter photographed the movements of the eyeball while subjects were reading at various suggested ages. The

---

[1] For example, K.I. Platonov and E.A. Prikhodivniy (1930) employed the Binet Simon test method. M. Kline and H. Guze (1951) worked with the so-called House-Tree-Person Test (H.T.P.)—drawing a house-tree-man. M. Suslova (1952) employed arithmetical problems. M. Parrish, R.M. Lundy and H.W. Leibowitz (1968) used test methods to elaborate illusionary perceptions. E. Barra and A.C. Moreas Passos (1960) used Rorschach's test. B. Stokvis (1955) on one occasion was able to compare the handwriting of a subject at a suggested age with the actual handwriting of the subject at that age.

film showed the instability of eye coordination in reading at suggested ages from 6 to 10. W. Roberts and D. Black found in one patient suffering from myopia, which had begun at the age of 12, that the suggested return to a younger age improved her vision, the improvement depending on the age she was supposed to be reliving. Her eyesight was examined by an ophthalmologist during the experiments. It is interesting to note that when direct suggestion under hypnosis was used without suggesting that she revert to a younger age, her eyesight did not improve.

A. As (1962) restored a language (spoken by a subject in childhood, but forgotten) in hypnotic age regression. H. Kupfer (1945) observed normal EEG when he regressed a patient suffering from epilepsy to the age he was before the disease began. But electroencephalographic investigations by Kupfer (1945), B. Schwartz *et al.* (1955), L. Ford and K. Ieager (1948), McCranie *et al.* (1955), and True and Stephenson failed to produce the characteristic features of the suggested age. Various vegetative functions at a hypnotically suggested younger age of subjects have also been investigated. H. Horvai and J. Hoskovec (1962) investigated the changes in the respiratory and pulse frequency as well as some reflexes of early age. They did not find physiological regression of these functions which put them on a level with those of people who really are the specified.[1]

We investigated (1955, 1959) the movements of the eyeball, handwriting and drawings of five hypnotized patients, two women and three men, between 20 and 30 years of age. Two of them were being treated for neurotic decompensation in thymopathic psychopathy, and the other three for mild neurotic disturbances. All five showed a fair degree of susceptibility to hypnosis.

The ophthalmological investigation in a normal waking state before and after the experiments showed no deviations in any of the subjects. In a somnambulistic phase of hypnosis, without additional suggestions, the eyeballs stayed immobile, staring forward or making small movements, but always associated, as in a normal waking state.

During suggestions to go deeper and deeper into the most profound sleep, a slight indication of nonassociation of the eye move-

---

[1] J.W. Gebhard (1961), A.J. Pates (1961), and T.X. Barber (1962) have described many of the various investigations in this field in reviews. M. Kline (1951), A. Moll (1924), R. Rubenstein and R. Newman (1954), and many other scientists have examined the results of the research into hypnotic age regression without reaching any convincing final conclusions.

ments could be observed at certain moments. The eyeballs seemed to begin to detach from each other and to move independently. This lasted only for very short periods of five or six seconds, but was repeated again in two or three minutes' time.

The direct suggestion: "Your eyes begin to move each one for itself, each independent of the other" did not result in disassociation. Only the maximum convergence was sometimes obtained. But when this occurred, the eye muscles grew tired very quickly, the eyes became moist and returned to their normal position.

But when the age of two days was suggested, the following was observed: the eye slits became unusually narrow and the eyeballs began to move slowly in a dissociated manner. Sometimes the movements stopped in a position of strabismus and then continued again. A pattern was obtained resembling the "floating" and squint eyes of the newly born (Figure 20). The dissociated movements were not emphatically expressed in all cases. They could be observed clearly in three of the subjects; in the other two there was an obvious attempt to simulate the strabismus of the newly born, but only for a few moments did it reach dissociation. A whole series of transitory states, starting from slight dissociation to the typical independent movement of each eye, was observed in the three subjects who manifested marked dissociation of the eyeball movements. We related this phenomenon to the dissociated movements of the eyeballs during natural sleep, which we were able to observe quite frequently and regularly in small children.

The eyeball movement phenomenon in suggested age regression under hypnosis was later also described by V.L. Raikov (1969). The general behavior of those hypnotized and under the suggestion of being two days, six months, one year or 8 years old was like their behavior when they were actually this age, although elements of their behavior when older quite clearly crept in. For this reason, we shall elaborate only the following results of our experiments.

One subject, during the period when he was at the suggested age of 8 years, spontaneously drew a picture of a girl with a mirror. Several months after this experiment, relatives of the subject, without his knowledge but at our request, looked through the family archives and found notebooks and drawings he had done at the actual age of 8, including one picture which was very much like the one drawn under hypnosis.

The theme and the execution of the drawing at the suggested age corresponded quite closely to the theme and execution of the

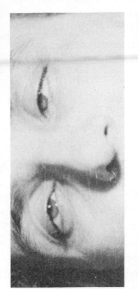
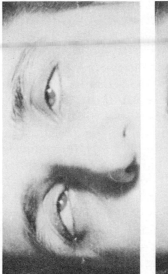
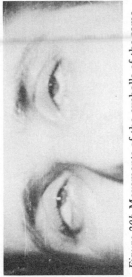

*Figure 20b* Movements of the eyeballs of the same subject at the hypnotically suggested age of two days.

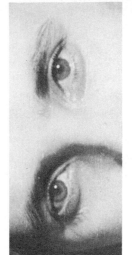
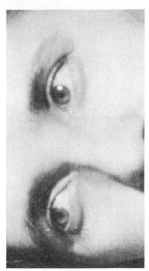
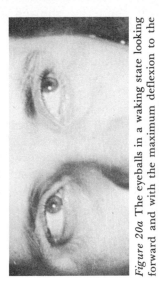

*Figure 20a* The eyeballs in a waking state looking forward and with the maximum deflexion to the right and to the left.

original drawing. The girl was the same size, and was the exact image of the girl in the old drawing; the straight lines were uncertain; the caption in block letters resembled the original caption; and the orthography was the same in both captions, the letter "b", which is not used in the new spelling, was used in spite of this in the caption written under hypnosis (Figure 21).

Five years later, the same experiment was repeated with the same person and the result of the second experiment did not differ in any essential point from the result of the first one.

The subject's relatives also brought a letter which was written when he was actually 8 years of age (Figure 22-a). At a suggested age corresponding to the exact age of the subject when the letter was written, he wrote the old letter from dictation without looking at the original (Figure 22-b). Then, under hypnosis without it being suggested that he was at a younger age, the letter was given to the subject for him to imitate the handwriting (Figure 22-d). Finally, the letter was dictated to him in a normal waking state (Figure 22-c).

The handwriting at the suggested age of 8 years bore a clear resemblance to the handwriting of the original letter, while his attempt to imitate the handwriting under ordinary hypnosis without suggestion of a change of age was unsuccessful.

Experiments carried out 5 years later, with the same subject and with the letter, showed some fluctuation in the results but remained reasonably convincing.

The dissociated movements of the eyeball obtained experimentally in a hypnotic age regression, going back to the age of a new-born baby, contradict Hering's motor law of the constant connectedness of the movements of the eyeballs. They and the dissociated eyeball movements, which we observed during natural sleep and in some neurotic states, represent a deviation from this law which cannot be simulated. It is also difficult to believe that such precise and spontaneous simulation in drawing the picture would be possible and all the more so seeing that the subject did not know we were going to look for a similar drawing in the family archives. The same holds good for the letter writing.

These experimental results permit a reexamination of the suggested hypnotic regression discussion. In the literature on this subject, several viewpoints have been formed. Kraft-Ebbing (1927) and V. Sreznevskiy (1924) hold the view that under the suggestion of a younger age there is an actual return to the suggested age—a reincarnation of the personality, Lowenfeld (1901), Young (1940),

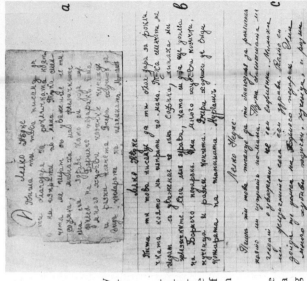

*Figure 22*

*a:*
A letter written by subject at the actual age of 8 years.

*b:*
Subjects handwriting at the age suggested under hypnosis, actually the same age as that of the subject when writing.

*c:*
Handwriting of the same subject in a normal waking state.

*d:*
Handwriting of the same subject under ordinary hypnosis. It was suggested that the handwriting of the old letter (a) should be imitated.

*Figure 21a* Drawing at the actual age of 8 years.
*b.* Drawing at the hypnotically suggested age of 8 years.

Horvai and Haskovec (1962) find that there is no personality reproduction, but a more or less successful playing of a role under
hypnosis.

J. Stuchlik (1965) compared hypnotic age regression with some
psychological features of dreaming. M. Erickson and L. Kubie (1941)
defined two types of regression: in one, the subject recalls and acts
past events, and in the other, the subject actually returns psychically
and physiologically to the suggested earlier functional level. All
experience after the suggested age disappears at the same time. A.
Weitzenhoffer (1953) distinguished three regressive types. To the
first type belongs the hypnotized subject who plays a role; to the
second, the subject who really returns to an earlier functional level;
and to the third, the subject who is a mixture of the first two types.
He expressed doubt as to what extent there can be a complete return
to an earlier functional level. According to him, this would mean
losing rapport with the hypnotist.

Without excluding those cases of completely conscious or unconscious hypnotic playing of roles, our experimental results show that
at certain moments and for certain functions true regression can be
reached. There is a return to an earlier functional level.

It is suggested that through eventual hypnotic hypermnesia, evidence is "collected" for the characteristic features of the suggested
age, which is afterward presented in the form of a play. Data may
arrive both from memories of one's own development and (especially
for the earliest ages) from memories of children of the given
suggested age whom the subject has observed. Such an explanation
of the matter, however, contradicts the following considerations.

1) If it is accepted as true, it would appear that whatever talent a
subject has it improves in an almost miraculous way under hypnosis.
A person who has never gone in for painting suddenly acquires the
ability to reproduce handwriting and drawings from memory with a
perfection that would be envied by the best artists. The hypermnesic
enlivening of ideas still does not presuppose the accurate
reproduction of them in handwriting or drawing to the same degree
of perfection.

2) It is even more difficult to posit this mechanism as an explanation for unassociated eyeball movements because they are impossible
to remember. Even if they are not recalled from one's own experience but stem from observing children, it is still impossible to

imitate the eyeball movements.

3) Why unassociated eyeball movements appear at a suggested age of two days, cannot be explained since these cannot materialize under ordinary hypnosis with the appropriate suggestion but without age regression.

4) The same consideration holds good in the case of the letter: it would have been impossible to write it under ordinary hypnosis without age regression.

It can be assumed that in its diffusion, the inhibiting process under hypnosis suppresses the actual memory traces and conditions are created for the "enlivening" of more deeply suppressed and older traces.

The hypermnesia mechanisms probably extend directly to the motor functions and to wider nerve structures. The bringing to life of old complexes of memory traces into a wider complex of structures is not always comprehensive and lasting, as the hypnotic process itself is not lasting. But this, in particular, is one of the prerequisites for the transistional reproduction of the personality.

The hypermnesia and ecmnesia which arise spontaneously and which are manifested in somnolent states offer no possibilities for their "control" and "guidance". But experimental hypnotic regression can be directed, deepened and discontinued by the physician. The profundity of the hypnosis can be fixed, can direct suggestion to the established hypnotic background and can revive past trace complexes more accurately and purposefully. These two components, hypnotic profundity and revived trace complexes, are to be found in the formula of suggestion itself. When a specific age is suggested to the hypnotized subject, the necessary depth of retention is formed, on the one hand, to suppress the newer and, probably, more inhibiting trace complexes, and on the other, to form a temporary link with the trace complexes of the respective age. For example, the suggestion: "Now you are 8 years old" contains the following two components, "everything after the age of 8 is nonexistent", and "there is an age of 8". That this is so is obvious from a number of experiments in which suggestion was divided up in this way.

In such cases, more accurate patterns of the suggested age were always obtained. The phenomenological richness and accuracy of the real regression depend on the harmonious inclusion of the whole complicated mechanism. When no connection is established with the trace complexes, and only the depth of the hypnosis is fixed, there is still regression but it coincides most accurately with a specific age period. It is well known that associations tend to shift to a lower level, where thinking becomes more primitive and more childish with deepening of the inhibiting process without suggested age. When an attempt is made, through suggestion, to establish a temporary connection with the trace complexes of a specific age, and the content necessary for inhibiting later trace complexes is not fixed, the type of regression in which the hypnotized person plays a role is induced.

In our examples, the drawings and handwriting coincide, and the eyes move in an unassociated manner only when the age regression has been successfully suggested. Probably, then, the two components are switched on simultaneously: one, the fixed profundity of hypnotic retention, and the other, the association with the trace complexes of the respective age. Our experiments demonstrate that the profundity of the hypnosis is of the greater importance for obtaining dissociated eyeball movements.

While a direct suggestion to deepen sleep to the maximum led to slight indications of dissociated eyeball movements, a direct suggestion to dissociate eyeball movements (without suggesting the age of a new-born baby) failed to produce any results. The same was observed with the letter writing; a suggestion to imitate the subject's own former handwriting (without suggesting the corresponding age) failed to produce any positive results.

This finding of ours has been corroborated by W. Roberts and D. Black who, suggesting to a myopic subject that he was younger than he really was achieved some improvement in his eyesight which became what it had been at the age they suggested. Direct suggestion under hypnosis without suggesting a younger age had brought no result. The suggestion that a subject is two days old would probably result in the maximum deepening of inhibition and, in this way, suppress the greatest possible number of trace complexes. Then, in accordance with our already emphasized view of the physiological mechanism of the dissociated eye movements, the suppression descends low in the mesodiencephalic region and blocks to various degrees the connection between the nuclei of the eye-raising nerves as is the case in ordinary sleep. For this reason, probably the maximum deepening of hypnotic sleep without suggested ages in some cases resulted in a slight tendency to dissociation, while direct suggestion of dissociation brought no results.

It can be suggested, therefore, that the earlier the age manifested, the deeper is the hypnotic retention for it to be able to include more and more of the later dynamic stereotypes. Here it is interesting to note the concepts of G. Bunge (1901), and V. Vaschide (1907) who believed that the more profound is one's sleep, the earlier is the period of one's life of which one dreams.[1]

Experimental hypnotic regression could also serve as a model in examining the mechanisms of clinical regression. The inhibiting background may occur here in a number of diseases which weaken the cortical tonus. Clinical regression appears in a more colorful form in puerilism, clinical ecmnesia and therapeutic ecmnesia of the abreacted psychotherapeutic methods. Therefore, it must be admitted that in puerilism and in some forms of clinical ecmnesia, the fundamental physiological mechanism, despite the quite frequent liveliness of the patient, is rooted in the diffusion of the process of inhibition, and this under specific conditions would result in the liberation (not fully and ultimately, of course) of older dynamic stereotypes on archaic (old) functional levels.

Above all, the problem of hypnotic age regression is closely connected with the problems of paraconscious mental activity. The experiments which seem to manifest an actual return to a younger age level show that the complex of conscious and unconscious contents of the human mentality at various earlier stages of individual development appears not only as a transformed current complex, but to a great extent is preserved in its earlier stages in the unconscious mental activity. What happens both in these experiments and in the experiments in which no earlier-age level is restored but only a notion of it is acted out, cannot be remembered after release from the hypnotic state. This shows that the complicated mental activity involved in these experiments remains outside the field of cons-

---

[1] When talking about the profundity of hypnotic retention, one should bear in mind the modern literature on electrophysiological research during sleep. This research into sleep suggests that it is a specific state of activity. The diffusion and intensification of the process of inhibition should be examined rather as a redistribution in a complicated functional structure, without precluding the possibility of further clarification. This holds good still more for hypnosis which many authors do not even consider to be a sleep-like state, but rather regard it as a behavioral sleep-like state which in its physiological characteristics is closer to the waking state than to sleep. Consequently, when we speak of the deepening of hypnotic sleep we must realize that we are using a term which in no case precludes future experimental clarification.

ciousness—in the regions of the unconscious mental activity—after the person comes out of the hypnosis. There are grounds to believe. that this unconscious mental activity plays a paramount role in the formation of the reactions and relations of the personality in health and sickness. To a large extent, the abreacting psychotherapeutic methods have been worked out on these grounds. Therapeutic ecmnesia—the return to younger functional states—is an attempt at spontaneous soothing of psychotraumatic experiences, which have not been fully lived through. They are not built into the features of the topical personal characteristics, but are sunk in the paraconscious mental activity.

Ecmnesia and age regression are very closely related to hypnotic hypermnesia because super-memory is one of the leading symptoms in them both. The clear recollection of seemingly forgotten events which happened when one was younger is most dramatically manifested in the altered personality as it returns to an earlier functional level. But hypermnesia, under hypnosis, can be observed also in an isolated form, without marked changes in other features of the personality. Hypnotic hypermnesia is most often observed in clinical practice as one of the leading symptoms, when abreacted psychotherapeutic methods are applied.[1] It can reveal many of the psychotraumatic circumstances which lie at the base of neurotic morbidity. E. Sharankov (1956), and others doubt the therapeutic value of hypermnesia by itself alone. There are serious grounds for such reservations.

Laboratory investigations of hypnotic hypermnesia clarified some of its features, but some difficulties were encountered in them. B. Huse (1930), M.B. Mitchel (1932), and P.C. Young (1925, 1926) showed that memory material which is not bound by sense and emotion cannot be memorized better under hypnosis than in an ordinary

---

[1] Already in Mesmer's time and even earlier—in temple medicine, for example— there were cases observed of abreaction through hypnotic recollection of forgotten psychotraumatizing events. Such hypermnesia was also observed by E. Breuer and S. Freud (1909), as well as by later proponents of psychoanalysis. Such clinical forms of hypermnesia were described by J.M. Bramwell (1913), H.E. Wingfield (1920), W. McDougal (1926), M. Prince (1914), and K.I. Platonov (1957). Hypnotic hypermnesia found a place in the abreacting therapeutic methods of M.M. Asatiani (1926), S.Y. Lifshits (1927), L. Frank (1927), N. Krustnikov (1929) and K. Cholakov (1933, 1940), as well as in the research work of the students of N. Krustnikov and K. Cholakov—E. Shehanova (1928, 1954), A.G. Atanasov (1969), T. Tashev (1957), V. Yonchev (1957, 1969), and others.

waking state. In measuring the short-term memory in some of these experiments, it was found that retroactive inhibition was not much different under hypnosis from what it was in an ordinary waking state. J.M. Stalnaker and E.E. Riddle (1932) obtained considerable hypnotic hypermnesia for verse. R. White, G. Fox and W. Harris (1940), B.G. Rosenthal (1944), and others also found that hypnotic hypermnesia occurs in the memorization of material which makes sense (verse, sentences, etc.), while material which makes no sense (isolated words, syllables, figures, etc.) is memorized equally under hypnosis and in an ordinary waking state. The recalling, under hypnosis, of forgotten events was described by R.M. Dorcus (1960), who showed how it was used successfully by the police to discover a crime.

Hypermnestic manifestations were observed in patients being treated for functional diseases by hypnosis, as well as in some experiments. For example, one subject was able to tell under hypnosis the number of steps he had climbed to come to the department without having counted them previously and without expecting that he would be asked to give the number of them.

Hypermnesia does not always occur in hypnotized persons. A number of the psychological features connected with its causation have not yet been clarified, and this gives rise to contradictory views. A.P. Slobodyanik (1966) quoted many authors who alleged that hypnotic hypermnesia does not exist, or even that the memory capacities decrease under hypnosis. The fact that not all investigators manage to achieve hypnotic hypermnesia shows the complexity of the phenomenon. Our investigations and the practice of suggestopedy have proved that hypermnesia can be found not only in a state of hypnosis, but in a suggestive atmosphere as well. In the hypnopedic experiments, the importance of suggestion also was not discerned.

In March 1965, we proved experimentally the correctness of our views. Hypnopedic methods were being used to teach Russian to 102 school children, aged 15–19, in a provincial town of Bulgaria. The new words, phrases and texts of each new lesson were read to the school children once in the evening before they fell asleep, to introduce them to the program which would be given them during the night. The same program was released on the loudspeakers in the dormitories four times in three successive readings, i.e., 12 times in all during their night's sleep from midnight to 5.00 a.m. The average memorization rate was 85 percent.

We were sent to check the results obtained with these school-children after they had already advanced considerably in their learning of this language; they had had 20 nights' training. This case was well fitted to demonstrate: first, that in hypnopedy there is a transformation from night sleep to hypnosis; and secondly, that suggestion alone is sufficient to obtain such results and it is not necessary to burden one's night sleep with tasks which are not suitable for it.

*Hypnopedy transforms sleep into a form of hypnosis.* To prove the correctness of this view we carried out the following experiment. We chose a group of 12 children, and told them to go to bed at 4.45 p.m. The program was then introduced to them on a loudspeaker, the same program which they were to be given during the night. Their instructor gave the daytime presentation of the material in the same way as it was presented in the night-time program. The children were told to relax in the same manner as they did in their regular hypnopedic night-time lessons. Near the end of the daytime broadcast of their lesson all the children fell asleep. Their sleep had the same qualities as an ordinary hypnosis—with rapport, general hypesthesia, catalepsy, hallucination, amnesia and posthypnotic hypermnesia—without the children knowing that such phenomena existed. At. 5.40 p.m. the program, which they usually heard 12 times during the night, was released on the loudspeakers three times in succession and in the voice of the instructor. At 6.15 p.m., the children were awakened by the sound of music in the same way as they were awakened from their night sleep.

The memorization program comprised 50 Russian words with their Bulgarian translation, 31 Russian phrases with their Bulgarian translation and a Russian poem.

On awakening, the children were immediately called for a control check because usually such checks were made in the morning after sleep. It was found that the material had been assimilated in the same manner as in their hypnopedic training at night—85 percent. It should be noted that the session lasted for only one and a half hours, and the material was given on the loudspeaker only three times while the regular night-time training continued from midnight to 5.00 a.m., and during that time the material was presented 12 times.

When the children were checked again the following day without any more study of the above daytime program, it was found that they had forgotten none of the material and everything was retained in their minds in just the same way as after the night-time session.

This experiment shows that hypnopedic training transformed night sleep into hypnosis and that the same thing could be brought about in the daytime by simulating the night-time conditions of hypnopedic training. Furthermore, with the experience gained from this experiment, we can assume that it is not the hypnosis, but the suggestive atmosphere which played the decisive role in the memorization.

*Suggestion by itself is sufficient to improve memorization and there is no need for hypnosis.* To prove this we carried out the following experiment (which proved to be of decisive importance) with the same hypnopedically trained schoolchildren. We put a group of 15 schoolchildren in a separate room. The new program was presented to them in the same way as it was given in the night-time session, but only before they fell asleep. And, without their knowing it, the program was not presented to them while they were sleeping, as it was to the children in the other dormitories. They had only the introduction prior to sleep.

In the morning, without being told about the change in the night-time experiment, they were examined. It was found that they had learned 78 percent of the material.

This experiment showed that program memorization is due neither to sleep nor to hypnosis, but to suggestion. In actual fact, the whole suggestopedic practice has already proved this.

Some characteristic features of paraconscious mental activity can be seen in hypnotic experiments with negative hallucinations when the hypnotized subject does not perceive real irritants but some information of their characteristic features, and their significance remains in his mental activity.

Some features of paraconscious mental activity also can be seen in experiments with posthypnotic suggestions. The carrying out of a suggestion to recite a given poem two hours after release from the state of hypnosis shows very clearly the possibility of a mental effect outside the scope of the consciousness. The subject carries out whatever has been suggested quite automatically, and remembers doing it without understanding why he has had to do it. We can consider that all amnesically concealed activities, i.e., activities which cannot verbally be accounted for after or at the time of their occurrence, enter for a specified time into paraconscious mental activity.

*Phase (Transitory) encirclement and nonspecific mental reactivity*

There are innumerable transitions from the clearly realized contents of the human mind to the uncontrollable automatic and unconscious mental activities. This understanding is not identical to the concept of the "secondary ego" or "double consciousness" of P. Janet (1903, 1923); nor can it be included in the attitude, active in its essence, of W. Wundt (1962), who rejects rather than accepts the existence of unconscious mental activity. Wundt is responsible for the analogy of consciousness with the optical field, where the clearest perception gradually passes to ever more shaded peripheral zones.[1] Shilder calls this zone a "sphere". Kretschmer does not include in the concept of "sphere" the elementary sensory stimuli or the qualities of the pronounced word (intonation, gesture, order, cry, pain, etc.). According to him, the spherical qualities represent the obscure sense of the word symbolism.

Along this line, Bekhterev dwells on the so-called passive perceptions which enter the general mental sphere when the active attention is absorbed by some other activity, i.e., in a state of absent-mindedness. In many cases, a stimulus unnoticed by the consciousness, or a dream, is recollected and after some time acquires sense. It often later acquires qualities of morbid autosuggestion. In such cases, K. Platonov (1957) speaks of secondary (consciously-verbal) second signalling processing.

In studying the problems of conscious and paraconscious mental activity, methodological omissions often occur quite imperceptibly. It is very important not to confuse the clinical, psychological, physiological and philosophical concepts of the conscious and unconscious. I.P. Pavlov emphasized that he would not deal with philosophical views on the conscious. He described the consciousnesss in physiological terms as a mobile region with optimal excitability along the large hemispheres. New conditioned reflexes are easily formed and the differentiation is made in that region. The activity of the other sections is what we usually call unconscious automatic activity.

Later, Pavlov wrote in relation to the possibility outlined in experiments of forming conditioned connections (ties); also, when the

---

[1] This idea in one or another form persists even today; for instance in the works of K. Cholakov (1933, 1940, 1947), and G. Welch (1959). According to P. Shilder (1950), and E. Kretschmer (1947), beyond the threshold of the consciousness there is no mental life.

conditioned stimulus does not precede the unconditioned one, i.e., when the stimulus falls on an inhibited cortex about the functions of the cortical sections related to the unconscious mental activity as follows:

The physiology of the large hemispheres would assimilate the situation, important in being applicable to man, that the formation of new connections in the cortex may occur not only in the regions of the hemispheres with optimal excitability but also in the parts of them which are more or less inhibited. This may not be realized (is not conscious) but it does take place and, under favorable conditions, may appear in the mind readily and be presented as an act originating in an unknown way.

It is natural that in man this mobile field with optimal excitability should include mainly the functional structures of the second signalling (conscious—verbal) system without forgetting its indestructible relation to the first signalling (emotional—pictorial) system. We cannot imagine human conscious activity without the "extra addition" of evolution, without speech and all its possibilities for generalization, abstraction, the building of higher concepts and human thinking. What the content of the consciousness, at a given moment, will be depends on what areas of the second signalling (conscious—verbal) system are located in the optimal excitability. When this "mobile light spot with queer outlines" darkens and disappears, the consciousness also becomes dark and disappears. This happens, for example, when we fall asleep and dream.

The idea of consciousness as a mobile field of optimal excitability, and in particular of "the very important situation applicable to man" that the formation of new connections in the cortex may also take place in the inhibited areas outside the "light spot", have still not been given sufficient attention in scientific literature. Most often, consciousness is identified either with the activity of the whole second signalling (conscious—verbal) system or the activity of the whole cortex, in general, without considering the field of optimal excitability. And the unconscious (paraconscious) mental activity, as far as its active existence is recognized, is most frequently "demoted" to the first signalling (emotional—pictorial) system (Ivanov—Smolensky) or even to the subcortex (A.T. Pshonik).

It is logical to consider that the conscious—verbal system, although outside the consciousness, also participates in cortical control. Thus, for example, there is justification in believing that all vegetative reactions for which "verbal account" can be obtained in a change of the functional level (e.g. under hypnosis) have felt some reflection, "information" in this system. The traces of this information in the ordinary, normal tonus of the cortex do not fall within the limits of the mobile field with optimal excitability. This does not mean, however, that they are not connected with the conscious—verbal system as long as they can manifest themselves and "be recalled" on other functional levels. The same also holds good for all the activities of the human organism which can be changed by way of verbal suggestion.

A number of examples can be given in the field of hypnosis showing that connections are established in the conscious—verbal system and outside the consciousness, outside the field of optimal excitability. Post-hypnotic suggestion, although unconscious, materializes with the obligatory participation of the conscious—verbal system.

The view that being unaware of reactions need not exclude the participation of the conscious—verbal system, of course, outside the field of optimal excitability, raises unconscious mental activity to the human level. Thus, it is freed from the domination of the physiologically older anatomic—physiological formations to which, with certain qualifications, the instinctive and emotional—pictorial system can eventually also be referred. The nonverbalized participation of the conscious—verbal system in many unconscious activities shows that there is an uninterrupted connection between the two signalling systems.

A. Pshonik (1952) "lowers" the paraconscious mental activity still further, alleging that "presensory stimuli" (both extero- and interoceptive) are imperceptible until they are included in the cortical connections. Once included in such connections they become perceptible, "sensory". Thus, unconscious (paraconscious) mental activity is related to anatomical formations located only lower than the cortex.

The existence of schematic functional dissociation "along the vertical" (inhibition of all cortical functions and independent activity of subcortical functions), with complete isolation of the secondary (human) signalling system and even of the cortex in general, is accepted in both cases. Dissociation "along the horizontal", i.e., participation of the higher human functions in the paraconscious mental activity, is not accepted as true. But such an understanding is not in accordance with the numerous facts.

Dissociation mainly "along the vertical" can, although very seldom, be observed in clinical practice. This is seen, for example, in the elementary impulse—instinctive unrealized and unconscious activities which are encountered most often in diffuse organic devastations of the cortical structural units. Far more complicated and of greater importance for understanding the nature of paraconscious processes, however, is the functional dissociation directed mainly "along the horizontal" (inhibition of some cortical functions and activation of other cortical functions), which is often met with in clinical practice. It is observed in transitory trance and somnambulic conditions connected with complicated activities, sometimes even going so far as participation in social life, travel and intellectual work.

These are cases of extreme degrees of pathologically increased functional dissociation "along the horizontal". A. Abashev-Konstantinovsky (1958) explains these pathological dissociations as a freeing of the automatisms from regulating effects. Elements of functional dissociation "along the horizontal" can also be detected in most of the activities of the normal healthy personality. All unconscious or insufficiently conscious mental and body activities which we do not take into account are an expression of this functional dissociation. When a paraconscious activity can be verbalized and become conscious through hypnosis or suggestion in a waking state, it is most logical to regard it as an expression of functional dissociation "along the horizontal". And when we take into consideration how many and how diverse these automatic insufficiently conscious activities are, it is easy to understand of what great importance is horizontal functional dissociation for the individual.

In order to understand this process physiologically, it seems that we must accept the fact that in the mosaic-like regrouping of physiological processes (the fields or structures over which the process of inhibition is spread) can also carry out informative, algorhythmical and control activity, as can the fields of optimal excitability. Speaking of "fields", however, we can no longer talk of some compact homogeneous excitable place in the central nervous system, but about dynamic structures and systems.

The best conditions for creating new connections are, of course, in the mobile "light spot" which, according to I.P. Pavlov, is a physiological expression of the psychological concept of consciousness. Excitability in this mobile "light spot" is optimal. However, it is very dynamic, changing its locale constantly. Psychologically this is expressed in the constant change in the content of consciousness (perceptions, sensations, ideas, thinking, etc.). Outside the field of optimal excitability are the enormous spaces of a wide-spread inhibiting process. The constant locality changes in the field of optimal excitability automatically result in changes in the area and intensity of the surrounding "shadow" of the inhibiting process. The unconscious and semi-conscious mental activities are preserved, combined, regrouped and further developed there. A considerable part of the paraconscious mental activity subsequently can become the object of consciousness (the mind), and vice versa: the content of the mind in every subsequent moment can pass into paraconscious mental activity. For example, while discussing at this moment the problems of the conscious and paraconscious mental activity, our knowledge of mathematics or our intention to do or not to do something concerning us personally, remains outside the reach of the mind. But both still exist, and at any given moment may reappear in the mind. Even now, as mention is made of them, they have reappeared and have arisen in front of each reader with the content and problems which are specific and different for each person. When we return to the subject under discussion, they will again sink into the system of the paraconscious mental activity. In general, it is just as impossible to separate conscious from paraconscious mental activity as it is to separate an illuminated object from its shadow.

Nevertheless, it is logical to think that there are certain laws governing the degree of inhibition of the separate functional fields. The sections of the brain related to activities which have the weakest connection with the content of the mind at a given moment are most probably subject to the most intensive process of inhibition, and it is the most difficult for them to recreate or restore any former connections. The more these functional fields approach the actual content of the mind, the lighter will grow the shadow of inhibition and the more improvement will there be in the conditions for creating new connections, thus preparing the field for the transition into optimal excitability. This probably results in the creation of transitory conditions from the fields of greatest inhibition to the field of optimal excitability. There is every reason to believe that in these transitory conditions intermediate thickenings of the process of inhibition, "phases" originate. Consequently, we can assume that the field of consciousness is surrounded by such a "phase (transitory) encirclement". A number of facts from life and from clinical practice and experimentation prove this concept. It is well known, for example, that sometimes when one is doing very concentrated mental work, very loud noises may go unnoticed, while a very weak sound may attract attention and disturb one's work.

Very similar is the mechanism of "being startled", something which can be caused by very weak stimuli when we are falling asleep. Such a deviation from the law of strength relations arises in transitory conditions between waking and sleeping, i.e., in phase (transitory) conditions In the cerebral cortex. While these transitory conditions at the time of falling asleep are understandable because they are a manifestation of the process of inhibition spreading over the consciousness, a process in which transitory conditions may arise, reactions through the same mechanism in active mental work can probably be explained by phase (transitory) encirclement of the field with optimal excitability.

Analogical facts are a regular phenomenon in the psychiatric clinic. Stimuli, often hardly perceptible and subliminal in respect to verbal contact, can cause stormy hallucinatory experiences while ordinary loud sounds or strong lights do not cause such reactions. This phenomenon is understandable in psychiatric clinical practice as it originates most often with those diseases which are accompanied by a slight veiling of the mind.

The existence of a transitory encirclement around the field of optimal excitation is also suggested by the physiological experiments with subliminal stimuli. For example, Pshonik's experiments have shown that presensory exteroceptive impulses as well as presensory interoceptive impulses do not establish conditioned connections very easily, but once such connections are established, they are practically inextinguishable. And G. Gershuni found in his experiments that conditioned reaction is considerably greater when the reflex runs subsensorily. The rather more difficult formation of the conditioned connection can be explained most probably by the conditioned stimulus falling in the inhibited background outside the field of optimal excitation. The impeded extinguishability and the greater magnitude of the reaction are a proof of an inertness of the excitation process and paradoxical reactiveness, i.e., "transitoriness".

The transition to the deeply inhibited regions (phase encirclement) is probably very dynamic. In a normal waking state it should represent a narrow transitory "strip", while in a state of increased inhibition it should spread widely, extending over the field of optimal excitation with different intensity. Such optimal excitation ceases to be optimal; it is overspread by transitory processes. Mentally, this is expressed in the veiling of the consciousness and the distortion of reactiveness.

Of course, such a working physiological hypothesis is of a schematic nature and it should be assumed that further experimental research is necessary.

Some kind of analytic—synthetic activity takes place not only in the center of the field with optimal excitation, but in the surrounding of it, as well, and gradually become denser transitory encirclement.

In every thought, in every feeling, in every perception and in every mental activity there exists one central, maximum, clear complex of experiences and many peripheral, obscure, background experiences. In the perception of speech, for example, the content, bearing the specificity, the basic thought, falls in the center of consciousness where it is subjected to critical analysis and logical processing and where the respective sensible answer is shaped. But we react not only to the sense specific for speech, but to a whole complex of accompanying and, in some cases, preceding or succeeding stimuli nonspecific for this speech. The number of these nonspecific stimuli is inconceivably large—gestures, gait, facial expression, expression of the eyes, diction, intonation, a number of ideomotor movements unnoticeable to the mind, environment, the person who speaks with his prestige, the physiological state of expectation or biological needs of the recipient and, in general, everything which for the moment is linked with the words that are spoken.

These factors which in themselves have no concrete sense can accompany anything that is spoken. For example, an angry intonation may be implied not only in words expressing anger, but also in those which express love.

Intonational warmth can be implied not only in words expressing warm feelings, but in words which in their sense also express hostility. The same applies to gestures, facial expression, etc. As a smile accompanies the telling of funny stories and anecdotes, so it can accompany the most severe words. Similarly, the same word, the same thought can be spoken by a great soldier, a genius, an authoritative comrade, a loafer, or a treacherous enemy. The nonspecific factors accompanying speech most often remain unnoticed, but they enter the mind, nevertheless, and play a significant role in shaping impressions, moods, decisions, relations, etc. This type of paraconscious mental activity has been called *nonspecific mental reactivity* (N.M.R.). It includes the "sphere" concept of Schilder and Kretschmer, but differs considerably from it. Above all, N.M.R. is not limited only to the "somnolent catathymic steamlike agglutination thinking" along the periphery of the mind. Here are to be found the elementary sensory qualities of words—intensity, the combining of sounds, intonation, etc. The necessary complex of stimuli from the social and natural environment must also be included. Our conception of N.M.R. differs considerably from the concept of "sphere", also in that we do not relate it to the periphery of the mind beyond which nothing exists. On the contrary, we think that N.M.R. begins under the normal conditions of the gradual transition of the conscious to the semiconscious, where transitory encirclement originates, and passes to the most obscure, distant and unconscious regions of mental life.

Specific mental reactivity is marked by clarity of ideas, inclination to thinking in ideas, intellectual abstractness, cohesion of logic, clearly and accurately perceived images through the receptors. On the other hand, N.M.R. bears the signs of insufficient awareness or complete unconsciousness, where unclear images, or specifically clear but emotionally saturated, images may originate. N.M.R. perceives the hidden sense in human speech. It builds up the instinctive sense of the veracity of the words we hear.

N.M.R. is the chief mechanism through which children establish their behavior in certain circumstances. Since their conscious logical recoding mechanisms are not yet developed, they rely on intuitional insight which is created through N.M.R. This is the reason that upbringing begins with the suggestive child—environment interrelations in the broadest sense.

In primitive man this intuitional insight also played a guiding role. It has features that have a great deal in common with the instinctive insight of many animals. It is an ancient interrelations mechanism which not only has not become rudimentary, but has further developed and, at the same time, has become more hidden and less easily perceptible.

The involuntary ideomotor movements, which are not perceptible through the listener's active attention and which accompany every thought and affix a sure imprint on expression, are easily recorded by N.M.R. no matter how skilfully one tries to conceal them. A similar role is played by all other nonspecific factors, such as intonation, gestures, etc. Thus, very often, without knowing how one does it, one detects falsity and deceit concealed behind brilliant convincing talk, behind warm smiles and even in the perfect hearty handshake, while, on the other hand, one can find warmth and loyalty underlying apparent roughness, derision, or awkwardness.

One of our patients discovered that his girl friend loved another man in the way she called this man "a fool". He felt that in the way she expressed and intoned the word there was something that reminded him of the way she used to express and intone what she said to him at the beginning of their love affair.

The great possibilities of nonspecific mental reactivity are realized on the widest scale in the arts. Unintrusive humaneness, harmony of form and color, the language of music, rhyme and rhythm reach not only the heart, but the mind of man as well, via a much shorter path than logical facts and arguments. Great art affects one indirectly through the N.M.R. and awakens feelings, thoughts and actions one does not always account for. W. Hilger (1928) quoted Jean-Francois Millet on the great masters of the Italian Renaissance:

These masters are like magnets, they have an incomparable power. They make one take their pain and joy upon oneself. When I saw a painting of an exhausted man by Michelangelo, the drooping muscles, the treatment of the surface and the modelling of this suffering exhausted body awoke a multitute of feelings in me. I suffered the same pain. I suffered and felt with his body and limbs, and I understood that any artist who could paint such a picture would be able to express in one single image everything that is good and everything that is bad in mankind.

Tenderness in art creates tenderness, meekness creates meekness, and force creates force. Through Wallenstein, Schiller voiced the thought: "I dare confront any enemy who is himself filled with courage and inspires courage in me".

In tracing the ideas underlying truly stirring works of art, one finds that the same ideas have been expressed by other artists, but that they have failed to exercise the same powerful effect. The imagination is not fired by every artist's work and the heart is not touched by every word that is written or spoken. The works of the great artists are necessary.

Not only the significance of the idea, not only the form in which it is expressed and the rhyme and rhythm of the expression are of importance for the perception of it, but also the manner in which utterance is given to it. The masters of speech know this very well. Great actors master to perfection the harmonious combination of all the means and elements of expression down to those that spring from N.M.R. While their voice rings with sincerity, they are not betrayed by a movement of hand, arm or leg denoting concealed insincerity.

In human relations, it is of exceptional importance not only what is said, but *how* it is said. The following anecdote is a good illustration of this: A father sent his son to study abroad. He did not hear from him for a long time. At last he received a letter from him, but he could not read it because he was illiterate. He took the letter to his neighbor, who was a butcher. The butcher read it in a rough, irritated voice: "Dear dad, send me some money". The father cut in angrily, crying: "Shame on him! Good-for-nothing! No letter for so long and then immediately asking me to send him money". He grabbed the letter and went home without hearing it to the end. A few days later he took the letter to another neighbor who was a baker. The latter began reading it in a gentle, pleasant voice: "Dear dad, send me some money . . ." Then the father smiled and said: "This is what I understand by a son's love for his father", and eagerly listened to the whole of the letter.

This anecdote is an illustration of the thought that intonation can change the sense of a text, as well as the behavior of a listener by making him more or less receptive. N.M.R. is an important element of the paraconscious mental activity.

## Anti-suggestive barriers

In its constant interrelation with the environment, the organism has worked out a number of self-protective devices. Not all the biological protective mechanisms have been fully clarified. The following, for example, are already known as biological barriers: the mechanical, thermic, infection, intoxication and other resistances of healthy skin, the bacteriocide properties in the mucous, blood coagulation and congenital and acquired immunity.

In his interrelations with environment, man also receives information very often which enters (is introduced) by suggestion, insufficiently conscious and insufficiently rationalized. It can be assumed that if man were to receive and react unconsciously to all the different (mental) effects from the environment, he would be helpless. But in the same way as the body has its physiological safe-guards, the personality has produced mental protection against harm-ful effects. This protection comes from the anti-suggestive barriers which accept or reject the various suggestive mental effects.

In psychological analysis one notices, first of all, the anti-sug-gestive barrier built by conscious critical thinking. When suggestion together with a greater or smaller conscious ingredient falls within the field of the consciousness, of critical thinking, it is weighed up carefully in all its aspects before being accepted. The critical, conscious assessment of the stimulation, which tends to be transformed into suggestion, is the first serious barrier destroying suggestion. *The critical logical barrier rejects everything which does not give an impression of well-intended logical motivation.*

A profound psychological analysis of a number of suggestive situations shows that outside the scope of the conscious critical thinking there is also an unconscious *intuitive—affective barrier* against any suggestions entering the mind. This anti—suggestive barrier springs from the congenital negativist setup in every man. An intuitive—affective barrier in a more complicated form exists in the small child before the complete development of the conscious—verbal system and conscious critical thinking. Children very often react in a negative way to suggestive effects. This mechanism of anti-suggestive reaction gradually weakens as the child grows older, but never disappears completely. Very often it even remains very much as it was in childhood, but it remains camouflaged by the new critical logic barrier which develops in the adult. *The intuitive—affective anti-suggestive barrier rejects everything which fails to create confidence and a feeling of security.*

Any stimuli that may have reached it in one or another way remain, for the moment, without any results. The personality often reacts to them in a way quite the opposite to what one has expected.

In rational types, the critical—logical barrier is more developed than in the emotional—imaginative types. "Men of art" possess more of the intuitive—affective barrier. In some psychasthenia and hysteria diseases these two barriers, one of which is predominant according to the type of individual, are pathologically hypertrophied. This impedes any suggestive therapeutic effect. At the same time, it prevents the correct suggestive balancing of the personality with the environment. The hypertrophy of the critical—logical barrier results in a *barrier of philosophizing,* while the intuitive—affective barrier results in a *barrier of negativism.*

Besides the logical and affective anti-suggestive barriers, there is also a third—the *ethical barrier.* It has been proved in experiments that *suggestions contradictory to the ethical principles of the individual are not realized.* The difficulties of the ethical barrier, however, are most often without great significance as suggestions are usually of no interest to the ethical nucleus of the personality. When medical practice does require that suggestions are made having some direct relation to the ethical barrier, it usually is with persons with loosened moral inhibitions. The ethical barrier is also morbidly manifested, especially in some neurotic diseases, in connection with importunate immoral thoughts and urges. In such cases, the conflict between the importunate immoral thoughts and actions and the increased ethical requirements of the sick man result in profound states of depression. To cope with the logical, affective and ethical anti-suggestive barriers requires not so much to overcome and impose something on them, but rather to bring the suggestion into harmony with their individual structure. The more a suggestion harmonizes with the logical requirements of the personality, with its congenital negativist resistance as an expression of affective vigilance, with its ethical nucleus, the quicker and easier is the suggestion realized. In actual fact, the *overcoming of barriers signifies harmonization with the barriers.* Otherwise, suggestion would be doomed to failure.

The three anti-suggestive barriers intertwine and mutually interact so intimately that, quite often, it is impossible to separate them from each other.

In medical practice, a patient's readiness to be treated by suggestion is of decisive importance in successfully overcoming the three anti-suggestive barriers. When such a patient has confidence in the physician, he relaxes and frees himself from the strain of the logical, negativist and ethical barriers and, thus, lessens their strength and gives easier access to therapeutic suggestions.

The teacher has to overcome the same anti-suggestive barriers in his work. If he manages to create confidence and to assist his students to relax calmly, he will create the necessary preliminary atmosphere which will ensure success in his work.

The properly directed utilization of suggestive means in pedagogical practice reveals the unsuspected reserve capacities of the human personality in the process of instruction. These latent reserves of the brain can be most clearly manifested in connection with the memory which, under suggestive conditions, can reach hypermnesia. But in order to get results from suggestopedic hypermnesia, the anti-suggestive barriers must be overcome to reach the unused reserves of the human mind. The whole suggestive conviction of the rather low capacities of human memory, which has been built into social and individual development, reinforces and hypertrophies, to a considerable extent, the anti-suggestive barriers in respect to memory. Therefore, suggestopedic hypermnesia comes not so much from suggestion of increased capacities but from desuggestion, from liberation from the historically and individually built up suggestion of the limited capacities of memory. If this were not so, suggestion would only evoke trust in possibilities but would give no actual results. In this complexity of the suggestive process, it *becomes clear that the suggestive process is always a combination of suggestion and desuggestion.* Desuggestive—suggestive connection occurs, thanks to the anti-suggestive barriers.

Desuggestion and the overcoming of the anti-suggestive barriers were observed in many experimental suggestopedic investigations. Manifestations of these barriers were found not only in the "micro-intervals" of suggestive instruction, but also in the total results obtained from most of the courses in which we tried to establish the relations between suggestive memorization and the volume of the material given. In the memorization experiments which we carried out in some of our suggestopedic courses for learning foreign languages, memorization programs of varying size were assigned in one session. In the written evaluative tests which were given in different variants, we assessed the level of memorization. The tests, for example, included the translation of words into the one or the other language in mixed order, or the translation of words chosen at random. To equalize the conditions in one of the experiments, only tests in which the course members wrote the Bulgarian translation of foreign words were considered. The data on 896 suggestopedic sessions are shown in Table 13 and Figure 23.

TABLE 13    *Relation Between Suggestive Memorization and Number of Words per Suggestopedic Session*

| Number of words given in session | Number of group sessions | Number of words not memorized per session | % of memorized words per session |
|---|---|---|---|
| Up to 100 | 324 | 3.9 | $92.2 \pm 2.98$ |
| 100 — 200 | 398 | 4.9 | $96.8 \pm 1.78$ |
| 201 — 400 | 93 | 20.6 | $93.1 \pm 5.26$ |
| 401 — 600 | 53 | 48.2 | $90.4 \pm 8.08$ |
| 1000 — 1200 | 28 | 42.0 | $96.1 \pm 7.32$ |

Memorization of the meaning of the words in sessions with under 100 lexical units was 92.2 percent of the total material. This percentage was evaluated on the basis of 324 tests. Memorization in sessions with 101 to 200 words in 96.8 percent. This percentage was obtained on the basis of 398 tests. The difference between the two

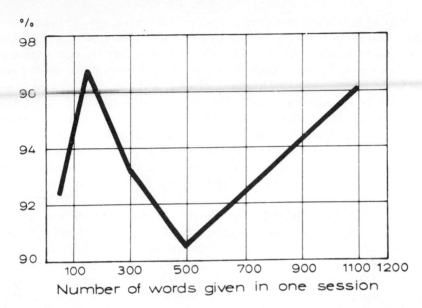

*Figure 23* Dependence of suggestive memorization on the volume of the suggestopedic sessions.

percentages, 4.6, is significant with probability of above 0.95.

It is obvious that the memorization percentage is related to the volume of material given in a session in a somewhat complicated way. The sessions with under 100 words showed a lower percentage of memorized words than those with from 101 to 200 new words. Memorization in sessions with 201 to 400 and 401 to 600 words dropped to the level of the sessions under 100 words, while sessions with 1000 to 1200 words rose to approximately the 101 to 200 memorization level. We obtained the curve in Figure 23 which illustrates the way in which memorization is related to the volume of material given in the suggestive session.

Here we will not examine the data's basic inconsistency with the concepts of conventional psychology on the relation between the level of memorization and the quantity of material given, or the newer concepts on the relation between the memory volume and the amount of information and symbols. Only the psychological reasons for getting lower results (though still high—above 90 percent) will be analyzed. We can assume that this curve is an expression of the counteraction exercised by the anti-suggestive barriers against the suggestive process. This barrier curve can be interpreted as follows:

the logical anti-sugestive barrier was not fully overcome at the under-100-words session. The students in these lesser-volume sessions were trying to memorize not only by suggestopedic, but by conventional methods, as well. As a result, the memorization methods were confused, no logical conviction was achieved, and the counter-action of logic was not overcome. Memorization, even at such a high level, can still be explained as the straining of one's capacities. However, when at the sessions from 101 to 200 new words are given, it is very difficult to explain memorization within the conventional framework. The logical counteraction is overcome and it is clear that new memorization mechanisms are switched on. But when the program is increased to over 200, then 300, 400 and 500 words, the students are faced by the rising affective barrier in the form of fear of the completely new, the barely acceptable, the incomprehensible, and what is contrary to any previous experience. This barrier exercises a counteraction to the process of memorization. When the sessions exceed 1000 new words in one day, both the logical and affective barriers have been overcome, and the students are confident that this is a completely new memorization technique which actually gives results, and calmly let themselves be carried along by it.

The existence of the three anti-suggestive barriers is biologically necessary, because otherwise human beings would be easily accessible to any kind of suggestion. This would expose them to health and psychological dangers. It is well known that many habits, many relations and many physiological directions can be changed by way of suggestion. Suggestion can treat mental and physical disorders, but in the absence of anti-suggestive barriers or weakened ones, suggestion can accidentally result in illness. The anti-suggestive barriers act as a filter when letting environmental stimuli into the paraconscious mental activity. Their mechanisms are built phylogenetically and ontogenetically in accordance with vitally important human needs.

It is sometimes believed that suggestion has to overcome the difficulties of conscious criticism, thus, making it out to be a kind of deception of the critical faculty. This idea is, in fact, not in agreement with the reality. On the contrary, the overcoming of the logical barrier in no way means a deception of the personality's critical thinking. The overcoming of the logical barrier requires, above all, that suggestion should contain elements of well-intentioned logical soundness. Motivated suggestion, to a great extent, provides such possibilities. Logically sound thought with the authoritativeness of its rational stability and unassailability exercises an additional sug-gestive effect. The suggestive influence of many authoritative persons, concepts, ideas, etc., is built on the same principle.

The negative barrier is also surmounted not by deception or force, but by understanding and confidence. The child's negativism is also found in the adult, but in a concealed form. Confidence, contact, positive affective resonance and authoritativeness facilitate the harmonic coordination of individual features with the negative barrier.

The ethical barrier is the nucleus of a man's ethical values created by his individual experience and suggestions should be in harmony with these requirements.

Until critical, though not always conscious objections are over-come, until natural negativism is surmounted and harmony with the basic ethical values and direction of the nucleus of the person is achieved, suggestion cannot rely on any positive results. In some cases of therapeutic practice the surmounting of these barriers proves very difficult, and days and months are needed to do it. In other cases it happens immediately. The surmounting of the anti-suggestive barriers is not a process of coercion, but a process of psychological resonance.

## PSYCHOLOGICAL STRUCTURE OF PERSONALITY AND TYPES OF SUGGESTION

The material we have treated, so far, shows that the personality is subjected to constant positive and negative suggestive effects. These effects are realized by way of the paraconscious mental activity. Their realization depends on the unconscious part of the setup, comprising attitude, motivation, expectancies, interests and needs; these, however, are refracted by the anti-suggestive barriers and to some extent they contribute to the shaping of these barriers. Thus, for instance, attitude and motivation reverberate mainly in the critical—logical barrier, carrying with them their emotional background. Expectancies and needs reverberate mainly in the intuitive—affective anti-suggestive barrier, but they are also accompanied by the res-pective reasoning. The setup and interests reverberate in the three anti-suggestive barriers, having an especially constructive effect on the ethical barrier.

These mediators in their links with the anti-suggestive barriers, are supplemented by the basic personality properties and processes such as perceptions, emotions, will, memory and intellect. They are also affected by the temperament and character of the personality. The complex interrelations of these characteristic personality features with the anti-suggestive barriers mean that suggestibility works in specific circumstances and for a specific person. Therefore, it is impossible to imagine the desuggestive–suggestive aspect of communication without the participation of the integrated personality. For instance, suggestion is introduced subliminally or by the peripheral perceptions. But, at the same time, it passes through the filter of the three anti-suggestive barriers in which all the personality's properties, qualities, processes, characteristic features are reverberated unconsciously. This means that the suggestion, which enters the personality peripherally through the second plane, exerts emotional, memory, intellectual and volitional influence. At the same time, it also relates to the expectancies, motivation, interests, etc., of the personality, until finally it is incorporated in the setup which through concentrative psycho-relaxation is reorganized for a given type of reserve reaction. An attempt to illustrate this global reactivity of personality to one or another suggestive effects is given in Figure 24.

It must be stressed, however, that suggestion always presupposes interrelations at a more or less unconscious level. Each activity and characteristic feature of the personality has its unconscious side. The peripheral perceptions, which always accompany the process of perceiving an object, have already explained this unconscious side in perceptions. They are perceived as the background to the object. This background information is essential in shaping the double plane suggestive behavior and the unconscious feedback which ensures the desuggestive–suggestive mechanisms.

Closely related to the problem of the suggestive importance of the unconscious peripheral background perceptions is the question as to whether attention is part of this process. It is clear that attention is not directed at these perceptions. They have no direct relation to volitional attention; nor do they to nonvolitional attention of the sort which participates in games or in other activities. This is because in most cases attention is realized. Only those moments when the personality is not aware of these perceptions can be described as peripheral unconscious perceptions. Such moments occur both in volitional and nonvolitional attention. These perceptions are the peripheral, double-plane, background

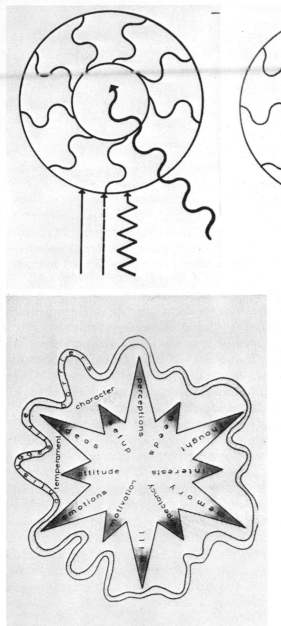

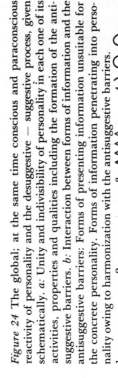

*Figure 24* The global; at the same time conscious and paraconscious reactivity of personality and the desuggestive — suggestive process, given schematically. *a*: Unity and indivisibility of personality in each one of its activities, properties and qualities including the formation of the anti-suggestive barriers. *b*: Interaction between forms of information and the antisuggestive barriers: Forms of presenting information unsuitable for the concrete personality. Forms of information penetrating into personality owing to harmonization with the antisuggestive barriers.

1. ⟶    2. ------⟶    3. ∿∿∿⟶    4. ∿⟶

*c*: Using a suitable form of interaction with the concrete personality in order to introduce a large amount of new information.

perceptions.

Data taken from literature show that special attention is paid to stressing the importance of vivid ideas in achieving suggestion. The explanatory mechanism refers to suggestion as auto-suggestion and conscious reactions. However, the possibility of the strictly logicalized conscious enlivening of ideas cannot explain a number of extraordinary suggestive phenomena. It doesn't matter whether the ideas will create suggestive or auto-suggestive effects. They must always be connected not only with the activity of the emotions, but with the whole unconscious sphere of the personality as a global mediator. For instance, the most vivid idea cannot provoke a suggestive effect if it is not connected with the unconscious basic setup of the personality: its attitude and motivation; with the personality's expectancy of "something" happening right now; with its interests and needs; as well as, with its characteristic emotional, intellectual and volitional qualities and the requirements of the temperament of the personality. At a given moment in these complicated interrelations, the ideas manage to transfer part of their activity into the unconscious sphere where, in complex interrelations with the anti-suggestive barriers, the final desuggestive—suggestive effect originates. The unconscious transformation of ideas into a suggestive result is especially clearly seen in ideomotor suggestions. Through them the ideas are transformed into a motor act without our being aware of it. Striving to follow authority's example is also, in most cases, a form of suggestive transformation of important ideas into a given effect.

Since the suggestive mechanisms are of an unconscious nature, a similar analysis can be made of all the personality's mediators. In accordance with this conception, the suggestive phenomena can be divided into three groups and the various desuggestive—suggestive techniques can be backed with arguments.

Suggestion has many and diverse varieties of expression. In some cases it is purposeful and in others it is the general suggestive background which influences the development of various processes in the personality. Quite often, suggestion is formed in speech, but it can also enter in unspoken ways. Though it is connected with paraconscious mental activity, suggestion sometimes also possesses a conscious ingredient. At present, the different types of suggestion can be determined phenomenologically according to the answers to the following three most essential questions:

1) At what is the suggestion aimed?

2) What role does speech play in the formation of the suggestion?

3) What is the degree of conscious participation in receiving the suggestion?

The types of suggestions can be grouped schematically by phenomenological criteria as follows:

a) According to the aim: (1) General suggestive background. (2) Purposeful suggestions.

b) According to the role played by speech: (1) Chiefly spoken suggestions. (2) Unspoken suggestions.

c) According to the degree of consciousness: (1) Suggestions with a conscious element in them. (2) Suggestions, without a conscious element in them.

Very often the conscious element of the suggestive effect comes so much to the fore that it is very difficult to discern the important mechanisms of the paraconscious mental activity behind it.

The conscious element, and even the awareness that a process of suggestion is taking place, is particularly marked in a number of shock methods and suggestion techniques. For example, Kaufmann (1916) applied sudden shock suggestions, which surprised the patients with their unexpected force and roughness. This therapeutic method is most often applied in time of war. D. Muller-Hegemann (1957) compared Kaufmann's method with the tortures described by Dostoyevsky in *Notes from the Dead House*. F. Kehrer (1916, 1917) softened Kaufmann's method slightly, beginning with forceful exercises and only in extreme cases resorting to painful galvanic current. Kretschmer (1947) also applied the painful faradic current or other stimuli to intensify suggestive effects. There are serious shortcomings in these methods so far as the patient is concerned. V. Danilevski (1924) and R. Tarkhanov (1886) emphasized the dangers of a strong affect no matter by what method it may be suggested and to illustrate this gave as an example a patient who lost consciousness in a suggested fear affect and whose cardiac activity and respiration stopped for half a minute. Such a psychoshock in patients with cerebral arteriosclerosis, vegetative lability, cardiovascular insufficiency, etc., may end in tragedy.

In contrast to the sudden shock methods in medicine, continuous, monotonous, rhythmical effects can also engage the N.M.R. and can result in overcoming the anti-suggestive barriers very easily. In these methods there are no dangers of psychoshock effect, and there is a conscious element for the conducting of the suggestive effect at the moment. Usually, the conscious realization of the suggestion process itself does not impede the realization of suggestion by these methods.

Elements of consciousness to different degrees in different persons can also be observed in the suggestive methods of logic confusion or disorientation used in medical practice. There, perplexing conversations, unclear associations and incorrect reasoning are employed. Apparent contradictions and speech disintegration hold sway. In the confusion thus created, suggestions can be presented confidently, rapidly and insisted upon. The patient has no time to assess them but reacts to them with relief, especially when they are clear and uncontradictory. A similar confusing technique was worked out by M. Erickson (1956) for the suggestive induction of hypnosis.

Many researchers employ medication which induces a feeling of relaxation, sleepiness or even actual sleep, in the hope that suggestibility will increase and even in some cases, increase the susceptibility to hypnosis. Thus, for example, ether was used by F. Starkey (1917), evipan by A. Hauptman (1934) and E. Stungo (1941), evipan and pentothal by A. Dick (1940), amytal-natrium by M. Teleshevska *et al.* (1955), and amytal caffein by A. Megrabyan and G. Safryan (1955) and others. But H. Eysenck's research (1947) showed that medicaments producing narcotic effects do not increase suggestibility in all persons, only in markedly suggestible neurotics. It seems that it is not the biochemical effects, but the motivation value of narcotics that is most often of decisive importance in such cases. However, in spite of the narcotic effect, in narco-suggestion there is some element of a conscious critical attitude toward the process of suggestion.[1]

A conscious element during suggestion exists to a certain extent in

---

[1] Some physiological methods which, like the narcotic effect, may result in a veiling of consciousness, do not entirely exclude the participation of a conscious critical attitude toward the suggestion presented to them. This is so, for example, in the first phases of the hyperventilation method employed by F. Stockert (1936), W. Sorgant and R. Fraser (1938) where alkalosis develops according to the way it did in J. Talbot's (1938) investigations. Elements of criticism also are not excluded in the first phases of the method proposed by J. Witlow (1948) for the facilitation of suggestion by pressing the two carotid arteries.

larvate (concealed) or indirect suggestion, which is most widely used in the so-called "placebo" therapy. In this treatment, the patient is given a neutral medication with the suggestion that it will exercise a therapeutic effect. The intonation and gesture with which the medicine is administered are the decisive factors. In such cases the physician requires not only knowledge, but also the art to engage the N.M.R. correctly.

The participation of the conscious element in motivated suggestion is similar. Motivation, the logic of suggestion, if well presented, creates confidence through observing the requirements of common sense. This increases the authoritativeness of the source of suggestion, and hence its suggestive power.

To satisfy the psychological needs of the expectancies of patients, we applied "the method of satisfying suggestions" (1963). This method is based on the mechanisms of indirect suggestion. Elements of consciousness of the suggestive procedure can also be detected in the patient when this method is used.

There are no elements of consciousness in suggestions without a conscious ingredient. The many suggestions which create the general suggestive background belong here.

This group of suggestive methods has not yet been sufficiently elaborated to be widely applied in practice. It has, however, its physiological and psychological foundations in experiments with subliminal, subsensory, and the first signalling stimuli, isolated from the second signalling system that has already been examined. In these suggestions no "explanatory" conscious element is sought. They act directly under ordinary conditions. In the so-called "whispering method" (1963), suggestive therapeutic effects are presented under the level of identification, and sometimes even under the level of hearing. The psychotherapeutic method of "somnolent breathing" (1963), in which subliminal signals enter the general suggestive background from the respiratory movements of the physician, can also be included in this group.

I.V. Strelchuk (1953) proposed a method which complied with the typological characteristics of the individual. But suggestion does not require compliance only with the typological features of the individual, especially, if we take into consideration the extreme variations, which are very rare and in which one of the first two anti-suggestive barriers is usually hypertrophied. Yet, on the other hand, the so-called direct suggestion very often does not bring the expected results.

Direct suggestion does not consider the structure of the individual, his way of thinking, his interests, his entire bearings and goals. For this reason, it is not always certain there will be lasting results. When suggestion enters one's mind as a ready-made solution, it clashes with the basic structure and requirements of the individual. And if the suggestions are alien to the principal bearings of the individual or are insufficiently motivated, they quickly fade away and lose their power to influence.

Suggestion should be the ultimate conclusion of a solid, logical structure. Unmotivated suggestions are threatened with the danger of remaining unrealized. In his time, L. Lowenfeld (1922) insisted on the good motivation of suggestions. This aspect is strongly emphasized in the method which K.I. Platonov (1957) called Bernheim-Bekhterev motivated suggestion in a waking state.

Proper motivation of suggestions not only ensures their lasting duration in many cases, but improves suggestibility, too. Simultaneously, in proper motivation of suggestions the ambitions and hopes of the personality are respected and even mobilized. It is quite clear today that P. Dubois' (1904) rational psychotherapy, which relies on the patient's intellect and logic, actually has many suggestive aspects.

In fact, motivation satisfies the need felt by the patient for explanation. The same is true in indirect suggestion, only here explanation is shorter and more visual. In both cases, the patient's critical thinking is satisfied.

To fight the hypertrophied, morbid intuition-affective barrier, the negativist barrier, a "method of reverse suggestions" has been worked out. Of the many patients treated in this way, especially characteristic was the case of E.. The therapeutic results achieved in this case were demonstrated on March 2, 1960, at the Psychotherapeutists' Seminar, in the City Psychoneurological Dispensary, in Sofia. The patient was 30 then and was suffering from severe hysterical neurosis, in which a severe dysphagia was the most strongly marked symptom. She could swallow practically no food and no liquids. She had reached a state of cachexia. She had been treated by all the methods known to medicine, but in spite of this she continued to be unable to eat and continued to lose weight. Any attempt to swallow caused spasms in the gullet musculature. All suggestions aimed at making her swallow more easily only resulted in aggravating her condition. An attempt to inject insuline subcutaneously resulted in inflammation and swelling—the patient showed supersensitivity. She could not endure any injection and was unable to take drugs orally. Treatment with clyster drug resulted in gastro-intenstinal disorders. Coming to such a dead end, we decided to employ the reverse suggestion method in an attempt to surmount the patient's strongly expressed negativism. We got quick results and steady convalescence followed. Fifteen years later, a follow up interview revealed no relapse.

M. Tantsyura (1956) overcame the hypertrhopied anti-suggestive barriers in some cases of obsession and compulsion by a method not requiring a struggle against the obsession, but by its repetition and exhaustion. It is not incorrect to say that all suggestive effect methods are ones to overcome the anti-suggestive barriers.

The psychological mechanisms for overcoming, i.e., for coordination and harmonization with the anti-suggestive barriers, are embedded in the nonspecific mental reactivity (N.M.R.). Their correct utilization, however, requires a good knowledge of the conditions which make N.M.R. more accessible, and of the qualities and peculiarities of the nonspecific factors which correspond to the N.M.R. Perfect use cannot be made of any method of suggestion without a profound knowledge of these.

The basic feature characterizing suggestion is the circumlocution of the critical analysis of the individual. Bekhterev expressed this as penetration into the "inner chambers through the backdoor". We believe this can be achieved by the various suggestive methods when the best use is made of N.M.R. It should be noted that, in the employment of suggestion in therapeutic practice, the patients are often aware of the fact that they are being treated by suggestion, but this does not make psychotherapy ineffective. The same is also true of suggestion in pedagogical practice. In suggestopedy, for example, all the students know that suggestion underlies their instruction. This does not make suggestopedy less effective. Furthermore, therapists have also been treated as patients by suggestion and in the suggestopedic courses there are students who are trained psycho-therapist specialists by profession. They are most familiar with what suggestion is and the mechanisms through which it works. As patients or students, the psychotherapists do not differ in the perception of the therapeutic or educational suggestions from other patients or students. The same is as true of psychiatrists and neurologists with a theoretical knowledge of psychotherapy as of psychologists and pedagogues.

Ninety-four evaluative tests of a group of 20 neurologists, psychiatrists, psychologists and pedagogues, who attended the suggestopedic foreign language courses, were processed separately. The average number of new words given in a suggestopedic session was 157, with the maximum number in one session at 1000 words. Of the 14,789 words or sentences given in the sessions, 14,252 were correctly recalled in the control tests. This was 96.37 percent of the material given. Four students of this group had sessions in each of which 1000 words were given. They were able to remember 97.50 percent of them correctly.

It was found in processing the control or evaluative tests of about 600 students in the language courses (consisting of people with different professions), that they hadsmemorized an average of 93 percent of the material taught. The above-mentioned specialists, who in their professional lives had to deal with suggestion, showed an even higher percentage of assimilation (96.37) and better results in the tests with 1000 words (97.5). This shows that knowledge of the characteristic features of suggestion in overcoming the anti-suggestive barriers may even improve the effectiveness of the process .of teaching and learning. Perhaps, it will be of interest to mention that the author of this book has also been taught in the suggestopedic courses he founded. Studying in these courses brought the same results for him as it did for the rest of the students. These facts show that a knowledge of the role that suggestion plays in a given process in no way hinders its realization. Such a knowledge does not deprive us of our nonspecific mental reactivity as, for example, knowledge of the laws of art does not deprive us of its beneficial suggestive effect. Music deeply affects us even when we know the principles on which it is built. Of course, some people are disposed to compulsive philosophizing, suspiciousness, abnormally intensified criticism, etc. These qualities can result in hypertrophy of the anti-suggestive barriers and this impedes the comprehensive acceptance of therapeutical or educational suggestions. But in such cases there are a number of ways to overcome the anti-suggestive barriers.

The significance of individual N.M.R. elements in overcoming the anti-suggestive barriers has been noticed by many authors. K.I. Platonov emphasized the suggestive power of intonation in physiological experiments and in iatrogenic phenomena. I. Simbaev (1958) wrote:

. . . Words exercise a suggestive effect only when they are pronounced in a solemnly expressive or commanding tone, i.e., when words affect not only through the nature of their sense, but also through the loudness, rhythm and timbre of the sound, through their affective nuance.

V. Myasishtev (1958) noted the significance not only of words, but of facial expression and pantomime. A. Weitzenhoffer (1953) attached importance to marginal suggestion entering through the epxression of the face and the intonation of the voice. These of course are only individual N.M.R. elements. The possibilities and range are much wider.

## SUGGESTION, HYPNOTIC STATE AND RESERVE CAPACITIES OF THE BRAIN

In psychotherapeutic literature the possibilities of activating the personality's reserve capacities are most often connected with inducing a special hypnotic state. Scientists working in the fields of hyp-nopedia, relaxation, alpha wave biofeedback, Alpha Dynamics, Silva Mind Control, etc., associate these reserve capacities not with the characteristic features of the process of communication, but with the induction of some kind of "state". Since all these trends proceed from the basic assumption that hypnosis is a kind of altered state of consciousness and that this "state" is of the greatest significance, we shall dwell briefly on this question.

Hypnosis has often been confused with suggestion. This is due probably to the fact that it still cannot be related to sleep and because for the first time suggestive phenomena had been observed in hypnosis.

Various alterations of a mental and purely somatic nature can also be brought about through suggestion, but their psychogenic—sugges-tive origin does not entitle us to identify them with suggestion itself. A suggestively caused alteration of the skin, for example, is no longer suggestion but something new which must be called by a different name. A suggestively produced erythema or ulcer is described as ery-thema or ulcer, not as "concentrated suggestion", although its name may carry some information about its genesis. Thus a behaviorally somnolent state such as hypnosis, although in most cases it is induced by suggestion, is also described as a "state". Nonetheless, the problem of the extent to which an approximation to the state of sleep can be induced by a suggestion to sleep is still of interest. Otherwise, we must assume that hypnosis is a compliance phenomenon where the hypnotized person pretends to be asleep. Even when this is assumed there is no way of explaining the appearance of the many hypnotic phenomena which cannot be simulated. Heightened suggestibility, for example, is considered to be an essential characteristic of hypnosis. Many scientists, however, have shown that most of the phenomena which can be observed during hypnosis can also be observed in suggestion in an ordinary waking state.

The hour-long surgical operation, which we have already described, and all the other suggestive phenomena in a waking state are examples of its possibilities. However, this does not mean that hypnosis as a special mental state does not exist. If suggestion (without hypnosis) can bring about all already known and characteristic hypnotic phenomena on the basis of conditioning, it is natural to expect that it can also induce some kind of special sleeplike state. A number of transitory states of consciousness—from a slight veiling of the mind to deep sleep and coma—are known to medical practice. Some of these states arise in both hysterical and healthy people when the surrounding atmosphere is affectively charged. Through the affective—eidetic mechanisms, suggestion can also induce these sleeplike conditions with different degrees of diffused inhibition. These sleeplike conditions are unlike sleep in that EEG changes do not necessarily take place in them.

The psychotherapeutic technique for the transformation of normal night sleep into hypnosis also testifies to some transition from the one state into the other, without intermediate awakening. The fact that hypnotized persons, if left alone, often do not wake up but pass from hypnosis into normal sleep refutes the idea of a simulated sleeplike state.

The experimental data given in the chapter on *Paraconscious Mental Activity during Hypnosis* also speak for the existence of hypnosis as a state.

Hypnosis is often called "suggested sleep", but it can also arise without suggestion. Experimental hypnosis of animals by I.P. Pavlov's method, for example, was induced under laboratory conditions without employing the complicated psychological methods of suggestion. A number of hypnotic phenomena such as catalepsy, dissociation of functions, somnolence, etc., were observed in hypnotized animals. In man, though very rarely, hypnosis can also come about without being suggested in advance. Many patients from the psychiatric clinics fall spontaneously into hypnotic states. But people who are sound in body and mind can also spontaneously fall into such states without suggestion. For example, when during natural sleep a person suddenly begins to converse with the people around him without waking, he is in a state of hypnosis, because hypnosis is a behaviorally somnolent state with rapport. This rapport, this connection with the environment, during hypnosis is used with suggestion for therapeutic purposes.

As there is hypnosis without suggestion, so there is suggestion without hypnosis. Where is the hypnosis in cases when we give the patient placebo and obtain therapeutical effects with only aqua distilata. There are many other methods of suggesting things in a waking state without bringing suggestion down to the level of a medical stratagem to fool the patient. In an EEG investigation of suggestibility, E.F. Mordvinov and A.A. Genkin (1969) discovered that suggestibility in hypnotic and waking states are two different phenomena with different realization mechanisms. Contrary to expectations, their EEG investigation showed that cerebral biocurrents under suggestion in a waking state are not related to conditions of increased inhibition and reduced tonus of the cerebral cortex as under hypnosis. They found that confidence, authority, interest and, in general, the positive suggestive setup of the experimental condition give quite a different EEG picture from that of passiveness in the hypnotized person. This feature of suggestion in the ordinary waking state, i.e., preserved critical faculties, consciousness and an active attitude toward the teaching process itself made it possible to develop the suggestopedic trend in education. Because suggestive interrelations materialize through the mechanisms of the unconscious, they find paths to the unconscious mental activity during the conscious activity of the participants in the process of teaching and learning. In this way, information is assimilated through two channels: the conscious one, ensuring criticism, and the unconscious one, ensuring ease of assimilation, by activation of the functional reserves of the mind.

Due to the inconvenience of hypnosis and sleep in memorization experiments, some researchers have tried to discover other states for this purpose. E.G. Reider and S.S. Libikh (1967), for example, tried out the possibilities of autogenic training and muscle relaxation to improve memorization. Under such conditions, they succeeded in improving memorization without, however, reaching hypermnesia. But they also wrote that there are elements of autosuggestion in autogenic training. They were inclined to ascribe the improvement in memorization capacities to autogenic training and muscle relaxation as states. The same holds true for controlled relaxation states, such as alpha wave biofeedback. We proved in our suggestopedic experiments that relaxation, though in the form of a very light pseudo-passiveness, to some extent plays the part of a suggestive placebo factor. In a number of experiments hypermnesia was obtained for a short time, even in the active part preceding the concert session. Our research into the role that suggestive factors play in sleep learning, into psychotherapeutical techniques and integral psychotherapy, into unconscious mental activity and suggestion in a waking state, as well as our whole experimental work on suggestopedy clearly show that reserve capacities are tapped mainly because of the unconscious—suggestive factors in the process of communication. It is true that some altered states, hypnotic, relaxed, somnolent etc., do sometimes play a part in this process, but it is chiefly in exerting an influence as a suggestive placebo factor and less so as a state per se.

The results obtained in a number of experiments with hypnosis might be due to the concentrative psychorelaxation originating by way of complex suggestive mechanisms and directed to man's reserve capacities. S. Krippner (1963), and W.L. Fowler (1961) improved the concentration of students in class by means of clinical hypnosis. G. Eisele and J. J. Higgings (1962), and F.J. Lodato (1964) lessened the fear of examinations or eliminated it entirely. H. McCord (1956) improved the mental abilities of a mentally retarded boy. McCord and C.I. Sherrill (1961) improved the calculation performances of a mathematician sixfold. T.X. Barber (1964, 1965-b, 1974) quite rightly considered that hypnosis was not necessary to obtain these results. He indicated the possibilities that high motivation offered. To ensure the genuiness of experiments he proposed that a tape recorder (1965-a) should be used in applying suggestive techniques. G. Kilman and E. L. Goldberg (1962) increased the concentration of students through hypnosis, and improved their recollection of visual perceptions. In experiments unlike those where relaxation, drowsiness and the relinquishment of initative are suggested, E.R. Oetting (1964) carried out research into hypnotic suggestions which restricted peripheral vision, concentrated the mind on definite goals and avoided it wandering from the subject by removing all distracting noises. In this way he obtained concentration in the process of learning through hypnosis. E.F. Hammer (1954) found that posthypnotic suggestions could be useful in teaching students who were susceptible to hypnosis. J.P. Das (1961), H.C. Selzberg (1960), and others found that memorization was better under hypnosis than in the ordinary waking state. Barber and P.D. Parker (1964) noted that instructions in which motivation for the task was given seemed sufficient to improve memorization and learning, and hypnosis seemed to them unnecessary. But motivating instructions have a suggestive side as well and sometimes this side grows stronger during hypnosis. In the age regression experiments, as already mentioned, we found that under hypnosis suggestions to imitate actions and phenomena characteristic of the subject's earlier age are not realized as successfully as direct suggestions for the subject's regression to the corresponding age. The suggested age regression possesses much greater suggestive and motivating power than does the direct suggestion (under hypnosis) for the manifestation of phenomena characteristic of earlier age periods. The general change in the personality's attitude influences the subject's compliance with the succeeding directed suggestion of the operator. Research into the possibilities for using some states of the personality for the purpose of tapping its reserve capacities have been mainly directed towards the field of hypnotism. But hypnosis cannot be applied in mass practice. S. Krippner (1970) writes:

The use of hypnosis in educational settings deserves additional study and further application. At this point no controlled research is available demonstrating the superiority of educational hypnosis over other task-oriented procedures . . . "Hypnosis is not a panacea and must be used in combination with other methods and techniques . . ."

(p. 459)

This cautious attitude toward the possibilities of hypnosis is fully justified. That is why the liberating—stimulating suggestopedic system, which has grown into an integral and original educational system suitable for the ordinary conditions of life, is becoming more and more popular, particularly as it is aimed at tapping the reserve capacities of students and schoolchildren.

The personality's reserve capacities, which are tapped and utilized under the desuggestive—suggestive (freeing-and-encouraging) conditions, can be of various kinds. Medical practice is interested in one kind of reserve capacities, while education is interested in another kind. The term "reserve capacities" is used for those capacities of both somatic and mental functions which are, for the ordinary man, an extraordinary phenomenon under certain circumstances. Some of these are, hypermnesia (supermemory) when the quantitative surpassing of the possibility of the ordinary human memory is great enough to bear the mark of a new law-governed regularity; anaesthesia (loss of sensibility), when it is not involved with the enduring of pain or a momentary painful irritation; and various suggested changes in organic functions which cannot be regulated by ordinary will power. The tapping of the personality's reserve capacities is due, on the one hand, to desuggestion, i.e., freeing a person from former limiting and discouraging suggestions and, on the other hand, to creative encouragement and suggestions. A great part of the reserve capacities tapped and manifested in the desuggestive—suggestive process may in the near future become normal, ordinary capacities of the personality. They may become a social norm. The social suggestive norm for one or another of the limitations of our capacities has kept these capacities down. One of the tasks of suggestology is to gradually establish new norms for the capacities of the personality. These capacities will develop not only in the desuggestive—suggestive (freeing-and-encouraging) creative communicative process, but also in the self-education process of individual people to their inner reorganization. This will, of course, be a long process because the social suggestive norm will constantly give shape and counteract the development, thus hampering it. However, this counteraction has its good side as well: it will ensure a gradual and smooth unfolding of the reserve capacities and it will protect us from indulging in too much enthusiasm which could also be harmful.

Not all the reserve capacities tapped by suggestology can or should be immediately applied in practice. A sharp conflict with the social suggestive norm may arise and if the specialists are not well prepared the work in this field may be delayed for years. In our suggestopedic experiments, for instance, we achieved the memorization of the meanings of 1000 to 1200 foreign words in one session. But these were isolated experiments. In mass practice, it was difficult to begin at once with such an enormous amount of material, an amount that was, and is, in such striking contradiction to the social suggestive norm. That is why for practical use we reduced the material given in one lesson most often to 250 to 300 new words. Man's greater possibilities to absorb much more material in learning were utilized by giving more grammar, discreetly, and almost unnoticed, and also by demanding a more plastic use of the assimilated material. In this way, the amount of material for learning, i.e., memory units, was considerably increased and surpassed the number of the new lexical units given overtly for memorization. At first, these additional memory units went unnoticed and, thus, the sharp conflict with the social suggestive norm for a student's capacities was avoided. When these facts are taken into consideration, various kinds of suggestopedic programs can be drawn up.

## MEANS OF SUGGESTION IN PRACTICE

Among the numerous methods of suggestion, the means to overcome the anti-suggestive barriers and to achieve desuggestion and suggestion are selected from the various elements of nonspecific mental reactivity. In this way, they ensure more direct informational algorythmic contact with the paraconscious mental activity. The ideal manner for directing the stream of suggestive information to the paraconscious mental activity would probably be, by way of subsensory (subliminal) stimulation through the weak signals. This, in practice, is difficult to achieve. There are grounds to believe that the development of experimental work in the field of subsensory stimuli will result in the possibility of using the results in educational practice. Even then, the means of suggestion used now will not lose their significance: they have been established spontaneously in centuries of practice.

Of these means, the most often employed are the peripheral effects where subsensoriness is not absolute but relative and situational depending on the direction of attention and consciousness. The best psychological conditions for peripheral effects are created by the diversity of N.M.R.

The means of suggestion shade off into each other in practice and it is nearly impossible to isolate them. They all employ various aspects of nonspecific mental reactivity and of paraconsciousness in general, where *peripheral subsensoriness is for the time being defined as a basic internal mechanism.* An enormous number of stimuli are pushed into the periphery of attention and consciousness in phylogenetic and ontogenetic experience. Their apparent deactualization and transformation into nonspecific stimuli not only do not preclude their participation in person—environment interrelations, but in actual fact turn them into an exceptionally reliable feedback. The information which the stimuli carry by peripheral subsensoriness serves as a reliability control. The regulation of the stream of this unconscious information creates conditions for running the processes on suggestive levels.

In creating these conditions, one of the most frequently employed schemes of the suggestive process is the *reversal* of part of the peripheral subsensoriness into consciousness and the *shifting* of part of the consciousness into the field of the peripheral. In this way the feedback is more or less controlled, which naturally assists harmonization with the anti-suggestive barriers and the realization of the suggestive process. An example of such a reversal in the foreign language suggestopedic courses is the directing of the students' attention not to vocabulary memorization and acquiring habits of speech, but to the act of communication. The means for the realization of an act of creation are not retained in the center of attention and consciousness, but are pushed to the periphery where their fixation in the long-term memory and their creative assimilation actually take place more quickly. At the same time, the personality occupies itself directly with the communicative stages of the learning process. Of course, for such pedagogical activity, the suggestopedic qualification of the instructors is necessary.

The description of the means of suggestion only through their logical sense as, for instance in psychotherapy, "Your eyes are closing", or "You become more and more relaxed", or "This is a very pleasant state", cannot give us a clear idea of the actual suggestive factors. In the complicated desuggestive—suggestive process, it is not so important what is said, but how it is said. It is not so important to verbally forestall hte natural physiological reactions and make conditioning possible, nor to offer the person logical arguments for attitude, motivation and the other mediators. It is much more important how all this is done; how the nonspecific mental activity, the unconscious peripheral and automated activity is engaged, and how the second plane is utilized in the entire suggestive situation. Within this aspect of the means of suggestion lies the very art of the scientific application of suggestology. In this way suggestology approaches and, in some places, almost becomes one with great art.

The numerous possible means of suggestion can be of a complex character, for instance, a work of art with a suggestive effect. They can also be of a more elementary character outwardly, for instance, the voice intonation of the person from whom the suggestion comes. But both the complex and the more elementary means must always be coordinated with the anti-suggestive barriers. One kind of intonation may be very suitable for one person and absolutely unsuitable for another. The case is much more complicated when one has to select the means of suggestion to be applied in work with a whole group. Theoretical and practical experience are indispensable in such a case.

For the purpose of clarity the means of the desuggestive—suggestive process can be divided conditionally into two groups: (a) means which can be used both suggestively and autosuggestively (meditatively) (b) means which can be used mainly suggestively, i.e., factors coming from outside. Infantilization and concert pseudopassivity belong to the first group. This group of means creates "a psychorelaxation state". This state should not be an end in itself. It must be connected with the personality's concentrative expectancy of the desuggestive—suggestive overcoming of the social suggestive norm and the tapping of reserve capacities.

Authority, double-planeness and some of the more distinct elements of double-planeness, such as intonation, rhythm, etc., (which should be discussed separately) belong to the second group of means.

It is through the second group of means, when they are harmonized with the anti-suggestive barriers, that the states characteristic of the first group of means are most often created. In some cases on the basis of association and fixation of the setup these means can achieve for a short time, results without creating states of infantilization and pseudopassiveness. It is also possible to achieve some desuggestive—suggestive results as if only by the concentrated and manifested participation of one or two of these means. Their simultaneous and complete participation is not always necessary, but it is absolutely imperative that they should not be in contradiction with each other.

The suggestive psychotherapeutic methods of various scientists include, intentionally or accidentally, some of these means or a combination of several of them. In the suggestopedic system, these means are used and the significance and power of each are sought, as well as, the most effective combination and dosage of them. We shall briefly discuss some of the most important means of suggestion without forgetting that these means are in complicated interrelations with each other.

## Authority (Prestige)

The concept of authority (not authoritarism!) as it is used in suggestology stands for the non-directive prestige which by indirect ways creates an atmosphere of confidence and intuitive desire to follow the set example. Guarantees of the reliability of the information carried by such kind of authority are associated, coded and symbolized in it.

There are various types of authority: authority of the personality, of sound logic, of the beauty found in the great works of art, etc. Here we are interested mainly in the authority of the teacher and that of the physician. Both the doctor's and the teacher's double-plane behavior should naturally and spontaneously create conditions for the developing of infantilization and concert pseudopassiveness similar to those of a good concert or performance. Thus the external conditions aid the personality's inner need for developing concentrative psychorelaxation directed to the reserve capacities.

In most cases, the person receiving the information does not realize that his receptivity has increased because of the increased authoritativeness of the source. He does not understand that, at a given moment, the informative process has begun to run at a higher level. More is received, understood and memorized than is usual because the source has increased authority. Enhanced authority exercising a suggestive effect is felt emotionally, to a great extent, like the other elements of N.M.R. with which suggestion operates. The N.M.R. is felt in a similar way in the various kinds of art in which the basic idea is perceived unnoticed during the emotional and aesthetic experience. The more convincing the N.M.R. means are in art, the more true to life and the more effectively selected they are, the greater is the ease with which the idea is perceived, i.e., the easier it is to overcome the anti-suggestive barriers. Consequently, enhanced receptiveness to the suggested content of information, although probably connected physiologically with local increased excitability of the respective structures, operates below the level of conscious mental activity. The role of authority in the communication process remains peripherally concealed, although it may have decisive importance in the ultimate results.

Experiments in this sphere were carried out in some of the comprehensive schools. A list of words from different poems was drawn up. These words were recorded on tape and presented to two groups of students. One of the groups, selected at random, was later told that the words were from the poetry of the celebrated Bulgarian poet P.K. Yavorov, the other group was not told from where the words had been selected. Then sheets of paper were distributed to the students asking them to write down the words they remembered. The results can be seen in Table 14.

The table makes it obvious that there was a considerable difference in the number of words memorized by the two groups. The statistical analysis of the material shows that the difference of

TABLE 14 Effects of Authority on Memorization

| Group | Informed | Number of subjects | Reproduced words Number of words | % |
|-------|----------|--------------------|--------------------------------|---|
| I | Words from P.K. Yavorov's poetry | 56 | 532 | $56.6 \pm 13.24$ |
| II | No author specified | 49 | 245 | $30.1 \pm 13.10$ |

memorization between the two experimental groups is statistically reliable at guaranteed probability over 0.99.

It was especially important that the authoritative source was announced at the end of the experiment. Consequently, the difference in memorization was due not to activating the aquisition but mainly to activating the reproduction.

Other experimental research into authority's influence on memorization have been carried out and all have given the same results. These experiments show that in schools authority plays an important role also in memorization, hence, the economic effect of establishing authoritative teachers and methods of teaching. In the suggestopedic foreign language courses at the Suggestology Research Institute, the role played by authority is very clearly marked. For example, a high percentage of words or phrases have been memorized and without manifested elements a suggestive effect other than authority — just considerably increased authority in individual groups. In a French language group, the meanings of 165 new words were memorized in this way on August 15, 1967. The average percentage of memorization for the whole group was 96.5 percent. Another group had class in the presence of specialists from abroad. From the very beginning, the factors creating authority were intensified. The control tests for the memorization of phrases and words showed an average group memorization of 96.3 percent.

In a number of similar experiments on the influence of authority (prestige), control tests were held of the students' ability to translate from a foreign language into Bulgarian, and from Bulgarian into a foreign language. In other cases, only the translation of pronounced words or sentences was recorded. Many times the control tests were in mixed order. The results in the different languages did not differ very much.

The results proved that memorization, when there is a considerable enhancement of the authority of the source of information, can, in some cases, be kept just as high as when the whole complex of suggestive means is employed. Of course, this does not signify that experimental and practical suggestology can abandon all the other means of suggestion and rely solely on authority, because it is neither easily achieved nor can it be maintained at a high level indefinitely. This is particularly true when the teacher has had no preliminary theoretical and practical training.

At the same time, the above-mentioned control tests proved that by relying mainly, or only on increased authority, the memorization can be maintained — high memorization of individual words, of whole sentences, and of specially selected isolated words which have no association with the mother tongue. Furthermore, memorization can be maintained at a high level not only when there is a previous associative setup from training prior to the experiment, but even when it has to begin with only the power of authority.

Authority contains considerable power to motivate in a concealed, concentrated form. Sometimes, the suggestive power of high motivation can be seen also outside the authority of the personality. Well argued speech convinces, on the one hand, by the very logic of the exposition and, on the other, through the direct suggestive power of the authority of brilliant motivation which impresses everyone. After assuming the proper setup, one is ready to accept some ideas immmediately with practically no logical processing. At the same time, motivation itself is built up from concepts containing different nuances of suggestively created contents for different times and different people.

It can be assumed, from the work in the suggestopedic courses and our experimental research into the role of authority in memorization, that the quantitative assessment of memorization in the future investigations of this problem will also supply a quantitative criterion for the qualities of the teacher. Such a criterion for the teacher can be obtained not only from the assessment of memorization but also from a number of other activities, and especially so from the students' creativity.Our experiments showed that under the guidance of a teacher with a liberating—stimulating, indirect and non-directive prestige the students' creativity is enhanced. The problem of authority is of special importance for all other sciences and aspects of life in which interpersonal relations exist.

*Infantilization*

Authority creates confidence in the reliability of expected results. This is how infantilization most often originates in the suggestive process. Sometimes infantilization develops without any external motive, due to inner inspiration born for instance from some idea, i.e., autosuggestively. The higher the inspiring and non-directive authority, the greater the developing infantilization; the two are, in most cases closely connected.

Sometimes infantilization develops without any external motive, due to inner inspiration born for instance from some idea, i.e., autosuggestively. Infantilization has nothing to do with the medical term "infantilism". It is a universal reaction of respect, inspiration and confidence which, without disrupting the level of the normal intellectual activity, considerably increases the perception, memory and creativity functions. In infantilization, perception, memorization and creative imagination seem to return, to some extent, to the more favorable level of the earlier age periods. It is well known that the child can memorize much more information than the adult. For a child, every new concept reveals new worlds. With the advance of age the memory functions and the flight of imagination begin to lose their significance in proportion to the growth of reasoning, which helps man logically understand the connections, interrelations and laws of nature, and society. The striving to develop the reasoning power results in minimizing and retarding the development of memory, emotions and imagination. Simultaneously, in the phylogenetic and ontogenetic aspects, a social norm is apparently established not only for the significance of the memory functions, but for their capacities, as well. Thus, imperceptibly, a suggestive conviction about the average level of human memory is formed. This suggestive norm is the major one removed in the suggestopedic courses; therefore, a process of desuggestion rather than suggestion takes place in these courses. Infantilization facilitates this process to a considerable extent. Infantilization can be observed in any pedagogical process. The group considerably facilitates infantilization and this creates an atmosphere of greater spontaneity. The concentration of the N.M.R. elements most often results in infantilization, which creates conditions for overcoming the anti-suggestive barriers. The logical anti-suggestive barrier is easily and unnoticeably overcome in developed infantilization in therapeutic or study groups. The perception of whatever is given in the program becomes, to a great extent, pleasant and emotional. The group has a feeling of growing confidence, which also facilitates the overcoming of the affective anti-suggestive barrier. If suggestive effect is in harmony with the ethical barrier, more favorable conditions are created for desuggestion and suggestion. Well-developed infantilization is a favorable base on which to develop the desuggestive-suggestive process.

Infantilization is not related to the libidinous infant—parent relations of Freud's psychoanalysis. In suggestive infantilization, a setup of confidence, a feeling of peace and receptivity is created— the same as that created in the pleasant atmosphere of a children's group. Infantilization does not mean a complete return to early age periods. It is rather a selective mental setup. This circumstance is of particular use. Life's experience and one's intellectual abilities are not reduced but rather supplemented by the plastic qualities of the earlier age periods, since these are liberated to a considerable extent.

In perceiving works of art, for example, infantilization through N.M.R. creates conditions for breaking away from the often uninspiring mental setup of critical logic and activates the effective—intuitive mechanisms. It leads both to aesthetic experiences and intellectual conclusions, but in a more direct, spontaneous and convincing manner.

There are various techniques for achieving a specific degree of infantilization. Apart from the serene attitude toward the process of teaching, the playing of roles is very often employed in suggestopedic work. At the very beginning, each member of the course is given a new name (one used in the respective foreign language he is going to learn) and a new life story. This approach creates a dramatic situation which liberates the members of the course from their social positions. It also facilitates the quick removal of the anti-suggestive barrier which, in its turn, stimulates the spontaneous and immediate expression of their abilities. Such play acting situations are of use in the suggestively built process of education for adults as well as for children. Considerable importance is also given to suggestive play acting in some psychotherapeutic methods. It has been used especially in most forms of group psychotherapy.

The playing of roles is often combined with singing, but all this should be carried with strict and proper timing. These play acting situations remove the existing setup of a person and create a new one closer to a child's setup.

In children, infantilization results in organization and consciousness in the process of teaching and creates a general atmosphere of easiness, spontaneity and absence of pressure. Memorization in children's suggestopedic courses in foreign languages is also high. The lessons are pleasant and the children appear to look forward to them. They have the feeling that the atmosphere is easy and pleasant with the grown-ups who are present and from whom they learn things without noticing—things for which they usually have to make great efforts and the learning of which is often bound up with insistance from adults and unpleasant discipline. In the suggestopedic courses, children do not feel compelled to imitate the adults in their apparent behavioral superactivity. As it has been shown, infantilization can be cultivated for autosuggestive purposes, too.

## Double-planeness

Double-planeness comprises the enormous signalling stream of diverse stimuli which unconsciously, or semiconsciously, are emitted from or perceived by the personality. Quite often, these unconscious signals possess great information value for the receiver. Imperceptible changes in facial expression, gait, speech, environment, etc., can play a decisive role in the formation of the suggestive result. Usually, this second plane in behavior is the source of the intuitive impressions which form many of our attitudes toward persons and situations incomprehensible even to ourselves. These are, in fact, N.M.R. factors. They can, to a certain extent, be controlled and directed in accordance with the requirements of the suggestive situation. Great actors master this art, and sometimes give convincing interpretations of characters even when their own internal balance is disturbed. This, of course, requires great effort and is a strain on them. The effort is not always successful. For this reason, actors and masters of other arts often prefer to appear less frequently and only when they are in good form. This rule is also observed by the skilled psychotherapist. He knows that he should appear before his patients only when he is in good form. Thus, through the second plane techniques of his activity, which are imperceptible to ordinary critical thinking, he inspires a feeling of ease and serenity in his patients, a feeling of confidence in their own quick recovery, and even a direct suggestion of recovery. This double-planeness in ordinary behavior should be mastered and used to influence and affect audiences, patients or students.

Purposeful employment of the "second plane" of behavior is

sometimes sufficient to begin building up authority on first sight, to win over students, patients or audiences and to inspire confidence. This gives rise to an atmosphere of infantilization and creates conditions for profound and efficient suggestive effects. No suggestion can have an effect and no authority can be built up if the words expressed are acceptable from the point of view of logic, but the numerous non-specific accompanying signals seem to speak just the opposite. It is absolutely necessary that double-planeness should be employed in art, medicine, teaching and life in general, in order to be able to ensure proper results from one's work. It is particularly useful for the physician and the pedagogue to understand the manifestations and possibilities of double-planeness, i.e., they must become artists in their profession. But it must not be forgotten that true artists are always sincere. Only when there is sincerity can double-planeness be mastered, and the desired suggestive effect achieved in the best way. This is the reason it must be emphasized that *no suggestive work should start without a mastery of the double-planeness of behavior.* Doctors, psychotherapists, teacher-suggestopeda-gogues, and men of art should be trained both theoretically and practically. If one's knowledge of double planeness is not perfected, a rush into practicing suggestion is doomed to failure. Double-planeness does not mean, however, artificial and theatrical acting or posturing; it must be the result not only of profound preliminary work, but of a great love for one's profession and for one's fellow men. It is only such double-planeness that can stand the test of time. A good knowledge of double-plane behavior ensures a quick buildup of authority and the suggestive connection, thus, creating conditions for the utilization of the reserve capacities of paraconscious mental activity.

## Intonation

Intonation is one of the elements of double-plane behavior. It also has marked significance for the buildup of authority and the establishment of the suggestive connection. Intonation in suggestology is usually understood as ordinary sound intonation. To a large extent this is due to its wide application in psychotherapeutic practice. Giving different nuances to the voice is, perhaps, the most often employed method because it is the handiest and the one easiest to "get the hang of". Other methods require some sort of organization and technique. They also involve certain difficulties of coordination which would be psychologically right in the ordinary therapeutic atmosphere. When a suggestion is put forward, the intonation in the voice makes whatever it is sound significant. At the same time, it convinces us of the authoritativeness of the source of information. Intonation also helps achieve double planeness in behavior. Solemn intonation is the kind most frequently employed. Special intonation also creates a particular attitude in those hearing it; it comes out of the framework of everyday life, and creates an atmosphere of expectation. The affective content of intonation facilitates a more profound emotional activation of the personality. A suggestive atmosphere is not created and the reserve mechanisms of unconscious mental activity are not liberated by every intonation and every condition. It is very important to emphasize that demonstrative intonation—if only for the sake of it and devoid of any content—not only fails to bring the expected results, but often diminishes the effect of the words because there is nothing behind the intonation. In this sense, intonation can be regarded not so much as external richness of tone, but as an expression of internal psychological content. Internal intonation, import and an atmosphere of expectation can also be created by some hardly noticeable external sound variation. Very often, a pause is richer in content than the effective sound shape of suggestive speech. Intonation, however, is not absolutely necessary to achieve high suggestive results. It only facilitates the suggestive process. A number of experimental researches into the suggestopedic methods for learning foreign languages have shown that this is so. In them, high memorization results, reaching genuine suggestive hypermnesia, were obtained without any special intonation when giving the material to be memorized. These experiments were made when the students were learning both individual words and phrases. The size of the program varied with the number of isolated new words or new words in phrases numbering from 100 to 1000. It should be noted that the students preferred intonational presentation of a new material: they found it more pleasant, not at all boring, and felt no uneasiness when they had to explain to themselves why they achieved such unusually high memorization results.[1]

In other experiments with special intonation, we got more lasting memorization than was achieved in the control group. The memorization of the experimental and control groups showed no significant differences. We dropped artificial intonation later on in our suggestopedic courses and retained only the artistic intonation in harmony with the music of the concert session. In this way, the intonation became more acceptable to the students.

Moderately artistic intonation increases the information value of the material given, engages the emotional and double plane aspects of the communicative process more actively, and creates an atmosphere of acceptable significance.

*Rhythm*

Rhythm is a basic biological principle, a reflection of the rhythms in nature. There are daily rhythms, seasonal rhythms and annual rhythms, affective vegetative reactions and, hence, mental life. There are also many cosmic rhythms affecting personality. The psychological significance of rhythm has been emphasized by many authors but, so far, no comprehensive experimentally motivated hypothesis has been offered. Nonetheless, rhythm finds empiric application in various spheres of life. Suggestive effects in medicine, commercial advertisement, pedagogical practice and other spheres are most often presented rhythmically. By feeling and experience, psychotherapists know that quite often the rhythmical repetition of therapeutic suggestive effects brings quicker results than the single "torpedo" or its antipole, the "gentle" suggestion. The various forms of rhythm in art can serve as examples of its deeply penetrating suggestive effect, particularly in music and dancing.

Rhythms have considerably greater effect when they are full of suggestive import, when they act with more than purely physical qualities, and are signals of authority and purposefulness of action. The magnitude of the interval between the separate rhythmically repeated stimuli is, of course, also significant. In the suggestopedic courses, the teachers fill in the intervals with psychologically pleasant meaningfulness and authoritativeness. The rhythmically correct

---

[1] The rhythmical intonational presentation, where "intonational swing" is created, was adopted at the beginning of the suggestopedic courses. In the first suggestopedic lessons, the new words were repeated 3 times—each time with a different intonation. With the same intonation we repeated each word that followed. Later, each new word was pronounced only once during the memorization session, but with intonational swing. Horizontal intonational swing was replaced by vertical intonational swing. The first type of intonation is declarative, somewhat resembling a headline or assigning a task but, at the same time, promising. The psychological content of the second type of intonation is the quiet expectancy with suggested import. The third intonation is solemn and generalizing.

intonational presentation of a program ensures a high degree of durable memorization. While, on the one hand, rhythm facilitates memorization by repetition, on the other, it impedes memorization by weakening the orientation reflex. This contradiction is overcome in the suggestopedic courses by the kind of intonation which gives greater plasticity and liveliness to the rhythmically presented program and thus maintains the orientation reflex at optimal level. The suggestive effect of rhythm is related mainly to the intervals in presentation of the separate memorization segments and not to their repetition.

A number of studies have shown that the interval between the segments of the memorization program has an effect on memorization volume. The interval can be better utilized in suggestopedic teaching, which creates better conditions for filling in the pause with psychological meaningfulness and expectation. The significance of the intervals (which vary in duration) changes in the suggestive process. When a saturated suggestive atmosphere is created, the interval can be considerably reduced without affecting the extent to which the suggestive program is learned. Thus, for example, hypermnesia of large programs was achieved in some suggestopedic courses in spite of the fact that the tempo was considerably reduced, mainly at the expense of the interval between the individual segments.

Rhythm combined with intonation to a great extent determines the suggestive effect of art.

## Concert pseudopassiveness (concert state)

In childhood new things are memorized more easily and, what is more important, without strain and effort. The memorization process itself takes an unconscious course in normal, calm perception. However, if the teaching is misguided, this normally spontaneous process in the individual development can involve great effort and strain. The natural mechanism of memorization is deformed. The maxim that everything can be acquired through work, although fundamentally true, is incorrectly understood and students get the idea that they must make extreme efforts to memorize. In these efforts they involuntarily activate many unnecessary memorization activities. This actually results in rapid fatigue and the reduction of their memory capacities. Quite often, when they have to memorize a large amount of material, they stiffen their body musculature and bring vegetative nervous system changes and mental strain. Their appearance is like that of those in a prestart condition: the person who has to memorize looks "active". But this "activeness" in memorization is wrongly demanded by many pedagogues who think it is a part of the pedagogical principle of activeness, which is, as a rule, correct. Activeness, however, in our opinion is not expressed in muscular contractions, vegetative changes and mental strain, but solely in the attitude toward the process of teaching and learning. An active and conscious attitude toward this process ensures its full utilization, but activeness in memorization can be expressed even in apparent external passiveness. This passiveness is like the passive children's perception and memorization. But behavioral passiveness in the adult is an expression of his superactive attitude toward the process of teaching. Such passiveness facilitates hypermnesia and liberates the intellectual activity to operate without any disturbing strain. This was the reason that we assumed that in our suggestopedic work, conditions are created for the development of creative pseudo-passiveness. It is an expression of internal superactivity, accompanied by the economizing of energy. That is why in educational suggesto-pedic courses, the fatigue experienced is considerably less than the norm and quite often does not exist at all. Therefore, passiveness and infantilization, in the sense they are used here, mean liberation from the parasitic supplementary activities which are unnecessary for the process of memorization itself.

One can be trained to acquire a state of pseudopassiveness which can also be created by supplementary means. It is unneces-sary to give preliminary instruction in autogenic training, relaxation or yoga savasana. What is required is only the setup of a serene, confident attitude toward the suggestive program being presented, and to be in the same state of mind as one would be in attending a concert. The listeners are behaviorally passive and make no intellectual efforts to memorize or understand; they allow themselves to apprehend the program of music emotionally. The physical and intellectual behavioral passiveness, as already mentioned, is not real passiveness because, at the same time as the music is apprehended, complicated internal processes take place, moods originate, assoc-iations emerge in the mind and ideas occur to one. All this is not tiring in the physically and intellectually passive climate. On the basis of such concert pseudopassiveness (concert state) with a built up setup for hypermnesia, the anti-suggestive barriers are much more easily overcome and the reserve capacities of the mind are released. The state of concert pseudopassiveness is created by meditative autosuggestion as well as by the mechanisms of authority and infantilization and those of intonation, rhythm, etc., but this state can be enhanced by creating a suitable musical background as is done in many suggestopedic sessions.

The structure of the suggestopedic foreign-language teaching process in its first variants was described in 1966. This structure comprised three phases: decoding (explaining the new material to be given in the session); the session; and elaboration (work on the material given in the session). Within the framework of these three phases we had to cover, in a quick tempo, the three specifically and mutually interacting stages of information, reproduction and production. To this end, the suggestopedic didactic pattern was created which allowed the utilization of the spontaneously originating placebo effect. The most important part of this pattern is the concert session. Research has shown that it acts through a double mechanism: on one hand, as a ritual placebo factor; and, on the other, as a readjusting psychological concert state. This is understandable in view of the participation of the associative factor in every mental act.

Under these conditions, the processs of suggestopedic foreign language instruction has been oriented to learning vocabulary, grammar, pronunciation, the more complicated relations in language structure, as well as enabling the students to switch over quickly, creatively and with ease to the respective language dynamic when new situations arise. It has become clear that suggestopedy not only improves memory processes (in the presence of the respective suggestive setup), but it is able to activate the whole creative personality in the process of teaching and learning (also in the presence of the respective suggestive setup).

Since the concert session comes to the fore in the suggestopedic pattern of the teaching process, it was decided to do some research into the role the session plays in learning the meaning of foreign words and sentences (the meaning of foreign words and sentences being the factor easiest to measure). A check was made of 164 students studying a foreign language in the suggestopedic courses. The results of the concert session were compared with the corresponding results of the decoding. Since the duration of the decoding and the duration of the concert session are different, it was calculated how many words and sentences were memorized per minute in each one of these phases of the teaching process. The results can be seen in Table 15.

TABLE 15    *Effectiveness of the Concert Session Compared with Decoding*

| Factors | Concert session | Decoding | Effectiveness of the concert session compared with the decoding |
|---|---|---|---|
| % of memorized words per min. | 1.17 | 0.54 | 2.17 times more |
| % of memorized sentences per minute | 1.10 | 0.44 | 2.50 times more |

Taking into consideration the fact that decoding comprises many suggestive elements, we can draw the conclusion that the difference would have been greater still if we had compared the results of the concert session with the results obtained in traditional teaching. This can easily be seen in a comparison of traditional teaching with the suggestopedic educational system taken as a whole, where the concert session is only one part of it.

These conclusions do not mean, however, that education should be carried out wholly in the form of concert sessions. The complex problem of the educational process, with its requirements for active communicativeness, cannot be solved in this way.

Concert pseudopassiveness can be obvious behaviorally. But it can also be unnoticeable, at first glance, and represent only a mental state which shows no external characteristic features. This can be illustrated by experiments in which material for memorization was given only in the so-called active part of the suggestopedic session. In spite of the absence of behavioral and apparently also of intellectual passiveness, hypermnestic results were achieved—something unthinkable under ordinary conditions. In such cases, pseudopassiveness is very unobtrusive. It is created by the presence of impressive authority and considerable infantilization factors. Pseudopassiveness in suggestopedy is built up by the special internal setup of serene memorization—without worry, strain or effort. It follows that on the background of some internal pseudopassiveness, memory processes again occur and these by themselves are demonstrative of activeness. Pseudopassiveness ensures great economy of suggestive processes, reduces fatigue and sometimes even results in relaxation.

## GENERAL CONCLUSION

From everything that has been said so far, the conclusion can be drawn that the suggestive is a constant and indivisible part of every communicative process. In some cases, it may increase to the extent of tapping the reserves of mind; in others, it may decrease; but it always participates in man's mental and emotional life. The term "suggestive" comprises the indivisible desugges- because, to a certain degree, we are always under the influence of some suggestions. Most of them we receive in early childhood when hardly any critical—logical and conscious thinking exists. And, because of the indivisibility of personality and because of the global nature of our reactions, even when we grow up the suggestive always participates in our most rational activity; as an emotional ingredient of each rational process; as peripheral perceptions in every activity; as unconscious automated actions; and, in general, as an unconscious ingredient of all qualities, processes and mediators of personality "refracted" by the anti-suggestive barriers.

The suggestive is realized through the paraconscious in all its variants. The suggestive can thus create new levels of the psycho-physiological manifestations of personality. These are of interest, above all, in medical and educational work and also in other spheres of life.

If we tried to apply our conception of suggestion and of sugges- tology to the most basic and familiar psychophysiological mechan- isms, we could say that suggestology is built up on the following three fundamentals: (1) interpersonal communications are always global and simultaneously conscious and unconscious; (2) all stimuli are associated, coded and symbolized; and (3) all stimuli are complex.

How well these conceptions are used in future developments and application depends on the theorist's views and the practitioner's experience. Personal experience is indispensable here, because suggestology is a science dealing with the art of activating desug- gestive—suggestive processes and, thus, tapping and making use of man's reserve capacities both under guidance and alone.

In conclusion, we should like to put forward the following defini- tion of suggestion: *Suggestion is a constant communicative factor which chiefly through paraconscious mental activity can create condi- tions for tapping the functional reserve capacities of personality.* In practice, suggestion cannot be separated from conviction, as the unconscious cannot be separated from the conscious. However, it should be borne in mind that the spontaneous unorganized use of suggestion has caused many setbacks in the personality's development. Suggestology elucidates the role of suggestion in this respect and provides ways of using its freeing and stimulating possibilities.

# Chapter 5

# Suggestopedy – An Experimental Method of Suggestology

Suggestology, for the present, has no great variety of experimental methods at its disposal. For this reason, when suggestopedy came into being and developed, our attention was directed not only toward practical results, but also to the possibility of employing suggestopedy as a method for experimental research into some of the aspects of the problems of suggestion. At the same time as we were able to shed some light on problems of unconscious mental activity, memory, the activation of creative processes and the reserve capacities of the personality.

## MEMORIZATION OF SUGGESTOPEDICALLY PRESENTED MATERIAL

We made our assessments chiefly from the results of written control tests. The tests were usually given the day after a suggestopedic session, without the students having done any homework. They were asked to give a partial or full translation of the material they had been given in the session. In the first half of the course, the translation was mainly from the foreign language into the mother tongue. In the second half, translation was more frequently from one's own language into the foreign language. The words in the tests were given at random.

The tests given were not on all the material, but on a great part of it. We have data on the number of words and sentences memorized by each student from the total 600—900 words and sentences given in the tests. The words and sentences included in the control tests are only a small part of the total number taught. Being chosen at random for the test, this small part satisfies the requirements for representative statistical research. Taking into consideration the considerable number of lexical units included in the tests, it can be said that the test figures for memorization are transferable to the total material studied. This claim acquires a greater value from the fact that the majority of the students showed a remarkable steadiness in achieving high results in the tests.

The percentage of the assimilation of the material taught was calculated for each student: percentage of memorized words, percentage of memorized sentences, average number of new words per school day, average number of words per suggestopedic session.

One example will be sufficient to explain how the calculations were made: Student P.M. in a German language group had taken seven tests. Out of the total 896 words given in the test, he knew 839, or 93.6 percent. Out of the total 1067 sentences he knew 1037, or 97 percent. Considering that the complete study program comprised 1600 words, and the tests comprised only 896 words, before transferring the results of the tests (93.6 words learned) to the total material taught, the random error had to be calculated. It was ±1.57 percent with a rank significance of 95 percent (error, 5 percent). In this case, the mean percentage of memorized words would vary from 92.03 to 95.17 percent. The percentage of the memorized sentences was 97, and the random error was ±1.02 percent.

In the experimental course attended by P.M., 1600 words were given in 31 school days. When P.M. memorized 93.6 percent, he memorized, on an average, 49 words per day and learned to use them correctly. In this experiment the 1600 words were given in 15 suggestopedic sessions. Calculations show that the student memorized, on an average, 100 words per session (about 45 minutes).

From the data provided by the above example, variations in percentage learned were calculated for all students. Table 16 shows the variations in the percentage of words learned by the students who completed the courses. It can be seen that most of the 416 students learned more than 90 percent of the material they were given. The average amount of material learned for all members of the courses was 93.16 percent.

Table 17 shows the basic statistical indices of the average number of words learned well enough for practical use in one study day and the memorized meaning of words in one suggestopedic session (the suggestopedic sessions were usually held every other day for 45 minutes).

These two indices depended largely on the scope of the study program, the distribution of the material by sessions, the number of days set aside for practice in speaking, etc. These are all connected with the philological tasks undertaken.

*TABLE 16   Variations in Average Percentage of Words Learned by Individual Students in the Courses*

| Percentage intervals | No of cases |
|:---:|:---:|
| 46 — 50 | 1 |
| 51 — 55 | 2 |
| 56 — 60 | 5 |
| 61 — 65 | — |
| 66 — 70 | 4 |
| 71 — 75 | 4 |
| 76 — 80 | 10 |
| 81 — 85 | 29 |
| 86 — 90 | 44 |
| 91 — 95 | 89 |
| 96 — 100 | 226 |
| Total: | 416 |

*TABLE 17   Summary Statistics for Students Who Were Given Suggestopedic Instruction*

| Indices | Memorization of material | Average number of words assimilated for practical use per schoolday | Average number of words memorized per suggestopedic session |
|:---|:---:|:---:|:---:|
| Arithmetical mean | | 61.46 | 108.40 |
| Variance | | 12.59 | 18.48 |
| Standard error ($p$ 0.95) | | 3.10 | 3.70 |
| Coefficient variation | | 20.48 | 17.00 |

Figure 25 shows graphically the distribution of the data of Table 16. The curve has no peak. The figure shows, to a considerable degree, the possibilities of the suggestopedic methods in improving the efficiency of memorization. It also shows the fact that these possibilities have not been exploited to the full extent in the experiments so far carried out.

TABLE 18   *Suggestopedic Memorization Dependent on Sex and Age*

| Age groups | Subjects | | % memorized words | |
|---|---|---|---|---|
| | Men | Women | Men | Women |
| Up to 20 yrs of age | 26 | 24 | 93.73 | 93.00 |
| From 21 to 30 | 40 | 52 | 94.50 | 95.38 |
| From 31 to 40 | 109 | 50 | 93.52 | 95.58 |
| From 41 to 50 | 81 | 27 | 90.59 | 89.85 |
| Over 50 | 14 | 4 | 90.36 | 92.25 |

## SUGGESTOPEDIC MEMORIZATION DEPENDENT ON SEX AND AGE

The extent to which age and sex can affect the process of learning can be used, to a certain degree, as a measure for assessing the power of suggestive hypermnesia and, hence, of the suggestopedic system. A study was made of 427 students in the courses, 157 women and 270 men, divided up into age groups.

The problem of assessing the effect of the suggestopedic system in relation to the students' age and sex was solved by comparing the mean percentages of memorized words. It was found that with men the mean percentage was 92.64 and with women 94.05. The difference of 1.41 percent is within the limits of the possible random error ($t = 1.03$).

The age characteristics in men and women (see Table 18 and Figure 26) show certain changes in the effectiveness of the applied method, changes dependent on their age. It was not our task to determine exactly between which ages significant differences in the number of memorized words occurred. Our task was to find out whether there was a law which governed difference in the amount of memorized material which might be due to the age factor. That is why we compared only those age groups where the differences were most clearly manifested. Such age groups with men proved to be the ones from 31 to 40 (93.52 percent) and from 41 to 50 (90.59 percent). The difference between the mean percentage of memorized words in these groups was 2.93 percent and it is statistically significant ($t = 2.86$, $P(t) > 0.99$). Analogical statistically significant differences between the average number of memorized words was also found with women—between the age group of 21 to 30 (95.38

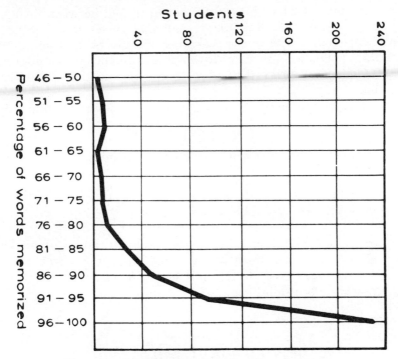

*Figure 25*   Average percentage of words memorized.

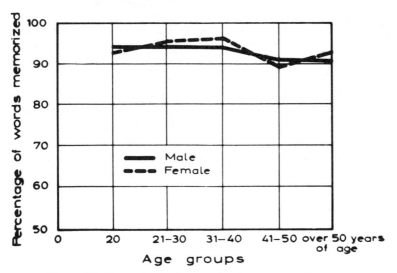

*Figure 26*   Dependence of memorization on sex and age.

percent) and that of 41 to 50 (89.85 percent), and between the age
group of 31 to 40 (95.58 percent) and that of 41 to 50 (89.85
percent) where the $t$-criterion is equal respectively to 2.12 and 2.14
($P(t) > 0.95$). This does not mean lower results in the older students,
because in comparison with other methods the result of 89.85 percent is high.

The results of the analysis gave us ground to draw the following
conclusions.

1) The amount of memorized material is not significantly affected
by sex.

2) The age factor is related to the amount of material memorized.
The highest results are found in students up to 40 years of age.

3) Some of the final values in the age group variation of results
are statistically and significantly different from the arithmetical
mean of the aggregate, but do not provide sufficient evidence to be
able to draw more profound conclusions from this fact.

## SUGGESTOPEDIC MEMORIZATION AND EDUCATION

It was interesting to check whether students with only a high school
education would, in learning the material for memorization, do
better or worse than those who had graduated from universities.
Of the 416 students involved in this experimental research, 120 had
graduated from high school. The knowledge we gained from this
research illustrates to what extent education affects the results of
suggestopedic instruction (see Table 19).

TABLE 19    Percentage of Memorized Words in Relation to Education of Students

| Education level | Number of subjects | % of memorized words |
|---|---|---|
| Higher education | 296 | 93.38 |
| High school education | 120 | 92.61 |
| Total | 416 | 93.16 |

The mean percentage of words memorized by students with higher education was 93.38 percent, and that of students with high school education was 92.61 percent; the difference of 0.77 percent is within the limits of the possible random error.

Consequently, it can be said that education plays no significant part in affecting the results of suggestopedic instruction.

## SUGGESTOPEDIC MEMORIZATION IN LEARNING VARIOUS FOREIGN LANGUAGES

Many kinds of subjects have been already taught by the suggestopedic method. Here we give only an account of the suggestopedic teaching of foreign languages, in particular the research we carried out to see whether suggestive memorization of different languages would be the same for all or would deviate. The results can be seen in Table 20.

TABLE 20     Percentage of Memorized Words Related to Language

| Language | % of memorized words |
|---|---|
| German | 95.00 |
| French | 94.40 |
| English | 92.40 |
| Italian | 95.60 |
| Total | 93.16 |

These are the mean percentages of the words memorized during the whole course of instruction, calculated from the data on each student who studied the respective language in the regular courses.

Here we shall assess whether the deviations observed in the different languages were significant in respect to the mean indices of the aggregate, where the arithmetical mean was 93.16, and the average dispersion coefficient was 8.12. We shall employ the criterion $t$.

For the German language group, criterion $t$ has a value of 1.86. Comparing it with the respective table, it is obvious that the alternative hypothesis is supported by a probability ranging between 90 and 95 percent. Although marginally significant, this probability is insufficient for unconditional adoption of the alternative hypothesis.

For the French language group, criterion $t$ has a value of 1.62. The null hypothesis is supported by a probability exceeding 10 percent. Therefore, neither it nor the alternative hypothesis can be accepted with certainty.

For the English group, *t* has a value of 1.88. With this value of the criterion, the alternative hypothesis cannot be accepted, although there is a probability ranging between 80 and 95 percent in its support.

The conclusion which can be drawn from these calculations is that the suggestopedic system of memorization has been tried out with success in different foreign languages. It is almost equally suitable for teaching any foreign language. The differences established in the results of the different groups cannot be unconditionally accepted as significant. This favorable conclusion we were able to draw about its usefulness in practice has been corroborated by the results of suggestopedic courses held in other countries.

## DURABILITY OF MEMORIZATION IN SUGGESTIVE HYPERMNESIA

One of the most frequently asked questions about suggestopedy is whether memorization in hypermnestic volume is lasting. Objections are usually raised to such a large amount of material being memorized, on the ground that it will be quickly forgotten again. Because of this criticism we decided to make experimental checks of the durability of memorization in suggestive hypermnesia.

The impression we got from these checks is that what was learned in the suggestopedic courses was lasting knowledge, not easily forgotten, even if it was not practiced. This being so, taking into consideration the pleasant suggestive atmosphere and the absence of fatigue, suggestopedic instruction has considerable advantages. Without examining in detail the problems of memory and the place of suggestopedic data in the research work on memory functions so far carried out, we shall briefly outline some of our principal researches into certain characteristics of suggestive hypermnesia.

### Durability of memorization in the first few days after the suggestive memorization session

During the suggestopedic courses, we were not always able to hold memorization control tests on the day after the session.

To standardize the material checked in our investigation, only the control tests in which the translation was from a foreign language into Bulgarian were taken into consideration. The data given in Figure 27 show that the percentage of errors gradually increases in the first few days after the suggestopedic session. These data could be employed in outlining whatever tendency there is to "forget" in the suggestopedic assimilation of the material.

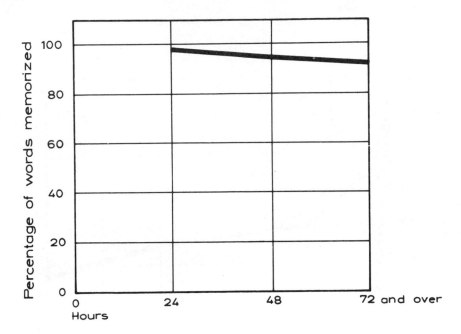

*Figure 27*    Dependence of memorization in the interval between session and control test.

The control tests show that even after 48 and 72 hours the students remember a large percentage of the words they have been given. Statistical investigations established that the difference between the first and second, and the second and third groups is smaller than the theoretically admissible chance error. Proceeding from this, we can conclude that there is no significantly expressed forgetfulness in the first days after the suggestopedic session.

Forgetting, under ordinary conditions, advances at a much faster rate than the tendency shown here. The curve for forgetting poetry, for example, drops to 73 percent after the first day. And as A.N. Sokolov (1967) pointed out,

When the volume of the meaningful material with sense is greatly increased, the curve of forgetting begins to approach the curve of forgetting nonsense material.

According to Ebbinghaus' well known classical curve, one hour after the memorization of senseless syllables, only 44 percent of them remain in the memory, with only 28 percent remembered 48 hours later (Figure 28).

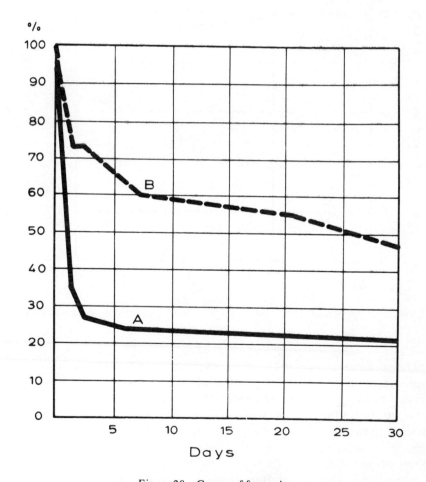

*Figure 28*   Curves of forgetting:
A: senseless syllables (after Ebbinghaus) and B: verses (after Boreas).
Reproduction (in percentage) of the material and memorized at different time intervals (after A.N. Sokolov).

This means that, according to Ebbinghaus' curve, the considerable amount of material given for memorization in the suggestopedic sessions could be expected to be forgotten. But, in fact, it has been proved that memorization of this material is more lasting than memorization of meaningful material under ordinary conditions. This super durability is characteristic of hypermnesia under suggestive conditions.

## *Durability of memorization tested at different times after students had completed courses*

After a number of students had graduated from the first suggestopedic course and joined the second, control tests were held on the material given in the first course. The results of these control tests were compared with the results of the control tests held immediately after the suggestopedic sessions. In the case of some students, after the second control test, words were read out aloud once by the teacher and a fresh check was made. The results of this check are shown on Table 21.

*TABLE 21    Percentage of Forgetting In Suggestive Memorization*

| | | | Results in % | |
| | | | Check before beginning new course | |
| Time from session to check | Number of students | After session | Without reading | With reading |
|---|---|---|---|---|
| 22 months | 4 | 93.5 | 57.0 | 81.00 |
| 12 months | 5 | 76.3 | 67.2 | 79.6 |
| 9 months | 4 | — | 85.2 | — |
| Under 6 months | 8 | — | 88.2 | — |

Taking into consideration the large number of words included in the material checked, we were even able to take individual students and the results of their tests as a separate psychological experiment. For example, B.A. took part in a large-scale experiment carried out in March 1966, with the presentation of 1000 new words. The control test after the session showed that he had memorized 98 percent of the material. In December 1967, an unexpected check based on the same 1000 words was made of the knowledge of the same student. He was able to reproduce 53.3 percent of these words correctly. After a single reading of the whole of the same material by the teacher, a fresh check was made. In this check, he was able to reproduce 73 percent. The large number of words on which the experiment with B.A. was based, as well as the great differences between the percentages in the comparisons we made, ensures quite high statistical reliability.

If we consider the curve of forgetting of different groups of students, we shall see that the process of forgetting becomes worse the more distant it is from the suggestopedic session (see Table 21 and Figure 29). However, two years after the suggestopedic course had ended, the members of it still remembered over 50 percent of the material they had been given. These results can be correctly evaluated if they are compared with the Ebbinghause curve.

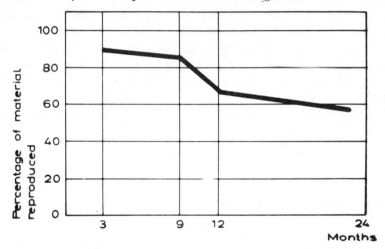

*Figure 29*    Reproduction of suggestopedically memorized material.

Figure 29 shows a remarkably even course, indicating another important difference from the established laws of forgetfulness. According to Ebbinghaus, the forgetting of syllables is a logarithmic curve, a logarithmic function of time.

Proceeding from our data, we can assume that forgetting after suggestopedic instruction is a linear function of time. These inferences received corroboration from much supplementary research into the knowledge retained by students who had taken suggestopedic courses. They were summoned specially to come for a check on what knowledge still remained in their minds at different periods after the completion of their courses. These members of former courses were called at random, and those who came did not know the reason for being asked to come. The results of one of these checks are shown in Table 22.

TABLE 22

| Subjects | % of reproduced memorized material | | Interval between the immediate and delayed check in months | Number of students who had not reviewed the material between the two checks |
|---|---|---|---|---|
| | Immediate check | delayed check | | |
| 24 | 92.6 | 82.4 | Up to 5 | 20 |
| 20 | 95.6 | 87.4 | From 8 to 16 | 13 |
| 3 | 97.7 | 50.4 | 22 | 3 |

These results corroborate the results shown in Table 21. In some groups, higher percentages for the durable nature of the memorization of the material learned suggestopedically were obtained. However, the tendency was always toward a delayed deterioration in the retention of the material (when it had not been reviewed, of course), and toward its very quick restoration when the occasion presented itself. The considerably high degree of retention of memorized material in many groups can be seen in Table 23.

The same high percentages of retention were also shown by some groups when a very large program was presented in one session. The memorization and retention of 500 isolated foreign words can be seen in Table 24.

TABLE 23    *Retention of Foreign Language Material*

| Subjects | Date of immediate check | Date of delayed check | Percentage of reproduced memorization material | | Reviewed material |
|---|---|---|---|---|---|
| | | | Immediate | Delayed | |
| L.T. | 17/11/63 | 4/3/66 | 100 | 100 | Little |
| A.M. | 17/11/63 | 4/3/66 | 96 | 96 | No |
| B.G. | 17/11/73 | 4/3/66 | 99 | 98 | Little |
| B.P. | 17/11/63 | 4/3/66 | 99 | 99 | No |
| V.V. | 17/11/73 | 4/3/66 | 100 | 100 | No |
| L.G. | 17/11/63 | 4/3/66 | 100 | 100 | No |
| E.R. | 17/11/63 | 4/3/66 | 100 | 100 | No |
| Z.M. | 17/11/63 | 4/3/66 | 100 | 99 | No |
| H.B. | 17/11/63 | 4/3/66 | 100 | 100 | Little |
| N.P. | 17/11/63 | 4/3/66 | 100 | 100 | No |

TABLE 24    Memorization and Retention of 500 Foreign words presented in a Single Session

| Subjects | Percentage of reproduced memorization material | | Interval between the two checks | Revised material or not |
|---|---|---|---|---|
| | Immediate check | Delayed check | | |
| H.B. | 100 | 95 | 3½ months | No |
| Z.M. | 100 | 100 | 3½ months | No |
| H.I. | 100 | 100 | 3½ months | No |
| A.I.M. | 100 | 98 | 3½ months | No |
| N.P. | 99 | 97 | 3½ months | No |

In another group a check was made of the retention not only of new foreign words, but of new phrases. Here again the general tendency of delay in the process of forgetting was proved (see Table 25).

All these investigations show that suggestive hypermnesia is subject to its own laws of forgetting, which are much more favorable for practical use than those governing the ordinary ways of memorization.

## Dynamics of forgetting after suggestive memorization of non-sense verbal material

Methods employing nonsense verbal material were developed to study the process of forgetting in suggestive memorization. The subjects were given 13 nonsense syllables to memorize.

The presentation of the syllables in a suggestopedic session took the principal place in the memorization of this material. Immediately after the suggestopedic session, checks were made for the dynamic tracing of the reproductiveness of the memorized syllables and also later, at different intervals. The subjects did not know when they had to undergo checks and how many checks there would be. The material was not available for them to review. This method was used in testing 133 students during suggestopedic instruction in a foreign language. The investigation was carried out in three variants:

1) Each member of a group (15 subjects) was given the same series of nonsense syllables. In the dynamic tracing in each subsequent check, all the subjects were examined separately.

Table 25    *Memorization and Retention of Foreign Words and Phrases*

| Subjects | Date of immediate check | Date of delayed check | Percentage of memoriza-tion material reproduced | | | |
| --- | --- | --- | --- | --- | --- | --- |
| | | | Immediate | | Delayed | |
| | | | words | phrases | words | phrases |
| Z.L. | 7/3/68 | 19/5/69 | 100 | 100 | 99 | 97 |
| V.T. | 18/2/68 | 19/5/69 | 97 | 100 | 84 | 84 |
| I.P. | 18/12/68 | 19/5/69 | 79 | 100 | 93 | 92 |
| V.P. | 18/12/68 | 19/5/69 | 100 | 100 | 97 | 94 |
| Z.P. | 29/3/69 | 19/5/69 | 98 | 100 | 98 | 94 |
| I.B. | 25/3/69 | 19/5/69 | 100 | 100 | 98 | 100 |
| N.P. | 25/3/69 | 19/5/69 | 100 | 100 | 100 | 100 |

2) Each participant in the experiment (a total of 40 subjects) was given a separate, individual series of syllables to memorize. Checks of the dynamic tracing of these subjects were made on numerous occasions.

3) Three groups (26 subjects in each group) memorized the same sequence of syllables. In the dynamic tracing, however, each subject was called for only one delayed check.

The results of these experiments are given in Figure 30.

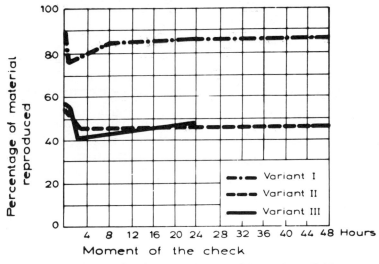

*Figure 30*    Results of the experiments with senseless syllables.

In the analysis of the data obtained from this research, the following important feature stands out: in all three variants of the experiment, a slight tendency toward declining reproduction of the material is noticeable. The minimum was reached in the first hours after the presentation of the material.

The decline mentioned above does not reach the size of declines observed in the nonsuggestopedic experiments of the Ebbinghaus type, and fluctuates between 10.4 and 15.9 percent in the different variants.

The tendency toward a decrease in reproduction in our experiments came to an end relatively quickly, and we did not observe that it continued beyond the third hour after the material had been given to the students.

In the three variants of this experiment, a tendency to form a reminiscent type reproductiveness curve was noticeable, i.e., in subsequent checks students tended to reproduce more and more of the material presented, and delayed reproduction approached reproduction in the immediate check.

The characteristic features of suggestive memorization, as seen in our experiments, are quite different from those of ordinary memorization and, in some indices, the results of our experiments are a direct contradiction of those obtained in ordinary memorization. This provides further grounds to justify the claim that forgetting in suggestive memorization has its own specific laws and patterns.

## SUGGESTOPEDY AND ORDINARY MEMORY

Memorization is a natural, spontaneous process. Not only does strain not intensify it but, on the contrary produces rapid fatigue. Such tiredness and exhaustion, however, are not observed in suggestopedic memorization.

In these circumstances it was important to investigate how suggestive hypermnesia, as reflected in learning by the suggestopedic method acts on the ordinary memory functions. In questionnaires, many of the students declared that their memory had been refreshed by suggestopedic instruction even for work outside the courses. It was necessary to investigate the level of ordinary memory before and after suggestopedic instruction. To do this we worked out and used the so-called "Hindi test". It consisted in the following:

Two groups of 100 words, each in the Hindi language, were selected. The words in both groups were equally difficult, words with equal numbers of syllables. Each group had the same number of nouns, adjectives, etc. The Hindi words with their Bulgarian translations were typed on sheets of paper. The sheets were left with the students and were to be memorized in one hour. The following day sheets of paper on which only the 100 Hindi words were written were given to the students who had to write the Bulgarian translation of the Hindi words. One of the sheets with the 100 words was given to the students on the first study day of the course, and the other one after the last suggestopedic session. In a number of courses, the words on the sheets and the sheets themselves were mixed up, but this did not change the results in any way.

The following are the results of the initial and final testing with 141 subjects.

At the beginning of the suggestopedic course, students learned, on an average, 33.9 percent of the words, and after the last session 50.2 percent. These data were statistically processed to ascertain the reliability of the differences. It was found that the difference of 16.3 percent was significant in a guaranteed probability of 0.999. The data make it possible for us to draw the important conclusion that suggestopedic instruction also has a very favorable effect on the mobilization of the memorization capacities of students in their extrasuggestopedic memorization.

## SUGGESTOPEDY AND THE INTELLECTUAL CAPACITIES

It was also necessary to investigate whether intellectual functions show any changes through suggestopedic instruction and to do this we employed various test methods. First, we made use of the "bigger-smaller" test. It consists of a specific number of unitype tasks. The subject has to draw a mental conclusion on the basis of two preceding pieces of information. The results of this test are shown in Table 26.

If we compare the percentages of tasks solved, we find that at the end of the suggestopedic course the students solved, on an average, 11.7 percent more problems than at the beginning of the course. It became clear during the statistical processing that this difference is significant.

In another experiment we modified Rubenstein's simple and complicated analogies tests. One hundred students were involved in the

TABLE 26    Results of the Investigation of Intellectual Functions with the
"Bigger—Smaller" Test

| Indices | Test applied | |
| --- | --- | --- |
| | At the beginning of the course | At the end of the course |
| Number of students | 226 | 226 |
| Total number of problems | 4342 | 4246 |
| Number correctly solved | 2762 | 3199 |
| Percentage correctly solved | 63.6 | 75.3 |

investigation.

The simple analogy test consists of the following: the students are given 10 problems. Each student must determine, by means of a given pattern, which one of five words corresponds to a given concept. The following results were obtained: at the beginning of the course, 62 percent of the problems were solved correctly; at the end of the course, 68 percent were correct. It was established statistically that the significance of this difference was supported by a probability of not less than 0.99 percent.

The complicated analogy test consists of the students having to determine the type of association between a pair of given concepts, by a given pattern. We set 12 such problems. Through this investigation we found that at the beginning and at the end of the suggestopedic course, the students solved on an average 43 percent of the problems correctly.

The results of the simple analogies test showed that during the suggestopedic instruction there was improved intellectual functioning, while the results of the complicated analogy test showed there was no intellectual activity change. A deeper positive change could have been expected if the period of instruction had been longer.

The activation and mobilization of the intellectual functions are especially favorable. They show that through suggestopedic instruction the memory, as well as, the intellectual reserves are utilized.

## SUGGESTOPEDY AND THE DYNAMICS OF SUGGESTIBILITY

We made tests of the suggestibility of students before the beginning and the end of the suggestopedic courses. We used the following test: At the beginning of the course, the students were given a picture to look at for one minute. Then the picture was removed and the students were given sheets of paper on which misleading questions were written about the nature of the picture. At the end of the course, another picture was shown to them and other questions were asked. Three questions were asked about each picture.

It cannot be claimed that this test reveals the whole suggestibility of the person. It can only give an idea of the local dynamic conditions of the general suggestive background, in so far as they are connected with suggestopedic teaching and learning. The results of the investigation of the suggestibility of the students at the beginning and at the end of the course are shown in Table 27.

TABLE 27     Results of Suggestibility Test at the Beginning and at the End
of the Suggestopedic Course

| Indices | At beginning | At end |
|---|---|---|
| Number of students | 236 | 236 |
| Number of misleading questions, total | 708 | 708 |
| Number of answers showing that students were misled, total | 240 | 96 |
| Average number misled | 1.02 | 0.41 |
| Percentage misled | 33.90 | 13.96 |

At the end of the suggestopedic course there is a clearly marked tendency to a reduction in the number of those who gave answers showing they had been misled by the questions. This means there was a tendency toward a reduction of susceptibility to suggestive effect.

Table 28 shows the answer analysis of the two groups in which the suggestibility of the students was investigated. The figure and percentage data given in the tables makes it possible to detail the suggestibility changes during suggestopedic training.

TABLE 28    *Table of Changes of Suggestibility During Suggestopedic Instruction*

| Number of answers showing students were misled | At beginning | At end |
|:---:|:---:|:---:|
| 0 | 78 | 162 |
| 1 | 94 | 53 |
| 2 | 46 | 20 |
| 3 | 18 | 1 |
| Total | 236 | 236 |
| Arithmetical Mean | 1.02 | 0.41 |

The difference between the results at the beginning and at the end of the course is significant. The significance of these differences is supported by a probability exceeding 0.999.

Table 29 shows that the majority of students in both groups exhibited a decrease in positive answers.

The study of suggestibility by the above test methods gives every reason to assume that suggestopedic instruction affects the students' suggestibility and most often results in a decrease in the general (background) suggestibility. The decrease in background suggestibility, at the end of the suggestopedic course, is probably an expression of suggestibility's concentrating mainly on increasing memorization during the process of instruction.

The dynamic changes and background-directed suggestibility interrelations during the suggestopedic process of teaching, and their association with suggestive hypermnesia, are only noted here. They will be the subject of further experimental elucidation.

## SUGGESTOPEDY AND STUDENTS' HEALTH

In suggestopedic instruction in foreign languages, the volume of material given in each lesson is considerable. In spite of this, it is easily learned by the students. It must also be borne in mind that the students in these courses are people who are already working in full-time jobs. They do not interrupt this work to take the course. They attend the course in their free time. That is why research was carried out to investigate the effect of suggestopedic instruction on the health of the students.

TABLE 29　Changes in Suggestibility During Suggestopedic Instruction

| Indices | Percentage |
|---|---|
| Less positive answers | 52.10 |
| Without change | 36.88 |
| More positive answers | 11.02 |

It is hardly necessary to point out that if the suggestopedic method had demonstrated its success in teaching, but at the expense of the students' health, we should have given it up altogether.

## Psychotherapeutic effect (Suggestopedy as Psychotherapy-through-Learning)

In a number of courses students at the beginning and end of the courses were asked to fill in special questionnaires. Their answers supply evidence about the state of their health at both times. The questionnaires of 396 students were processed (Table 30).

TABLE 30　Changes in State of Health During Suggestopedic Instruction

| Groups | Number of persons | Percentage |
|---|---|---|
| Negative effect | 0 | 0 |
| No noticeable effect | 327 | 82.6 |
| Positive effect | 69 | 17.4 |

The statistical investigation of the effect of suggestopedic instruction on the state of health of students, from evidence supplied by them, allows us to draw the following conclusions:

1) It can be claimed with certainty that suggestopedic instruction has no unfavorable effect on the health of students.

2) In a comparatively small percentage of students, suggestopedic instruction had a favorable effect on some functional disorders.

3) A number of complaints of a neurotic nature disappeared during instruction, giving grounds for the elaboration of methods for group psychotherapy for neurotic patients, by means of suggestopedic instruction.

Besides answering the special questionnaires, the students often gave spontaneous expression to their impressions of the changes they felt during suggestopedic instruction. Some of their impressions were given in written form. Most often their letters referred to a favorable effect on some neurotic complaint. The following are several excerpts from the hundreds of letters we have received.

I.V., German course, November 1967:

Before I joined the course I felt nervous and irritable. It was difficult for me to go to sleep. A few days after I started the course I found that I had become calmer and fell asleep more easily . . . .

### E.S., French course, April, 1966:

I was suffering from a nervous disorder before the course, but now I am fine. I sleep much better now.

In other letters students have described how they overcame psychotraumatic experiences and how this influenced their mood and activity.

S.T., German course, November 1967:

Thanks to your course, I was able to get back to my normal state after a shattering experience which had been depressing me for several years . . .

In some letters the students have written of the favorable influence of the suggestopedic system on their character.

I.V., German course, November 1967:

. . . In general, in the days which I have spent here, I have gained confidence and trust in my own abilities.

E.I., German course, November 1967, wrote that the migraines she had been suffering from for many years no longer occurred:

. . . but this seems to me to be very little in comparison with the other encouraging feelings which I experienced. In the Institute I felt far away from all worries and trouble. I felt reborn, or intoxicated if you like. I find that I now have a wish to be better to everyone, and that I have begun to contemplate life and the reality which surrounds me more philosophically.

### D. E., German course, November, 1967:

For 30 days, while sitting in my armchair in the Suggestology Institute, I felt uplifted, refreshed and freed from petty, everyday matters. Worries and unpleasant things lost their biting quality, the impossibly difficult things became easier, and I became fitter for work in my occupation and able to make the extra effort almost beyond my strength. From the armchair one seems to perceive that people can be better, things less complicated, and life more beautiful.

These letters are of special value as they were written spontaneously, out of an inner wish and a need felt by the former students to express their feelings.

Owing to these and a number of other positive psychotherapeutic results obtained in suggestopedic courses, suggestopedy becomes a psychotherapy-through-learning system with considerable potentialities. The global approach to personality, the 'volumely' (not linearly) organized instruction, the simultaneous utilization and activation of the conscious and paraconscious functions, the simultaneous participation of man's mental and emotional sides, the simultaneous participation of the left and right hemispheres of the brain, as well as that of the cortex and subcortex—all these are of great importance for the global and many-sided influence of suggestopedy over the personality. In this respect an extremely favorable effect on the suggestopedic educational and curative complex is exerted by the indivisibly integrated elements of music-psychotherapy and art-therapy in general, sociopsychotherapy, suggestive-motivational indirect and non-directive psychotherapy, psychodrama, autosuggestive meditation psychotherapy, concentrative psychorelaxation and the free creative instruction under the conditions of controlled infantilization and concert pseudopassiveness.

Data obtained from the working capacity tests, and from investigation of the dynamics of the bioelectrical activity of the brain of neurotics during suggestopedic instruction, indicate that—in spite of the considerable amount of material given to the students in the lessons and the quick rate of the work—the one month's course does not lead to any kind of fatigue. Though the neurotics' average mark at the end of the course is slightly lower than that of the healthy students, the difference is not significant. Thus suggestopedy proved to be a psychotherapy-through-learning system whose results deserve consideration.

But it is also of importance that suggestopedy has considerable psychohygienic and psychoprophylactic possibilities. In our (Bulgarian) school experiment comprising of sixteen schools, a number of investigations were carried out in order to determine what the effect of suggestopedy on children was. In the course of two years (1975—76 and 1977—78) 2,300 first and second graders were examined by a commission of twelve psychotherapists and four university professors. It was established that in the suggestopedic schools neurotic disorders in children have decreased by half compared with those in the control schools. At the same time the schoolchildren have learned a material twice as much as that given to the children in the control schools, and they have achieved that without any homework and under the conditions of a shortened working week. The psychotherapuetic, psychohygienic and psychoprophylactic sides of suggestopedy were experimentally studied and corroborated by I.Z. Velvovski (1971, 1975) and later by other authors too.

## Pulse and blood pressure

The changes in the pulse and blood pressure in mental work have been studied by M.V. Antropova *et al.* (1955), P. Balevsky *et al.* (1968), B. Vuzvuzova (1966), K. Georgiev and D. Iliev (1958), K. Georgiev and P. Balevsky (1961), T. Gotsev and A. Ivanov (1949, 1950), D. Daskalov (1958), S. Zotov (1955), V.G. Krizhanovsky (1957), M.R. Mogendovich and A.G. Markin (1955), E.S. Rutenberg (1959), B. Yanev and Z. Ivanova (1959), A. Binet and V. Henri (1968), and others. Although the data are not always along the same line, it is generally believed that short strenuous mental work is accompanied by an increase in pulse frequency and a rise in blood pressure, while longer but steadier, less intensive mental activity brings a slight delay of the pulse and a drop in the maximum blood pressure.

By measuring the pulse and blood pressure of 157 students before and after lessons (P. Balevski), it was found that in 49 percent of them the pulse was slower at the end of the class, in 28 percent it was quicker and in the other 23 percent there was no change. The maximum blood pressure dropped in 53 percent of the students, rose in 28 percent and showed no change in the other students. The changes, both toward a rise and toward a drop, are only slightly marked and are within the framework of the average daily fluctuations. When the data obtained from all the investigations is analysed, a tendency can be observed toward a delay of an average five beats per minute in the pulse, and an average drop of four divisions of the mercury column in the blood pressure (Figures 31 and 32). The changes in the minimum blood pressure are not statistically significant. Even on days when the sessions were long, the changes in the students' pulse and blood pressure were only slight. Thus, for example, after a long

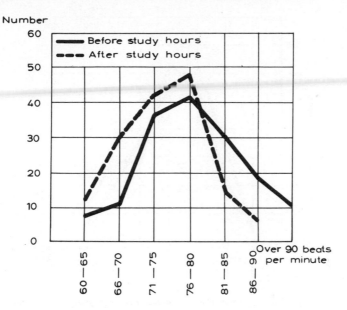

*Figure 31*   Changes in the pulse rate.

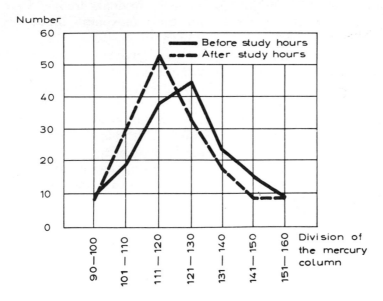

*Figure 32*   Variations in the maximum blood pressure.

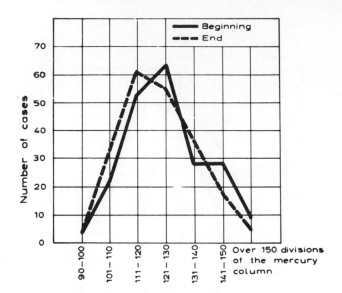

*Figure 33*   Average data on the maximum blood pressure at the beginning and at the
end of the course.

session for the memorization of the meaning of 600 foreign words, held on June 27, 1967, the pulse of the students dropped from 80.2 beats per minute to 74.3, and their maximum blood pressure remained unchanged.

At the end of the courses, there was an average drop of 2.8 units of the mercury column in maximum blood pressure (Figure 33). The changes in the minimum blood pressure and pulse were insignificant. In conclusion, it can be said that the changes in the pulse and blood pressure of the students were only slightly expressed. A tendency toward a delay in the pulse, a drop in the maximum blood pressure at the end of the courses (as compared with the beginning) was noticed. This proves that the suggestopedic method, in spite of the large volume of material given in the lessons, does not burden the cardiovascular system of the students.

## Capacity for mental work

The methods chosen for research into the capacity for mental work were quite different. In compliance with the scientific research plan of the Institute, P. Balevski carried out investigations with the proof-reading test in Amfimov's modification, problems set for solving by mental arithmetic, the measurement of the electrical sensitivity of the eye, and the latent period of simple motor reaction to strong and weak sound stimuli were selected. Here are given the most important data obtained in this research.

In the proof-reading test, which lasted for two minutes, students had to cross out all examples of one given letter and underline another one. On days with sessions for the consolidation of what was to be memorized, the proof-reading tests were given three times to the students—before classes, and before and after a session; on days without a session, twice: before and after classes. Altogether, 1485 proof-reading tests were held, with the investigation covering 24 groups of students.[1]

In order to see whether there were any changes in the capacity for mental work and in the reactivity of the students after one month of classes, 439 students were given proof-reading tests at the beginning and end of the course, and 221 students took part in five minute tests to solve mental-arithmetic problems. The dynamics were also traced on the working capacity of 17 other groups, comprising 172 students altogether. New variations of the suggestopedic method were used in teaching these groups.

The data obtained from all these investigations were processed by means of analysis of variance, and were checked for significance of difference.

As can be seen in Figures 34 and 35 on days without a session at the end of the day's lessons, the number of letters examined decreased from 365 to 345, or by 5.05 percent, and the number of errors increased from 6.25 to 7.05, or by 12.8 percent.

On those days on which there was a session and on which, before it, the students showed a tendency toward a decrease in their working capacity, there was, after the session, an increase in the accuracy and quickness of the student's work, even surpassing that shown before the lessons began. Thus, it can be seen that the sessions contribute to the restoration of the mental working capacity of the students in spite of the fact that the teaching process actually continues.

The laws and patterns described above have also been corroborated by evidence obtained from the processing of data on individual cases. Before the sessions, a slight decrease in the number of letters checked was noticed in about 50 percent of the students, and also a tendency toward an increase in errors. After lessons, on

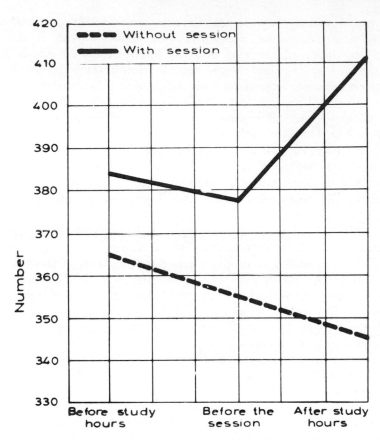

*Figure 34*    Average number of letters examined.

days without a session, such initial phenomena of reduced working capacity were observed in 58 percent of the students. Conversely, on days with sessions, the percentage of students with reduced working capacity after lessons decreased instead of increased. Thus, at the end of the day's lessons when there had been a session, initial phenomena of reduced working capacity were observed in only 30 to 35 percent of the students. The difference in the percentage of students with reduced working capacity on days with sessions and on days without sessions are statistically significant $(P>0.99)$.

The data obtained in the proof-reading tests coincided with objective statements made by the students expressing their feelings. They declared, in the inquiry sheets they had to fill in and in daily checks,

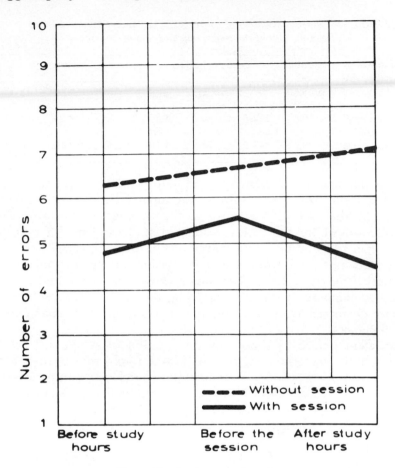

*Figure 35*   Average number of errors.

that they were in the best of spirits after a session—even when the lessons had been rather long. Thus, for example, on June 27, 1967, after a session for the memorization of 600 French words, the students did not feel in the least tired. On the same day, before the lessons the students checked on an average 419 letters each, and showed on average 3.9 percent errors. After the session, which lasted several hours, the average number of letters the students checked rose to 519 and the percentage of errors dropped to 2.4. When the students were examined a day or two after, it was found that on an average they had assimilated 94 percent of the given words.

At the end of the courses, the students showed greater speed and

TABLE 31    *Average Number of Letters Checked and of Errors in Proof-Reading Test at the Beginning and End of Courses*

| Time of investigation | Number of subjects | Letters checked | | avge | | | Errors | | avge |
|---|---|---|---|---|---|---|---|---|---|
| Beginning of course | 305 | 332.6 | 66 | 3.80 | 4.84 | 2.94 | 0.17 |
| End of course | 305 | 347.6 | 72 | 4.10 | 4.33 | 2.20 | 0.13 |

accuracy in their work than they did before the courses began ($P>$ 0.99, see Table 31). The results of the mental arithmetic test were similar. At the end of the courses, the number of the problems correctly solved by the 221 investigated students was 7.3 percent higher than the number they solved at the beginning.

The data obtained from the investigation of the eye electrical sensitivity (rheobasis) of 210 students show that at the end of the course, as compared with the beginning, the ocular rheobase of the students decreased from 51.2 microamperes to 47.2 microamperes, or by 6 percent.

The latent period of simple motor reaction to strong and weak sound stimuli was also investigated. It was found that both before and after lessons the students reacted more quickly to comparatively strong stimuli, i.e., the law of intensity was not violated. Balancing or paradox reactivity, which would have been the expression of more clearly manifested fatigue, were not detected either on days with or without a session.

This research showed in a convincing way that the working capacity and the reactivity of the organism in suggestopedic teaching and learning do not follow the laws of ordinary teaching and learning, especially on the days of suggestopedic instruction with sessions. Therefore, it can be said that desuggestive—suggestive teaching and learning take place in the presence of new and favorable physiological laws.

## SUGGESTOPEDIC INSTRUCTION AND CEREBRAL BIOELECTRICAL ACTIVITY

Research work was organized in order to search more deeply into the physiological mechanisms governing the effectiveness of the suggestopedic system and its favorable effect on the working capacity and reactivity of the organism. This research was carried out jointly with our assistants P. Balevski and E. Stomonyakov, and was aimed at establishing the effects of suggestopedic lessons on the cerebral bioelectrical activity of the students.

Although much research work has been done on the bioelectrical activity of the brain in mental work, the most suitable EEG criteria to assess mental strain and fatigue are still being sought. A. Glass (1964) and Gray Walter (1966) and others most frequently made use of the changes of alpha rhythm in the electroencephalogram (EEG), i.e., its depression as a criterion. K. Kiryakov (1964) also noted a depression of alpha waves after continuous mental strain (after operators, controllers and others had had 9 to 12 hours on duty) and their replacement by rapid fluctuations or by slow fluctuations with rapid wave accumulation. G. Lange, V.N. de Strom van Louwen and P. Verre (1962) found, in some subjects, no depression in mental strain, only an alpha rhythm fluctuation, but in others they noted an intensification of beta activity. J. Volavka, M. Matousek and J. Roubicek (1967) found that beta waves are more closely related to changes in cerebral activity than are the other types of waves. Research into the changes in the cerebral bioelectrical activity of students under the effect of teaching have, up to now, been on a very small scale. Y.M. Pratusevich and N.M. Korzh (1961), Y.M. Pratusevich *et al* (1909, 1964), and others found no well expressed or stable changes in the "spontaneous" electroencephalogram under the effect of the strain of instruction, although they established such changes by the method of conditioned reflexes and in their research into the assimilation of light stimuli. V. Yonchev (1959/60) found EEG changes in students during examinations.

The visual study and manual processing of electroencephalograms have provided only scanty data on cerebral activity changes in mental work, especially when the work was not very continuous or intensive. It has become evident from the investigations of V.A. Kozhevnikov and R.M. Meshterski (1963), S. Ormandjiev *et al.* (1967), G. Walter (1966) and J.R. Richl (1963) that the possibility of studying the changes in the functional condition of the cerebral cortex has become considerably greater since multichannel analyzers were introduced into neurophysiology.

On the other hand, the works of R. Mackey (1965), G. Walter (1966), A.G. Simons and N.R. Burch (1960) have made it clear that the recent introduction of telemetric instruments in electrophysiology has facilitated remote investigation of the changes in human cerebral biocurrents under the conditions of the natural experiment. It has become possible for us to study an extended span of cerebral activity directly in the process of mental work without immobilizing the students or hindering the normal process of teaching. These instruments, which at present are used mainly in hospital clinics and in examining athletes, pilots and astronauts, can also become very useful in teaching.

In our research we used a 12-channel Galileo polyphysiograph, an ART-1000 electric signal analyzer, and a 4-channel telemetric instrument made by the Alvar firm (Televar). This research was comprised of the following:

a) Analysis of interperiod interval of EEG-wave in various types of mental work (with subjects),

b) Analysis of EEG of students before suggestopedic classes, before a session and after a session.

c) Telemetric recording and analysis of EEG of students during their lessons,

d) Assimilation of light stimuli by the cerebral hemispheres before classes, before and after a session;

e) Investigation of changes in evoked potentials of visual stimuli in the course of the day's lessons,

f) Telemetric investigation of the EEG of students while sleeping during the night which followed a day of lessons.

The following are the detailed analyses of these investigations.

*Analysis of the interperiod interval of the EEG waves in various types of mental work*

Before starting the investigation of the students, the interperiod interval of the EEG-wave of 15 subjects was investigated while they were doing different kinds of mental work: solving problems mentally, doing a proof-reading test, translating from a foreign language, memorizing a text, etc;, in the course of 2 to 80 minutes. A total of 155 histograms were recorded. These preliminary investigations showed that in the above-mentioned types of mental work, the alpha and theta waves decrease as the beta waves increase. Figure 36 shows typical histograms of the time interval of the EEG-

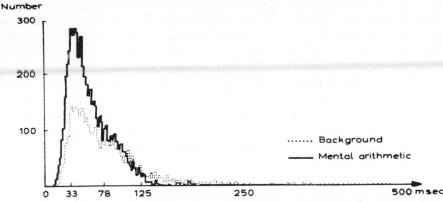

*Figure 36*     Histograms of the interperiod intervals of the EEG waves at rest and while doing mental arithmetic.

waves at rest, with open eyes, and doing mental arithmetic. Intervals with a continuation of 33 to 78 milliseconds correspond to the beta waves, from 79 to 125 to alpha waves, from 124 to 250 to theta waves, and from 251 to 500 to delta waves. Although the frequency and interval analysis cannot be made identical, the majority of researchers assume that interval analysis data give a sufficiently clear idea of the frequency distribution of EEG. The analyses, when students were at rest and when they were solving problems, were made in the course of five minutes from left occipitoparietal output. The histogram processing in Figure 36 shows that, at rest, alpha rhythm formed 31 percent of the total number of waves with a frequency of 2 to 30 Hz, beta waves formed 57 percent, theta waves 11 percent, and delta waves 1 percent. In mental arithmetic, alpha rhythm decreases to 24 percent, theta rhythm to 3 percent, and beta rhythm increases to 73.4 percent, while delta waves disappear completely (Table 32).

*TABLE 32     Alpha, Beta, Theta and Delta Indices of Subject V.K., At Rest and In Doing Mental Arithmetic, May 17, 1969*

| EEG waves | At rest | In solving problems % |
|-----------|---------|----------------------|
| Alpha | 31 | 24 |
| Beta | 57 | 73.4 |
| Theta | 11 | 3 |
| Delta | 1 | — |

The processes of the restoration of cerebral rhythms after mental work were also studied. It was established that in short-term mental work, not exceeding 10 minutes, cerebral activity returns to its initial level, on an average, after five or six minutes. Intensive mental work for 15 to 30 minutes requires 10 to 15 minutes for restoration. After intensive mental work exceeding one hour, restoration to the initial EEG level is observed only after 20 minutes or more. There are, however, considerable differences in the time needed for restoration. For example, after a ten minute proof-reading test, full restoration of the beta and theta waves in the subject L.Y. only came after 20 minutes (Table 33).

*TABLE 33    Alpha, Beta and Theta Indices of Subject L. Y. At Rest, In Proof-Reading and After The Test, November 19, 1968*

| EEG waves | At rest % | In proof-reading test % | 10 minutes after the test % | 20 minutes after the test % |
|---|---|---|---|---|
| Alpha | 55 | 30 | 54 | 56 |
| Beta | 30 | 60 | 38 | 28 |
| Theta | 15 | 10 | 8 | 16 |

Therefore, EEG-index wave changes were observed not only directly in the process of mental work, but also on its completion, i.e., a rather lengthy post-effect was observed.

## Analysis for interperiod interval of EEG waves of students being taught by the suggestopedic method

A five minute analysis (in test lab) was made of the EEG of the left occipito-parietal output of 117 students, aged 18—63, who were sitting with eyes closed. 350 histograms were taken; 256 channels were used, with elementary analysis time of one or two milliseconds..

The investigations revealed individual differences in the EEG changes under the effect of teaching. On the basis of the data, it was possible to divide the students up into several groups. Figure 37 illustrates the dynamics of cerebral bioelectrical activity most frequently encountered in the course of the lessons. As can be seen from the histograms, the alpha waves decrease after the first three academic hours, and the beta waves increase. After the session, the beta waves decrease somewhat under the initial level, and the alpha

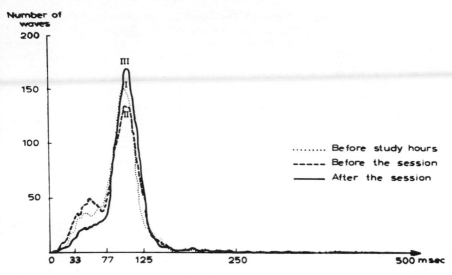

*Figure 37* Histograms of the interperiod intervals of the EEG waves before study hours, before the session and after the session (group I).

waves increase above the initial level. The changes in the theta and delta waves are insignificant. A similar dynamic was observed in 56 percent of the students. A second group of students (30 percent) reacted by increasing the alpha waves after the first three study periods. After the session, in some of the students cerebral bioelectrical activity was partially restored to the initial level (Figure 38) and, in the others, the alpha waves increased still more. In the third group of students, the distribution of waves did not change. A tendency toward an ever more clearly expressed acceleration or delay of cerebral activity in the course of the study periods was observed in individual cases. The difference in the reactivity of the students was probably an expression both of their individual features and of the effect of a number of internal factors and external environmental circumstances.

The data obtained on the students' cerebral bioelectrical activity was processed in order to see what percentage of them had increased, decreased, or not changed their alpha and beta indices during the lessons. It was found that, after the lessons without a session, in 57 percent of the students the beta waves had increased and in 38 percent they had decreased. On the days with a session, an increase of beta waves after the lessons was detected in only 25 percent, while in 70 percent the beta waves had decreased ($P > 0.99$). Reciprocal changes were also established in respect to alpha waves (Table 34).

TABLE 34    *Percentage of Increased, Decreased and Not Changed Alpha and Beta*
            *Indices After Lessons with and without a Session*

| EEG waves | Increased | | | | Decreased | | | | No change | |
|---|---|---|---|---|---|---|---|---|---|---|
| | After lessons without session | By what % | After lessons with session | By what % | With-out session | By what % | With session | By what % | With-out session | With session |
| Alpha | 42 | 8.6 | 66 | 8.9 | 54 | 7.3 | 26 | 5.2 | 4 | 8 |
| Beta | 57 | 6.5 | 25 | 3.8 | 38 | 7.7 | 70 | 6.9 | 5 | 5 |

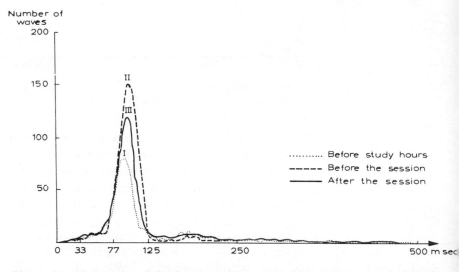

*Figure 38*    Histograms of the interperiod intervals of the EEG waves before the
              study hours, before the session and after the session (group II).

There was, therefore, a significant difference in the dynamics of
the cerebral bioelectrical activity of students on days with a session
and on those without one.

*EEG telemetric investigations*

The EEG investigations made before the lessons, before the session,
and after the lessons made it possible to see the residual effect of
mental strain, but not its immediate effect on the cerebral bioelectrical activity of students. To obtain some idea of the changes in

the distribution of the EEG-waves during the lessons under the conditions of a "natural experiment" with eyes open, 150 EEG telemetric recordings of students were taken by means of 4-channel telemetric instruments and electrodes fixed with collodion. A miniature transmitter, to which the electrodes were connected, was fixed to the head of each student by means of an elastic band. Neither the transmitter nor the band hindered the process of learning, and students soon forgot them. At the same time as the recording was made, an interval analysis of EEG waves was made with an ART-1000 analyzer.

*TABLE 35    Changes in the Alpha, Beta and Theta Indices in the Course of Lessons*

| EEG waves | Ist hour | 2nd hour | 3rd hour | Session |
|-----------|----------|----------|----------|---------|
| Alpha | 31 | 30 | 30 | 40 |
| Beta | 55 | 55 | 56 | 47 |
| Theta | 14 | 15 | 14 | 13 |

It is evident from Table 35 that there were slight changes in the EEG indices during the first three study hours, while during the concert session the alpha index increased from 31 to 40, and the beta index decreased from 55 to 47. The same dynamic of cerebral bioelectrical activity was also established by R. Noncheva in school-chidren being taught algebra and geometry, according to the suggestopedic system.

The results of the telemetric investigations supplement the data obtained from the EEG investigations of the students, and make it possible to get a comprehensive idea of the nature of cerebral bioelectrical activity during suggestopedic instruction.

The first characteristic feature noted in these investigations was that the strongly marked increase in beta waves and reduction in alpha waves, typical of intensive mental work, were absent in the EEG of students during suggestopedic instruction in a foreign language. The changes registered were typical of mental work of low intensity, although the suggestopedic method is, in fact, associated with the giving of an enormous amount of information in the lesson.

It was found that the concert state was characterized by the alpha rhythm increasing over its level before classes, and the beta rhythm dropping under its initial level.

*Assimilation of light stimuli*

The assimilation of light stimuli was one of the tests used to investigate the functional state of the brain. The synchronization of the excitation of the individual neurons underlies the assimilation of the stimulation rhythm. Moreover, it seems that synchronization affects only that group of neurons which operates in a rhythm close to the rhythm of the light stimuli, or a multiple of this rhythm. This became clear from an investigation of the interperiod intervals of the encephalograms, at rest, and on the presentation of light stimuli. Figure 39 shows an encephalogram of left occipitoparietal output at rest and with the presentation of light stimuli with a frequency of 5 cycles per second. We get a visual impression of the full reorganization of the encephalogram into the rhythm of the presented stimuli. However, in the histograms in Figure 40 it is seen that, in the so-called assimilation of a given rhythm, all the frequencies registered in the background recording are also present. Only the number of waves with a period of 200 milliseconds (5 Hz) and their multiples, multiples, about 10 Hz, show an increase.

Our aim was to trace the changes in the assimilation of stimuli by the students' cerebral cortex during the lessons, and compare the data we obtained with the data from other investigations of the functional state of the cerebral cortex.

With the aid of a Galileo photostimulator, light stimuli of 5, 8, 11, 14, 17, 20, 23 and 26 Hz were applied to subjects with closed eyes for 10 seconds during each frequency. The investigations were carried out in a darkened room. The photostimulator was positioned 40 cm from the eyes. We counted the waves which coincided with the moment of applying the light stimuli· and calculated the coefficient of synchronization for each frequency, after which the rhythm assimilation curve was drawn. A comparison was made of the curves of 40 students of both sexes, from 17 to 55 years of age, before lessons, before a session and after a session.

It was found on analyzing the individual curves that, after the first three study periods, the percentage of stimuli assimilation decreased in 28 of the 40 students and in 12 it increased. It was just the opposite after sessions: the majority of the students improved stimuli assimilation, mainly, in respect to slow and rapid frequencies. The data on the average percentage of assimilation of light stimuli are given in Figure 41. A slight decrease in the assimilation of stimuli was established before sessions and a tendency toward restoration to

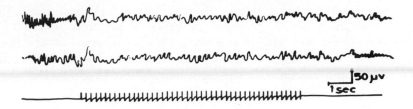

*Figure 39*    EEG at rest under stimulation with the frequency of light signals, 5 cycles
per sec.

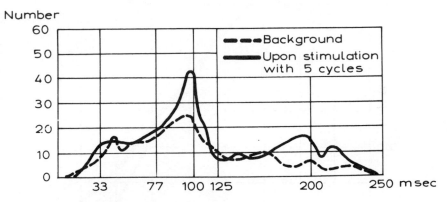

*Figure 40*    Histograms of the inter-period intervals of the EEG waves at rest and
under stimulation with a frequency of 5 cycles.

the initial data after sessions. In general, changes in the assimilation
of stimuli in lessons were only slightly expressed. This was apparent
from the fact that in the three investigations the maximum assimilation remained for 11 Hz. This also suggests that the well expressed
phenomena of fatigue were absent among students during the day's
lessons. Taking into consideration that it was also found that there
was a slight increase in cerebral cortex excitability after the first
three periods in the majority of the students, it can be concluded
that an increase in excitability affects the stimuli—assimilation
rhythm of the cerebral cortex unfavorably, while a decrease of
cerebral excitability raises the percentage of the assimilation of
stimuli. On the other hand, according to Pratusevich (1964) and
other researchers, there is a better assimilation of light stimuli by the
left hemisphere when one is in a fresh, unwearied state, and by the
right hemisphere when one is tired. G.A. Sergeev, L.P. Pavlova and
A.F. Romanenko (1968) found that in a serene untired state the left

hemisphere assimilated rhythms of from 12 to 16 Hz better than the right hemisphere which, however, assimilated rhythms of 6—10 Hz better than did the left. It was found to be reversed in states of fatigue, i.e., better assimilation of slow rhythms by the left hemisphere and rapid rhythms by the right hemisphere (Figure 41).

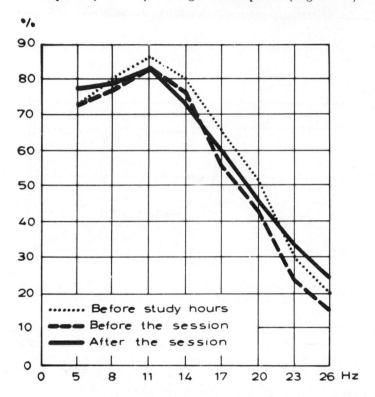

*Figure 41*    Assimilation of photic stimulations before the study hours, before the session and after the session.

Comparative research into rhythm assimilation by the left and right hemispheres in 30 students showed that the left hemisphere assimilated rhythms with a frequency of 11—14 Hz better than did the right, while the right hemisphere assimilated the rhythms of 5, 8, 17, 20, 23 and 26 Hz better than the left (Figure 42). In the course of the day's lessons, no significant change was established in this initial asymmetry, which also showed that there were no clearly marked phenomena of fatigue in the students.

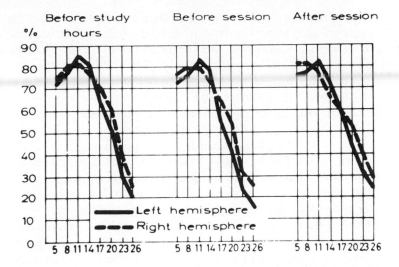

*Figure 42*    Assimilation of the photic stimuli by the left and right hemispheres of the brain before study hours, before and after the session.

## Evoked potentials

A number of reports in literature have revealed the fact that evoked potentials in the human brain depend on the state of one's attention. According to J. Garcia-Aust, J. Bogacr and C. Vanzulli (1964), M. Heider, P. Spong and D. Lindsley (1964, 1965), the amplitude of the evoked potential increases when the attention is not fixed on the stimuli, and its latent period shortens, while any distraction of attention by stimuli results in changes diametrically different. M.P. Kudinova and M.S. Mislobodski (1968), R.M. Chapman and H.R. Bragdon (1964) and others described more complicated and contradictory changes in the parameters of the evoked potentials when the attention was drawn or distracted from the stimuli. Kudinova and Mislobodski wrote about very typical changes in the evoked potentials. The question arose as to whether evoked potentials in the cerebral cortex could serve as a test for any changes in the attention that might occur under the effect of teaching. To find the answer to this question, a study was made of the amplitude and time characteristics of evoked potentials of light stimuli before lessons, after the first three study periods and after the sessions, as well as during the sessions themselves. Twenty-six students of both sexes from 20 to 55 years of age, were involved in the research which was carried out in a darkened room with the subjects' eyes closed. The evoked potentials were conveyed monopolarly. The active electrode was located 2 cm above and to the left of the occiput stem, and the indifferent on the processus mastoideus. Light stimuli were presented by a Galileo photostimulator, at random, with a frequency ranging from 0.1 to 1 Hz. The photostimulator reflector was located 40 cm away from the eyes of the subject under investigation. The intensified potentials from the Galileo polyphysiograph with a time constant of 0.3 seconds were fed, so as to become averaged, at the input of the ART-1000 electric signal analyzer with a minimum analysis time of 2 milliseconds with no delay. The average evoked potentials of 40 stimuli were registered on paper by means of an XY-Cimagraph.

The changes in the time appearance of the maximum values of the separate components of evoked potentials before lessons, before a session and after a session are given in Table 36. The data on 26 students are given as averages. There are only slightly expressed changes but, nevertheless, after the first three study periods there appears to be a tendency towards shortening, and after the sessions, towards lengthening the time to the maximum of the individual potential components. The same is true for the total duration of the evoked potential. This is probably an expression of the slightly increased excitability of the cerebral cortex of the students after the first three study periods and then, after the session, of a decrease in this excitability until it disappears altogether, as was also seen in the investigations we carried out by other methods—EEG interperiod interval analysis, rheobase, and the latent period of the motor reaction.

TABLE 36   *Average Latent Time in milliseconds to the Maximums of the Positive and Negative Components of Evoked Potentials Before Lessons and Before and After a Session*

| Time of investigation | Peaks | | | | | | | |
|---|---|---|---|---|---|---|---|---|
| | $N_1$ | $P_2$ | $N_2$ | $P_3$ | $N_3$ | $P_4$ | $N_4$ | $P_5$ |
| Before lessons | 43 | 55 | 72 | 99 | 126 | 170 | 235 | 260 |
| Before session | 41 | 55 | 71 | 99 | 124 | 169 | 233 | 258 |
| After session | 42 | 58 | 74 | 103 | 127 | 169 | 235 | 262 |

After the first three study hours the evoked potential amplitude increased the increase in the peaks $N_3$ and $P_4$ being expressed the best (Figure 43). The amplitude from peak $N_3$ to peak $N_4$ increased from an average 15.7 to 18.6 microvolts, or by 11.2 percent. After the session the amplitude between the two peaks is 15.8 microvolts, i.e., it practically returns to the initial level, or what it was before lessons.

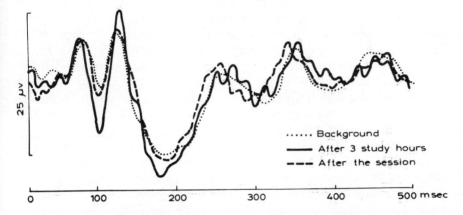

*Figure 43*   Evoked potentials after 3 study hours and after the following session.

The data obtained from the investigation of the students' evoked potentials are in accord with the data on the other factors investigated. With increased strain on the cerebral cells (increased beta activity), the evoked potentials increase in amplitude, and their latent periods are reduced. When the strain is decreased (increased alpha activity), the latent time of the evoked potential returns to the initial level or is slightly extended, and the amplitude of some of the peaks, mainly the peak $N_3$, decreases or recovers its initial value completely. If these preliminary data are confirmed by later research the evoked potentials could be used for the investigation of the functional state of cerebral cells.

## EEG telemetric investigation of students while sleeping in the night after the day's lessons

It has been found that the psychological and physiological effects of suggestopedic instruction are very favorable. Recently we began researches into the night sleep of students who had had suggestopedic lessons during the day. According to V.N. Kasatkin (1967), M. Jouvet (1967), Y. Maximov (1967) and others, paradoxical (rapid) sleep forms from 25 to 29 percent of the night's sleep. Researchers have noted a certain sequence in the appearance of paradoxical sleep during the night, usually at one hour intervals. Paradoxical sleep appears four or five times during the night and has a duration of from 10 to 60 minutes. It appears that always after loss of rapid sleep, a compensatory increase is observed the following night. In experiments in which the subject is continually deprived of rapid sleep, the initial symptoms of mental disorders appear. In the physiological interpretation of paradoxical sleep, a number of hypotheses have been put forward. One of these is that during this sleep and in the dreams frequently associated with it, the information obtained during the day is processed. But there is still no certain experimental proof that this is so.

If during paradoxical sleep the day's information is processed, its duration should lengthen if the volume of information has been large. As in suggestopedic instruction in foreign languages a considerable amount of new information is received by the student every day, it could be expected that while the course lasts the duration of the students' paradoxical sleep would exceed the duration before the beginning of the course, and that certain changes would occur in the distribution of the various phases of sleep.

To check this hypothesis, preliminary researches were carried out into the sleep of four students for three nights before the course began and for six nights during the course in a specially equipped dormitory. For seven continuous hours (from midnight to 7 a.m.) the EEG of the students' left occipitoparietal output and the EOG of both their eyes were simultaneously registered with an 8-channel Televar and an 8-channel Galileo portable encephalograph. An analysis was also made of the EEG interperiod intervals in the various stages of sleep of individual subjects with an ART-1000 analyzer. On awaking, the students were asked about their sleep and their dreams.

The data were analyzed for every hour from midnight to 7 a.m. The ABC stages were grouped together as comparatively superficial sleep and stages D and E as comparatively sound sleep. The students' adjustment to the new environment had an effect on the length and profoundness of sleep only in the first of the three nights before the course, when the average length of sleep was 4 hours 12 minutes. On the second night it reached 6 hours 14 minutes and on the third, 6 hours 39 minutes. During the course the average length of sleep was 6 hours 28 minutes, so the data obtained in the second and third nights before the course can be compared with those obtained during the course.

It was found that periods of rapid eye movement (REM) occurred several times during the night, and that individual differences were clearly marked. Often, but not always, the REM were accompanied by typical EEG changes, i.e., low amplitude, rapid rhythm. Table 37 shows the EEG indices for one of the subjects in a waking state and in a state of paradoxical sleep. It is evident that the alpha and beta waves were well expressed during paradoxical sleep.

*TABLE 37    EEG Indices in a Waking State and During Sleep in the Paradoxical State*

| EEG waves | Waking state | Paradoxical sleep |
|-----------|--------------|-------------------|
| Alpha | 54 | 42 |
| Beta | 41 | 30 |
| Theta | 5 | 23 |
| Delta | — | 5 |

The students' sleep was most profound in the first two or three hours of the night, after which it became increasingly superficial. A slight deepening of sleep was observed again between 4 and 6 a.m. but not in all the students. Paradoxical sleep showed undulation during the night. One was struck by the counter-phase pattern of the curves of paradoxical sleep before and during the course (Figure 44). There were no strongly marked differences in the data prior to and during the course. During the night when the courses were being held, the average length of the ABC stages in relation to the total length of sleep decreased from 60 to 58 percent and of stages D and E from 30 to 27 percent. The duration of paradoxical sleep increased from 10 to 15 percent (Figure 45).

The EEG data on the continuation of paradoxical sleep and the subjective data obtained from the students in recounting their dreams at night do not always coincide. There were cases of students who reported they had dreamed little during a considerable length of their paradoxical sleep, and vice versa. It should also be noted that in comparison with the data given in literature on this subject, the results we obtained in our investigation of paradoxical sleep showed

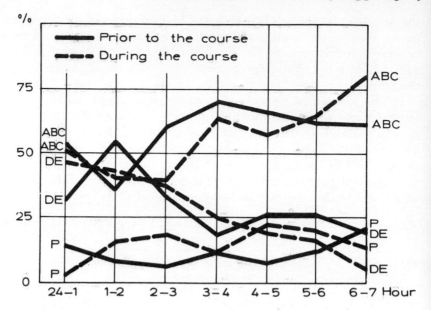

*Figure 44*    Duration of the different phases of sleep in the night.

relatively low indices but the stages ABC relatively high ones.

As a result of the above-mentioned preliminary investigation of the students' sleep, we were able to establish the fact that there was a tendency for the duration of paradoxical sleep to increase during the period of the courses and for the hours in which this sleep is most frequent to shift. To what extent these findings are regular and not accidental will become apparent in future research in which more students are involved. However, the tendency is favorable, and is in line with the results of other investigations.

## SUMMARY

The researches carried out to see the effect of suggestopedic instruction showed that besides pedagogically highly efficient, suggestopedy is conducive to the well-being of the students from the point of view of physiology, psychology and mental work. The data obtained from all the experimental methods point in the same direction. This makes the data on the changes we observed all the more reliable.

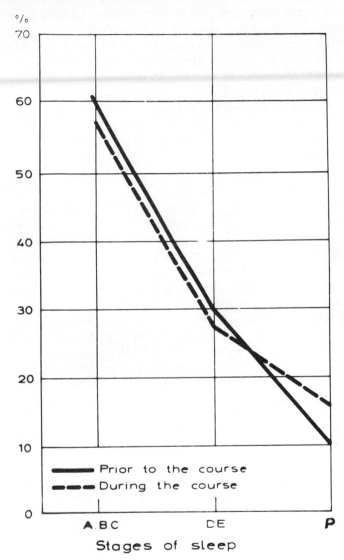

*Figure 45* Duration of the different stages of sleep before and during the course.

Suggestopedy is safe from the point of view of health and even has a favorable psychotherapeutic effect on some functional disorders. The strain felt in learning unknown study material is abolished in suggestopedic instruction. In spite of the rapid rate of work and the large volume of material given to learn, the psycho-physiological changes are only very slightly expressed. They corres-pond to the characteristic changes that come from doing mental work of low intensity. In the first three study hours, the functional state of the cerebral cortex of the students is characterized by a slight intensification of excitability as compared with the initial condition. During the time of the session the alpha index in most cases increases above its initial level, and the beta index decreases. During the sessions we have a state of the most markedly expressed mental relaxation in a waking state. This state of specific rest explains the improvement of the students' working capacity after the session — an improve-ment in as much as there is sometimes a slight decrease in some students' working capacity after the first three study periods.

It can be concluded that hypermnesia is not necessarily bound up with strenuous mental bioelectric activity and great strain. Hypermnesia can be achieved in states of concentrative pseudo-passiveness with an increased alpha rhythm.

N. Viner (1961) attributes a special role to alpha rhythm in the mechanism of the preservation of excitability traces by coding in the time of sequence events. M. Bresye (1962) regards alpha rhythm as a biological time clock; it is a standard of time to account for events. Sergeev, Pavlova and Romanenko (1968) also consider that the reserve capacities of the brain can be judged from the alpha index. This hypothesis is difficult to defend because in some of the subjects tapping of personality's reserve capacities was observed without any increase of the alpha-rhythm. Thus the bioelectrical activity of the brain, no matter how important it is for experimental studies, seems to be more of the nature of a by-product of the personality's mental changes.

However, from the point of view of practice, it is of great importance that suggestopedy has proved not only absolutely harmless to man's health but even able to function by itself as a psychotherapeutic, psychohygienic and psychoprophylactic system. Under the conditions of this psychotherapy-through-learning the personality's creative reserve capacities are released and some new (reserve) law-governed psychophysiological processes are activated.

# Chapter 6

# Characteristics of the Desuggestive–Suggestive, Liberating–Stimulating System

The desuggestive–suggestive pedagogical system–suggestopedagogy, or suggestopedy, as it is called–has also been developed on the basis of the general theory of suggestion already outlined.

A detailed description of the methical side of this system will be the subject of another book.

The main aim of teaching is not memorization, but the understanding and creative solution of problems. However, the main obstacle encountered in teaching is memorization, automation and the assimilation of the material presented. Teaching methods have so far been in accordance with the accepted "restricted" capacities of the human personality. The existing social and historical norms for the level of human memory and speed of automation, as well as, the methods of memorization and automation created by them have established a suggestive setup which, in actual fact, delays the expansion of mental abilities. In these circumstances, one of the most important tasks of suggestopedy has been to free, to desuggest and to explain to all students that human capacities are much greater than expected, and to provide liberating–stimulating methods to bring these locked-up human resources into play. The present suggestopedic system has proved that this is possible.

It must be underlined, however, that suggestopedy stimulates not only the memory, but the whole personality–its interests, perceptions, creativity, moral development, etc.

The suggestive pedagogical system is considerably more humane and puts no burden upon the student. The humane principle in suggestopedy is vitalized by the student's considerably increased capacities for memorization and automation of the material taught, and the greater creative plasticity in their use of this material in practice. All this encourages and inspires the student. The organization of this process has great advantages. It is in agreement with the psychotherapeutic demands of suggestology for liberation from discrete micro psychotraumata, for desuggestion of incompatible ideas about the limits of human capacities and for the positive, comprehensive stimulation of personality. This psychological organization can be applied to any process of teaching and learning, provided that the specific features of the subject to be studied are taken into account. The training of qualified specialists is, of course, of paramount importance.

## SUGGESTOPEDY IN THE GENERAL PRACTICE OF TEACHING

In the historical development of the science of teaching, many obvious psychotraumatic factors have been understood, condemned and even eliminated in practice.

It is not difficult to diagnose overt didactogeny—when students are harassed and oppressed by the teacher to such a degree that a physician's intervention becomes necessary. Then psychotherapeutic and psychopedagogical measures have to be taken. There is, however, a *covert didactogeny* which is widespread. It is due to the fact that both teachers and the organizers of public educational systems often have no knowledge of suggestology. Covert didactogeny manifests itself in bowing to *the social suggestive norm in regard to the restricted capacities of students and to the maxim that "knowledge is not easily come by"*. Here is the source of lack of self-confidence, the necessity for endless, senseless repetitions, unnecessary analysing (often made to be an end in itself) and, above all, the poor results in school work. This covert didactogeny is created by the teachers' requirements, by curricula, by parents' fears for their children's future. Getting rid of covert didactogeny means getting rid of the social suggestive norm which has been accepted in regard to the restricted capacities of children making their entry into school life.

All this shows the social significance of suggestopedy in creating an atmosphere of profound psychological understanding, in which the personality is liberated and stimulated from early childhood. Hence, the necessity for all those who work in this sphere to have a well-developed sense of responsibility. From this point of view, suggestopedy could become a universal educational system applicable to every level of school and university life (Figure 46).

*Figure 46*  The first experimental suggestopedic course in Moscow was carried out by specialists of the Suggestology Research Institute (Sofia) in 1969.

Experimental testing of the suggestopedic system in a number of primary schools and other educational establishments in Bulgaria and Austria, as well as, in a number of schools and institutes in the USSR, the USA, Canada, France, Hungary and other countries, has been very promising (Figure 47).

The rapid increase of this experimental research is understandable in view of the present situation in educational science. Today, it is more than ever clear that there is a need to speed up and improve the methods of instruction and education without any additional burdening of the nervous system, and without any harmful effects. It is known from official data, that overfatigue, neurotic conditions and overt or covert didactogeny (illness or suppression of the development of children due to the teachers' tactless approach) are assuming great dimensions in schools. All this holds good on a world scale.

*Figure 47* Canadian specialists being trained to teach by the suggestopedic educational system at the Suggestology Research Institute, Sofia, 1972.

Contemporary improvements of various kinds in pedagogical methods do not solve the teaching, educational and psycho-hygienic complex in such a way as to respond to or "stand up" against the situation created by the stormy technological development. Very often, it is even forgotten that instruction is the result of the mutual effect of the individual and the environment. It is the result of communication and, at the same time, one of its requirements. We are taught and educated by the environment and for the environment in which we live and are to live. A better knowledge, therefore, of individual and communicative psychology is a fundamental pre-requisite for the proper organization of the teaching and educational process. The person undergoing instruction is no cybernetic robot. A number of unconscious, emotional and intuitive factors influence the way he masters knowledge, habits, skills and practical experience.

Psychotherapeutic studies have shown that the basic mechanism, which ensures the uncovering of the reserves of the person under-going treatment, is suggestion. It does not possess only a restricted clinical value. Suggestion plays a part in every ordinary communica-tive process. It is particularly intensified and well organized in the various arts: music, the fine arts, acting, etc. It plays its part also in teaching, though, most often, it is left unorganized and unutilized by the teacher.

The suggestopedic teaching system has more or less organized the paraconscious suggestive factors in the pedagogic, communicative, learning process. It creates emotional impetus, high motivation and the setting up of reserves in the global approach to the pupil. In reality, it is a desuggestive—suggestive teaching system. This means that it does not rely on putting "suggestive pressure" on the pupils. It frees man of the numerous overt, or unnoticeable, negative, restricting and inhibiting suggestive factors in every process of learning. This is why, in the first place it is "desuggestive" and, in the second place, "suggestive" because in no communicative process is there "void space" —the interactions are always at a nonreasoning, intuitive, emotional and more or less, unconscious level as well. It will be a different matter if, in the future, this paraconscious automatic aspect of the communicative  process is consciously self-controlled by the personality.

Instead of creating conditions for the joyous satisfaction of one of the fundamental needs of the personality—*the thirst for knowledge* —by taking into consideration the law-governed working of the cerebrum, teachers often seem to want "to teach the brain how to work".

The following are some of the features in pedagogical practice that are in contradiction to fundamental physiological and psychological law-governed regularities of the personality:

1) It is well known that there is no case where the brain functions only with its cortical structures or only with the subcortex or with one of the hemispheres either. The functional unity of the two hemispheres, and the cortical—subcortical system with the reticular formation is indissoluble. This means that in teaching practice, the emotional—motivational complex, the setup, the imaginative thinking and the logical abstraction should be simultaneously activated, in complex and indivisible unity. Frequently, however, there are the following two types of deviations from this natural pattern: (a) the instruction is addressed only to the cortical structures, or only to the left hemisphere, of the pupil who is regarded as an emotionless cybernetic machine; (b) the pupil is regarded as a psychophysiological entity, but the teaching is not global, i.e., not simultaneously cortically—subcortically directed, but is in stages, the

emotional–subcortical–reticular stage, the emotional–imaginative stage and the abstract–logical "cybernetic" stage.

2) It is well known that the analytical and synthetic activity under normal conditions take place simultaneously–there is not a purely analytical stage and a purely synthetic stage. This dialectically simultaneous and indivisible bond of the physiological process has its own psychological expression as well. It also lies at the base of cognition–from the general to the particular (as an element of the general) and, again, to the general. These natural regularities, are, however, "corrected" in pedagogical practice in one of the following variations: (a) elements are studied in isolation from the meaning in its entirety–they are made automatic by tiresome exercises and then only subsequently are connected up systematically into a whole, (b) the whole is studied without taking into consideration the constituent elements, and mistakes are made because of this. In both cases, an attempt is made to divide the natural simultaneousness of the analytical–synthetic process.

3) In every communicative process, a human being participates simultaneously at numerous conscious and unconscious levels. This natural state is utilized in mass teaching practice, most often, in one of the following variations: (a) the principle of consciousness in the learning process is formalized and turned into a fetish. The pupils have to assimilate and automate every element of the material in a strictly conscious and reasoning manner, irrespective of whether it could be mastered, to a certain degree, spontaneously and unconsciously at the first perception of the globally given lesson; (b) importance is attached only to the unconscious and intuitive capacities of the student, while the need for a conscious finalizing and creative reassessment of the material is neglected.

The organization of the process of learning in conformity with these psychophysiological law-governed principles, and with the fundamental need of the personality–"the thirst for knowledge"– and with a number of other characteristics of the normal man or woman from the standpoint of suggestology, in point of fact, represents the desuggestive–suggestive line in pedagogy. It takes into account the direction indicated in suggestology in the *general theory of communication,* because the process of learning is an organized and purposeful communicate system. Suggestopedy seeks ways to overcome the public suggestive norm. It reveals reserves through

*Figure 48* The global conscious—paraconscious interpersonal communications, given schematically. $L_1$: personality. $L_2$: personality. C: conscious activity. N: paraconscious activity. a: automated unconscious functional structures within the framework of the conscious activity.

organizing the paraconscious components as well in the conscious—unconscious complex. In this activity, it relies also on the *theory* arising out of suggestology—that of the paraconscious foundation of long-term memory, automation, intuitive—creative activation and global stimulation of the personality. In this way, it is striving to respond ever more to the natural psychophysical, law-governed regularities of the whole personality.

The fact that the psychophysiological principles underlying suggestology are taken into consideration creates prerequisites for tapping of a distinctly formed reserve complex in the student. This reserve complex which suggestopedy reveals has the following characteristic and indispensable features:

1) The system always involves tapping the reserves of the student's memory and intellectual activity, his creativity and, in general, his whole personality. There can be no suggestopedia unless the complex reserves have been tapped.

2) The process of instruction is invariably accompanied by an atmosphere that produces an effect of relaxation or, at least, of no fatigue. There is no suggestopedia when students become tired.

3) Suggestopedic training is always a pleasant experience.

4) It has a good effect from the educational point of view, in that it softens the aggressive trends in the student and helps him in the process of social adaptation.

5) It has a marked psychoprophylactic and psychotherapeutic effect in cases of functional disturbances or of functional com-

ponents of organic diseases. It could be used as psychotherapy-through-learning also.

## PRINCIPLES AND MEANS OF
## SUGGESTOPEDY

In suggestopedy the revealing of the reserve complex is realized by the simultaneous observance of the three suggestopedic principles and the simultaneous use of the three suggestopedic groups of means. Apart from taking the peculiarities of age and the pedagogical tasks into account, the principles of suggestopedy are: (1) "joy, absence of tension and concentrative psychorelaxation", (2) "unity of the conscious and the paraconscious and the integral brain activity", and (3) "the suggestive link on the level of the reserve complex."

The principle of "joy and absence of tension and concentrative psychorelaxation" requires a joyful freedom in the process of learning, in which the outward conduct of the pupils is not a simulation of concentrated attention and of good behavior. Pseudopassivity in conduct, without falling below the requirements for good behavior, does not impede the high inner motivation and positive setup in respect to the material that is studied. According to this principle, mental relaxation and "concentration without tension" are taken for granted. The emotional unjamming creates conditions for calm intellectual-mnemonic and creative activity without anxious tension, which is tiring and energy-consuming to a high degree. Most frequently, this tension comes from the lack of confidence in one's ability to understand, memorize and utilize the material given in the lesson.

Under the conventional conditions of studying, when this principle is not observed, the educational process is accompanied with a great deal of tension. This tension is a result of some unnecessary, one might say parasitic, movements of the muscles of the student's face and his whole body—as if in this way he were trying to help himself. All the muscles are strained in order to "aid the brain". The vegetative-endocrine system is in a characteristic stress state. Emotions showing anxiety and tension appear. Mental activity wanders, making all kinds of associational combinations in order to help itself. Not believing in its own capacities, the personality tries "to catch" everything that will be of help in making understanding and memorization easier. If at this moment the student finds "a "a key", he heaves a happy sigh and is relieved for one minute. At an examination, for instance, what a pitiful, tragic sight is the student in his unconscious superfluous straining to recollect the things he has learned and to motivate his answers.

If the student in his individual work, or while working with his teacher, had observed the principle of "joy, absence of tension, and concentrative psychorelaxation", he would have had confidence in his own abilities.

Observance of this principle makes "teaching students how to learn" imperative for the instructor.

It must be emphasized, however, that this principle does not mean passiveness in the sense of submission, lack of will-power and the absence of a critical attitude. It presupposes calmness, steadiness, self-confidence and trust. That means an absence of parasitic psychological and physiological activities, and well directed self-control which does not cause fatigue.

The principle of "the unity of conscious and paraconscious and integral brain activity" or of "totality" requires that teaching and learning should be organized in such a way as to utilize the conscious reactions and functions of the student, as well as his paraconscious activity. At the same time, this implies the integral and purposeful participation of the two brain hemispheres of the student and his cortex and subcortex in the process of instruction. The suppression of the unconscious functions, in the so-called consciously directed process of learning is not in compliance with the natural indissoluble dialectical bond between the conscious and paraconscious processes. This principle also calls for meaning to be given to the simultaneous total participation of the cortical and subcortical structures, as well as to analysis and synthesis. The observance of this principle brings the learning process closer to the regular natural psychological and physiological make-up of the pupil. It raises consciousness to a still higher level.

The fact that this principle is observed in suggestopedic classes does not mean that, under ordinary conditions of study, the paraconscious functions remain nonutilized. This is practically impossible. But, the suggestopedic educational system does not oppose the educational process to the natural unity of conscious and paraconscious functions. What is more, the suggestopedic system tries to find all the possible ways to receive unconsciously, retain, process and creatively utilize information, as well as to utilize all the possibilities of conscious mental activity. And all this is done in indivisible unity globally.

The principle of "the suggestive link on the level of the reserve complex" requires the reconstruction of the process of instruction in such a way that mutual relations, similar to those existing in group psychotherapeutical practice, are created. The level of the suggestive link is measured by the degree to which the reserves of the student have been tapped. The qualitatively different character of these reserves (a new type of assimilation of the material, a considerably larger scope and durability of what has been assimilated, higher creativity a positive psychohygienic and psychotherapeutic effect, useful educational influence, etc.) turns them into a reliable criterion for the realization of this principle.

The principle of "suggestive link on the level of the reserve complex" makes it imperative that the educational process should always run at the level of the reserve capacities of personality so far not utilized. This cannot be achieved, however, if the above-mentioned principles are observed independently of each other. What is more, the isolated observance of these principles does not lead to the creation of a new suggestive social norm for the student's capacities. On the contrary, the old social norm is reinforced and fixed. For instance, many good teachers create a joyful and pleasant atmosphere in the schoolroom; to all appearances it seems as though they were abiding by the first suggestopedic principle. And, indeed, one remembers these teachers; it was pleasant to work with them. One learns one's lessons a little bit better with them than with other teachers. But still they have not got so far as the suggestopedic principle of joy, absence of tension and concentrative psychorelaxation. First of all the assimilation of the material in this pleasant atmosphere, does not reach the rate of the reserve complex with the new laws governing the processes and the paradoxic positive psychohygienic effect of suggestopedic instruction. Of particular importance is the fact that these pleasant lessons, given by good-hearted teachers, do not wipe out the old limiting social suggestive norm. On the contrary, this norm is reinforced. This reinforcement of the old norm comes from the use of old didactic approaches, the absence of systematic utilization of the paraconscious factors, and of any organized efforts to direct the whole educational process to the reserve capacities of the student. In these circumstances, one gives one's smiling confirmation to the validity of the brain's limited capacities and backs up the accepted ideas that studying can only be made more pleasant. Such a smiling confirmation of the old norms, in spite of the gentle approach, can be of little advantage. Under suggestopedic conditions, joy springs not so much from the pleasant outward organization of the educational process, but rather from the easy assimilation of the material and the easy way it can be used in practice. The observance of the three principles simultaneously, in every moment of the educational process, makes learning joyful and easy and leads to the tapping of complex reserves.

These principles are realized through the indivisible unity of the three groups of suggestopedic means: (1) psychological, (2) didactic and (3) artistic.

The psychological means are one aspect of the other two groups of means, but they also possess a specific additional significance for suggestopedic instruction in primary schools. They require that teachers should have  theoretical and practical training to enable them to utilize the emotional stimulus and the peripheral perceptions. Numerous experiments have shown that considerably high percentages of peripheral perceptions are apprehended, without loss of energy, and that they extend the scope of the assimilated and automated material in the long-term memory.

Both in perceptions and in thinking, paraconscious processes accompany each conscious activity, giving it depth and perspective. This is due to a great extent, not only to their relevant, but also to their irrelevant character and to the personality's concentration at any given moment. Teachers must be familiar with the numerous variants of unconscious perceptual and thinking processes, so that they are able to utilize them in the educational process. Therefore, the psychological means for observing the unity of the three suggestopedic principles make it imperative for teachers to be theoretically and practically well-trained. In the process of "teaching students how to learn", the teacher must not only give them the respective material, but he must also teach them how to help themselves in learning it.

The didactic means call for the generalization of the meanings of the codes and the enlarging of the teaching units. The enlarged teaching unit makes it possible to get an overall view of all the material studied, while the generalization of the codes makes it possible, besides this, to overcome the seeming limitation of short-term memory. This principle demands a great deal of common sense in teaching, the avoidance of repeated exercises on details, and the gradual introduction of new subjects for study.

The generalization of the codes brings education to a meaningful level from the very beginning—and at each stage of the educational process. At the same time, it helps to reveal the general laws in which the particular laws are included. There is another important and characteristic feature of suggestopedy involved here: while attention is drawn to the consciously understandable, generalized unity and its sense, the processes of paraconscious perception and thinking process the implied elements included in the general code. For instance, in teaching foreign languages, the students' attention is directed to the whole sentence, to its meaningful communicative aspect, to its place and role in a given humorous everyday situation. At the same time, pronunciation, vocabulary and grammar remain to some extent on the second plane. They are also assimilated, but the well-trained teacher draws the students' attention to them only for a short time and then goes back quickly to the sense of the whole sentence and situation. A considerable part of these elements are learned along with the whole structure, without special attention being paid to them. It is namely in this that teachers must show their skilfulness.

For example, in teaching children to read, they do not first learn the separate letters, then later join them to form syllables, words and sentences. Nor are they taught by the so-called "whole-word" method, where no interest is shown in the letters that form the words. The children learn meaningful units—words and short sentences. They discover the letters in pictures on the second plane together with the words, as though they were doing a picture-puzzle, and then in writing lessons. Here also the experience of the teacher—suggestopedist is of particular importance.

The artistic means of suggestopedy introduce a special kind of liberating—stimulating didactic art (music, literature, acting, etc.) into the process of teaching and learning. These are not illustrative stages in the process of learning, but are built into the contents of the lesson (Figure 49).

The artistic means are used not only to create a pleasant atmosphere during the process of receiving, memorizing and understanding the basic information given in the lesson, but also to enhance the emotional impetus, the suggestive setup, attitude, motivation, expectancies. By means of the art, adapted or specially created for suggestopedic instruction, part of the material is immediately assimilated. After this, the teacher's work becomes easier and more pleasant (Figure 50).

*Figure 49* Suggestopedic didactic — aesthetic puppet show in a classroom of the experimental school in Vienna, Austria.

*Figure 50* Suggestopedic didactic — aesthetic theatre in one of the experimental schools in Bulgaria — an actor is helping the pupils with their class work.

A number of studies have been carried out in our experimental schools to check this. Table 38 shows the results obtained after didactic suggestopedic performances of little plays specially written to give new material in mathematics in the first grade.

TABLE 38    First Graders' Assimilation of Mathematical Material Taught by
Means of Art

| Number of schoolchildren | Kind of test | % of correctly solved problems |
|---|---|---|
| 1312 | Before performance | 57.00 |
| 1312 | After performance | 74.00 |

As can be seen from Table 38, immediately after the performance the children had learned a considerable amount of the material without noticing it. The difference is statistically significant ($p.> 0.001$).

In teaching other subjects, both in the case of children and adults, the didactic suggestopedic performances always give good results if they are correctly organized.

Table 39 shows the results of such performances in teaching English in one of the primary schools.

TABLE 39    Primary Schoolchildren's Assimilation of English Taught by Means of
Art

| Kind of test | Number of school children | Maximum possible correct answers | Correct Number | answers % |
|---|---|---|---|---|
| Before performance | 302 | 985 | 49 | 4.9 |
| Immediately after performance | 295 | 965 | 130 | 13.5 |
| Delayed check — the following day | 278 | 913 | 216 | 23.7 |

Table 39 shows that without making any effort (only by coming into contact with didactic art), the children assimilated part of the material. And the amount of the material they had assimilated increased the following day, without their having been able to do any homework on it, or repeat it. The suggestive law of recollection, which has already been mentioned, is manifested here. All differences are statistically significant ($p.> 0.001$).

It is of interest to point out that experimental checks, involving the solving of problems and tasks similar to those given in the performances, have shown very good results. The children not only memorize, but transfer the knowledge they acquire in these performances to other similar problems and tasks. Our investigations in the role of the concert session in language courses for adults showed, as mentioned above, that it is in this stage that the largest percent of the new material is assimilated in the long term memory.

The suggestopedic means, like the suggestopedic principles, should not be applied independently. At each stage of the educational process, one specific means may prevail, but always in close connection with the other means. Therefore, we can speak both of the unity of the three suggestopedic principles and of the unity of the three groups of means by which these principles are observed. For example, when children come into contact with only the means of didactic art, they cannot make use of the knowledge acquired in the performance of the little plays if, at the same time, the other two groups of means have not been applied in the process of instruction. If, on the other hand, only didactic means are used, the material is not assimilated and fatigue appears among the children.

On the basis of these very briefly described principles and groups of suggestopedic means, specific approaches and a definite organization of the process of instruction have been worked out. A comprehensive suggestopedic school system should comprise all subjects in the curriculum, including the technical ones, and should also take into account all the educational and psychohygienic aspects of the process of instruction and learning. Experimental work can start with those subjects which are the most difficult for children to master, beginning from the first form of the primary school. Then follows the stage for the comprehensive organization of instruction in the other subjects taught in the first form, and then for the entire primary school. Suggestopedic instruction can also be gradually organized in the upper classes of schools and in universities.

## THE SUGGESTOPEDIC FOREIGN LANGUAGE SYSTEM

Forms for the teaching of all subjects to pupils and students of all ages have been worked out on the basis of suggestology and, with the observance of the continuous unity of the three principles and the three groups of suggestopedic means. The suggestopedic system for learning foreign languages has become the most popular. It is being used with success or experimented in a number of universities, institutes and language centers in Bulgaria, the USSR, the USA, Hungary, Canada, the German Democratic Republic, Austria, France, Sweden, Colombia, and other countries.

In its development, the suggestopedic system of instruction in foreign languages has been checked experimentally with a number of variants. Here we shall dwell only very briefly on our former experiments in order to make the present state of the suggestopedic foreign language system comprehensible.

*Yoga, relaxation, autogenic training, hypnosis, sleep learning, alphawave bio-feedback, Silva Mind Control and other controlled and uncontrolled states of the consciousness and instruction in foreign languages*

Wide circles of the public and many specialists are convinced, as mentioned above, that in teaching and learning, particularly in the teaching and learning of foreign languages, the personality's reserve capacities can be revealed and brought into play only under exceptional states of the consciousness.

Objectification of these states of the consciousness is sought along various lines, in Hatha-Yoga, Raja-Yoga, Karma-Yoga and other varieties of yoga, in muscle relaxation, in autogenic training, in hypnosis, in natural sleep, in the constant state of alpha and other brain waves—controlled either by means of electronic devices or by special psychic training. The unfolding of a new type of personality with new and higher capacities for learning are sought mechanically in such special states. As already mentioned, we carried out experimental research along all these lines from yoga to alphawave biofeedback, and we found that it was not external phenomenology, behavior or the subjective accounting for something "special" on which all these systems, were based but the inner desuggestive—suggestive complex. All these techniques can lead to revealing the reserve capacities of the mind, if they carry an inner desuggestive—suggestive charge. Otherwise, they have no particular effect. In this sense, one could say that suggestopedy is built up on the basis of yoga techniques. Suggestopedy has also to a certain extent some relations to other special techniques, but only when they have been given an inner desuggestive—suggestive sense and when they create a constant setup to reserves through concentrative psychorelaxation. The question of the direct and associative effects of different yoga systems will be discussed in detail in our next book.

Since it is not the outward behavior but the inner state which is of decisive importance in revealing the reserve capacities of the personality, then in any system of instruction of a new type this should be taken into account. Thus, the external factors will acquire the meaning of a desuggestive—suggestive ritual, of a particular kind of "placebo", of necessary objectification of the inner setup, relations, motivations, needs and expectations. Therefore, all kinds of external desuggestive—suggestive rituals can be introduced into the suggestopedic educational system. But here the question immediately arises as to which ritual, which "placebo" situation will be the most suitable for pupils and students, on a mass scale, under the present conditions of life. Everyone does not believe in yoga, everyone cannot have confidence in hypnosis, everyone does not wish to apply ritual techniques and some cannot do so. Therefore a ritual "placebo" system must be chosen which will be acceptable to all people today. This means that the ritual "placebo" systems will change dynamically in accordance with the times. Their desuggestive—suggestive strength weakens with the years. New times create conditions for building up new desuggestive—suggestive ritual "placebo" systems. Thus, in their evolution, human beings will reach a point at which they will need no external ritual "placebo" objectification in order to create the desired inner state. Then suggestopedy will become autosuggestopedy on a mass scale. Only very few people can make use of autosuggestopedy at present.

On the basis of these conceptions and bearing in mind the present conditions, we have organized a desuggestive—suggestive, suggestopedic, ritually-meaningful and placebo-associative global system of teaching and learning which, in our opinion, is the most acceptable and which has the best prospects of lasting. The external factors in this system are pleasant, never irritating and acceptable from the point of view of general culture and life. At the same time, the positive effects are made use of in their conscious—paraconscious unity and also the possibility of associating them, something which is inseparable from each stimulus.

## The suggestopedic session

In every suggestologically well organized communicative process there is a leading procedure with a ritual or "placebo" meaning. The other stages are more or less subordinate to this focus. It is so, for example, in psychotherapy when, after holding some "special" session, the patient's recovery is expected. In suggestopedy, ritualization and placebo-associating are focused in the so-called suggestopedic session.

The conviction that the new material which is to be learned will be assimilated, automated and creatively processed without strain and fatigue is suggested in the weight and solemnity given to the carrying out of this session. This session must, above all, facilitate the memorizing and psychohygienic sides of teaching and learning, although these are of necessity bound up with the personalities of the teachers and students. The suggestopedic session must be adapted to the subject taught and to the age of the pupil or student. Such a session for little children is quite different from one for grown-ups. For children its functions are taken up by the didactic performance. One of the most important of the peculiar characteristics of the suggestopedic session is that it is a source of aesthetic pleasure for pupils and students.

In the numerous experimental variants, the details of the suggestopedic session have been worked out and fixed. For example, at the beginning, it was divided up into an "active" part and a " 'passive' " or "concert" part. In the active part of the session, the teacher read the new words with special three-stage intonation. In the concert part of the session, the new lexical material was read quietly, with pre-classical or classical music (specially selected as suitable and experimentally checked) playing in the background. With this variant the students used to be trained in muscle relaxation.

On the basis of the results of our experimental research, the passive part of the session, with the muscle relaxation then practiced, was dropped and only the concert part of it retained with the students in a state of mental pseudopassivity as they would be at a concert—listening serenely to the musical program and to the new material being given them to learn. This creates the same atmosphere and conditions which prevail at a musical recital. The music is no longer the background to the session, but in its effect has the normal force of music at a concert. The teacher must be able to modulate the tone and pitch of his voice to be in harmony with the particular features of the music. In this form the concert session has proved sufficient for attaining concentrative psychorelaxation even without resorting to exercises in muscle relaxation and rhythmical breathing.

The active session was dropped because it did not produce the same satisfactory results as the concert session. At the same time, it constituted a danger of insufficiently trained teachers intoning unsuitable material and creating some external conditions similar to those for inducing a light form of hypnosis, something which has to be avoided altogether in suggestopedy. For the same reasons, all monotonous sounds and utterances were eliminated from the sessions, as well as, the shading of the light in the rooms with curtains.

The recital-like character of the session has the following advantages over all other types of "special" procedures, sessions etc:

1) The session is acceptable from the point of view of the ordinary level of culture and of practical experience—in this respect resembling certain forms of art.

2) There are no procedures even slightly resembling hypnosis nor does the student feel any undesirable suggestive pressure on his personality.

3) The liberating, stimulating, desuggestive—suggestive influence of specially selected music, recitation and histrionic mastery, adapted to the requirements of suggestopedic teaching and learning, are used.

4) Ritualization of the musical—theatrical performance, with its rich possibilities of additional positive associating and revised according to the requirements of the educational process, is utilized.

5) At the same time as the pupils and students are learning, their aesthetic interests are aroused and their ethical development is improved.

6) Instruction is made pleasant, is never tiring and stimulates students' motivation.

Now the suggestopedic session in the regular foreign language courses for adults comprises two parts. In the first part, the students listen to classical music of an emotional nature; while, in the second part, they listen to classical music of a more philosophical nature.

The new material that is to be learned is read or recited by a well-trained teacher, once during the first part of the concert—solemnly, slowly, with clear diction, and once during the second part of the concert—closer to the normal way of speaking. At the same time, the teacher must, while taking into account the peculiar features of the music when reading the material and dual-planewise with intonation and with behavior, get a feeling of conviction across to the pupils or to do this the teacher must be properly trained.

The musical program for each session is chosen by our fellow-researcher E. Gateva. Its effect is experimentally checked both in the electrophysiological laboratory and in the foreign language courses. The following musical compositions are included in our programs:

1) (A) Joseph Haydn, Symphony No. 67 in F major, and No. 69 in B major. (B) Archangelo Corelli, Concerti Grossi, op. 4, 10, 11, 12.

2) (A) Joseph Haydn, Concerto for Violin and String Orchestra, No. 1 in C major, and No. 2 in G major. (B) J.S. Back, Symphony in C major, and Symphony in D major, J.C. Bach, Symphony in G minor, op. 6, No. 6, W.F. Bach, Symphony in D minor, C.P.E. Bach, Symphony No. 2 for String Orchestra.

3) (A) W.A. Mozart—Haffner Symphony, Prague Symphony, German Dances. (B) G. Handel, Concerto for Organ and Orchestra, J.S. Bach, Choral Prelude in A major, and Prelude and Fuge in G minor.

4) (A) W.A. Mozart, Concerto for Violin and Orchestra, Concert No. 7 in D major, (B) J.S. Bach—Fantasy in G major, Fantasy in C minor and Trio in D minor, Canonic Variations and Toccata.

5) (A) L.V. Beethoven, Concerto No. 5 in E flat major for Piano and Orchestra, op. 73. (B) Antonio Vivaldi, Five Concertos for Flute and Chamber Orchestra.

6) (A) L.V. Bethoven, Concerto for Violin and Orchestra in D major. (B) A. Corelli, Concerto Grosso, op. 6, No. 3, 8, 5, 9.

7) (A) P.I. Tchaikovsky, Concerto No. 1 in B flat minor for Piano and Orchestra. (B) G.F. Handel, The Water Music.

8) (A) J. Brahms, Concerto for Violin and Orchestra in D major, op. 77 (B) F. Couperin, Le Parnesse et l'Astree, Sonata in G minor, J.P. Rameau, Pieces de Clavecin No. 1, 5.

9) (A) F. Chopin, Waltzes, (B) G.F. Handel, Concerto Grosso, op. 3, No. 1, 2, 3, 5.

10) (A) W.A. Mozart, Concerto for Piano and Orchestra No. 18 in B flat major.
(B) A. Vivaldi, The Four Seasons.

The whole material for the first course comprising of 2000 lexical units, all the basic grammar of the respective foreign language, with a view to achieving a satisfactory level of reading, speaking and aural comprehension habits and skills is divided up into ten thematic dialogues with entertaining plots and sub-plots. One of these dialogues is read at each session.

In principle the sessions for the second and third courses are not essentially different from those for the first course.

## The suggestopedic foreign language system in relief

As was mentioned above, the suggestopedic foreign language system has been molded with its own definite features standing out in high relief and with the different stages focusing in the suggestopedic session. In this way, not only the direct desuggestive—suggestive factors are made use of, but also the associating that invariably accompanies them.

There are three principal phases of the suggestopedic lesson in a foreign language: the pre-session phase, the session phase and the post-session phase.

The pre-session phase takes two academic hours (90 minutes). In this phase the students are made familiar with the most important new material for the first time. The organizing of this "first encounter" with the material is of particular importance in creating a positive set-up of reserve capacities. A great part of the material is memorized during this phase; anticipation of the next phase, the session phase arouses pleasant emotions in the students. The teacher explains the new material and deciphers the thematic dialogue. In doing this, he must suggest through his behavior that the assimilation of the new material has already begun and all is pleasant and easy. Already during the deciphering, which is a stage in the giving of the primary information, the following stages should be noted: fixation, reproduction and new creative production. Thus, the setup is not created for fixed memorization of the global units of the respective language without the possibility of creatively processing them and breaking them in for use. Some of the students can repeat some of the new passages, others can use them in new variants, while others again can link them up with the material already learned.

The next phase comprises the session itself. It lasts for one academic hour (45 minutes) and with it, the day's lessons come to an end. At the beginning of the session, all conversation stops for a minute or two, and the teacher listens to the music coming from a tape-recorder. He waits and listens to several passages in order to enter into the mood of the music and then begins to read or recite the new text, his voice modulated in harmony with the musical phrases. The students follow the text in their textbooks where each lesson is translated into the mother tongue. Between the first and second part of the concert, there are several minutes of solemn silence. In some cases, even longer pauses can be given to permit the students to stir a little. Before the beginning of the second part of the concert, there are again several minutes of silence and some phrases of the music are heard before the teacher begins to read the text. Now the students close their textbooks and listen to the teacher's reading. At the end, the students silently leave the room. They are not told to do any homework on the lesson they have just had except for reading it cursorily once before going to bed, and again before getting up in the morning.

The post-session phase comprises various elaborations of the material to activate its assimilation. The primary elaboration, secondary elaboration, generalization of the material and the final etudes make up this phase.

The primary elaboration takes place the day after the session. It ensures the reproduction of the material given in the session. It comprises imitation of the text, questions and answers, reading, etc. It is of special importance that the teacher should give each student the possibility of taking part in what he knows the best. The students must be stimulated without being given a false impression that they know more than they really do. The students must be made to feel that the material will gradually emerge in their mind and that they will be able to reproduce above 90 percent of it. Already, in this phase, they may, depending on the level of the group, make a transition to the stage of creative transformation of the new material and of its use in practice. This must be done carefully and as spontaneously as possible, in order that those students who still cannot cope with the new material do not lose their self-confidence and become depressed.

The secondary elaboration takes place in the first periods of the second day, after the session. In this elaboration the material is activated, without any forcing on the part of the teacher, to such an extent that it is possible to make new combinations with it and new creative productions. The students listen to new emotionally saturated musical compositions on the tape-recorders. An extra text, a monologue, is read. The students engage in conversation on given themes, and are given small roles to play. The playing of these little scenes should take place, however, only when the students themselves agree to take the roles. The teaching and learning thus acquires sense and meaning. In the general emotional stir caused by the play-acting, the language side of the lesson is forgotten and the students use the phrases heard in the session without searching their minds for them or analysing them. After they have used the phrases, the teacher can draw attention to them for a second or two, if some mistakes are repeated. Mistakes made in conversation should not be corrected immediately, but a situation should be created in which the same words or phrases or similar ones are used by other students or by the teachers themselves. Not only in this phase, but during the whole course the students should never be made to feel embarrassed by the mistakes they make. That is why the correction of mistakes is considered one of the most important things in the art of giving suggestopedic instruction.

The generalization of the material takes place twice during the whole course. It is mainly grammatical, but the grammar is included in new texts with interesting plots.

In the middle of the course the students might have a particular kind of practical experience in speaking the language they are learning in real hotels, restaurants, the street and in other places. This is intended to encourage them by showing that they can cope in the foreign language in real-life situations.

The last day of the course is dedicated to a performance in which every student is included—the level to which he has learned the material given in the course and his own wishes being taken into consideration. The students themselves think up an interesting play in which most of the themes they have studied are included. Their acting enhances their self-confidence in speaking the foreign language. They can invite spectators to form an audience. The roles and the plot of the play are planned, but the conversation between the characters in the foreign language is done *ex tempore,* since they use the whole vocabulary learned in the course with the oral auto-matism and the mastery of the grammar acquired in the course.

The pre-session phase, the session phase and the post-session phase stand out in the basic high relief picture of the suggestopedic foreign language course. The picture is, however, enriched by a number of supplementary factors which give breadth to the high relief, and which strengthen the associating sense of ritualization and the placebo factors. These factors can be enumerated in the following way, without making a deep analysis of the psycholgocial meaning and peculiarities of each one of them:

## Preliminary psychological preparation

1) The release of information, which is restrained, scientifically written and of a noncommercial nature, in the press.

2) On would-be students' first and subsequent visits to the Institute to arrange the formalities necessary for those joining the course, they are met by members of the staff who are kindly and polite, with the right measure of restraint, never curious, but confident in their professions. They find a pleasant, easy atmosphere, without any extravagance and with proper organization of the work in the Institute.

## Psychological preparation the first day of the course

1) A test is held to check the level of the students' knowledge and to divide them up into groups according to the results of the test. One group consists of beginners and another group consists of students who know a few words or separate phrases. In the tests, care must be taken not to hurt the feelings of any of the students. Tests are not administered for the purpose of revealing features of the students' personalities about which they would not wish others to know.

2) After the students have been divided up into groups, a member of the staff reads the initial instructions to each group. These instructions contain information about the work that is going to be done in the course. It is explained to the students that, during the session, they are not to make any efforts to memorize the material, but to listen quietly to the concert. They are told to take part in the course as though it were a pleasant game of cultural occupation. They are not to force the learning process by going over the material again and again. They are to try to learn it in the way that children learn new things—without being worried about the mistakes they make at the beginning. They are reminded that they should not go in for self-

analysis during the course, but should judge the effect of the teaching by the results which will be seen the last day or even some days after the end of the course. It is explained to them that mastery of the material is not a matter of ability, but one of adaptation to the favorable climate for learning created in the course. The students are reminded that this kind of adaptation is hindered by psychotrauma during the period of the course by excessive self-analysis and disturbances in hearing, but even under any of these circumstances a considerable part of the material is mastered. The students are assured that the course has no harmful effects on their health, but just the contrary—nervous disorders are often cured by this psychotherapeutic—psychohygienic educational process.

3) Before the beginning of the course each student is given a name that is used in the language he is going to study. He is also given a new biography. In this way, the students become actors and actresses. They are forbidden to talk about their real names and professions and, further, are not to ask each other questions about themselves.

## Current psychological maintenance

1) All the staff of the Institute with whom the students come in contact should show or suggest confidence in the teachers and the method.

2) Fastidiousness in teachers' manners, dress and reactions.

3) Proper organization for the strict observance of the ritual stages of the teaching process: excellent recordings of the musical compositions, putting on the music at the proper time, beginning and ending the lessons exactly on time, the maintenance of a high cultural level in the etudes and the little plays which the students perform. Alcoholic drinks are banned in the Institute as is improper behavior and sexualization or misunderstood modernization of the etudes.

4) A solemn attitude toward the session.

5) The giving of written tests at different stages to reassure the students in regard to the progress they have made in the respective language. A tactful attitude toward poor test papers, if there are any.

6) The global presentation of the material that is to be learned, without insistently drawing attention to the different elements of which it is formed. The elements should be mastered imperceptibly in a meaningful whole in different variants, and only at the end should the elements be analyzed.

7) A tactful attitude toward mistakes by varying a student's repetition of that part of the material in which he has slipped up, or by other students' repetition of it, without anyone feeling that these are variants introduced for the purpose of correcting the mistakes.

8) Maintenance of an enthusiastic emotional tone, without overplaying it.

## Final psychological presentation

1) A final written and oral test of the knowledge, skill and habits acquired during the course.

2) The final performance of a dramatic presentation to show that the students can make use of the knowledge they have gained. The play is chosen by the students themselves, but the teacher takes care that it is in accordance with their language abilities, psychological stimulus and has is sound from the aesthetical and ethical points of view.

3) A final lecture given by the principal of the Institute to all the groups about the results achieved in the courses, about the students' future work and about the use they can make of the knowledge, skills and habits they have acquired in the Institute.

## The independent work of pupils and students

A basic requirement of the suggestopedic system of teaching and learning is that didactogeny should be avoided, even in the most insignificant forms, such as pupils' or students' fear of the difficulties that may arise in learning the material. This insignificant form of didactogeny is very common. It forces students into endless repetition and tiring memorization of meaningless component elements of the relevant parts of the text they are learning. To avoid this while in the transitional period of overcoming the old social suggestive norm, and establishing a new suggestopedic one, the independent work of both pupils and students must be carefully organized so that they do not go back to the traditional ways and frustrate the effectiveness of suggestopedic instruction itself. It cannot be taken for granted that pupils and students will work out a suggestopedic suggestive norm rapidly and easily for their own capabilities, because they are under the unceasing influence of the mass social suggestive norm which has already been accepted. At present, only very few would be able to undertake suggestopedic self-training successfully. It is, therefore, necessary that the independent work of the students should be properly organized.

At present, those students learning foreign languages by the suggestopedic system do almost no homework. They are recommended to read the new material they are given in the lessons only cursorily —for 15 or 20 minutes in the evening, before going to bed, and again in the morning as one's first task for the day, much in the way one goes over a newspaper. They should not repeat words and expressions they do not know, but only read for the purpose of gaining information. They are not recommended to read for longer periods than 15 or 20 minutes, because they will be running the risk of getting involved in analyses and repetitions. This time-restricted homework shifts the burden of acquiring the material to the class-room and this enhances the effectiveness of the system.

When individual students have more free time than the others, and they wish to make use of it to study the respective foreign language more intensively, they can be given additional recommendations as to how to work. For instance, to listen to recordings of belletristic literature or ordinary foreign-language talks. The important thing is that these recordings are not the conventional type of exercises for the repetition of lessons and for memorizing lexical and grammatical elements. They must be whole meaningful texts (not of a fragmentary nature) and, above all, interesting. It is important that no analysis and no translation of all the different elements of these recordings are made. They must be listened to for the sake of the music of the foreign speech. The meaning of the speech should be left to surface in the minds of the students, by itself, without stress and without any unpleasant efforts. In the beginning the recordings should be listened to while one is actively engaged in doing some work. Adapted reading matter can also be read in addition to listening to recordings. But even in the reading of these adapted stories, the separate words, the meaning of which may not yet be absolutely clear to the students, should not be dwelt upon. The important thing for the student is to grasp the general meaning at the beginning and, thus, be able to read a greater number of pages in a given time.

In teaching the spelling of a foreign language, the system worked out by our fellow-researcher, K. Pashmakova could be applied. She recommends the use of peripheral perceptions, as well as interesting and meaningful texts. By this we do not infringe in any way upon the general suggestopedic sense of teaching and learning but, on the contrary, make use of the unconscious factors.

It is important that, in all these cases of more intensive home-work, the principles of suggestopedy are observed. Instruction must be global. Analysis of the elements that make up a text must always be linked with the whole of the text and made only after the elements have, to a certain degree, been mastered. The unconscious processes must be made use of.

Students must study alone only when it gives them pleasure to do so.

## The suggestopedic textbook

The suggestopedic textbook must be in accordance with the principles of suggestopedy. This means that the material for each new lesson must be given in large portions and the theme of each lesson must be complete and given globally. The material must be presented in meaningful aggregates, and must be communicative. The textbook should have motivational force, and should be entertaining and interesting for the students. Its psychological structure should be given prominence and stressed, while the language problems must be "smuggled" in unobtrusively without alarming and worrying the students. The textbook must suggest how easy it is to learn the respective language. It must have the features of a particular kind of literary or literary—musical work. The ten principal lessons, included in the textbook, each complete in itself, must be governed by one single idea featuring many themes, the way it is in life. One must not feel that the material in each theme has been arranged for the purpose of instruction, in spite of the fact that some grammatical explanations are given. There must be a light-hearted story running through the material in the textbook and the plot must turn on the emotional content of the story. Traumatic themes and distasteful lexical material should be avoided. The heroes of the story must have definite character traits. Grammar should be given in natural situations, and unobtrusively. The textbook must be up to all modern requirements in regard to the choice of lexical material.

As an example of one kind of a suggestopedic foreign-language textbook (By E. Gateva), Lesson One, for beginners studying a foreign Western language (Italian) has been included here. The material given in this lesson has to be assimilated in a kind of ritual-cycle, featuring a pre-session, a session and a post-session phase (Figure 51 and Figure 52).

## THE SUGGESTOPEDIC SYSTEM FOR THE TEACHING OF READING, WRITING AND MATHEMATICS IN THE FIRST GRADE OF THE PRIMARY SCHOOL

Instruction in all subjects, for students in all age groups, can be reorganized on the basis of the principles of suggestopedy and its available means. Here we are giving a short general scheme for the teaching of reading, writing and mathematics in the first grade of the primary school. A detailed account of the suggestopedic system for primary schools will be given in another book.

### Preliminary preparation and organization

1) Teachers must be made familiar with the basic requirements for teaching according to the suggestopedic system. They must realize that it will be necessary for them, in some cases, to work off the cuff, at their first glance at the material, contrary to the conventional didactic principles. They will have to overcome their internal resistence and the influence of routine, and will have to strictly observe the new requirements. When they have gathered experience, it will then be difficult for them to revert to the old conventional ways and they will have no wish to do so.

2) The preparation of posters, which are used as teaching aids and hung on the wall, is necessary.

For the purpose of learning to read, we prepare large color pictures with scenes from the world of children, such as a picture of a bear, a stork or a kitten. The word corresponding to the picture, or a short sentence describing the meaning of the picture, is written in large typed letters under the picture. The first letter of the word is inscribed and interwoven into the picture in a semi-concealed way (Figure 53).

*Figure 51a*

*Figure 51b*

*Figure 52*

## PARTE PRIMA

"E CANTERÒ DI QUEL SECONDO REGNO
DOVE L'UMANO SPIRITO SI PURGA
E DI SALIRE AL CIEL DIVENTA DEGNO"

(Dante, Purgatorio, Canto I)

### QUADRO PRIMO

### CONOSCENZA IN AEREO

L'aeroporto di Berlino.
La famiglia Walter parte per Roma.
L'aèreo è pieno di viaggiatori.

*Giovanni Civinini:*
Scusi, signore.
E'libero questo posto?

*Il dott. Walter:*
Si, prego...
Ma che sorpresa...
Lei è il signor Civinini,
il famoso càntante
della Scala di Milano.
Lei non mi conosce.
Ma io La conosco.
Sono un amico
di Suo padre.
Suo padre è un uomo
di grande ingegno.

*G.C.:*
Lieto di conóscerla.
Con chi ho l'onore?

*Il dott. W:*
Mi chiamo Richard Wálter.
Sono mèdico,
psicoterapèuta di Berlino.

| | |
|------|-------|
| (sono | siamo |
| sei | siete |
| è | sono |
| | èssere) |

Ecco il mio biglietto
da vísita.

        *il* biglietto — *i* bigliett*i*
        *un* biglietto — *dei* biglietti)

*G. C:*
Grazie.
Ecco il mio.
Lei parla l'italiano
molto bene.

        parl-o     parl-iamo
        parl-i      parl-ate
        parl-a     pàrl-ano

                      parl-*are* 1)

        (il francese, l'inglese, il tedesco,
        lo spagnolo, il búlgaro, l'ungherese
        il russo, il greco, il giapponese . . .)

*Il dott. W:*
Grazie.
Ho studiato all'Università
di Roma.
Ho studiato insieme a Suo padre.
Signor Civinini,
Lei ha un grande successo
a Berlino.
Lo spettàcolo dell'Aida
è meraviglioso.

        *lo* spettàcolo — *gli* spettàcoli
        *uno* spettacolo — *degli* spettacoli)

*G. C.:*
Il successo non è
soltanto mio.
Canto con i miei colleghi:
Lucia Vittorini
e suo marito Giuseppe Pellico.
Ottimi cantanti.
Ottima coppia.
Un matrimònio felice.
Hanno sei bambini.

        (ho       abbiamo
        hai    avete
        ha      hanno

                   avere)

Anche loro ritòrnano.
Viàggiano in treno.
Ma si perde tanto tempo.

*Il dott. W:*
Si,
e noi abbiamo sempre fretta.
Perché?

*G. C:*
Lei ha ragione.
Chi sa perché?

*Il dott. W:*
Mi permetta di
presentarLe la mia famiglia
La signora Walter è regista.

*G. C.:*
Tanto piacere, signora.

*La signora Walter:*
Mio marito parla spesso
di Suo padre. Le piace la città di Berlino?

*G. C:*
Si, mi piace molto.
E'una bella città.

*Il dott. W:*
Posso presentarLe
la signorina Elsa,
mia figlia?
E'studentessa.
Studia canto al Conservatorio.

*G. C.:*
Parla anche Lei l'italiano?

*Elsa:*
Certamente, lo parlo.
I musicisti pàrlano l'italiano.
L'italiano non è difficile.
E'fàcile.
E'una lingua bella e sonora.
Chi vuole cantare,
l'italiano deve parlare.

*G. C.:*
Proprio cosi...

*Il dott. W.:*
Alle nostre spalle
sono seduti
i nostri figli.
Sono studenti,
sono bravi ragazzi.
Il maggiore si chiama Franz —
Francesco.
Suona pianoforte.
Il minore si chiama Emil —
Emilio.
Dipinge.

*G.C.:*
Io non sono sposato.
Ho trent'anni.

*(l'anno — gli* anni
*un* anno — *degli* anni)

Viaggio troppo.
Da cinque anni
àbito a Milano
con mia madre, con mio padre
e con mia sorella.
Sono nato a Roma.
Roma mi manca continuamente.
E'diventata proprio un museo.
Ma io ho bisogno
della sua bellezza.
Mia madre ha cinquant' anni.
Mio padre ha cinquantatré.
Mia sorella ha vent' anni.

(*la* sorella — *le* sorelle
*una* sorella — delle sorelle)

E'molto intelligente.
Assomiglia al babbo.
Studia filologia romanza.
Siete già stati in Italia?

*Il Dr:*
Dopo i miei studi
ci sono stato
alcune volte
per ragioni di servizio.
Ai congressi
ci incontriamo con Suo padre.
Molti anni fa

sono venuto a casa Sua.
Lei era bambino.
Conosco tutta la Sua famiglia.
L'anno scorso
sono stato a Roma.
L'Italia è un bel paese.
E'il piú ricco museo
d'Europa.
Adesso sono invitato
al Congresso degli psicoterapeuti.
I miei vèngono
per la prima volta.
Vogliamo fare un giro.
Un giro per l'Italia.
Vogliamo visitare
i luoghi cèlebri.

G. C.:
Quanto tempo rimanete?

Il Dr.:

*Il dott. W:*
Dieci giorni.

G. C.:
Dunque ci rivedremo.

*Il dott. W:*
Si.
Ed i Suoi fratelli?

G. C:
Gianni è ingegnere in chìmica.
Lavora in uno stabilimento industriale
a Torino.


Sua moglie è professoressa
in una scuola primaria.
Hanno quattro figlie.
Luigi è giurista.
Lavora in una ditta
commerciale.
La moglie è ragioniera
in una ditta d'importazione
e d'esprotazione
Carlo è professore
in una scuola mèdia.

Insegna lèttere.
Si è laureato recentemente.
Sua moglie è molto gióvane.
Hanno un bambino.
Vìvono a Pádova.

*La signora Walter.*
Siete una sòlida famiglia.

*Elsa:*
Signor Civinini,
quando possiamo sentirLa?

*G. C:*
Ecco il mio programma
per la pròssima settimana:
lunedì canto nella Traviata,
martedì nella Norma,
mercoledì canto nella Sonnàmbula,
giovedì non canto;
è il mio giorno di riposo.
Venerdì ho un concerto.
Avrà luogo a Roma.
Sàbato canto nel Barbiere di Siviglia.
Domènica nel Rigoletto.

*Elsa:*
Babbo,
forse il Rigoletto . . .

*Il Dr:*
Forse . . .
Ecco viene la hostess.
Ci porta qualcosa
da bere.
Avete sete?

*La hostess:*
Prego, signora,
che cosa desidera?
Una tazza di tè,
una tazza di caffè,
una tazza di caffelatte,
un bicchiere di birra
o di vino rosso o bianco,
oppure succo di frutta.
Ci sono anche:
limonata, aranciata,
spremuta d'arancio,

spremuta di limone,
gazzosa.

*La signora Walter:*
Per favore, un succo di frutta.

*La hostess:*
Prego, signora.
E Lei, signore?

*Il dott. W:*
Vorrei un caffé
senza zúcchero.

*Elsa:*
Un'aranciata, per favore.

(*l'*aranciata—*le aranciate*
*un'a*ranciata—delle aranciate)

*G. C:*
Preferisco un tè
con limone.

*Francesco:*
Vorremmo del vino rosso.

*La signora Walter:*
Ma che vergogna!
Scusi, signorina,
i ragazzi schèrzano.
Vògliono dell'acqua
minerale.

*Francesco:*
Emilio,
non siamo adulti,
noi?
Sono stufo!
Ci tràttano sempre
da bambini.
Non è vero?

*Emilio:*
Eh si!
Ma che cosa possiamo fare?

*G. C:*
Sono stupefatto!
Parlate benissimo l'italiano.
Con una corretta pronuncia.
Dove l'avete imparato?

*Elsa:*
All'Istituto
per la ricerca scientifica
di mètodi nuovi
con un sistema psicològico.
In un mese.

*G. C:*
Impossibile!

*Elsa:*
Perché no?
Lei sa il caso di Toscanini:
in un giorno
ha imparato a memoria
tutt'un'òpera.

*G. C:*
E'vero, è vero.
Vorrei imparare il tedesco.
Ho bisogno di
questa lingua.

*Il Dr:*
Sono amico del Direttore
dell'Istituto.
Quest'anno
in settembre
cominciamo un lavoro insieme.
Viene con me?

*G. C:*
Volentieri!
Mi interessa molto!
Che bell'occasione!
La ringrazio.

*Il dott. W:*
Prego!
Non c'è di che!

*Francesco:*
Sentite la música?
Chi canta?


*Elsa:*
E'la voce del signor Civinini.
Mamma,
ti voglio tanto bene!
Mamma,
tu mi aspetti sempre.
Guardo il tuo viso
un po'invecchiato.
capisco molto bene
i tuoi sacrifici,
la gioia, il dolore,
l'amor per tutti noi,
nascosto nel tuo cuore.
E cerco, cerco sempre
la strada bella e vera,
e vengo innocente
a riposàr da te . . .


Terra mia cara,
bella ed antica!
Guardo le montagne,
il cielo piú sereno,
i laghi, i fiumi,
le valli,
il mare piu azzurro—
l'ànimo agitato
trema di giòia pura.
Terra mia cara,
abbraccia con amore,
con fede e speranza
un figlio che torna!

*G. C:*
Siamo arrivati.
Ecco la mia patria.
Fra poco
siamo a Roma—
la città eterna.
Ragazzi, vedete laggiú?

(vedo      vediamo
vedi       ved—ete
ved—e     vèd—ono
              ved—ere      2)

Ecco Roma.
Fra poco viene il pullman.
Siamo all'aeroporto.
Il controllo dei passaporti.

*L'impiegato:*
Prego, signore,
il Suo passaporto.
Grazie.
Oh il passaporto non è valido!

*Il dott. W.:*
Impossibile!
Lei sbaglia.
Il mio passaporto è prorogato
per un anno.
Ecco il visto d'ingresso
e d'uscita.

*L'impiegato:*
Scusi, signore.
Tutto in règola.
Riempia, per favore,
questo mòdulo:

---

Cognome
Nome
Nome del padre
Nome della madre
Nazionalità
Professione
Luogo di nascita
Domicilio
Luogo di partenza
Denstinazione
Frontiera
Data
Firma

---

*Il doganiere:*
Di chi è questa valigia?

*Il dott. W.:*
La valigia è mia.

*Il doganiere:*
Per favore,

deve aprire.
Che cosa è questo?


*Il dott. W.:*
Un film.
Partécipo a un Congresso
di medicina a Roma.
La mia esposizione
viene acompagnata
dal film.

*Il doganiere:*
Va bene, va bene.
Porta dei regali?
Ha valuta?
Ha denaro?
Quanti soldi ha?

*Il dott. W.:*
Ho degli assegni,
ho un po'di lire.
Devo scrivere qui?

                          (devo        dobbiamo
                          devi         dovete
                          deve         dèvono
                                              dovere)


*G.C:*
Mi dispiace,
ma dobbiamo lasciarci.
Parto sùbito per Milano.

                          (parto       partiamo
                          parti        part—ite
                          parte        pàrtono
                                              part—ire      3)

Buon giorno.
Vi àuguro salute,
felicità e divertimenti.

*Il dott. W.:*
Grazie. Altrettanto.

*G.C:*
Qual è il vostro albergo?

*Il dott. W:*
Hotèl Leone.
In via Vittorio Vèneto.

*La signora Walter:*
Tanti saluti alla famiglia!

*Emilio:*
Tante belle cose!

*Francesco:*
Fra una settimana
ci rivedremo.

*Elsa:*
Buon viaggio!

*Tutti:*
ArrivederLa!

*Il dott. W.:*
Ora dobbiamo cercare
un tassi.
La città si trova
lontano da qui.

*Francesco:*
Ecco un tassi.
Scusi, è libero?

*L'autista:*
Si.
Dove?

*Il dott. W.:*
L'albergo Leone
in via

*L'autista:*
Vittorio Veneto.
Va bene.
Andiamo.
La famiglia Walter arriva al centro di Roma.
La bellezza della città impressiona.

*Il dott. W.:*
Cari miei,
respirate l'ària di Roma.

*Francesco:*
Con l'odore di benzina.

*La signora Walter:*
La civilizzazione ci porta
di tutto.

*L'autista:*
Questo è vero, signora.
Guardate il tràffico!
Senza disciplina ed órdine
non possiamo vìvere.

| (posso | possiamo |
|--------|----------|
| puoi | potete |
| può | pòssono |

potere)

Siamo arrivati.

*Il dott. W.:*
Quanto Le devo?
L'autista indica la somma, la riceve e se ne va.
La famiglia entra nell'albergo.

*Il dott. W.:*
Buona sera.
Vorrei tre càmere
con bagno.
Due a due letti,
una a un letto.

*L'albergatore:*
Le ha prenotate?
No?
Quanto tempo vuole rimanere?

| (voglio | vogliamo |
|---------|----------|
| vuoi | volete |
| vuole | vògliono |

volere)

Dieci giorni?
Dove desidera le camere?
Al primo, al secondo,
o al terzo piano?

*Il dott. W.:*
Le preferisco al secondo piano.

| (prefer — isc — o | preferiamo |
|-------------------|------------|
| prefer — isc — i | preferite |
| prefer — isc — e | prefer — isc — ono |

prefer — ire        3)

Quanto còstano le camere?

*L'albergatore:*
Ogni camera costa
40,000/quarantamila/lire.

*Il dott. W.:*
Con colazione?

*L'albergatore:*
Senza colazione.

*Il dott. W.:*
E'troppo per me.

*L'albergatore:*
Ma come mai, signore,
il nostro albergo è
di prima classe.
Vuole vedere le camere?
Il facchino viene con Lei.
Rocco, súbito!

*Il dott. W.:*
No, grazie.
Prendo le camere.


*La cameriera:*
Buona sera.
Mi chiamo Mirandolina.
Sono a vostra disposizione.
Le camere sono còmode
e tranquille.
Danno sul giardino.
Accendiamo la luce!
Guardate, tutto è nuovo:
il tappeto, le tende,
le poltrone.
Il pavimento è pulito
e lúcido.
Sul letto c'è un cuscino.
Ma nel cassettone ci sono
altri cuscini.
Ci sono anche le fèdere,
le lenzuola e le coperte.
L'armadio per i vestiti.
L'attaccapanni.
C'è uno spècchio.
Il soffitto e le pareti
della camera

sono alti.
C'è aria.
Sul tavolino ci sono
i giornali.
Sono di oggi.
Vicino alla finestra
c'è una tàvola
con alcuni libri.
Accanto al letto
c'è un comodino.
Sul comodino c'è
una lampada da notte.
Il telèfono.
Ci sono una radio
e un televisore.

*Francesco:*
Funzionano?

*La cameriera:*
Credo di si.
Sul balcone c'e
una sedia.
Nella stanza da bagno
avete tutto il necessàrio:
sul lavabo ci sono
i saponi. L'asciugamano.
Ecco la vasca e la doccia.
I rubinetti per l'àcqua
calda e fredda.
Posso aprire le finestre?

*La signora Walter:*
Grazie, grazie, signora,
Lei è molto gentile.

*La cameriera:*
Ai Suoi órdini, signora.
Buona notte!

*Elsa:*
Ho sonno.

*Il. dott. W.:*
Non avete fame?

*Elsa:*
Non ho fame.

*Francesco:*
Voglio raccontarvi
una barzelletta.
Sentite!
Rossini era un gran buongustàio.
Una dama dell'aristocrazia
lo invita a cena.
Un'altra dama gli chiede:

*La dama:*
Maestro;
non si ricorda di me?

*Rossini:*
Mi dispiace,
ma non ricordo.
Dove ci siamo visti?

*La dama:*
In casa della marchesa Rattazzi.
Lei sedeva accanto a me.
Non si ricorda?

*Rossini:*
L'ho dimenticato.

*La dama:*
Ma come è possibile?
Abbiamo mangaiato
un mgnifico pollo
alla panna.
Ricorda?

*Rossini:*
Ah, il pollo delizioso!
Ricordo benissimo . . .

*Elsa:*
Com'è bella la música
di Rossini:
"Una voce poco fa . . ."

GRAMMATICA

1. Fonetica
   L'alfabeto italiano
   Particolarità della pronuncia di alcune consonanti
   Le consonanti doppie
   L'accento
   L'apocope
   L'elisione

2. Morfologia e sintassi
   L'articolo determinativo ed indeterminativo
   Il nome: genere e numero
   I verbi ausiliari: essere ed avere
   I pronomi personali: soggetto
   Verbi regolari della I, II e III coniugazione. Presente
   Particolarità delle coniugazioni: cercare, pregare, cominciare,
                     mangiare, vincere, dipingere
   I verbi irregolari: potere, dovere, volere
   La forma negativa dei verbi
   La forma interrogativa dei verbi
   Le preposizioni semplici ed articolate
   L'articolo partitivo
   Il verbo impersonale: c'è, ci sono
   L'aggettivo
   Participio passato
   Passato prossimo

3. Lessicologia
   Presentazione
   Professione
   Famiglia
   Lingue straniere
   I giorni della settimana
   Bevande
   Paesaggio
   All'aeroporto: il controllo dei passaporti, la dogana
   All'albergo

## PATRIZIA

Vorrei raccontarvi della mia amica Patrizia.

La conoscete? No?

Patrizia è studentessa. Abita e studia a Roma. Studia violino al Conservatorio. E'una brava violinista e una brava ragazza. Non perde il suo tempo. Studia anche alcune lingue: il tedesco e il russo. Parla benissimo il francese, l'inglese e lo spagnolo. Conosce bene il greco e il latino. E'molto intelligente.

E'nata a Como. Como è una bella città vicino al lago omonimo; l'antica colonia romana, la patria dei due Plinii, di Volta . . . A Como abita suo padre con un'altra figlia e con il figlio maggiore.

La sorella di Patrizia si chiama Giulia. Ha dieci anni. Bella bambina! Il fratello maggiore si chiama Benedetto. E'medico. Un bravo psicoteraupeuta. L'altro fratello si chiama Cesare. E'professore di italiano. Abita a Napoli. Suona pianoforte e canta. E'un poeta e musicista. Scrive per il teatro d'opera. Spesso viaggia ma ritorna sempre a Napoli. Gli piace il cielo sereno, il mare azzurro e tranquillo. Ama molto anche Como. Si ricorda della montagna, del lago, dei fiumi, delle valli. Prende il treno e arriva a Como.

La sorella ed i fratelli di Patrizia assomigliano al padre. Patrizia assomiglia alla madre. Sua madre era napoletana.

segue

Ti voglio tanto bene

Mamma, ti voglio tanto bene !

Mamma, tu mi aspetti sempre...

Guardo il tuo viso un po' invecchiato, co —

nosco molto bene i tuoi sacrifici, la

gioia, il dolor, l'amor per tutti noi, na —

scosto nel tuo cuor. E cerco, cerco sempre la

strada bella e vera, e vengo innocente

a riposar da te .

## Terra mia cara

Terra mia cara, bella ed antica !

Guardo le montagne, il cielo più sereno, i

laghi, i fiumi, le valli, il mare più azzurro —

L'animo agitato trema di gioia pura .

Terra mia cara, abbraccia con amore, con

fede e speranza un figlio che torna !

## GRAMMATICA

*Quadro primo*

### FONETICA

*L'alfabeto italiano*

| | | | |
|---|---|---|---|
| A a | a | M m | emme |
| B b | bi | N n | enne |
| C c | ci | O o | o |
| D d | di | P p | pi |
| E e | e | Q q | qu |
| F f | effe | R r | erre |
| G g | gi | S s | esse |
| H h | acca | T t | ti |
| I i | i | U u | u |
| L l | elle | V v | vi/vu/ |
| | | Z z | zeta |

K, k/cappa/, X, x/ics/, Y, y/i greco/, W, w/doppia vi/ — Queste lettere si incontrano in voci non italiane.

### IN ITALIANO NON SOLO LE VOCALI TONICHE, MA ANCHE QUELLE ATONE VANNO PRONUNCIATE CON NITIDEZZA E PRECISIONE.

Le vocali atone non si dileguano mai, nè si degradano, nè sfumano. La melodia propria della lingua italiana, il fascino musicale dell'italiano è insito in quel principio di chiarezza, nettezza, purezza: stabilità di timbro di ogni vocale.

### PARTICOLARITÀ DELLA PRONUNCIA DI ALCUNE CONSONANTI

| | | |
|---|---|---|
| *c* | ce | *ce*rtamente, feli*ce*, suc*ce*sso |
| | ci | *Ci*vinini, Lu*ci*a |
| | ca | *ca*ntante, S*ca*la, domeni*ca* |
| | co | *Co*nservatorio, ec*co*, Pelli*co* |
| | cu | *cu*ore, s*cu*ola |
| | cia, cio | comin*cià*mo, sacrifi*cio*/i atona non viene pronunciata |
| | chi, che | *chi*edere, mar*che*sa |
| *g* | ge | dipin*ge*, intelli*ge*nte |
| | gi | *gi*ro, re*gi*sta |
| | ga, go, gu | ra*ga*zzo, *Ri*goletto, *gu*ardo |
| | gia, gio | viàg*gia*no, *Gio*vànni /i atona non viene pronunciata/ |
| | ghe, ghi | colle*ghe*, colle*ghi* |
| | gli | gi*gli*o, bi*gli*etto |
| | gn | si*gn*ore, inge*gn*o, monta*gn*a |
| *h* | | *h*o, *h*ai, *h*a, *h*anno, *h*ostess/h non viene pronunciata mai/ |
| *q* | qu | *qu*ando, ac*qu*a, tran*qu*illo |

| s | | a/sempre, studentessa,<br>posto, respirare<br>b/ francese, casa<br>slavo, sbagliare |
|---|---|---|
| | sce | conoscenza |
| | sci | cuscino, scientifico |
| | sca, sco, scu | Scala, preferisco, scusi |
| z | | a/ zucchero, zero<br>b/ servizio, ragazzo, scherzano |

## LE CONSONANTI DOPPIE

Babbo, ragazzo, abbracciare, repubblica

## L'ACCENTO

...:  Parole piane:

| 2  1 | 2  1 | 2  1 | 2  1 |
|---|---|---|---|
| signore, | cantante, | mare, | rosso |

2.  Parole tronche:
città, università

3.  Parole sdrucciole:

| 3  2  1 | 3  2  1 | 3  2  1 | 3  2  1 |
|---|---|---|---|
| telefono, | libero, | zucchero, | parlano |

## L'APOCOPE/ *Troncamento/*

buon giorno/buono giorno/
gran buongustaio/grande buongustaio/

## L'ELISIONE

trent' anni/trenta anni/
l'amico/

## MORFOLOGIA E SINTASSI

L'articolo determinativo e indeterminativo
Il nome: genere e numero

*Maschile*

| *Singolare* | *Plurale* |
|---|---|

1.  Nomi che terminano in—o
A/ *il/ un/* davanti a nomi che cominciano con
consonante tranne la Z.

Il/ un/ biglietto                           I /dei/ biglietti

Il quadro, il successo, il marito, il matrimonio,
il figlio, il ragazzo, il museo, il congresso, il giro,
il luogo/ i luoghi/, il giorno, il bambino.

| *Singolare* | *Plurale* |
|---|---|

b/ *lo/ uno/* davanti a nomi che cominciano con
s + consonante, ps, z

*lo/ uno/* spettacolo                              *gli/ degli/* spettacoli
lo stabilimento, lo specchio, lo psicologo, lo
zucchero

C/ *l'/ un/* davanti a nomi che cominciano con
vocale

*l'/ un/* anno                                      *gli/ degli/* anni
L'italiano, l'aeroporto, l'istituto, l'albergo/gli
alberghi/, l'amico, / gli amici/

2.  Nomi che teminano in — e
    il/ un/ padre                                  i/ dei/ padri
    il cantante, il viaggiatore, il direttore, il
    professore, lo studente, lo scrittore, l'autore

3.  Nomi che terminano in — a
    il/ un/ musicista                              i/ dei/ musicisti
    il college, il pianista, il poeta, il sistema, lo
    psicoterapeuta

4.  Nomi che terminano in consonante:
    il/ un/ film, bar                              i/ dei/ film, bar

5.  Particolarità del plurale
    *il* lenzuolo                                  *le* lenzuola
    il frutto                                      le frutta

*Femminile*

| *Singolare* | *Plurale* |
|---|---|

1.  Nomi che terminano in — a
    a/ *la/ una/* davanti a nomi che cominciano con
    consonante
    *la/ una/* sorella                             *le/ delle/* sorelle
    la strade, la famiglia, la signora, la lingua, la
    ragazza, la tazza, la sorpresa, la bellezza, la gioia,
    la valigia
    b/ *l'/ un'/* davanti a nomi che cominciano con
    vocale
    *l'/ un'/* aranciata                           le/ delle/ aranciate
    l'italiana, l'opera, l'amica/ le amiche/, l'uscita,
    l'acqua

2.  Nomi che terminano in — e
    la/ una/ madre                                 le/ delle/ madri
    la moglie, la cantante, l'importazione,
    l'occasione, la canzone, la voce, l'ungherese,
    la francese
    la scrittrice/ lo scrittore/                   le/ delle/ scrittrici

3.   Nomi che terminano in — o
la/ una/ mano                                          le mani
la radio, l'auto                                        le radio,  le auto

4.   Plurale dei nomi tronchi:
la/ una/ città                                          le/ delle/ città

# I VERBI AUSILIARI: ESSERE ED AVERE

I pronomi personali — soggetto

|  |  |  | *Essere* |
|---|---|---|---|
| 1. | /Io/ | *sono* | italiano. |
| 2. | /Tu/ | *sei* | un bambino! |
| 3. | /Egli/Lei/ | *è* | inglese. |
|  | /Ella/Lui/ | *è* | italiana. |
|  | /Lei/ | *è* | molto gentile. |
| 1. | /Noi/ | *siamo* | a Roma. |
| 2. | /Voi/ | *siete* | studenti. |
| 3. | /Essi/Loro/ | *sono* | ragazzi. |
|  | /Esse/Loro/ | sono | ragazze. |
|  | /Loro/ | sono | molto gentili. |
|  |  |  | Lei   e   Loro — forme   di cortesia |

|  |  | *Avere* |  |
|---|---|---|---|
| 1. | *Ho* | un figlio. |
| 2. | *Hai* | un fratello? |
| 3. | *Ha* | due fratelli. |
| 1. | *Abbiamo* | molti amici. |
| 2. | *Avete* | tanti libri! |
| 3. | *Hanno* | grandi successi. |

## VERBI REGOLARI DELLA I, II e III CONIUGAZIONE. PRESENTE

|  | *I coniugazione* |  | *II coniugazione* |
|---|---|---|---|
| cant—*are* | | cred—*ere* | |
| 1.  cant—*o* | cant—*iamo* | credo | cred*iamo* |
| 2.  cant-*i* | cant-ate | cred*i* | cred—ete |
| 3.  cant-a | cant-ano | cred-e | cred-ono |
| studiare | abbra*cciare* | perdere | permettere |
| presentare | pre*gare* | scrivere | pia*cere* |
| suonare | via*ggiare* | prendere | sedere |
| lavorare | ritornare | *potere* | dipingere |
| abitare | parlare | *dovere* | rivedere |
| mancare | entrare | *volere* | vivere |
| assomigliare | chiamarsi | chiedere | ricevere |
| invitare | ineressarsi | vedere | accendere |
| visitare | comin*ciare* | rima*nere* | |
| portare | laurearsi | *conoscere* | |
| scherzare | diventare | | |
| scusare | insegnare | | |
| trattare | entrare | *III coniugazione* | |
| imparare | indi*care* | | |
| ringraziare | respirare | part—*ire* | |
| aspettare | proro*gare* | | |
| guardare | partecipare | part*o* | part*iamo* |
| riposare | acompagnare | part*i* | part—ite |
| tremare | lasciare | parte | part*ono* |
| tornare | augurare | | |
| arrivare | trovare | | |
| sbagliare | impressionare | preferire | aprire |
| firmare | man*giare* | capire | sa*lire* |
| desiderare | prenotare | | *venire* |
| raccontare | costare | | sentire |
| ricordare | funzionare | | riempire |
| dimenticare | | | |
| cer*care* | | | |

## PARTICOLARITÀ DELLE CONIUGAZIONI

### *I coniugazione*

| Cer*care* |  | comin*ciare* |  |
|---|---|---|---|
| cerco | cer*chi*amo | comin*cio* | comin*ci*amo |
| cer*chi* | cercate | cominc*i* | comin*ci*ate |
| cerca | cercano | cominc*ia* | comin*ci*ano |
| pre*gare* | | man*giare* | |
| prego | pre*ghi*amo | man*gio* | man*gi*amo |
| pre*ghi* | pregate | mang*i* | man*gi*ate |
| prega | pregano | mang*ia* | mangiano |

## Il coniugazione

| Vincere | | Verbi irregolari | |
|---------|---------|----------------|---------|
| Vinco | vinciamo | *potere* | |
| vinci | vincete | posso | possiamo |
| vince | vincono | puoi | potete |
| dipingere | | può | possono |
| dipingo | dipingiamo | *volere* | |
| dipingi | dipingete | voglio | vogliamo |
| dipinge | dipingono | vuoi | volete |
| rimanere | | *vuole* | *vogliono* |
| rimango | rimaniamo | *dovere* | |
| rimani | rimanete | devo | dobbiamo |
| rimane | rimangono | devi | dovete |
| conoscere | | deve | devono |
| conosco | conosciamo | | |
| conosci | conoscete | | |
| conosce | conoscono | | |

## III conigazione

| capire | | salire | |
|--------|---------|--------|---------|
| capisco | capiamo | salgo | saliamo |
| capisci | capite | sali | salite |
| capisce | capiscono | sale | salgono |

## LA FORMA NEGATIVA DEI VERBI

Giovedi *non canto,* è il mio giorno di riposo.

## LA FORMA INTERROGATIVA DEI VERBI

Sentite la musica?

## LE PREPOSIZIONI SEMPLICI ED ARTICOLATE

*a*

Abito *a* Milano.

| | | | |
|---|---|---|---|
| a + il = al | a + i = ai | a + la = alla | a + le = alle |
| a + lo = allo | a + gli = agli | a + l' = all' | |
| a + l' = all' | | | |

Studia *al* Conservatorio.

*da*

*Da* cinque anni abito a Milano.

| | | | |
|---|---|---|---|
| da + il = dal | da + i = dai | da + la = dalla | da + le = dalle |
| da + lo = dallo | da + gli = dagli | da + l' = dall' | |
| da + l' = dall' | | | |

Vengo *dall'*aeroporto.

*di*

Sono amico *di* Suo padre.

| | | | |
|---|---|---|---|
| di + il = del | di + i = dei | di + la = della | di + le = delle |
| di + lo = dello | di + gli = degli | di + l' = dell' | |
| di + l' = dell' | | | |

Le pareti *della* camera sono alte.

*in*

Viaggiano *in* treno.

| | | | |
|---|---|---|---|
| in + il = nel | in + i = nei | in + la = nella | in + le = nelle |
| in + lo = nello | in + gli = negli | in + l' = nell' | |
| in + l' = nell' | | | |

*Nell'*armadio per i vestiti ci sono molte stampelle

*su*

*Sulla* tavola ci sono i giornali. / su + la = sulla/

*per*

Vengono *per* la prima volta.


## L'ARTICOLO PARTITIVO

Vogliono *dell'acqua* minerale.
*Non* vogliono acqua minerale.


## IL VERBO IMPERSONALE *c'è, ci sono*/ci + essere — 3 persona/

Sul letto *c'è un* cuscin*o*
Nell'armadio per i vestiti *ci sono* molte stampelle


## L'AGGETTOVO

1. Lo spettacol*o* è meraviglio*so*.
   Gli spettacol*i* sono meraviglio*si*.
   La camer*a* è comod*a* e tranquill*a*.
   Le camer*e* sono comod*e* e tranquill*e*.

2. Francesco è un ragazz*o* intelligent*e*.
   Francesco ed Emilio sono due ragazz*i* intelligent*i*.
   Elsa è una ragazz*a* intelligent*e*.
   Elsa e la sua amica sono ragazz*e* intelligent*i*.


### PARTCIPIO PASSATO

| I coniugazione | II coniugazione | III coniugazione |
|---|---|---|
| *I coniugazione* | *II coniugazione* | *III coniugazione* |
| cant — are | cred — ere | part — ire |
| cant — ato | cred — uto | part — ito |

PASSATO PROSSIMO

Ho cantato            Abbiamo cantato
Hai cantato           Avete cantato
Ha cantato            Hanno cantato

Abbiamo mangiato un magnifico pollo alla panna.

Sono partito/maschile/, partita/femminile/        Siamo partiti, — e
Sei partito, — a                                  Siete partiti, — e
E' partito, — a                                   Sono partiti, — e

Siamo arrivati.

| *Avere* | | | *Essere* | |
|---|---|---|---|---|
| ho | avuto | abbiamo | avuto | sono stato, — a | siamo stati, — e |
| hai | avuto | avete | avuto | sei stato, — a | siete stati, — e |
| ha | avuto | hanno | avuto | è stato, — a | sono stati, — e |

Hanno avuto grande successo.        Siete stati in Italia?

*Figure 53*

In mathematics, we produce mathematical posters featuring the basic laws rules and algorithms which are to be studied. Such posters can be used for the writing lessons.

3) Preparation of appropriate readers, textbooks, etc., is needed.

4) The formation of a small musical didactic theatrical ensemble (eventually for T.V. or cinema show), with whose help each new section of the curriculum, is introduced. The choice and rehearsing of the players and singers is of particular importance for carrying out this part of the lesson suggestopedically, naturally and unaffectedly.

5) There should be a division of the material into rather large, and meaningfully connected global units. The entire quantity of mathematical material for the first grade (twice larger than that given in ordinary schools), for instance, is given in five or six lessons. In the reading lessons, we begin immediately with the reading of words or short sentences together with the peripheral perceptions of the letters.

6) Special scripts and music are to be written for the didactic theatrical performance which might be filmed and video-taped. Books with pictures where the stories of the same performances are related must be prepared.

7) Familiarizing and training teachers is necessary for work with the musical form, in which part of the lesson is given. Teachers must realize the educational, as well as the direct significance (from the point of view of learning) of the musical compositions of the pre-classical and classical period chosen to accompany the delivery of the new material. They must unobtrusively turn the music on at difficult moments in the teaching and learning of new material. Teachers must be on guard against showing a formalistic attitude toward the use of music in the lessons.

8) The parents should be instructed on how they should play their role in the educational process. Parents must be clever enough to organize their children's free time properly, particularly when these children have no obligations to do homework, especially in the first half of the school year. Parents must help to encourage motivation and arouse the interest to learn in their children. If they are unable to do this, it is better not to interfere and not to insist on their children doing tiring exercises at home, but rather to urge them to utilize what they have learned at school in the practical everyday

tasks of the family—going shopping, writing letters, reading books, etc.

For example, parents are sent the following instructions:

Your child is going to be taught, in the present school year, according to a new method in which the following factors have been taken into consideration.

1) The life-long significance to the child of his (or her's) first experience of school work—the problem of the child *deriving pleasure from being taught and learning* emerges as a basic consideration. Children, freed from any possible fear of being made to learn by force, begin to like their instruction and, after this, begin to like learning things independently by themselves.

2) The delicate health of children of this age—in connection with this factor there is an absolutely basic requirement, *to decrease and then do away with the unpleasant experiences* involved in teaching and learning. It is necessary to eliminate those psychological factors which sometimes lead to nervous break-downs in children.

3) The growing avalanche of information which will confront children when they grow up—this makes it necessary that they should receive knowledge in a more systematized way. Therefore, according to the suggestopedic system, the material is given first in a more generalized form, after which we return to the separate, still unmastered elements. In this suggestopedic instruction *use is made of the leverage provided by the arts,* operas, theaters, concerts, etc. by means of which the contents of the new material is introduced. After this, the material is reviewed and elaborated on in detail.

In view of the above considerations, will you please take the following attitude toward your child:

1) In the presence of your child, avoid expressing any unfavorable opinions about the school, the teachers and the teaching methods. Make your criticism and your remarks directly to the school management.

2) When you speak about the schoolwork in the presence of the child please say how easy and pleasant it is.

3) Do not forget that your child will have no homework to do. The entire material will be assimilated in school. You, however, should show interest in what has been taught to the child. Send the child to do some of the shopping or, in other ways, show your child that he (or she) can make use of what has been learned at school. Provide him with interesting books to read, without forcing him (or her) to read them. You can also ask your child to write a letter, from time to time, to friends and relations. Always encourage your child, and if he (or she) does not know something in the lessons, show the child that the material is easy and that he (or she) is going to master it.

4) If in the second half of the school year the child is given easy tasks to do for homework, bear in mind that these are not obligatory. The child itself must have the desire to do them. Do not resort to force or threats in connection with

these tasks, but try encouragement.

5) Do not give your child any extra unpleasant and monotonous exercises.

6) Create a happy, peaceful atmosphere in your home. Take your child for hikes, give him (or her) the chance to play, and teach your child to help in the house. Generally, provide him (or her) with conditions for development outside the school life.

## Learning to read in the first grade

Learning to read in the first grade is in the following stages:

1) From the very first day of school about half of the picture posters, with the words written underneath them and the first letter of the respective words half-concealed in the pictures, are hung as decoration in the class room. The entire alphabet is given in this way and also the more difficult letter combinations. The posters are placed in the pupils field of vision. They are left hanging for two days, without the children's attention being drawn to them.

2) At the end of the second day of school, the posters are taken down and shown to the children in random order with the pictures themselves concealed and only the written words showing for the children to read. A situation for playing games is created. At first in chorus and then separately, the children have to answer the following questions: (a) Which picture was above this word (or sentence)? (b) The word (or sentence) of which picture is this? (c) What is this word (or sentence)?

3) The other half of the posters are hung in the class room for another two days. Then the teacher proceeds in the same way with them as he did with the first half. It is obligatory to realize all this in the atmosphere of a game.

4) All the words and sentences contained on the posters are written separately without the pictures. They are to be read quickly in random order by the first-grade group, first in chorus, and afterwards separately by each child.

5) The words and sentences already learned are combined in short new sentences, each with one new word. The sentences are connected in a plot, and they are read in chorus and from time to time, by individual pupils. The children are not allowed to read

separate letters or syllables. Only the whole word is read, or the whole sentence. However, the teacher does suggest in passing, that the words are composed of letters, yet one does not stop to dwell on the letters when reading. Here, too, the teacher goes on to the quick reading of slides and quick-reading contexts are held.

6) Next is the didactic opera or theatrical performance, usually filmed or videotaped. A part of the words already learned, and also some of the new words, are given in the performance as a way of unravelling the most interesting parts of the plot. All the children join in the chorus and thus "help" the actors who suggest that reading is pleasant and easy. The same performance comprises some mathematical material. Note that the previous day a book with illustrations containing the play of the same performance was read by the pupils.

7) Small songs and poems already learnt by heart by the children and made up primarily of words already familiar and of a pleasant nature are sung or read in chorus and individually. The children must follow the place in the text with their first finger even when the word is unknown to them. Note that the whole of the above described stages takes about ten days.

8) The reading of the first entertaining book—the suggestopedic primer, specially worked out on the basis of the picture posters and containing mainly words already known.

9) The reading of other booklets, adapted to the level of knowledge of the children and containing both familiar and unfamiliar words, is the next stage. The reading is in chorus, but the teacher stops from time to time and waits for the children to continue alone. Sometimes the teacher only lowers his voice, and then raises it again as soon as he notices that the children need his support. The texts should be short, emotional and rhythmical. The speed of the reading should increase gradually, but steadily. The aim is to teach the children how to read quickly, fusing the short words with the long ones and avoiding breaking the words up into syllables. At given moments, the chorus reading is switched to individual reading. Each text is read, at the most, only twice. Thus, the pupils are prevented from memorizing it. After they have read the text, the children re-tell, very briefly, what they have read in order to avoid mechanical reading. There should be no reading of texts without a plot and with-

out a positive emotional quality.

After reading the beginners' series of booklets, with texts adjusted to the children's capability, we pass on to reading suitable booklets available in the book shops. The aim is to read in chorus and individually *as many books as possible.* The children's attention is not kept fixed on one book for any length of time and the teacher keeps going on quickly to the next one.

Conditions are created for bringing more *variety into the repetition* by the continual introduction of more and new material for reading. Those pupils who are already well advanced can be left to do quiet individual reading of more difficult booklets, the contents of which they can narrate afterwards to the class. Meantime, the class continue to read one new book after another in chorus. A transition is gradually made to increasingly expressive and artistic reading.

*General survey:* The method here described for learning to read has, at first glance, features in common with the method for learning whole words. However, this is only outwardly, in the external phenomenological similarity. We can list a number of features in which the method for learning to read differs essentially from this method. Primarily, the suggestopedic system for learning to read differs from the method for learning whole words in the unity of the three principles of teaching and learning. In the former method, the following more essential differentiating traits should be noted:

a) The pooling of the material in words and short sentences in the suggestopedy is always harmonized with the psychological and artistic means of expression.

b) The whole word or sentence is learned, to a large degree, peripherally and without worry or strain for the pupils, and without any waste of time. It is presented to them by means of the posters, which serve as decoration for the room without attention being drawn to them, and by the reading or singing of memorized passages and and by opera or theatrical performances specially prepared for the purpose.

c) The pupils do not dwell for any appreciable length of time on one and the same short sentences to change only a word here and there. They pass on very quickly to new texts and booklets.

d) The pupils assimilate the word as a whole, but it is cursorily suggested to them that it be composed of letters. The initial letters of the words are incorporated in the posters as a hidden element of the pictures. The visual–auditory analysis goes to the second plane simultaneously with the cognitive stimulus of the first plane, the word or short sentence as a unit full of meaning.

e) The synchronous group reading, as a stage in suggestopedic instruction, with its chanting features, rhythm and accelerated tempo, and with the "conducting" of the children by the teacher occasionally modulating his voice and speaking in a low tone, is of a suggestopedic nature and adds to the naturalness of the method.

In a word, the suggestopedic system for learning to read is a natural method which, in many respects, is similar to the processes by which small children learn to speak. Children learn to read several times quicker by this method than by the other method used at present. This also suggests that there are very essential differences involved.

## Learning to write in the first grade

Learning to write by the suggestopedic system has also been brought up to a meaningful level by introducing global didactic units and by observing the unity of the three principles and three groups of suggestopedic means. In the performance of little theatrical scenes, difficulties in writing are not neglected. The plan for one writing lesson taken in one period is as follows: (1) The teacher writes a short meaningful, emotional sentence on the blackboard leaving some space between the letters and the words. (2) The teacher makes a brief analysis of its contents and structure — words, letters and capital letters. (3) The pupils write down the whole sentence in their notebooks. (4) The teacher checks the independent work of the pupils, points out the mistakes and makes them write out the incorrectly written words and letters again—but only once. (5) Then the pupils write out the whole sentence again. (6) After this, they write the same sentence as it is dictated to them. (7) Then another sentence with the same words is dictated to the pupils and written down. (8) Gradually, they go on to more complicated texts and dictations.
Note: Teachers should be careful to see that the pupils do not find

the writing lessons tiresome. Writing material should be included in in the theatrical performances. Pleasant texts should be given for copying and the musical accompaniment should be turned on often.

## Teaching mathematics in the first grade

In teaching mathematics to pupils in the first grade, one should seek to give the new material globally, as well as, to find a link with the other subjects. In drawing and manual work, for example, it is possible to introduce, in an unobtrusive way, a number of things the pupils have learned in their lessons in mathematics. In this way, the children will begin to feel that a knowledge of mathematics is indispensable and, at the same time, extremely interesting. Such links between mathematics and physical culture and all other subjects can easily be found. For example, in physical culture, the children can count themselves, or certain numbers of children can be added to a game or taken out of it. The links with the other subjects should be sought unobtrusively and in a captivating way, so that the children do not feel they are engaged in mathematical exercises.

The mathematical material for the first grade comprises everything that is in the official curriculum for the first and second grades of the other schools. A part of the material for third grade is also included. The whole material is divided up, according to its functions, into six themes. Each theme is studied in the following four stages:

*First stage:* The most essential of the new themes are first given in theatrical, operatic or recital-like scenes. The performances of these shows are prepared in advance by the actors and actresses of the suggestopedic didactic theatre or is videotaped. Some of the most essential examples of the respective mathematical theme are skilfully built into the plot of each play. The plays must be interesting for the children and must not make them feel it is being used for mathematical exercises. The mathematical examples must not weigh on the performance and hinder its normal fascinating development.

These examples must come into operation at the most thrilling emotional moments of the performance, as the form for the means of the denouement. The children in the audience must gradually be drawn into the play in the course of the performance. Thus, they imperceptibly become actors and actresses in the play and often show creative initiative which improves the performance. An illustrated booklet containing the story of the performance has been read the previous day.

At this stage, and before beginning each new theme, posters which depict the most essential problems must be hung on the classroom walls. By analogy, whole sections of mathematical problems can be solved from these posters. Teachers should, however, pay no attention to these posters; they should hang there on the walls as decoration for the classroom. It has been proved that such material is assimilated with more lasting results and without loss of effort and time.

*Second stage:*  The following day (in one period in the classroom) the children re-tell the contents of the play or even re-play some passages, never failing to mention the didactic problem included in it as the means of unravelling the plot. Then an extra song is sung or a poem is learned by heart—the song or the poem containing an essential variant of the mathematical example given in the performance.

*Third stage:*  The following day (in two periods in the classroom) the whole theme is given in a generalized way. The lesson begins with going over the plot of the theatrical performance and the didactic songs and poems. Following this the teacher goes over to didactic games. The material, which is large in volume, is all subject to one and the same functional principle, which must be pointed out to the children. For example, it must be explained to the children that when we add 6 to 7, we add it in the same way as we add 16 to 7, or 46 to 7, or 136 to 7, and so on.

*Fourth stage:*  In the next few days (one period per day), there follows the consolidation of the material taught, deepening the children's knowledge and solving creative tasks. Short control tests are given periodically to see the degree to which the material has been mastered and what extra help is necessary for the different pupils.

The teacher goes on to the next theme only when the control tests show that the pupils have mastered, on an average, 70 or 75 percent of the material.

Of essential importance is the ability of the teacher to suggest to the pupils, through his conduct, that the material is extremely easy to master, and to create a bright, pleasant atmosphere in the classroom. Homework is not given, because it suggests that there are many difficulties to master and because, through homework, parents are inclined to force their children to learn.

If a child on his or her own initiative wants to solve mathematical tasks at home and then show them to the teacher, the child should be encouraged, provided that no one insists on his or her doing such tasks every day, except in those cases when he or she expresses a wish to do so.

Introduction to the material during the first year should take place imperceptibly and in a manner that is pleasant for the children. Parents should be instructed to send their children shopping, and to ask for an exact account of the change they bring back after paying for their purchases. In general, all cases in which the children's knowledge acquired at school can be practically applied must be made use of by the parents. The children, however, should not ever think that this is a form of testing their knowledge.

The mistakes which the children make at first should be very tactfully corrected, sometimes imperceptibly, or they should even be overlooked. Stress should be laid on the correct solving of problems, these should be underlined and encouraged.

Children must periodically be taken "sightseeing" to institutes which are interesting to them. Here they can see for themselves how important and interesting it is to study mathematics. These visits should take place at the very beginning of the school year, so that positive motivation can be triggered off at once. Contact with the workers in such institutes must be for the purpose of refracting the mathematical work done there through the prism of the child's world-vision and within the framework of the children's abilities in mathematics.

The problems that the children are given to solve should not be formally molded, only for the sake of the mathematical material itself. In their verbal shaping, there should always be settings which are interesting and thrilling for children's mental make up. Thus the child must be interested in the solution of the problem itself. For instance, if there are several soccer fans in the class, some *real figures* can be taken in respect to goals and scores and members of the teams and, on this basis, carry out a mathematical check up which would stir the fans of the different teams. In this way, a multitude of mathematical tasks can be invented.

The material is increased on the basis of analogy. At the same time, due regard is paid to the requirements for uniting opposite operations. With the expansion of codes and methodical units, the requirements of the didactic means of suggestopedy are duly observed and, at the same time, the meaningfulness is enhanced. This helps to further the motivation of the pupils.

Strict differentiation of the means, the different stages, the themes and the subjects leads to their being brought into opposition. This makes the instruction less effective. In teaching first graders mathematics, it is necessary that unceasing internal integration is achieved in the following directions:

1) *Integration of the means.* The psychological, didactic and artistic sides of the suggestopedic means of instruction should always go hand in hand. It is not right, at certain times, to pay attention only to the didactic means and, at others, only to the artistic ones, or again, in a third case, only to the psychological ones. At every moment of suggestopedic instruction, use is made of the whole complex of these means. This is regardless of the fact that, in some stages, prominence is given, for example, to the artistic or the didactic sides. If, in the first stage, the stress falls only on the pleasure derived from the performance and the didactic material is left as only a formally fulfilled obligation, then this stage becomes self-purposive. It has little significance for the whole process and is unable to play a sufficiently positive role in assisting the learning of the new material. Similarly, if in the third stage the stress is laid only on strict instruction, the effect of the artistic means is lost and the teaching and learning acquires a conventional nature.

2) *Integration of the different stages.* The four teaching stages should, in the subject matter, be a continuation of one another. Elements of one stage should be contained, to a lesser degree, in the next one. Essential elements of the first and second stages should be contained in the third stage and, at the same time, a transition to the fourth stage should be made possible. The teacher should begin with the story, the performance and the song, then switch over to the didactic material; and then, again and again, go back to the play, to art and to the emotions. These elements also should not be missing in the fourth stage, no matter how strong is the tendency to make it a dry review and fixation of the material taught.

3) *Integration of the themes.* The separate themes should not be linked together, just for the sake of transition. It is indicated in each theme that it contains the themes taken before, and the prerequisites are created for the next one. Thus, for example, the study of multi-

plication should not remain isolated in the first theme. It can be illustrated, enriched and more thoroughly mastered by giving the children a variety of examples taken from the next themes. Similarly, geometrical material is imperceptibly introduced, in the very first theme, in the form of illustrations that are easily understood by the children. While teaching the children the composition of numbers which forms the second theme, a natural link can be found with addition and subtraction which are given in the third theme. Moreover, addition should be compared with multiplication while addition and subtraction, like multiplication and division, should always be taken together for the sake of comparing one with the other. The generalized laws are then expressed by using letters. Therefore, every moment of instruction in mathematics gives meaning to all previous examples and creates the prerequisites for the next ones.

4) *Integration of the subjects.* Integration also must be realized in regard to the other subjects—reading, writing, manual work, drawing, physical education and singing. In teaching each one of these subjects, we can introduce elements of mathematics in a natural way, as in everyday life.

Comprehensive integration in teaching reveals the maturity and experience of a teacher. It does not cancel out the tasks set for the respective study period, but links what is being studied with real life. In this way, the suggestopedic teaching of mathematics becomes a really global instruction system. The link between school knowledge and the family lies in this globality and the channelling of this knowledge to social necessities.

All this should create joy in learning because a multitude of depressing psychic factors are overcome. The basic need of the human personality—the unquenchable *thirst for information,* is satisfied.

## THE RESULTS OF SUGGESTOPEDIC INSTRUCTION

The results of suggestopedic instruction in teaching different subjects have been published in a number of papers on the problems of suggestopedy and reported at conferences and symposia in Sofia (1971), Moscow (1974), Ottawa (1974), Los Angeles (1975), and

Washington, D.C. (1975) (Figure 54).

The experience accumulated so far shows that steady results, identical in the different countries, can be expected when the suggestoedic system of teaching and learning has been properly organized.

The very important accompanying effects of a psychohygienic, a psychotherapeutic and a cultural nature will not be discussed here. We shall dwell briefly only on the immediate educational possibilities of suggestopedy.

*Results of the suggestopedic foreign language system of teaching*

There can be different variants of the suggestopedic foreign language system, from courses with several lessons a week, to courses of whole days' "immersion" in the suggestopedic foreign language atmosphere. The leading factor is not the number of lessons, but the psychological organization of the process of instruction. The most widely spread variant is the one-month course—24 working days with four lessons a day, or 96 lessons in the whole course without obligatory homework. In the time when the students have no suggestopedic lessons, they go to work. In the suggestopedic courses with all-day "immersion", the material given in the 96 lessons in 24 working days is taught and learned in 10 days. In other courses, the same material is taught in lessons given every other day or every two days. In such courses, the process of teaching and learning, though very pleasant and equally efficient, lasts respectively longer. The same holds good for suggestopedic courses, both in universities and schools, where there are no possibilities of changing the curriculum to introduce an intensified form of foreign language instruction. Under such conditions the process of instruction can be prolonged to cover a whole academic year. However, the volume of the material taught and assimilated will be much larger than the volume usually taught and assimilated in this period of time. All the characteristic features of the suggestopedic system of instruction will be present in the prolonged course, a fact of great importance from the point of view of psychohygiene and education.

If we take the 24 days' foreign language course with four lessons a day as the basic pattern, the following results can be expected: (1) The students assimilate, on average, more than 90 percent of the vocabulary which comprises 2000 lexical units per course; (2) More than 60 percent of the new vocabulary is used actively and fluently in everyday conversation and the rest of the vocabulary is known at translation level; (3) The students speak within the framework of the whole essential grammar; (4) Any text can be read; (5) The students can write, although making some mistakes; (6) The students make some mistakes in speaking, but this does not hinder the communication; (7) Pronunciation is satisfactory; (8) The students are not afraid of talking to foreigners who speak the same language; (9) The students are eager to continue studying the same foreign language and, if possible, in the same way.

This also is true for beginners who have never learned the foreign language before. It stands to reason that in teaching students who have some preliminary idea of the language, the results will be much better. The assimilation of the new material in the following second and third course takes place approximately at the same speed.

If we compare the average number of words per lesson (according to official data), given according to the different methods of teaching foreign languages, we obtain the data shown in Table 40.

TABLE 40    Data on Language Units per Lessons in Different Methods

| Methods | Duration of course in number of lessons | Number of lexical units given in the course | Number of students in a group | Average number of words per lesson |
|---|---|---|---|---|
| Audiovisual | 270 (first course) | 1500 | 8 — 12 | 5.55 |
| Audiolingual | 500 (total) | 3500 | 8 — 12 | 7.00 |
| Conventional | 840 (total) | 4500 | 8 — 10 | 5.35 |
| Suggestopedic system | 96 (first course) | 2000 | 12 | 20.80 |

The data given in Table 40 show that on an average four times more new words are given per lesson in suggestopedic instruction than in instruction by other methods. It is exceptionally important to point out that these words are not only given but they are assimilated in class along with the corresponding grammar, phonetics, reading, etc. One great advantage of the suggestopedic system is the absence of obligatory homework.

*Effectiveness of the suggestopedic teaching of reading to the first grade*

Experimental work was organized in an experimental and a control school in Sofia, in schools in the villages of Dragalevts (experimental), and in Simeonovo (control), with approximately identical conditions as regards the number of pupils and their social composition.

On the second school day, the initial level of reading of every pupil of the experimental (122nd) school and the control (139th) school in Sofia were recorded on tape. In that school year, the classes in the experimental school were divided up, according to the level of the children's preliminary skill and knowledge in reading. This homogenizing of the classes facilitated the simultaneous development of all the children in the same class. For instance, in the Class 1—c, 65.62 percent of the children could read freely, while the other children read by pronouncing the words in syllables. This created favorable conditions for passing on immediately to second-grade material in the Bulgarian language. Only 6 percent of the children in this group could not read, but they were admitted into it on the insistence of their parents. When somewhat more attention was paid to them, they caught up quickly with the other children.

In Class 1-a, however, none of the children could read. This enhanced the value of the work of the teachers, because there were no children "feeling bored". The level of the children of the Class 1-b fell in between the levels of the other two classes.

It is necessary to point out here that it was clear to the parents and the entire teaching staff that the children were not divided up according to their intellectual abilities, but only on the basis of the standard of their preliminary skill in reading.

In the control school, the children were left, as is usual in mass practice, in heterogenous groupings.

At the end of the school year, the individual final level was again taken and recorded on tape. The final results of these studies are given in Table 41.

As can be seen from this table, the average percentage for the experimental pupils and the control pupils at the final level favor the experimental ones. It must be taken into consideration, however,

TABLE 41   Initial and Final Levels of Reading in the First-Grade Classes of the 122nd (Experimental) and the 139th (Control) School

| School | Class | Type of control test | Number of pupils | Did not know the letters | Knew the letters | Could spell | Could read in syllables | Could read word by word | Read freely |
|---|---|---|---|---|---|---|---|---|---|
| | | | | % | % | % | % | % | % |
| | I-a | Initial 17.9.73 | 34 | 23.53% | 52.94% | 17.65% | 5.88% | — | — |
| | | Final 21.5.74 | 33 | — | — | — | — | 18.18 | 81.82 |
| 122nd (experimental) | I-b | Initial 17.9.73 | 36 | — | — | 19.44 | 77.78 | — | 2.78 |
| | | Final 21.V.74 | 38 | — | — | — | — | 3.57 | 96.43 |
| | I-c | Initial 17.9.73 | 32 | — | 6.25 | — | 28.13 | — | 65.62 |
| | | Final 21.V.74 | 27 | — | — | — | — | 3.70 | 96.30 |
| | Avge. % | Initial | 102 | 7.84 | 19.61 | 12.74 | 38.24 | — | 21.57 |
| | | Final | 88 | — | — | — | — | 9.09 | 90.91 |
| | I-a | Initial 18.9.73 | 24 | 25.00 | 33.33 | 12.50 | 12.50 | — | 16.67 |
| | | Initial 17.5.74 | 23 | — | — | — | — | 34.78 | 65.22 |
| 139th (control) | I-b | Initial 18.9.73 | 26 | 11.54 | 30.77 | 19.22 | 34.62 | — | 3.85 |
| | | Final 17.5.74 | 24 | — | — | — | — | 41.67 | 58.33 |
| | Avge. % | Initial | 50 | 18.00 | 32.00 | 16.00 | 24.00 | — | 10.00 |
| | | Final | 47 | — | — | — | — | 38.30 | 61.70 |

that 90.91 percent of the pupils in the experimental schools could not only read freely, but also had a considerable advantage over the other children because they had already read a number of books—something which could be assumed only in the case of 61.70 percent of the control pupils ($p < 0.001$).

As the average percentages at the initial level of the experimental group were slightly better than the initial level of the control group, we made a comparison between the control group with the two classes of the experimental school, which at the initial level had low standards of knowledge and skill. Their average percentage at the initial level proved even lower than the average percentage at the initial level of the control group. Of the experimental pupils, 1.43 percent read freely and of the controls, 10 percent. In the other indices, the figures are more varied and more difficult to assess. The final level of the experimental group, however, shows an average, percentage of 88.53 percent for those "reading freely", while in the control group it is 61.70 percent ($p<0.001$) (See Table 42).

TABLE 42    *Input and Output Levels of Reading in the First-Grade Classes of the 122nd (Experimental) and the 139th (Control) School*

| School | Class | Type of control test | Number of pupils | Did not know the letters % | Knew the letters % | Could spell % | Could read in syllables % | Could read word by word % | Read freely % |
|---|---|---|---|---|---|---|---|---|---|
| | | Input 17.9.73 | 34 | 23.53 | 52.94 | 17.65 | 5.88 | — | — |
| | I-a | Output 21.5.74 | 33 | — | — | — | — | 18.18 | 81.82 |
| 122nd (experimental) | I-b | Input 17.9.73 | 36 | — | — | 19.44 | 77.78 | — | 2.78 |
| | | Output 21.V.74 | 28 | — | — | — | — | 3.57 | 96.43 |
| | Avge % | Input | 70 | 11.43 | 25.71 | 18.57 | 42.86 | — | 1.43 |
| | | Output | 61 | — | — | — | — | 11.47 | 88.53 |
| | I-a | Input 18.9.73 | 24 | 25.00 | 33.33 | 12.50 | 12.50 | 12.50 | — |
| 139th (control) | | Output 17.5.74 | 23 | — | — | — | — | 34.78 | 65.22 |
| | I-b | Input 18.9.73 | 26 | 11.54 | 30.77 | 19.22 | 34.62 | — | 3.85 |
| | | Output 17.5.74 | 24 | — | — | — | — | 41.67 | 58.33 |
| | Avge. % | Input | 50 | 18.00 | 32.00 | 16.00 | 24.00 | — | 10.00 |
| | | Output | 47 | — | — | — | — | 38'30 | 61.70 |

In order to see more clearly what happened to the children who could not read when they were admitted to the school, we separated them, both from the experimental and the control schools and thus obtained the data of Table 43. From this table it is perfectly clear that these children ended the school year with a considerable lead in proficiency over the children in the experimental group. In the experimental group 75 percent of the children were able to read freely, as compared with 45 percent in the control group ($p<0.05$).

*TABLE 43    Initial and Final Reading Levels of Pupils Without Preliminary Knowledge at the 122nd (Experimental) and the 139th (Control) School*

| School | Group | Type of control test | No. of pupils | Did not know the letters % | Knew some letters % | Read word by word % | Read freely % |
|--------|-------|---------------------|---------------|-----------|------------|-----------|--------|
| 122nd (experimental) | 1st | Initial 17/9/73 | 26 | 30.77 | 69.23 | — | — |
| | | Final 21/5/74 | 24 | — | — | 25.00 | 75.00 |
| 139th | | Initial | 25 | 36.00 | 64.00 | — | — |
| | | Final | 21 | — | — | 55.00 | 45.00 |

Since it could have been argued that the children in the experimental school read better, but that it was mechanical reading and that they did not understand the text, we held a control test at the end of the year to check their reading of a text and their understanding of the contents of what they had read. In this research we took for comparison the most backward experimental class at the initial level, Class I-a, and all the children in the control classes. Table 42 shows the considerable difference at the initial level between Class I-a of the experimental school and the average percentages of the control school. Class I-a had an initial level of 23.53 percent of those who could not tell the letters and 52.94 percent of those who knew individual letters. The percentages in the control classes were 18 and 32 percent respectively, including 10 percent of the children who read easily. Despite these adverse initial positions at the input levels, the output level for mental reading and for the re-telling of the story produced the results given in Table 44.

It can be seen that the experimental pupils read the text more quickly and with a better retelling.

The data on the results of reading in the two village schools are similar: the experimental (50th) school and the control (64th) school.

Table 44    Mental Reading and Retelling the Contents at the End of the 1973/1974 Academic Year

| School | Class | No of pupils | Good retelling of the text read mentally | | Understanding of the contents along the main lines | | Average time of the pupil reading the text in secs. |
|---|---|---|---|---|---|---|---|
| | | | No. of pupils | % | No. of pupils | % | |
| 122nd. (experi-mental) | I-a | 30 | 20 | 66.67 | 10 | 33.33 | 31.37 |
| 139th (control) | I-a | 23 | 11 | 47.83 | 12 | 52.17 | 32.43 |
| | I-b | 21 | 11 | 52.38 | 10 | 47.62 | 40.76 |
| Average | | 44 | 22 | 50.00 | 22 | 50.00 | 36.41 |

The results achieved in reading, mathematics and other subjects which had been checked by a number of commissions made the Ministry of Education adopt a resolution for extending the school experiment beginning with the 1975/76 academic year. The Institute was given 16 experimental schools with a total of 1500 first graders.

146 specialists and researchers were in charge of the pedagogical and medical control of these schools. These specialists came from different institutions, viz., Sofia University, the Higher Medical Institutes in Sofia, Pleven and Plovdiv, the Educational Research Institute, psychoneurological dispensaries of different towns, the Ministry of Education itself etc. The Suggestology Research Institute was mainly in charge of the methodological purity of the experiment.

By the end of the school year the data concerning the pupils' health were more favorable in the experimental than in the control schools. The sociometric investigations showed a considerably better psychological microclimate in the experimental schools. The results in reading (obtained under conditions of five-day week and no homework) were as follows: For 99 lessons the pupils in the experimental schools assimilated 91.5 percent of the material envisaged for two academic years while those in the control schools (with six-day week and regular homework) assimilated 79.5 percent of the material envisaged for one academic year.

For 99 lessons the pupils of the experimental schools assimilated a material which in the ordinary school is envisaged to be covered in 334 lessons.

The following academic years the first graders achieved the same good results in reading, and these results have been repeatedly corroborated. There remain some methodological and organizational problems to be solved now.

*Effectiveness of the suggestopedic teaching of mathematics to the first grade*

The suggestopedic teaching of mathematics to the first grade meets all the requirements for the development of mathematical thinking in children, while the program covers a considerably greater amount of material than the one envisaged by the Ministry of Education. The instruction and learning of the material was carried out without the children having to do homework.

In the 1972/1973 academic year, the pupils took the material for the first-grade and the greater part of that for the second-grade in one school year, with a smaller number of hours set aside for the study of mathematics than those planned by the ministry.

The commission of experts, appointed by the principal of the school found, as early as March 13, 1973, that

. . . the material that had been studied had been well assimilated and was more than adequate for completing the school year of the first-grade.

Of the problems chosen and given by the commission for solving, 78 percent were solved by the children. At the end of the year, the first graders' test in second-grade mathematics showed that 66 percent of the examples and 64 percent of the problems had been solved.

The question most often raised in that year was whether the children were acquiring lasting knowledge in mathematics. For this reason control tests of the same material were made in the experimental and the control school before and after the winter holidays. The information in Table 45 gives the end results. Whereas, the experimental groups both before and after the holidays solved 72 percent of the problems, the control groups solved 65 percent before and 36 percent after the holidays ($p < 0.001$).

The data on the initial and final level (1973/74 academic year) in the experimental (122nd) school in comparison with the control

TABLE 45    *Retention of the Material Taught in Mathematics After the Winter Holidays in the First Grade — 1972/1973 School Year*

| School | Type of control test | Time | % of correctly solved problems |
|---|---|---|---|
| 122nd (experimental) | Addition and subtraction with decimal transition up to 20 | Before holidays | 72 |
| | | After holidays | 72 |
| 139th (control) | Addition and subtraction with decimal transition up to 20 | Before holidays | 65 |
| | | After holidays | 36 |

TABLE 46    *Input and Output Levels in Mathematics in the First Grade of the 122nd (Experimental) and the 139th (Control) School*

| Test | School | Type of control test | Control date | Problems solved | |
|---|---|---|---|---|---|
| | | | | Number of pupils | % |
| Addition and subtraction with and without decimal transition up to 20 | 122nd | Initial | 17/9/73 | 100 | 36.13 |
| | 139th | Initial | 18/9/73 | 52 | 33.17 |
| Control test of all the first-grade material: addition and subtraction with and without decimal transition | 122nd | Final | 31/1/74 | 77 | 86.64 |
| | 139th | Final | 13/5/74 | 45 | 63.18 |
| Control test of second-grade material: addition and subtraction up to 1000, multiplication and division up to 100 | 122nd | Final | 22/5/74 | 87 | 77.39 |
| | 139th | Final | 14/5/74 | 46 | 5.28 |

(139th) school can be seen in Table 46. It is clear that already, on January 31, the pupils in the experimental school solved 86.64 percent, and in the control school 63.18 percent of the problems taken from second-grade material were solved in the experimental group, while in the control group the pupils solved about 5.28 percent of this material ($p<0.001$).

In the 50th school the experiment began on November 12, 1973. At the initial level, the data obtained from the experiment in it were more unfavorable than the data obtained in the control school. At the final level, this time with second-grade material, the pupils in the experimental group solved 65.83 percent of the problems, whereas, in the test on the same second-grade material, the pupils in the control school succeeded in solving only 1.04 percent of the problems ($p<0.001$) (See Table 47).

*TABLE 47     Initial and Final Levels of the First-grade Classes of the 50th (Experimental) and the 64th (Control) School in the 1973/74 School Year*

| School | Type of control test | Test on material studied: addition and subtraction with decimal transition up to 20 | | Test on second-grade material(addition and subtraction up to 1000: multiplication and division up to 100) | |
|---|---|---|---|---|---|
| | | Number of pupils | % correctly solved problems | Number of pupils | % correctly solved problems |
| 50th (experimental) | Input: 12/11/73 Output: 8/5/74 | 48 — | 29.00 — | — 40 | — 65.83 |
| 64th (control) | Input: 17/11/73 Output: 9/5/74 | 32 — | 33.98 — | — 32 | — 1.04 |

The results obtained are of significance because of the complexity of the problems solved and also because of the durability of the assimilation of the material and the creative character of the problems solved. Above all, one must stress the fact that the children entered the sphere of mathematics with pleasure and high motivation. It can be expected that this will have a particularly good influence on their further development in this sphere.

The results obtained in mathematics were further corroborated by the large scale school experiment already mentioned. In the 1975/76 academic year 1500 first graders from the 16 experimental schools (with five-day week and no homework) assimilated 80.3 percent of the material envisaged for the first grade. For the same period the control first graders assimilated 63.3 percent of the same material. The experimental first graders assimilated 81 percent of the material envisaged for the second grade, while the control second graders themselves assimilated 66.4 percent of this material. Or, in other words, for 100 lessons the pupils from the experimental schools have assimilated a material in mathematics which according to the curriculum should be covered in 289 lessons (without taking into account the additional time necessary for doing homework), and what is more they have assimilated this material on a better level than that of the control pupils.

The results obtained in mathematics in the 1975/76 year have been corroborated by the results achieved in the following academic years.

*Results of the suggestopedic teaching of all subjects taught in the tenth grade of high school*

In the school year 1970/71, a representative form of tenth grade students was taught by the suggestopedic system in the Suggestology Research Institute in Sofia. The curriculum had to be in accordance with all the requirements of the program of the Ministry of Education. On the basis of the principles and means of the suggestopedic system, a concrete program for teaching all subjects was worked out (Figure 55).

As a result of the instruction carried out in this way, all the medical, psychohygienic and educational effects of suggestopedy were established.

The material given in the lessons was assimilated under the following conditions: (1) The daily program was reduced in time; (2) No homework was given; (3) The school year was shortened by two months. The results were reported at the First International Suggestology Symposium (1971), in Varna, Bulgaria.

Good educational and psychohygienic results were obtained in the suggestopedic teaching of the different subjects studied in high schools, universities, and in qualification courses for adults both in Bulgaria and abroad. It should once more be pointed out that good results depend on the good organization of suggestopedic instruction.

*Possible mistakes in work with suggestopedy*

The surprising effectiveness and the seeming simplicity of the suggestopedic educational system attract many nonspecialists, speculators
and specialists with dubious motives. This is easy to understand and
it throws no discredit on suggestopedy itself, if suggestopedy is
officially established on the necessary, professionally protected
level. It is a similar case with psychotherapy. Today it is an important and basic medical discipline, in spite of the fact that there are
different variants in which it is put to dubious use or misused
by people who have nothing to do with medical science.

Even now, when suggestopedy is beginning to be discussed and
conditions are being created for people to eventually become
acquainted with it, an unsound interest is in most cases evinced—a
sort of "gold rush"—and one can hear the most incredible
descriptions and explanations of it.

On the one hand, the information on suggestopedy available is
still insufficient and, on the other, it is difficult to understand and
accept information which is in contradiction to the social suggestive norm and these facts give rise to a wrong interpretation of it
and a wrong attitude toward it. If the basic principles and means
of suggestopedy are properly understood and accepted by those who
organize suggestopedic work, this will lead to corollaries on a large
scale and of great importance for social development. The influence
of suggestopedy would go far beyond the framework of the educational systems.

The question of just who will be pioneers is also of importance.
It is not only good specialists in teaching the respective subjects
that are needed, but people who are suitable in every respect.

With the basic difficulties of suggestopedy in mind, we shall
here dwell briefly on some of the mistakes that are, or could be, made
in the present and future use of suggestopedy in general practice.

*Eclectic combination of different educational systems*

One often comes across specialists who for different reasons and
from different standpoints may approve suggestopedy, but who
begin to seek purely mechanical ways of combining it with other
educational systems. They fail to see that suggestopedy is built on
specific principles which are indivisibly united and which are realized
in indivisible unity with the means of suggestopedy in order to tap

the reserve complex of the student. Each system has its own merits within the framework of its own principles, goals and tasks. Phenomenological and mechanical combination, without taking into consideration the psychological principles and specific tasks of suggestopedy, most often leads to the lowering of its effectiveness. It is important to stress that the lowering of effectiveness does not involve only the assimilation of the material taught, but suggestopedy's positive educational effects and its favorable medical ones as well without which we cannot speak of a tapped reserve complex which is the aim of suggestopedy. Any eclectic combination of suggestopedy with other methods brings a risk of lower effectiveness and of fatigue in the students.

## Selecting the concert program

There may be different opinions about the music of the concerts included in suggestopedic instruction and attempts may be made to change the pieces for other ones. The music included in the suggestopedic course is checked experimentally in the laboratories of the Institute. It answers many requirements not only in regard to the assimilation of the material but also in regard to its role as an educational, cultural and psychohygienic factor. The fact that some students do not like the particular music that is played is not of essential importance. The effect of the music is not very closely connected with the taste of the listeners. Therefore, we do not recommend the changing of the music without making a profound preliminary study of its educational effect, its psychohygienic significance and its aesthetic qualities, to see if they are positive and lasting and, of course, the possibility of its facilitating the sound and creative assimilation of the material under joyful conditions and in the absence of tension.

## The place of games and sketches

There is also a danger of some teachers turning the suggestopedic process of teaching and learning into a time only for playing pleasant games and performing theatrical sketches. Making the external effect of the games and sketches an aim in itself may cause the effectiveness of suggestopedy to decrease. At the same time, since the group comprises different kinds of people, there is a danger of their establishing unsound and not quite refined relations. Therefore, the games and the sketches should be only one element in the lessons and they should, above all, be under the constant control of the teacher. When using different techniques the teacher should keep to the basic requirements for highly cultured organization of the instruction.

## The teacher's prestige

Suggestopedy, let us emphasize again, requires that the teacher should have a great deal of prestige. This does not mean that he should act in an overbearing manner with his students. The teacher's prestige should be understood as a readiness to share his experience and knowledge with his students, and he should set an example to be followed. This kind of prestige should create conditions for emotional deblockage; it should free the students of any oppressive factors and stimulate their progress. The teacher's relations with the students should be cultural and refined. He should teach them how to learn and how to educate themselves. Only in this way can the teacher make his global, positive, creative and stimulating influence felt.

It is very important for the teacher to strictly observe proper ritualization in the structure and organization of the process of instruction. Teachers who underrate the degree to which the strictness of the ritual must be observed may get poor results in their teaching and hinder the general development of suggestopedy.

*General conclusion:* An understanding of the nature of suggestopedic principles and means in their indivisible unity, their strict observance, devotion to the cause of suggestopedy and awareness of its importance for the future ensure that mistakes are avoided and that the suggestopedic system is not discredited. Each teacher must bear in mind that any discrediting of his suggestopedic work is not confined only to his group, but has much wider repercussion.

## CONCLUSION

It is hardly necessary to point to all the prospects that suggestology and suggestopedy offer. The fact that suggestopedy is becoming popular all over the world is a confirmation of its importance. We consider that the main question now is how to go further. In our opinion, the most important procedure is to continue organizing the work in this field under the management of state and international institutions and with the participation of trained specialists from institutes of high repute, otherwise programs will be implemented on nonprofessional amateur levels. We believe that the good results which suggestology and suggestopedy achieve will be made use of by those countries and organizations which understand the importance of these questions and that they will now create conditions for the proper development of suggestopedy.

# Bibliography - English

Adler, A., *Uber Den Nervosen Charakter.* Wiesbaden, 1912.
Adler, A., *Praxis und Theorie der Individualpsychologie.* München, 1924.
Adler, A., *Menschenkenntnis.* Leipzig, 1927.
Adley, W.R. and D.F. Lindsley, On the role of subthalamic area in the maintenance of brain-stem reticular excitability. *Exp tl. Neurol,* 1959, **1, 407—426.**
Agnew, H.W., W.B. Webbs and R.L. Williams, The effects of stage four sleep deprivation. *EEG Clin. Neurophysiol,* 1964, **117,** 68—70.
Allen, D.T., Die Individualtherapie in der grossen Gruppe. *Abstracta in Group Psychotherapy, 4th International Congress.* Vienna, 1968, 247.
Allport, G., *Personality: a physiological interpretation,* New York, 1937.
Allport, G., *The Nature of Personality.* New York, 1950.
Ancona, L., Azione psicodisletica e azione psicosintetica di farmaci psicoattivi (LDS 25). *Medicina Psicosomatica,* 1968, **13,** No. 1-2, 137—141.
Antonelli, F., Sperimentazione clinica del fluoretione su pazienti neurodistonici e psicosomatici. *Medicina Psicosomatica,* 1968, *13,* No. 1-2, 142—147.
Arduini, A. and M.G. Arduini, Effect of drugs and metabolic alterations on brain-stem arousal mechanisms. *J. Pharmacol. Exper. Ther.,* 1954, **110,** 76—85.
Arnold, M.B., On the mechanism of suggestion and hypnosis. *J. Abnorm. Soc. Psychol.,* 1964, **41,** 107—128.
As, A., The recovery of forgotten language knowledge through hypnotic age regression' A case report, *Amer. J. Clin. Hyp.,* 1962, **5,** 24—29.
Asch, S.F., The doctrine of suggestion, prestige and imitation in social psychology. *Psychol. Reviews,* 1948, **55,** 250—276.
Asch, S.E., *Social Psychology.* New York, Prentice Hall, 1952.
Asch, S.E., Studies of independence and conformity I. A minority of one against a unanimous majority. *Psychological monographs, general and applied,* 1956, **70,** 9.
Aschley, W.R., R.S. Harper and D.L. Runyon, The perceived size of coins in normal and hypnotically induced economic states, *Amer. J. Psychol.,* 1951, **64,** 564—572.
Aserinsky, F. and N. Kleitman, Regularly occurring periods of eye motility, and concomitant phenomena during sleep, *Science,* 1953,**118,** 273—274.
Astruck, P., Uber psychische Beeinflussung der Herztätigkeit und Atmung in der Hypnose. *München. Med. Wchnschr.,* 1922, 173.
Aveling, F. and H.L. Hargreaves, Suggestibility with and without prestige in children. *British J. Psychol.,* 1921—22, **12,** 53—75.
Azam, E., *Hypnotisme.* Paris, 1887.

Babinsky, J.F. and J. Froment, *Hysteria or pithiatism.* University of London Press, 1918, 11, 161.

Baldissera, F. and M. Mancia, Spinal inhibition during deep sleep. *Cortico-subcortical relationship in sensory regulation.* Havana, 1965, 17 — 18.

Barber, T.X., Hypnotic age regression' A critical review. *Psychosom. Med.,* 1962, **24**, 286 — 299.

Barber, T.X. and P.D. Parker, Hypnosis task-motivating instructions, and learning performance. *J. Abnorm. Psychol.,* 1964, **69**, 499 — 504.

Barber, T.X., The effects of "hypnosis" on learning and recall: Methodological critique. *J. Clin. Psychol.,* 1965-a, **21**, 19 — 25.

Barber, T.X., Experimental analyses of "hypnotic" behavior, A review of recent empirical findings. *J. Abnorm. Psychol.,* 1965 — a, **70**, 132 — 154.

Barber, T.X., N.P. Spanos and G.F. Chaves, *Hypnosis, Imagination and Human Potentialities.* New York, 1974.

Barker, W. and Bergwin, S, Brain wave patterns during hypnosis, hypnotic sleep and normal sleep. *Arch. Neurol. Psychiat.,* 1949, **62**, 412 — 420.

Barlett, F.C., *Remembering A Study in Experimental and Social Psychology.* Cambridge Univ. Press, 1932.

Barra, E. and A.C. Moraes Passos. The Rorscharch test in a case of age regression under hypnosis. *Boletim da divisao nacional do Brasil da Sociedade Internacional de Hypnose Clinica e Experimental,* 1960, **2**, No. 1-2.

Baruk, H., *Psychoses et Nevroses.* Paris, 1958.

Baudouin, Ch., *Suggestion and Autosuggestion.* London, 1922 (I-ère Edit. Française. 1920).

Bsaglia, F., The therapeutic community as psychiatric ideology. Psychodramatis et communitatis therapeuticae. *Congressus Internationalis tertius. Abstracta.* Praga, 1968, Vo. 6.

Benton, A.L. and A. Bandura, "Primary" and "secondary" suggestibility. *J. Abnorm. and Soc. Psychol.,* 1953, **48**, 336 — 340.

Berenda, R.W., *The Influence of the group on the Judgements of Children,* New York, Columbia Univ., 1950.

Berger, E. and L. Loewy, Les yeux pendant le sommeil. *J. d'anat. et Physiol.,* 1898, **34**, 364.

Berger, R., Tonus of extrinsic laryngeal muscles during sleep and dreaming. *Science,* 1961, **134**, 840.

Berillons, E., *Hypnotisme Expérimental' La Dualité cérbrale et l'indépendance Fonctionnelle des deux Hémisphères cérébraux.* Paris, 1884.

Berlucchi, G., L. Maffei, G. Moruzzi and P. Strata, Mécanismes hypnogènes du tronc de l'encéphale antagonistes du système réticulaire activateur. *Neurophysiologie des etats de sommeit.* Paris, 1965, 89, 10.1.

Bernheim, H., *De la Suggestion et de ses Applications á la Thérapeutique.* Paris, 1888.

Bernheim, H., *Neue Studien über Hypnotismus. Suggestion und Psychotherapie.* (Paris, 1890) Ubersetzung S. Freud, Leipzig und Wien, 1892.

Bernheim, H., *Hypnotisme et suggestion.* Paris, 1910, 3-ème édition.

Berreman, J.V. and E.R. Hilgard, The effects of personal heterosuggestion and two forms of autosuggestion upon postural movement. *J. Soc. Psychol.,* 1936, **7**, 289 — 300.

Beron, P., *Panépistème Electrostatique.* Maillet-Bachelier, Paris, 1861, Vol. I.

743—744.

Bertin, E., Sommeil, Diet, Encycl. de med., **181, v. 10,** 262—276.

Bertone, C., G. Leone and L. Pacilli, Correlazioni fra techniche analgesiche e metodische di preparazione al parto. *Atti del lo Congresso Nazionale della Societa Italiana di Psicoprofilassi ostetrica.* Roma, 1967-a, 22.

Bertone, C. and L. Pacilli, Orientamenti ed attifudini dell ostetrico pratico sul problema della psicoprofilassi. *Atti del 1° Congresso Nazionale della Societa Italiana di Psicoprofilassi ostetrica.* Roma, 1967-b, 25.

Bier, W., Beitrag zur Beeinflussung des Kreislaufes durch psychische Vorgänge. *Ztschr. f. Klin. Med.,* 1930, **113, 762.**

Binet, A. and V. Henri, *La Fatigue Intellectuelle.* Paris, 1898.

Binet, A., *La Suggestibilité.* Paris, 1900.

Binswanger, L., *Nervenarzt,* 1951, **1,** 35—40.

Blake, H. and R.W. Gerard, Brain potentials during sleep. *Amer. J. Physiol.,* 1937, **119,** 692—703.

Blake, H., R.W. Gerard and N. Kleitman, Factors influencing brain potentials during sleep. *J. Neurophysiol.,* 1939, **2,** I, 48—60.

Bleuler, E., *Textbook of psychiatry.* New York, Macmillan, 1924, 10, 162, 188.

Bonvallet, M. and P. Dell, Contrôle bulbaire du système activateur, *Neurophysiologie des états de sommeil.* Paris, 1965, 133—148.

Bostroem, A., Handbuch der Geisteskramkheiten, Bd. 11. Allgemeine Teil 11, 1936.

Bour, P., Psychodrama und Körperbewusstsein. *Abstracts in Group Psychotherapy, IV International Congress.* Vienna, 1968, 293.

Bradley, P.B., The effect of some drugs on the electrical activity of the brain in the cat. *EEG & Clin. Neurophysiol.,* 1953, **5,** 471.

Braid, J., *Neurophynologie.* London, 1883, Paris, 1884.

Bramwell, J. M., *Hypnotism.* Wm. Rider and Son, 1913.

Braun, E., *Hdb. d. Geisteskrank.,* 1928, **5,** 112—226.

Bremer, F., Cerveau "isolé" et physiologie du sommeil. *C.R. Soc. de Biol.,* 1935, **118,** 1235—1241.

Bremer, F., L'activité cérébrale au cours du sommeil et de la narcose. *Bull. Acad. Roy. Med.,* 1937, **4,** 68—90.

Bremer, F. and C. Terzuolo, Nouvelles recherches sur le processus du réveil. *Arch. Int. Physiol.,* 1953, **61,** 86—90.

Bremer, F. and C. Terzuolo, Contribution à l'étude des mécanismes physiologiques du maintien de l'activité vigile du cerveau. Intersection de la formation réticulée et de l'écorce cérébrale dans le processus du réveil. *Arch. Int. Physiol.,* 1954, **62,** 157—178.

Breuer, J. and S. Freud, *Studien über Hysterie.* Leipzig-Wien, 1909.

Brind, A.B., Psychodrama and the pivotal concept of spontaneity. *Psychodramatis et communitatis therapeuticae. Congressus Internationalis tertius, Abstracta.* Praga, 1968, 9.

Brind, A.B. and N. Brind, Psychodrama und der Gruppenprozess. *Abstracts in Group Psychotherapy, IV International Congress,* Vienna, 1968, 289.

Brissemoret, A. and A. Joanin, Sur l'action narcotique des carbures alycycliques et sur les propriétés somnifères de la cholestèrine. *C. R. Soc. de Biol.,* 1911, **71, 715.**

Brown-Sequard, Le sommeil. *Arch. de Physiol.,* 1889, **1,** 323.

Brown, W., Individual and sex difference in suggestibility. *University of California Publiction in Psychology,* 1916, **2,** 291—430.

Bruner, J.S. and C.C. Goodman, Value and need as organizing factors in perception. *J. Abnorm. Soc. Psychol.*, 1947, **42**, 33 — 44.

Buchwald, N.A., *et al.* The "caudate" spindle. *EEG & Clin. Neurophysiol.*, 1961, **13**, 509 — 518, 519 — 524, 525 — 530, 531 — 537.

Bülow, K., Respiration during sleep. *Neurophysiologie des Etats de Sommeil.* Paris, 1965, 535 — 552.

Bunge, G., *Lehrbuch der Physiologie*, 1901, Bd. I, 241 — 258.

Burgess, T.O., Hypnodontia — Hypnosis as applied to dentistry. *Brit. Jr. Med. Hypnotism*, 1952, **3**, 62.

Burgess, T.O., Hypnosis in dentistry. *Experimental Hypnosis.* Edit. by Leslie M. LeCron, New York, 1956, 322 — 351, Paris, *A. Maloine*, 1909 — 1911, 1, **XV** 86, **II** 993.

Burlingham, D.T., *Psychoanal. Quart.*, 1935, **4**, 69.

Burnett, C. T., Splitting the mind. *Psychol. Monogr.*, 1925, **34**, No. 2.

Cajal, S.R., Hystologie du système nerveux de l'homme et des vértébrées. Paris, *A. Maloine*, 1909 — 1911, **1**, XV, 986, 993.

Calderaro, G., Metodo di allenamento ad intervalli "Dry fire"; Tipo di allenamento psicosomatico nello sport del tiro a segno. *Atti del Simposio Internazionale di Medicina Psicosomatica sportiva.* Roma, 1967, 33 — 39.

Carmichael, L., H.P. Hogan and A.A. Walter, An experiment study of the effect of language on the reproduction of visually perceived forms. *J. Exptl. Psychol.*, 1932, **15**, 73 — 86.

Cartaz, A., Le centre du sommeil. *La nature*, 1901, **1**, 115.

Carter, L.F. and K. Schooler, Value, need and other factors in perception. *Psychol. Review*, 1949, **56**, 200 — 207.

Caruso, I.A., Das Microsoziale Modell in der Neurose und in der Neurosentherapie (Abatracta), *Psychodramatis et communitatis therapeuticae; Congressus Internationalis tertius.* Praga, 1968, 12.

Casler, L., The improvement of clairvoyance scores by means of hypnotic suggestion. *J. Parapsychol.*, 1962, **26**, 77 — 87.

Caspers, H., Shifts of the cortical steady potential during various stages of sleep. *Neurophysiologie des états de sommeil.* Paris, 1965, 213 — 224.

Charcot, J.M., *Sur les Divers Etats Nerveux Déterminés par l'hypnotisation chez les Hystériques.* Paris, 1882.

Charcot, J.M., *Leçons du mardi à la Salpétrière.* Paris, 1888, 1889.

Chapman, R.M.H. and R. Bragdon, Evoked responses to numerical and non-numerical visual stimuli while problem solving, *Nature*, 1964, 203.

Chari, C.T.K., Quantum physics and parapsychology. *J. Parapsychol.*, 1956, **20**, 166 — 183.

Chari, C.T.K., Remarks on some statistical and information theoritic models for ESP. *J. Amer. Soc. Psychic. Res.*, 1966-a, **60**, No. 2.

Chari, C.T.K., *Quantephysik und Parapsychologie* Darmstadt, 1966-b.

Chari, C.T.K., On information-theoretic approaches to ESP. *Int. J. Parapsychol.*, 1966-c, Vol. VIII, No 4, 533.

Chari, C.T.K., ESP and "semantic information" *J. Amer. Soc. Psychic. Res.*, 1967, **61**, No. 1.

Chauvin, R., ESP and size target symbols. *J. Parapsychol.*, 1961, **25**, 185 — 189.

Chertok. L., *L'hypnose.* Paris. 1965.

Chevreul, A., *Personal communication.* 1954.

Cirrincione, A., Psichiatria, Medicina Psicosomatica e igiene mentale. *Atti del Simposio Internazionale di Medicina Psicosomatica Militare*. Roma, 1967, 7.

Clemente, C.D. and M.B. Sterman. *Cortical Synchronization and Sleep Patterns in Acute Restrained and Chronic Behaving Cats Induced by Basal Forebrain Stimulation EEG & Clin. Neurophysiol.* Suppl. 24, 1963, 172—187.

Coffin, T.E., Some condition of suggestion and suggestibility: a study of certain attitudinal and situational factors, influencing the process of suggestion. *Psychol. Monogr.*, 1941, 4, 53.

Cohn, R.C., Training von Gruppentherapeuten in interaktionellen Seminaren (Abstracta). In' *Group Psychotherapy, IV International Congress.* Vienna, 1968, 271.

Cox, W.E., Three-tier placement P.K. *J. Parapsychol.*, 1959, 23, 19—29.

Cook, S.W. and R.E. Harris, The verbal conditioning of the galvanic skin reflex. *J. Exptl. Psychol.*, 1937, 21, No. 3.

Cramer, H. and E. Wittkower, Affective Kreislaufveranderungen unter besonderer Berucksichtigung der Herzgrösse. *Klin. Wchnschr.*, 1930, 9, 1290.

Cratty, B.J., Individual motives and group performance. *Atti del Simposio Internazionale di Medicina Psicosomatica sportiva.* Roma, 1967, 75—76.

Damasiewicz, M., St. Grochmal and A. Pachalski, Les facteurs psychosomatiques au cours d'une réeducation sportive des handicapes physiques. *Atti del Simposio Internazionale di Medicina Psicosomatica sportiva.* Roma, 1967, 77—79.

Danilovic, B., Les mécanismes obsessionnels dans la conduite de la cure psycho-dramatique. *Psychodramatis te communitatis therapeuticae, Congressus Internationalis tertius.* Praga, 1968, 14, Abstracta.

Darwin, E., *Zoonomia.* London, 1801, 1, Sect. 18.

Das, J.P., R. Rath and R.S. Das, Understanding versus suggestion in the judgement of literary passages, *J. Abnorm. Soc. Psychol.*, 1955, 51, 624—628.

Das, J.P., Learning and recall under hypnosis and in the waking state, A comparison. *Arch. Gen. Psychiat.*, 1961, 6, 517—521.

Davis, H., P.A. Davis, A.L. Loomis, E.N. Harvey and G. Hobart, Human brain potentials during the onset of sleep. *J. Neurophysiol.*, 1938, II, 24—38.

Delhaugne, F. and K. Hansen, Die suggestive Beeinflussung der Magenund Pankreas-sekretion in der Hypnose. *Deutsche Arch. f. Klin. Med.*, 1927, 157, 20.

Dement, W. and N. Kleitman, Cyclic variations in EEG during sleep and their relation to eye movements, body motility, and dreaming. *EEG & Clin. Neurophysiol.*, 1957, 9, 679—690.

Dement, W. and N. Kleitman, Relation of eye movements during sleep to dream activity Objective method for study of dreaming. *J. Exptl. Psychol.*, 1957-b, 53, 339.

Dement, W., The occurrence of low voltage, fast electroencephalogram patterns during behavioral sleep in the cat. *EEG & Clin. Neurophysiol.*, 1958, 10, 2, 291—296.

Dement, W., Studies on the function of rapid eye movements (paradoxical) sleep in human subjects. *Neurophysiologie des états de sommeil.* Paris, 1965, 571—611.

Demole, V., Pharmacodynamie et centres du sommeil. Mise en évidence des composantes automatiques neurovégétatives basiliaires et volitionnelles corticales. *Revue Neurologique,* 1927, I, 850—852.

Derbolowsky, U. Die Drei-Satz-Technic beim Rollenspiel in der gruppenzentrierten analytischen Psychotherapie. *Psychodramatis therapeuticae, Congresus*

*Internationalis tertius.* Praga, 1968.

Derbolowsky, G., Bemächtigungstherapie als Möglichkeit analytischen Arbeitens bei klinisch durchgeführten Psychotherapiengruppen. (Abstracta). In' *Group Psychotherapy, 4th International Congress.* Vienna, 1968, 245.

Deutsch, F. and E. Kauf, Uber die Ursachen der Kreislaufänderungen bei Muskelarbeit. *Ztschr. f. d. Ges. Exper. Med.,* 1923, **34,** 71.

Deutsch, H., *Imago,* 1926, 12, 418.

Deutsch, M. and H.B. Gerhard, A study of normative and informational social influences upon individual judgement. *J. Abnorm. Soc. Psychol.,* 1955, **51,** 629 — 636.

Devaux, E., Anesthésie chloroformique et cédémie. *C.R. Soc. de Biol.,* 1910, **69,** 416.

Dick, A.V., Hypnosis in Psychotherapy, *BRIT: Med. J.,* 1940, 1, 865.

Dolezal, V. and M. Hausner, Metacommunitative analysis of Psychodrama. *Psychodramatis et communitatis therapeuticae; Congressus Internationalis tertius.* Praga, 1968, 18.

Dorcus, R.M., Recall under hypnosis of amnestic events. *Int. J. Clin. Exptl. Hypnosis,* 1960, **7,** 57 — 61.

Dubois, R., Le centre du sommeil. *C.R. Soc. de Biol.,* 1901, 229.

Dubois, R., *Les psychonévroses et leur traitement normal.* Paris, 1904.

Dubois, R., Hydration. *Dict. de Physiol.* (Richet), 1909, **8,** 674 — 705.

Duke, J.D., Intercorrelational status of suggestibility tests and hypnotizability. *Psychological Record,* 1964, **14,** 71 — 80.

Duneker, K., Experimental modifications of children's food preferences through social suggestion. *J. Abnorm. Soc. Psychol.,* 1938, **83,** 489 — 507.

Economo, C.V., Der Schlaf als Lokalisationsproblem. *Jahreskurse für ärztliche Fortbildung,* 1929, Heft 5, 31 — 46.

Ehrewald, J., *Télépathy and Medical Psychology.* New York, 1948.

Eisele, G. and J.J. Higgins, Hypnosis in educational and moral problems. *Amer. J. Clin. Hypnosis,* 1962, **4,** 259 — 263.

Eisenbud, J., *Psychiat. Quart.,* 1948, **I,** 21.

Eisenbud, J., Psychiatric contributions to parapsychology. *J. Parapsychol.,* 1949, **13,** 247 — 262.

Elefteery, D.G., Heranziehung von Personal und Verwaltung zu Gruppenpsychotherapie und Psychodrama (Abstracta). *Group Psychotherapy, IV International Congress.* Vienna, 1968, 291.

Enke-Kerschland, E., Untersuchungen zur Gruppendiagnostik in der psychosomatischen Klinik. *XVIth International Congress of Applied Psychology,* Amsterdam, 1968, Reviews, Abstracts, Working Groups, 197.

Erickson, M.H. and L. Kubie, The successful treatment of a case of acute hysterical depression by return under hypnosis to a critical phase of childhood. *Psychoanal. Quart.,* 1941, **10,** 592 — 609.

Erickson, M.H., Deep hypnosis and its induction. *Experimental Hypnosis.* New York, 1956.

Estabrooks, G.H., A contribution to experimental telepathy. *Bulletin, Boston S.P.R.,* 1927, **5,** 1 — 30.

Evans, F.J., Suggestibility in the normal waking state. *Psychological Bulletin,* 1967, **67,** No. 2, 114 — 129.

Evarts, E.V., Photically evoked response in visual cortex units during sleep and waking

*J. Neurophysiol.*, 1963, **26**, 2, 229–248.

Evarts, E.V., Temporal patterns of discharge of paramidal tract neurons during sleep and waking in the monkey. *J. Neurophysiol.*, 1964, **27**, 2, 152–171.

Evarts, E.V., Neuronal activity in visual and motor cortex during sleep and waking. *Neurophysiologie dés états de sommeil.* Paris, 1965, 189–209.

Eysenck, H.J., Suggestibility and hysteria. *Journal of Neurology and Psychiatry,* 1943, **6**, 22–31.

Eysenck, H.J. and W.D. Furneaux, Primary and secondary suggestibility: An experimental and statistical study. *J. Exp. Psychology,* 1945, **35**, 485–503.

Eysenck, H.J., *Dimensions of Personality,* London, 1947.

Faaboirg-Andersen, K., Electromyographic investrigation of intrinsic laringeal muscles in humans. *Acta Physiologica Scandinavia,* 1957, **41**. Suppl. 140.

Fahler, J., ESP card test with and without hypnosis. *J. Parapsychol.,* 1957, **22**, 179–185.

Fahler, J. and R.J. Cadoret, ESP card test of college students with and without hypnosis. *J. Parapsychol.,* 1958, **22**, 125–136.

Fangel, C. and B.R. Kaada, Behavior "attention" and fear induced by cortical stimulation in the cat. *EEG & Clin. Neurophysiol,* 1960, **12**, 575–588.

Favale, E., C. Loeb, G.G. Rossi and G. Sacco, EEG-synchronization and behavioral signs of sleep following low frequency stimulation of the brain stem reticular formation. *Arch. Ital. Biol.,* 1961, **99**, 1–22.

Ferenci, S., Introjection und Ubertragung. *Jb. Pschoanal. Psychopath. Forsch.,* 1909, 422–458.

Fischer, J., *Konflikty a Neurosy u Dety.* Praha, 1959.

Fischer, V.E., *An introduction to Abnormal Psychology.* New York, Macmillan, 1937, 162.

Fischgold, H. and B. A. Schwartz, A clinical electroencephalographic and polygraphic study of sleep in the human adults. *The Nature of Sleep.* London, 1961, 209–236.

Fodor, N., *Psychiat. Quart.,* 1947, **21**, 171.

Ford, L.F. and G.I. Ieager, Change in the EEG in subjects under hypnosis. *Dis. Nerv. Syst.,* 1948, **9**, 190__192.

Forel, A.L., *La Psychologie des Névroses.* Genève, 1925.

Forwald, H., A continuation of the experiments in placement P.K. *J. Parapsychol.,* 1952, **16**, 273–283.

Forwald, H., A study of psychokinesis in its relation to psychical conditions, *J. Parapsychol.,* 1955, **19**, 133–154.

Foster, H., New standpoint in sleep theory. *Amer. J. Psychol.,* 1900–1901, 12, 157–177.

Foulkes, D. and A. Rechtschaffen, Presleep determinants of dream content: effect of two films. *Percept. & Motor Skills,* 1964, **19**, 983–1005.

Fowler, W.L., Hypnosis and learning, *Int. J. Clin. Exp. Hypnosis,* 1961, 9, 223–232.

Frank, L., *Die psychokatartische Behandling nervöser Störungen,* Leipzig, 1927.

Frankl, V., *Theorie i Therapie.* Wien. 1956.

Freeman, G.L., Mental activity and the muscular processes. *Psychol. Review,* 1931, **38**, 428–449.

Freeman, J.A., An experiment in precognition. *J. Parapsychol.,* 1962, **26**, 123–130.

Freeman, J.A., Sex differences in precognition tests. *Parapsychology Today.* New York, 1968 (Second printing), 160.

French, J.D., M. Verzeano and H.W. Magoun, A neural basis of the anesthetic state. *Arch. Neurol. Psychiatr.* (Chicag.), 1953, **69,** 519—529.

Freud, S., *Das Ich und das Es.;* 1—8 Tausend, Leipzig-Wien-Zürich, 1931.

Freud, S., *Jenseits des Lustprinzip,* Leipzig-Wien-Zürich, 1921.

Freud, S., *Int. J. Psycho-Anal.,* 1922, **3,** 283.

Freud, S., Zur Psychopathologie des Alltagslebens, *Uber Vergessen, Versprechen, Vergreifen, Aberglaube und Irrtum;* **9,** Aufl. Wien, 1923.

Freud, S., *Gesammelte Schriften.* Leipzig-Wien-Zürich, 1924, (Bd. IV).

Freud, S., *Kleine Beiträge zur Traumlchre,* Leipzig-Wien-Zürich, 1925-a.

Freud, S., *Studien zur Psychoanalyse der Neurose )(1913—1925).* Leipzig-Wien-Zürich, 1925-b.

Freud, S., *Die Frage der Laienanalyse,* Leipzig-Wien-Zürich, 1926.

Freud, S., *Vorlesungen zur Einführung in die Psychoanalyse (1917),* Wien, 1930-a (31-35, Tausend).

Freud, S., *Vorlesungen zur Einführung in die Psychoanalyse (1917),* Wien, 1930-b (31-35, Tausend.

Freud, S., *New Introductory lectures on psychoanalysis.* London, 1933 (p. 304).

Freud, S., *Int. J. Psycho-Anal.,* 1943, **24,** 71.

Fromm, E., *Man for himself,* Chicago, 1947.

Furneaux, W.D., The prediction of susceptibility to hypnosis. *Journal of Personality,* 1946, **14,** 281—294.

Furneaux, W.D., Hypnotic susceptibility as a function of waking suggestibility. *Experimental Hypnosis,* by Leslie Lecron. New York, 1956.

Gall, I., Frères chinois. *Nature,* 1901, **1,** 351.

Garcia-Austt, J. OBogacr and C. Vanzulli, Effects of attention and inattention upon visual evoked response. *EEG & Clin. Neurophysiol.,* 1964, **17,** 136.

Gebhard, J.W., Hypnotic age regression, A review. *Amer. J. Clin. Hypn.,* 1961, **3,** 139—168.

Genevay, J., Hypnopédie. *Revue du son,* Janvier, 1959, 69.

Genevay, J., La nuit hypnopédique. *Revue du son,* Fevrier, 1959, 70.

Gerald, Yeo. *The nervous mechanism of hypnotism,* London, 1884.

Gerebtzoff, M.A., Des effets de la stimulation labyrintique sur l'activité électrique de l'écorce cérébrale. *V.R. Soc. de Biol.* (Paris), 1939, **131,** 807—813.

Gerebtzoff, M.A., Recherches sur la projection corticale du labyrinthe. *Arch. Internat. Physiol.,* 1940, **50,** 59—99.

Gernsback, H., Ralph 124C41. *Modern Electrics,* 1911, **4,** 165—168.

Gernsback, H., The birth of hypnopaedia. *Journal of the Sleep-learning Association,* 1967, **4,** 21—26.

Gernsback, H., Sleep learning. *Radio-Electronics,* July, 1962.

Gessler, H. and K. Hansen, Hypnotische Beeinflussung der Warmeregulation. *Zentralbl. f. Inn. Med.,* 1927, **48,** 658.

Gheorghiu, V.L., Probleme metodologice ale artcetarü sugestiei si sugestibilitatü, *Revista de psihologie.* 1966, **3,** 377.

Gibbs, F.A. and E.I. Gibbs, *Atlas of electroencephalography.* Cambridge, Mass., 1941.

Gidro, F.L. and M.K.Bowerbuch, A study of the planter response in hypnotic age regression. *J. Nerv. Ment. Dis.,* 1948, **107,** 443—458.

Gigon, A., Uber den Einfluss der Psyche auf koperliche Vorgänge, Hypnose und Blutzucker. *Schweiz. Med. Wchnschr.,* 1926, **56,** 749.

Gilchrist, J.C. and L.S. Nesberg, Need and perceptual change in need related objects. *J. Exptl. Psychol.*, 1952, 44, 369—376.

Glaaer, F., Uber den klinischen Nachweis psycho-physischer Reaktionen, Die Appetitsaft-leucocytosen. *Med. Klin.*, 1924, 20, 535.

Glaser, F., Psychische Beeinflussung des Blutserumkallspiegels. *Klin, Wchnschr.*, 1924, 3, 1492.

Glass, A., Mental arithmetic and blocking of the occipitalrhythm, *EEG & Clin. Neurophysiol.*, 1964, 16, 595.

Goldberg, F.H. and H. Fiss, Partial cues and the phenomenon of "Discrimination without awareness". *Perceptual & Motor Skills*. 1959, 9, 243—251.

Goldiamond, I., The hysteria over subliminal advertising as misunderstanding of science. *Amer. Psychologist*, 1959, 14, 598—599.

Goldiamond, I., The relation of subliminal perception to forced choice and psycho-physical judgments, simultaneously obtained. *Amer. Psychologist*, 1954, 9, 8, 378—379.

Goldiamond, I., Perception. *Experimental Foundations of Clinical Psychology*, 1962, 280—340.

Goldiamond, I., Response bias in perceptual communication. *Disorders of Communication*, 42. Research Publications, A.R.N.M.D., 1964, 334—363.

Goldsmith, M., *Franz Anton Mesmer*. New York, 1934.

Gould, L.N., Verbal hallucinations and activity of vocal musculature. An electro-myographic study. *Amer. J. Psychiatr.*, 1948, 105, 5.

Gould, L.N., Auditory hallucination and subvocal speech. Objective study in a case of schizophrenie. *J. Nerv. & Mental Disease*, 1949, 109, 5.

Grasset, D., *L'hypnotisme et la Suggestion*. Paris, 1904.

Graubard, L.E., Sociometry and Adolescent Groups (Abstracta). *Psychodramatis et communitatis therapeuticae; Congressus Internationalis tertius*. Prague, 1968, 33.

Grella, J.J., Effect on ESP scoring of hypnotically induced attitudes. *J. Parapsychol.*, 1945, 9, 194—202.

Grumes, F.V., An experimental analysis of the nature of suggestibility and of its relation to other psychological factors. *Studies in Psychology and Psychiatry at the Catholic University of America*, 1948, 7, No. 4.

Grings, W.W. and R.A. Lockhart, Effect of "anxiety-listening" instructions and differential set development on the extinction of GSR. *J. Exp. Psychol.*, 1963, 66, No. 3.

Gubisch, W., *Hellseher, Scharlatane, Demagogen: Kritik an der Parapsychologie. München, 1961.*

Guerra, A. and A. Cirrincione, Medicina reabilitativa e psicosomatica. *Atti del Semposio Internazionale di Medicina Psicosomatica Militare*. Roma, 1967, 179.

Haider, M., P. Spong and D. Lindsley, Attention, vigilance and cortical evoked potentials in humans. *Science*, 1964, 145, 180.

Haider, M., P. Spong and D. Lindsley, Selective attentiveness and cortical evoked responses to visual and auditory stimuli. *Science*, 1965, 148, 395.

Hall, H., *The Spirutalists*. New York, 1963.

Haller, A. von, *Anfangsgründe der Physiologie*, 1772, B.V.S., 1137, 1189.

Hammer, A.G., F.J. Evans and M. Bartlett, Factors in hypnosis and suggestion. *J. Abnorm. & Soc. Psychol.*, 1963, 67, 15—23.

Hammer, E.F., Post-hypnotic suggestions and test performance. *J. Clin. Exp. Hypnosis*, 1954, 2, 178—185.

Hammond, W., Lectures on sleep. *Gillard's Med. Journ.*, 1880, **29**, 125—157.

Hansel, E.M., *ESP: A Scientific Evaluation.* New York, 1966.

Harvey, D., *About Yoga.* London, 1960.

Haskovec, L., Localisation de la conscience. *Rev. Sci.*, 1911, **1**, 456.

Hauptman, A., Versuche zur rascherem Herbeifuhrung einer Hypnose. *Klin. Wsch.*, 1934, **13**, 437—439.

Hawkins, D.R., H.B. Puryear, C.D. Wallace, W.B. Deal and E.S. Thomas, Basal skin resistance during sleep and "dreaming". *Science*, 1962, **136**, **3513**, 321—322.

Heidenhein, R., *Hypnotism or Animal Magnetism.* London, Paul Trench & Trubner, 1906.

Heilig, R. and H. Hof, Beiträge zur hypnotischen Beeinflussung der Magenfunktion. *Med. Klin.*, 1925-a, **21**, 162.

Heilig, R. and H. Hoff, Uber hypnotische Beeinflussung der Nierenfunktion. *Keutsche Med. Wchnschr.*, 1925-b, **51**, 1615.

Henoque, A., Circulation pendant le sommeil. *Dict. Encycl. d. Méd.*, 1881, kl. 10. 276—298.

Hering, E., *Die Lehre vom binocularen Sehen.* Leipzig, 1868.

Hernandez-Peon, R., A cholinergic hypnogenic limbic forebrain-hindbrain circuit. *Neurophysiologie des états de sommeil.* Paris, 1965, 63—84.

Heron, J.W. and M. Abramson, Hypnosis in Obstetrics (A psychological preparation for childbirth). *Experimental Hypnosis,* Edit. by Leslie M. LeCron. New York, 1956, 284—302.

Hess, W.R., *Die funktionelle Organisation des vegetativen Nerven-systems.* Basel, 1948.

Hess, W.R., *Das Zwischenhirn.* Basel, 1949.

Hess, W.R., The electroencephalogram in sleep. *EEG & Clin. Neurophysiol.*, 1964, **16**, 1/2, 44—55.

Heyer, G., Die Magensekretion beim Menschen unter besonderer Berücksichtigung der psychischen Einflüsse. *Arch. i. Verdaungs-krankheiten*, 1921, **27**, 266.

Heyer, G.R., *Praktische Seelenheilkunde.* München, 1935.

Hiebel, G., M. Huve and P. Dell, Analyse neurophysiologique de l'action centrale de la d-amphétamine (Maxiton). *Sem. Hôp.* (Paris), 1954, **30**, 1880.

Hilgard, E.R., *Hypnotic Susceptibility.* New York, 1965.

Hilgard, E.R., R.K. Campbell and W.N. Sears, Conditioned discrimination: the effect of knowledge of stimulus-relationships. *Amer. J. Psychol.*, 1938, **51**, No. 3.

Hilger, W., *Die Suggestion.* Jena, 1928.

Hill, L., Arterial pressure in sleeping. *J. of Physiol.*, 1898, **22**, XXVI.

Hirschlaff, L., *Hypnotismus und Suggestiontherapie.* Leizig, Barth, 1919.

Hodes, R. and W.C. Dement, Depression of electrically induced reflex ("H-reflex") in man during low voltage EEG "sleep". *EEG and Clin. Neurophysiol.*, 1964, **17**, 617—629.

Hollos, J., *Imago*, 1933, **19**, 529.

Hombravella, J.F., L'entrainement psychotonique en psychosomatique. *Atti del Simposio Internazional di Medicina Psicosomatica sportiva.* Roma, 1967, 40—42.

Horetzky, O., Psychodinamische Beziehungen in der nonverbalen Einzel-Gruppen-psychotherapie (Abstracta). *Group Psychotherapy, 4th International Congress.* Vienna, 1968, 313.

Horvai, J. and J. Haskovec, Zu Manchen Fragen der sogenannten experimentalen hypnotischen Altersregression, Psychiatrie, Neurologie und med. *Psychologie,*

1962, **14,** 6, 215—221.

Hull, C.L., *Hypnosis and Suggestibility.* New York, Apleton Century, Crofts, 1933.

Humphrey, B.M., Paranormal occurrences among preliterate peoples. *J. Parapsychol.,* 1944, **8,** 214—229.

Humphrey, B.M., ESP and intelligence. *J. Parapsychol,* 1945, **9,** 7—16.

Humphrey, B.M., Success in ESP as related to form of response drawings: I. Clairvoyance experiments. *J. Parapsychol.,* 1946-a, **10,** 78—106.

Humphrey, B.M., Success in ESP as related to form of response drawings' II GESP experiments. *J. Parapsychol.,* 1946-b, **10,** 181—196.

Humphrey, B.M. ESP score level predicted by a combination of measures of personality. *J. Parapsychol.,* 1950, **14,** 193—206.

Humphrey, B.M., Introversion-extroversion ratings in relation to scores in ESP tests. *J. Parapsychol.,* 1951, **15,** 252—262.

Humphrey, B.M. and J.F. Nicol, The exploration of ESP and human personality. *J. Amer. Soc. Psychic. Res.,* 1963, **47,** 133—178.

Humphrey, B.M., ESP tests with mental patients before and after electroshock treatment. *J. Soc. Psychic. Res.,* 1954, **37,** 159—266.

Huse, B., Does the hypnotic trance favor the recall of faint memories *J. exptl, Psychol.,* 1930, **13,** 519—529.

Huttenlocher, P.R., Evoked and spontaneous activity in single units of mesencephalic reticular formation during sleep. *EEG & Clin. Nerophysiol.,* 1961-a, **13,** 2, 304.

Huttenlocher, P.R., Evoked and spontaneous activity in single units of medical brain stem during natural sleep and waking. *J. Neurophysiol,* 1961-b, **24,** 5, 451—468.

Jacobson, E., Electrical measurements of neuromuscular states during mental activities. *Amer. J. Physiol.,* 1930, 91, 2.

Jacobson, E., *Progressive Relaxations.* University Chicago Press, 1938.

James, W., *The Principles of Psychology,* Vol. 2, New York, Holt, 1890.

Janet, P., *Rev. Phil.,* 1886, **21,** 190.

Janet, P., *L'automatisme psychologique.* Paris, 1903.

Janet, P., *Major symptoms of hysteria.* New York, Macmilan, 1907, 161, 174.

Janet, P., *Les Névroses.* Paris, 1909.

Janet, P., *L'état Mental des Hystériques.* Paris, 1911.

Janet, P., *La Médecine Psychologique.* Paris, 1923.

Janet, P., *Eléménts de Psychlogie Pathologique,* Vol. 7. Paris, 1925.

Janet, P., *Les Médications Psychologiques,* Vols. 1, 2, 3. Paris, 1925/28.

Janet, P., *History of Psychology as Autobiography,* Vol. 1. Worcester, Mass., 1835.

Jaspers, K., *Allgemeine Psychopathologie.* Berlin, 1948.

Jasper, H.H., Some relationships between the waves of the cortex. Excerpta Med., 5th. Int. Congr. *EEG & Clin. Neurophysiol.,* 1961, 1—2.

Jennes, A.F. and C.L. Wible, Respiration and heart action in sleep and hypnosis. *J. Gen. Psychology,* 1937, **16,** 197.

Jepson, J., Evidence for clairvoyance in card-guessing. *Proc. Soc. Psychic. Research, 1929,* **38,** 223—268.

Jokl, E., Motivation in sport. *Atti del Simposio Internazionale di Medicina Psicosomatica sportiva.* Roma, 1967, 7—20.

Jouvet, M., Telencephalic and rhombencephalic sleep in the cat. *The nature of sleep.* London, 1961, 188—208.

Jouvet, M., Recherches sur les structures nerveuses et les mécanismes responsables des différentes phases du sommeil physiologique. *Arch. Ital. Biol.*, 1962, 100, No. 2, 125—206.

Jouvet, M., Etude de la dualité des états de sommeil et des états de la phase paradoxale. *Neurophysiologie des états de sommeil.* Paris, 1965, 397—446.

Jouvet, M., Neurophysiology of the states of sleep. *Physiol. Review*, 1967, **47,** 2.

Jouvet, M. and D. Jouvet, A study of the neurophysiological mechanisms of dreaming. *EEG & Clin. Neurophysiol.*, 1963, Suppl. 24, 133—157.

Jouvet, M., M. Jeannerod and J. Mouret, Mechanisms of the rapid eye movements during paradoxical sleep. *Corticosubcortical relationship in sensory regulation.* Havana, 1965, 39—41.

Jung, C., *Psychologische Typen.* Zürich, 1921.

Jung, C., *Das Untewusste im normalen kranken Seelenleben.* Zürich, 1926.

Jung, C., *Die Beziehung zwischen dem "Ich" und dem Unbewussten.* Zürich, 1928.

Jung, C., *Uber die Psychologie des Unbewussten.* Zürich, 1943.

Kahn, E., *Hdb Geisteskrank*, Vol. 5. 1928, 227—478.

Kanthamani, B.K., A study in differential response in language ESP test. *J. Parapsychol.*, 1965, **29,** 27—34.

Kanthamani, B.K., ESP and social stimulus. *J. Parapsychol.*, 1966, **30,** No. 1.

Kanzov, E., Changes in blood flow of the cerebral cortex and other vegetative changes during paradoxical sleep periods in the unrestrainted cat. *Neurophysiologie des états de sommeil.* Paris, 1965, 231—237.

Kaufmann, I., Die planmässinge Heilung komplizierter psychogener Bewegung-störungen bei Soldaten in einer Sitzung. *Münch. Med. Wschr.*, 1916, 22.

Kehrer, F., Uber Entstehung und Behandlung der Kreigsneurosen, Vortrag. Ref. *Ztschr. f. d. Ges. Neur, u. Psychiat*, 1916, H. 12, 7.

Kehrer, F., Zur Frage der Behandlung der Kriegsneurosen. *Ztschr. f. d. Ges. Neur, u. Psychiat.*, 1917, H. 1—2, 36.

Kelman, H. C., Effcts of success and failure on "suggestibility" in the autokinetic situation. *J. Abnorm. Soc. Psychol.*, 1950, **45.** 267—285.

Kilman, G. and E.L. Goldberg, Improved visual recognition during hypnosis. *Arch. Gen. Psychiat.*, 1962, **7,** 155—162.

King, H.E., C. Landis and J. Zubin, Visual subliminal perception where a figure is obscured by the illumination of the ground. *J. Exptl. Psychol.*, 1944, **34,** I, 60—69.

Klages, L., *Die Grundlagen d. Charakterkunde.* Leipzig, 1926.

Klapman, J.W., *'Group Psychotherapy.* London, 1946.

Kleinsorge, H. and G. Klumbies, Herz und Seele (Hypnose und Elektro-kardiogramm). *Deutsche Med. Wchnschr.*, 1949, **4,** 37.

Kleitman, N., The nature of dreaming. *The Nature of sleep.* London, 1961, 349—374.

Kleine, M.B. and H. Guze, *Brit. J. Med. Hypnot.*, 1951, **2,** 7710.

Kline, M.V., Hypnosis and age regression' A case report. *J. Genet. Psychol.*, 1951, **78,** 195—206.

Knepler, E., Soziodrama in der amerikanischen Gemeinschaft. *Abstracts in Group Psychotherapy, 4th International Congress.* Vienna, 1968, 283.

Koffka, K., *Die Grundlagen der psychischen Entwicklung.* München, 1925.

Köhler, W., *Gestalt Psychology,* London, 1930.

Krech, D. and R.S. Grutchfield, *Theory and Problem of Social Psychology.* New York, McGraw Hill, 1948.

Krestnikov, N., Die heilende Wirkung künstlich hervorgerufener Reproduktionen von pathogenen affectiven Erlebnissen. *Arch. f. Neur. u. Psychiatrie,* 1929, Bd. 88, 3.

Kretschmer, M. and R. Krüger, Uber die Beeinflussung des Serumkalgehaltes in der Hypnose. *Klin. Wchnschr.,* 1927, **6,** 695.

Kretschmer, E., *Körperbau u. Charakter.* **10,** Berlin, 1931.

Kretschmer, E., *Medizinische Psychologie.* Stuttgart, 1956.

Krippner, S., Hypnosis and reading improvement among university students. *Amer. J. Clin. Hypnosis,* 1963, **5,** 187—193.

Krippner, S., Hypnosis as verbal programming in educational therapy. *Academic Therapy,* 1971, **7,** 5—12.

Kronthal, P., Uber dem Schlaf. *Zbl.,* 1907, Bd. 26.

Kubota, K., Y. Swamura and Y. Niimi, Monosynaptic reflex and natural sleep in the cat. *J. Neurophysiol.,* 1965, **28,** I, 125—138.

Kupfer, H.I., Psychic concomitants in wartime injuries. *Psychosom. Med.,* **7,** 15—21.

Kurka, E., Zur Beeinflussung der Stimme durch inneres Sprechen bei maschineller Schreibarbeit, Autoreferat zur Diss. *Zeitschrift Universität Halle, Ges. Sprachw.,* 1959, **8,** 6.

Kurka, E., Inneres Sprechen und Stimme. *Proceedings of the Fourth International Congress of Phonetic Science,* Helsinki, 1961.

Langheinrich, O., Psychische Einflusse auf die Sekretionsstätigkeit des Magens und des Duodenums. *München Med. Wchnschr.,* 1922, **69,** 1527.

Leal, R.M., Methoden der Gruppenpsychotherapie. Spezifische Probleme der gruppenanalytischen Arbeit (Abstracta). *Group Psychotherapy, 4th International Congress.* Vienna, 1968, 329.

LeCron, L.M., A study of age regression under hypnosis. *Experimental Hypnosis,* edited by Leslie M. LeCron. New York, 1956.

Lefevre, L., *Les phénomènes de suggestion et d'autosuggestion.* Paris, 1903.

Levine, M., Electgrical skin resistance during hypnosis. *Arch. Neurol. & Psychiat.,* 1930, **24,** 973.

Levine, R., I. Chein and G. Murphy, The relation of the intensity of a need to the amount of perceptual distortion A preliminary report, *J. Psychol.,* 1942, **13,** 283—293.

Liebault, L., *Du sommeil provoqué et des états analogues,* 1886, Edit. 1, 1889, Edit. 2.

Liebault, A.A., *Le sommeil provoqué.* Paris, 1889.

Lissak, K., G. Karmos and E. Grastyan, A study of the so-called "paradoxical phase" of sleep in cats. *Excerpta Med., 5th Int. Congr., EEG & Clin. Neurophysiol.,* 1961, 57—58.

Lissmann, H. and H. Machin, Electric receptors in a nonelectric fish. *Nature,* 1963, **199,** 88.

Lodato, F.J., Hypnosis as an adjunct to test performance. *Amer. J. Clin. Hypnosis,* 1964, **6,** 271—273.

London, P., J.E. Hart and M.P. Leibovitz, EEG Alpha rhythms and susceptibility to hypnosis. *Nature,* 1968, **219,** No. 5149, 71—72.

Loomis, A.L., E.N. Harvey and G. Hobart, Brain potentials during hypnosis. *Science,* 1936, **83,** 239.

Louise Maron, A. Rechtschaffen and E.A. Wolpert, Sleep Cycle during napping. *Arch. Gen. Psychiatry,* 1964, **II,** 503—508.

Löwenfeld, L., *Der Hypnotismus.* Wiesbaden, 1901.

Löwenfeld, L. *Der Hypnotismus.* München, 1903.

Löwenfeld, L., *Hypnotismus und Medizin.* München, 1922.

Löwy, M., Bemerkungen zur Lehre von der Hypnose und zur Pulsbeeinflussung in derselben. *Monatschr. f. Psychiat. u. Neurol.,* 1918, **44,** 169.

Lozanov, G., Deviations from Herring's law of the movements of the eyeballs. *Bulletin of the Institute of Psychology, Bulgarian Academy of Sciences,* 1918, **44,** 169.

Lozanov, G., *Integral Psychotherapy.* Report at the Psychosomatic Week, Rome, September 1967-a.

Lozanov, G., Anaesthetization through suggestion in a state of wakefulness in the course of abdominal operation. Report at the Psychosomatic Week, Rome, September, 1967-b.

Lozanov, G., Suggestopedia and memory, *Proceedings of the International Psychosomatic Week,* Rome, 1967-c, 535 — 539.

Lozanov, G., A common curative mechanism of suggestion underlying all psychotherapeutic methods. *Groups Psychotherapy, 4th International Congress.* Vienna, 1968, 221 — 233.

Lozanov, G., Zur Frage der experimentellen hypnotischen Regression. *"Hypnose— Aktuelle Probleme in Theorie, Experiment und Klinik".* VEB Gustav Fischer Verlag, Jena, 1971.

Lozanov, G., Psychotherapie und Gesellschaft. Kongres Materialen zum 7 Kongress der Gesellschaft für ärztliche Psychotherapie der DDR, April, 1973.

Luchkardt, A.B. and R.L. Johnston, Studies in gastric secretion of gastric juice under hypnosis. *Am. J. Physiol.,* 1924, **70,** 174.

Lundholm, H., An experimental study of functional anesthesias as induced by suggestion in hypnosis. *J. Abnorm. Soc. Psychol.,* 1928, **23,** 337.

Lundholm, H. and H. Loewenbach, Hypnosis and the alpha activity of the electroencephalogram. *Character a. Personality,* 1942, **2,** 145 — 149.

March, L.C., Group treatment of the psychoses by the psychological equivalent of revival. *Ment. Hyg.,* 1931, **15,** 328 — 349.

Marchand, H., Cholesterine et sommeil. *Compt. Rend. Soc. de Biol.,* 1912, **72,** 615.

Marcus, H. and E. Sahlgren, Uber die Einwirkung der hypnotischen Suggestion auf die Funktion des vegetativen Nervensystems. *München. Med. Wchnschr.,* 1925, **72, 381.**

Marinesco, G., O. Sager and A. Kreindler, Etudes électroencéphalographiques pendant le sommeil naturel et hypnotique. *Bull. Acad. Med.* (Paris), 1937, **117,** 273—276.

Marino, A., Psychosomatic Medicine and Psychopharmacology (Introductory report). *Medicina Psicosomtica,* 1968, **13,** No. 1 — 2.

Markov, M., G. Lozanov and P. Kircev, Uber einem durch Suggestion in wachem Zustand hervorgerufenen und geheilten Urtikariaanfall. *Allergie und Asthma,* 1962, Band 8, Heft 1.

Marx, H., Untersuchungen über den Wasserbaushalt. *Klin. Wchnschr.,* 1926, **5,** 92.

Mausner, B., The effect of prior reinforcement on the interaction of observer pairs. *J. Abnorm. Soc. Psychol.,* 1954, **49,** 65 — 68.

Mauthner, L., Pathologie und Phsyiologie des Schlafes. *Wien, Med. Wschr.,* 1890, Bd. 40.

McAllister, W.R. and Dorothy E. McAllister, Effect of knowledge of conditioning upon eyelid conditioning, *J. Exptl. Psychol.*, 1958, **55,** No. 6.

McCay, A.R., Dental extraction under self-hypnosis. *Med. J. Australia*, 1963, June 1, 820—822.

McCord, H., Hypnosis as aid to teaching a severely mentally retarded teen-age boy. *J. Clin. Exp. Hypnosis*, 1956, **4,** 21—24.

McCord, H. and C.I. Sherrill, A note on increased ability to do calculus post-hypnotically. *Amer. J. Clin. Hypnosis*, 1961, **4,** 124.

McCranie, E.J. and H.B. Crasilnech, The conditioned reflex in hypnotic age regression. *J. Clin. Exp. Psychopath*, 1955, **16,** 120—123.

McCranie, E.J., H.B. Crasilnech and H.K. Jeter, The EEG in hypnotic age regression. *Psychiat. Quart.*, 1955, **29,** 85—88.

McDougall, W., *An Introduction to Social Psychology.* London, Methuen, 1908.

McDougall, W., Suggestion. *Encyclop. Brit.*, 1911, 162.

McDougall, W., *Outline of Abnormal Psychology.* New York, Charles Scribner's Sons, 1926.

McGinnies, E., Discussion of Howe's and Solomons's note on "Emotionality and perceptual defense". *Psychol. Review*, 1949, **56,** 244—251.

Meier, G.W. and R.J. Berger, Development of sleep and wakefulness patterns in the infant rhesus monkey. *Exptl. Neurol.*, 1965, **12,** 257—277.

Mitchell, M.B., Retractive inhibition in hypnosis. *J. Gen. Psychol.*, 1932, **7,** 343—358.

Miraglia, F., La preparazione psicologica del ginecologo al fini dell'assistenza psycoprofilactica. *Atti del I Congresso Nazionale della Societa Italiana di Psicoprofilassi ostetrica.* Roma, 1967, 111.

Moll, A., *Der Hypnotismus.* Berlin, 1907.

Monnier, M., M. Kalberer and P. Krupp, Functional antagonism between diffuse reticular and intralaminary recruiting projections in the medical thalmus. *Exptl. Neurol.*, 1960, **2,** 271—289.

Monnier, M., L. Hösli and P. Krupp, Moderating and activating systems in mediocéntral thalamus and reticular formation. *EEG & Clin. Neurophysiol.*, Suppl. 24, 1963, 97—112.

Morgan, J.B., *The Psychology of Abnormal people.* New York, Longmans, 1936, 162.

Moreno, L.T., Wechselwirkende Grupenpsychotherapie und Psychodrama in einer Familie (Abstracta). *Group Psychotherapy, 4th International Congress.* Vienna, 1968, 253.

Moruzzi, G. and H. Magoun, Brain stem reticular formation and activation of EEG. *EEG & Clin. Neurophysiol.* Montreal, 1949, 455—473.

Moruzzi, G., Reticular influences on the EEG. *EEG & Clin. Neuro-physiol.*, 1964, **17,** 2—17.

Moss, A.A., Hypnodontis. *Experimental Hypnosis*, Edit. by Leslie M. LeCron, New York, 1956, 303—319.

Motokizawa, F. and B. Fujimori, Fast activities and DC potential changes of the cerebral cortex during EEG arousal response. *EEG & Clin. Neurophysiol.*, 1964, **17,** 630—637.

Mühl, A., *Automatic Writing.* Dresden and Leipzig, 1930.

Mühl, A., *Automatic Writing and Hypnosis' Experimental Hypnosis.* New Uprl. 1956.

Müller-Hegemann, *Psychotherapie.* Berlin, 1957.

Müller, J., *Handbuch der Physiologie*, 1840, Bd. II, Abt. **3,** 579—588.

Mundle, C.W.K., Some philosophical perspectives for parapsychology. *J. Parap-*

*sychol.*, 1952, **16,** 257—272.

Murphy, G. and L.A. Dale, Concentration versus relaxation in relation telepathy. *J. Amer. Soc. Psych. Res.*, 1943-a, **37,** 2—15.

Murphy, G., Psychical phenomena and human needs. *J. Amer. Soc. Psychic. Res.*, 1943-b, **37,** 163—191.

Murphy, G., Spontaneous telepathy and the problem of survival. *J. Parapsychol.*, 1943-c, **7,** 50—60.

Murphy, G., An outline of survival evidence. *J. Amer. Soc. Psychic. Res.*, 1945-a, **39,** 2—34.

Murphy, G., Difficulties confronting the survival hypothesis. *J. Amer. Soc. Psychic. Res.*, 1945-b, **39,** 67—94.

Murphy, G., Field theory and survival. *J. Amer. Soc. Psychic. Res.*, 1945-c, **39,** 181—209.

Murphy, G., Psychical research and the ind-body relation. *J. Amer. Soc. Psychic. Res.*, 1946, **40,** 189—207.

Murphy, G., The place of parapsychology among the sciences. *J. Parapsychol.*, 1947-a, **13,** 62—71.

Murphy, G., Personality appraisal and the paranormal. *J. Amer. Soc. Psychic. Res.*, 1947, 3—11.

Murphy, G., Psychical research and personality. *J. Amer. Soc. Psych. Res.*, 1950, **44,** 3—20.

Murphy, G., Current developments in psychical research. *J. Amer. Soc. Psychic. Res.*, 1952, **46,** 47—61.

Murphy, G., Progress in parapsychology. *J. Parapsychol.*, 1958, **22,** 229—236.

Murphy, G., A qualitative study of telepathic phenomena. *J. Amer. Soc. Psychic. Res.*, 1962, **56,** 63—79.

Murphy, G., Lawfulness versus caprice: Is there a law of psychic phenomena? *J. Amer. Soc. Psych. Res.*, 1964, **58,** 238—249.

Naquet, R., M. Denavit, J. Lanovi and D. Albe-Fessard, Altérations transitoires ou définitives de zones diencéphaliques chez le chat. *Leurs effets sur l'activité électrique corticale et le sommeil' Neurophysiologie des états de sommeil* (Paris), 1965, 107—130.

Narikashvili, S.P., Some data on the synchronizing mechanism of the lower brain stem. *Cortico-subcortical relationship in sensory regulation.* Havana, 1965, 55—56.

Neisser, U., *Cognitive Psychology.* New York, Meridith, 1967.

Nicard, M., *Le sommeil normal.* Lyon, Thèse, 1904.

Notterman, J.M., W.N. Schoenfeld and P.J. Bersch, A comparison of three extraction procedures following heart rate conditioning. *J. Abnorm. Soc. Psychol.*, 1952, **47,** No. 6.

O'Connor, P.J., Psychosomatic disease in military aviation. *Atti del Simposio Internazionale di Medicine Psicosomatica Militare.* Roma, 1967, 89.

Oetting, E.R., Hypnosis and Concentration in study, *Amer. J. Clin. Hypnosis,* 1964, 7, 148—151.

Oppenheimer, L., Zur Physiologie des Schlafes. *Arch. f. (Anat. u.) Physiol.,* 1902, 68—102.

Orne, M.I., The mechanism of hypnotic age regressions' an experimental study. *J. Abnorm. Soc. Psychol.,* 1951, **46,** 213—225.

Osis, K., A test of the occurrence of a psi effect between man and the cat. *J. Parap-*

*sychol.*, 1952, **16**, 233—256.

Osis, K. and E.B. Foster, A test of ESP in cats. *J. Parapsychol.*, 1953, **17**, 168—186.

Osis, K., Precognition over time intervals of one to thirty-three days. *J. Parapsychol.*, 1955, **19**, 82—91.

Osis, K., ESP over a distance of seventy-five hundred miles. *J. Parapsychol.*, 1956, **20**, 229—232.

Oswald, I., Sleep mechanisms: recent advances, *Proc. Roy. Soc. Med.*, 1962, **55**, 910—912.

Oswald, I., R.J. Berger, R.A. Jaramillo, K.M. Keddie, P.C. Olley and G.B. Plunkett, Melancholia and barbiturates, A controlled EEG, body and eye movement study of sleep. *Brit. J. Psychiat.*, 1963, **109**, 66—78.

Paillard, J., Cortical activity and control of proprioceptic afferences in humans. *Cortico-subcortical relationship in sensory regulation.* Havana, 1965, 59—60.

Parrish, M., R.M. Lundy and H.W. Leibonitz, Hypnotic age-regression and magnetudes of the Ponzo and Poggendorff Illusions. *Science*, 1968, **159**, 3821, 1375—1376.

Passouant, P., Séméiologie électroencéphalographique du sommeil normal et pathologique. *Rev. Neurol.*, 1950, **83**, 545—559.

Patrie, F.A., The genuineness of hypnotically produced anaesthesia of the skin. *Am. J. Psychol.*, 1937, **49**, 435.

Pederson-Krag, *Psychoanal. Quart.*, 1947, **16**, 61.

Peerbolte, M., *Tijdschr. voor Parapsychologie*, 1937, **3**, 121.

Penaloza-Rojas, J.H., M. Ellerman and N. Olmos, Sleep induced by cortical stimulation. *Exptl. Neurol.*, 1964, **10**, 140—147.

Petrov, P.D. Traikov and I.Z. Kalendjiev, A contribution to psychoanaesthetization through hypnosis in some stomatological manipulations. *British J. of Medical Hypnotism*, 1964, **15**, 4, 8—16.

Phinney, J.N., Learn while you sleep. *Journal of the Sleep-learning Association*, 1967, **4**, 3, 27—31.

Pichon, J-le, Peut-on apprendre en dormant? *Science et Vie*, 1960, **511**, 99—100.

Pompeiano, O. and J.E. Swett, EEG and behavioral manifestations of sleep induced by cutaneous nerve stimulation in normal cat. *Arch. Ital. Biol.*, 1962, **100**, 311—342.

Postman, L., J.S. Bruner and E. McGinnies, Personal values as selective factors in perception. *J. Abnorm. Soc. Psychol.*, 1948, **43**, 142—154.

Prados, M., The use of pictorial images in gruop psychotherapy. *Amer. J. Psychother.*, 1951, **5**, 196—214.

Pratt, J.G., Towards a method of evaluating mediumistic material. *Boston Soc. Psychic. Res., Bull.*, 1936, 23.

Pratt, J.G., Larger preference in P.K. tests with dice. *J. Parapsychol.*, 1947, **11**, 26—45.

Pratt, J.G. and E.B. Foster, Displacement in ESP card tests in relation to ESP performance. *J. Parapsychol.*, 1950, **14**, 37—52.

Pratt, J.G., Methods of evaluating verbal material. *J. Parapsychol.*, 1960, **24**, 94—109.

Pratt, J.G., On the question of control over ESP: The effect of environment on psi performance, *J. Amer. Soc. Psychic. Res.*, 1961, **55**, 128—134.

Pratt, J.G., The group method in the treatment of psychosomatic disorders.

*Sociometry,* 1945, **8,** 323—331.

Prince, M., *The Unconscious.* New York, Macmillan, 1914.

Prokop, O., *Wünschelrute, Erdstrahlen und Wissenschaft.* Leipzig, 1957.

Prokop, O., *Medizinischer Okkultismus.* Jeana, 1962.

Purkinje, J.E., Wacher Schlaf, Wagner's Handworterbuch. *d. Physiol.,* 1846, Bd. III-2, 412—480.

Rao, R.K., The preferential effect in ESP. *J. Parapsychol.,* 1962, **26,** No. 4.

Rao, R.K., Studies in the preferential effect. II. A language ESP test involving precognition and "intervention". *J. Parapsychol.,* 1963-a, **27,** No. 3.

Rao, R.K., Studies in the preferential effect. I. Target preference with types of targets unknown. *J. Parapsychol.,* 1963-b, **27,** No. 1.

Rao, R.K., Studies in the preferential effect. III. The reversal effect in psi preference. *J. Parapsychol.,* 1963-b, **27,** No. 4.

Rao, R.K., The psychological picture of psi Res. *J. Philos. and Soc. Sci.,* 1963-a, I, Part I.

Rao, R.K., Studies in the preferential effect. IV. The role of key cards in preferential response situations. *J. Parapsychol.,* 1964-a, **28,** No. 1.

Rao, R.K., The differential response in three new situations. *J. Parapsychol.,* 1964-b, **38,** No. 2.

Rao, R.K., Five years report of Seth Schan Lal Memorial Institute of Parapsychology by S.C. Mukherjee. *J. Parapsychol.,* 1964-c, **28,** No. 1.

Rao, R.K., ESP and the manifest anxiety scale. *J. Parapsychol.,* 1965-a, **29,** No. 1.

Rao, R.K., The bidirectionality of psi. J. Parapsychol., 1965-b, **29,** No. 4.

Rao, R.K., *Experimental Parapsychology; A Review Interpretation.* Springfield, Illinois, USA, 1966.

Rechtschaffen, A., E.A. Wolpert, W.C. Dement, S.A. Mitchell and C. Fisher, Nocturnal sleep of narcoleptics. *EEG & Clin. Neurophysiol.,* 1963-a, **15,** 559—609.

Rechtschaffen, A., G. Vogel and G. Shaikum, Interrelatedness of mental activity during sleep. *Arch. General Psychiatry,* 1963-b, **9,** 536—547.

Rechtschaffen, A., P. Verdone and J. Wheaton, Reports of mental activity during sleep. *Canad. Psychiat. Assoc. J.,* 1963-c, **8,** No. 6, 409—414.

Rechtschaffen, A. and P. Verdone, Amount of dreaming, effect of incentive, adaptation to laboratory, and individual differences. *Percept. & Motor Skills,* 1964, **19,** 947—958.

Rechtschaffen, A. and A.B. Louise Maron, The effect of amphetamine on sleep cycle. *EEG & Clin. Neurophysiol.,* 1964, **16,** 335—338.

Rechtschaffen, A. and D. Foulkes, Effect of visual stimuli on dream content. *Percept. & Motor Skills,* 1965, **20,** 1149—1160.

Reding, G.R. and W.C. Rubright, A. Rechtschaffen and R.S. Daniels, Sleep-patterns of tooth-grinding: its relationship to dreaming. *Science,* 1964, **145,** No. 3633, 725—726.

Reiter, P.J., The influence of hypnosis on somatic fields of function. *Experimental Hypnosis,* edit. by Leslie M. Le Cron. New York, 1956, 241—263.

Rheinberger, M. and H. Jasper, Electrical activity of cerebral cortex in unanesthetized cat. *Amer. J. physiol.,* 1937, **119,** 186—196.

Rhine, J.B., *Extrasensory Perception.* Boston, Bruce Humphris, 1934.

Rhine, J.B., The effect of distance in ESP tests. *J. Parapsychol.,* 1937-a, **1,** 172—184.

Rhine, J.B., Some basic experiments in extrasensory perception, a background. *J. Parapsychol.*, 1937-b, **1**, 70—80.
Rhine, J.B., Conditions favoring success in psi tests. *J. Parapsychol.*, 1938-a, **12**, 58—75.
Rhine, J.B. ESP tests with enclosed cards. *J. Parapsychol.*, 1938-b, **2**, 199—216.
Rhine, J.B., Terminal salience in ESP performance. *J. Parapsychol.*, 1941, **5**, 183—244.
Rhine, J.B. and B.M. Humphry, P.K. tests with six, twelve and twenty-four dice per throw. *J. Parapsychol.*, 1944, **8**, 139—157.
Rhine, J.B., Telepathy and clairvoyance reconsidered. *J. Parapsychol.*, 1945, **9**, 176—193.
Rhine, J.B., The source of the difficulties in parapsychology. *J. Parapsychol.*, 1946-a, **10**, 162—168.
Rhine, J.B., Hypnotic suggestion in P.K. tests. *J. Parapsychol.*, 1946-b, **10**, 126—140.
Rhine, J.B., A digest and discussion of some comments on telepathy and clairvoyance reconsidered. *J. Parapsychol.*, 1946-c, **10**, 36—50.
Rhine, J.B., The question of spirit survival. *J. Amer. Soc. Psychic. Res.*, 1949, **43**, 43—58.
Rhine, J.B., Psi phenomena and psychiatry. *Proc. Roy. Soc. Med.*, 1950, **43**, 804—814'
Rhine, J.B., *A Brief Introduction to Parapsychology.* Parapsychology Duke University.
Rhine, J.B., Telepathy and human personality. *J. Parapsychol.*, 1951, **15**, 6—39.
Rhine, J.B., The problem of psi-missing. *J. Parapsychol.*, 1952, **16**, 90—129.
Rhine, J.B. and J.G. Pratt, A review of the Pearce—Pratt distance series of ESP tests. *J. Parapsychol.*, 1965, **18**, No. 3.
Rhine, J.B. and J.G. Pratt, A review of the Pearce—Pratt distance series of ESP tests. *J. Parapsychol.*, 1954, **18**, 165—177.
Rhine, J.B., A quarter century of the Journal of Parapsychology, A brief review. *J. Parapsychol.*, 1961, **25**, 237—246.
Rhine, J.B., The shifting scene in parapsychology. *J. Parapsychol.*, 1962, **26**, 293—307.
Rhine, J.B. and J.G. Pratt, *Parapsychology, Frontier Science of the mind.* Springfield-Illinois, 1967.
Rhine, J.B., Introductory comments. *Parapsychology Today.* New York, 1968, 25.
Rhine, L.E., Conviction and associated conditions in spontaneous cases. *J. Parapsychol.*, 1945, **15**, 164—191.
Rhine, L.E., Subjective forms of spontaneous psi experiences. *J. Parapsychol.*, 1953, **17**, 77—114.
Rhine, L.E., *ESP in Life and Lab: Tracing Hidden Channels.* New York, 1967.
Rhine, L.E., Parapsychology, then and now. *Parapsychology Today.* New York, 1968, 244.
Richet, Ch., *Rev. Phil.*, 1888, **25**, 435.
Richet, Ch., Circulation cérébrale. *Dict. de physiol.*, 1897, Vol. 2.
Richet, Ch., *Thirty Years of Psychical Research.* New York, 1923.
Richl, J.R., Analog analysis of EEG activity. *EEG & Clin. Neurophysiol.*, 1963,

15, 1039—1042.

Roberts, W.H., On a measured change in vision in a regressed myopic subject. Unpublished report to Leslie M. Le Cron.

Roheim, G., *Psychoanal. quart.*, 1932, 1, 277.

Roffwag, H., W. Dement and C. Fisher, Observations on the sleep-dream patterns in neonates infants, children and adults. *Problems of Sleep and Dream in Children and Adults.* Oxford, 1963.

Rojas-Bermudes, J.G., Das Psychodrama. (Abstracta). *Group Psychotherapy, 4th International Congress.* Vienna, 1968, 285.

Rosenthal, B.G., Hypnotic recall of material learned under anxiety- and non-anxiety-producing conditions. *J. Exptl. Psychology*, 1944, 34, No. 5, 369—389.

Rosenzweig, M. and L. Postman, Frequency of usage and the perception of words. *Science*, 1958, 123, 263—266.

Rosenbaum, E., *Warum mussen wir schlafen?* Diss, Berlin, 1892.

Rossi, G.F., Sleep-inducing mechanisms in the brainstem. *EEG & Clin. Neurophysiol.*, 1962, 14, 428.

Roth, B., The clinical and theoretical importance of EEG-rhythms corresponding to states of lowered vigilance. *EEG & Clin. Neurophysiol.*, 1961, 13, 395—399.

Rothballer, A.B., The effect of phenylephrine, methamphetamine, cocaine and serotonin upon the adrenaline-sensitive component of the reticular activating system. *EEG & Clin. Neurophysiol.*, 1957, 9, 409—417.

Rubin, H.E. and E. Hatz, Auroratone films for the treatment of psychotic depression in an army general hospital. *J. Psychol.*, 1946, 2, 333—340.

Rubenstein, R. and R. Newman, The living out of "future" experiences under hypnosis. *Science*, 1954, 119, 472—473.

Ryzl, M., Precognition and intervention. *J. Parapsychol.*, 1955, 19, 192—202.

Ryzl, M., Training the psi faculty by hypnosis. *J. Soc. Psych. Res.*, 1962-a, 41, 234—252.

Ryzl, M. and J.G. Pratt, Confirmation of ESP performance in a hypnotically prepared subject. *J. Parapsychol.*, 1962-b, 26, 237—242.

Ryzl, M. and J. Ryzlova, A case of high-scoring ESP performance in the hypnotic states. *J. Parapsychol.*, 1962, 26, 153—171.

Ryzl, M. and J.G. Pratt, Confirmation of ESP performance in the hypnotic states. *J. Parapsychol.*, 1962, 26, 153—171.

Ryzl, M. and J.G. Pratt, A repeated calling ESP test with sealed cards. *J. Parapsychol.*, 1963-b, 27, 161—174.

Ryzl, M. and J.G. Pratt, The focusing of ESP upon particular targets. *J. Parapsychol.*, 1963-c, 27, 227—241.

Ryzl, M., A review of hypnotic ESP experiments in Prague. Paper read at the Seventh Annual Convention of the Parapsychological Association, Oxford University, 1964. (Abstract) *J. Parapsychol.*, 1964-a, 28, 285—286.

Ryzl, M., Model parapsychologicke kommunikace. *Sdelovaci technika*, 1964-b, 8, 299—302.

Ryzl, M., A working model of ESP communication. *J. Parapsychol.*, 1965-a, 29,

Ryzl, M. and J. Beloff, Loss of stability of ESP performance in a high-scoring subject. *J. Parapsychol.*, 1965-b. 29, 1—11.

Ryzl, M., J.A. Freeman and B.K. Kanthamani, Further testing of an outstanding subject. *J. Parapsychol.*, 1965, 29.

Ryzl, M., Soji Otani, An experiment in duplicate calling with Stepanek. *J.*

*Parapsychol.*, 1967, **31**, No. 1.

Ryzl, M., Precognition scoring and attitude towards ESP. *Parapsychology Today.* New York, 1968, **135**.

Sailaja, P., A confirmatory study of the role of key cards in language ESP tests. Papers read at the Eighth Annual Convention of the Parapsychological Association, New York, 1965.

Salzberg, H.C., Effects of suggestion on performance. *Int. J. Clin. Exp. Hypnosis, 1960*, **8**, 251 — 258.

Samelson, F., Conforming behavior under two conditions of conflict in the cognitive field, *J. Abnorm, Soc. Psychol.*, 1957, **55**, 181 — 187.

Sanford, R.H., The effects of abstinence from food upon imaginal processes: a preliminary experiment. *J. Psychol.*, 1936, **2**, 129 — 136.

Sarbin, T.R., Mental age changes in experimental regression. *J. Personality*, 1950, **19**, 221 — 228.

Satow, L., *Hypnotism and Suggestion.* London, 1923, 162.

Schaffer, L.F., *The Psychology of Abnormal People.* New York, Longmans, 1936, p. 162.

Scheibel, M.E. and A.B. Scheibel, Structural substrates for integrative patterns in the brain stem reticular core. *Reticular formation of the brain; Henry Ford Hospital Symposium.* Boston, Little Brown and Co., 1958.

Schazillo, B.A. and N.P. Abramov, Uber die Wirkung der Hypnose auf das Verhältnis der K und Ca Elektrolyte in Blutserum. *Ztschr. f. d. Ges. Neurol. u. Psychiat.*, 1928, **112**, 54.

Schilder, P., Uber Gedenkenentwicklung. *Z. Neurol.*, 1950.

Schlag, J.D. and F. Chaillet, Thalamic mechanismus involved in cortical desynchronization and recruiting responses. *EEG & Clin. Neurophysiol.*, 1963, **15**, 1, 39 — 62.

Schmeidler, G.R., Predicting good and bad scores in a clairvoyance experiment. A preliminary report. *J. Amer. Soc. Psych. Res.*, 1943, **37**, 103 — 110.

Schmeidler, G.R., Position effects as psychological phenomena. *J. Parapsychol.*, 1944, **8**, 110 — 123.

Schmeidler, G.R., Comparison of ESP scors with Rorschachs scored by different workers. *J. Amer. Soc. Psych. Res.*, 1949, **43**, 94 — 97.

Schmeidler, G.R., ESP performance and the Rorschach test: A survey of recent experiments. *J. Soc. Psychic. Res.*, 1950, **35**, 323 — 339.

Schmeidler, G.R., Personal values and ESP scores. *J. Abnorm. Soc. Psychol.*, 1952, **47**, 752 — 762.

Schmeidler, G.R., Agent precipient relationships. *J. Amer. Soc. Psych. Research*, 1958, **52**, 47 — 69.

Schmeidler, G.R., Contemporary psychologists view on Parapsychology today. *Parapsychology Today.* New York, 1968, 195.

Schneider, P.B., Die Neutralität in der analytischen Gruppenpsychotherapie (Abstracta). *Group Psychotherapy, 4th International Congress.* Vienna, 1968, 233.

Schultz, J. H., *Die seelische Krankenbehandlung (Psychotherapie).* Jena, 1930.

Schultz, J.H., *Hypnose-technik.* Jena, 1935.

Schultz, J.H., *Das autogene Training.* Leipzig, 1954.

Schultz, J.H., *100 jahre medizinische Psychologie,* Munch. med. Wschr., 1958, **1**.

Schultz, J.H. and W. Luthe, Autogenic training. *Proceedings of the Third World Congress of Psychiatry, Montreal, Canada, 4—10 June, 1961,* 1, 191 — 200.

Schultz, J.H., *Autogene Training*. Stuttgart, 1964.

Schutzenberger-Ancelin, A., Das dreigegliederte Psychodrama' Gruppenanalyse, Gruppendynamic und Psychodrama (Abstracta). *Group Psychotherapy, 4th International Congress*. Vienna, 1968, 281.

Schwartz, B.A., EEG et mouvements oculaires dans le sommeil de nuit. *EEG & Clin. Neurophysiol.*, 1962, **14**, 126—128.

Schwarz, B.E., R.G. Bikford and W.C. Rasmussen, Hypnotic phenomena including hypnotically activated seizures studied with the EEG. *J. Nerv. Ment. Dis.*, 1955, **122**, 564—574.

Servadio, E., *Imago*, 1935, **21**, 489.

Shaw, L.J., Hypnotism in dental work. *Brit. J. Med. Hypnotism*, 1949, **1**, 38.

Sherif, M., *The Psychology of Social Norms*. New York, 1936.

Silverman, R.E., Eliminating a conditioned GSR by reduction of experimental anxiety. *J. Exptl. Psychol.*, 1960, **59**, 2.

Simons, A.G. and N.R. Burch, Telemetry and automatic analysis of the electroencephalogramm under simulated flight conditions. *EEG & Clin. Neurophysiol.*, 1963, **15**, 165—166.

Smith, A.A., R.B. Malbo and C. Ahagass, An electromyographic study of listening and talking. *Canadian Journal of Psychology*, 1954, **8**, No. 4.

Smuts, J., *Holism and Evolution*. New York, 1926.

Snyder, F., The new biology of dreaming. *Arch. Gen. Psychiat.*, 1963, **8**, 381—391.

Soal, S.G., Experiment in supernormal perception at a distance. *Proc. Soc. Psych. Res.*, 1932, **40**, 165—362.

Soal, S.G., Fresh light on card guessing some new effectivs. *Proc. Soc. Psychic. Res.*, 1940, **46**, 152—198.

Soal, S.G., The experimental situation in psychical research. *J. Parapsychol.*, 1949, **13**, 79—100.

Soal, S.G., Some aspects of extrasensory perception. *Proc. Soc. Psychic. Res.*, 1951, **49**, 131—153.

Soal, S.G. and F. Bateman, *Modern Experiments in Telepathy*. New York, Yale University Pres, 1954.

Sorgant, W. and R. Fraser, Inducing light hypnosis by hyperventilation. *Lancet*, 1938, **235**, 778.

Stalnaker, J.M. and E.E. Riddle, The effect of hypnosis on long delayed recall. *J. Genr. Psychology*, 1932, **6**, 429-440.

Starkey, F.R., Aether hypnosis in psychotherapy. *Med. Res.*, 1917, **91**, 631.

Starr, A., Das Psychodrama als dynamischer Weg zur Ausbildung (Abstracta). *Group Psychotherapy, 4th International Congress*. Vienna, 1968, 279.

Steckel, W., *Der telepatische Traum*. Berlin, 1921.

Stern, W., *Differenzielle Psychologie*. Leipzig, 1911.

Stern, W., *Menschliche Persönlichkeit*. Leipzig, 1922.

Stern, W., *Allgemeine Psychologie auf personalistischer Grundlage*, Berlin, 1935.

Stern, W., *Handbuch klinischer Psychologie*. Zürich, 1954-1955.

Stocker, G., Psychological preparation and physiological adjustment in hypnopaedia. *Journal of the Sleep-Learning Association*, 1967, **4**, 3, 11—15.

Stockert, F.G., Die Psychologie der Hypnose. *Nervenarzr*, 1936, **3**, 462—467.

Stokvis, B., Der Einfluss der Hypnose auf den Pls. *Schweiz. Med. Wchnschr.*,

1938, **19,** 764.

Stokvis, B., *Hypnose in der ärztlichen Praxis.* basel—New York, 1955.

Straub, Zur psychodramatischen Behandlung von Zwangsneurosen Psychodramatis et communitatis therapeuticae (Abstracta). *Congressus Internationalis tertius.* Praga, 1968, 59.

Strumwasser, F., Long term recording from single neurons in brain of unrestrained mammals. *Science,* 1958, **127,** 469—470.

Stuchlik, J., Dos tipos funndamentales de sugestion. *Archivos Panamenos de Psicologia,* 1965, **I,** No. 3—4, 246—252.

Stukat, K.G., *Suggestibility (factional and experimental analysis).* Stockholm, 1958.

Stungo, E., Evipan hypnosis in psychiatric outpatients. *Lancet,* 1941, **240,** 507—509.

Swaardemaker, H., Periodische Lebenserscheinungen. *Erg. d. Physiol.,* 1908, **7,** 1—26.

Swerenz, G., *Magie, Sternenglaube, Spiritismus.* Leipzig, 1956.

Talbot, J.H., *et al.* Acid-base balance of the blood of a patient with hysterical hyperventilation. *Arch. Neurol. Psychiat.,* 1938, **39,** 973—987.

Tarchanoff, I., Observation sur le sommeil normal. *Arch. Ital. de Biol.,* 1894, **21,** 318.

Tatarelli, G., Medicine Psicosomatica e Igiene Mentale Nell'ambito della Marina Militara. *Atti Simposio Internazionale di Medicina Psicosomatica Militare.* Roma, 1967, 61.

Tenhaef, W.H.C., Parapsychological research in the Netherlands. *Proc. Parapsychol. Institute of the State University of Utrecht,* 1960, No. 1.

Tenhaef, W.H.C., The method of introspection. *Proc. Parapsychol-Institute of the State University of Utrcht,* 1965, No. 3.

Jenhaef, W.H.C., On the Personality Structure of Paragnosts, *Proc. Parapsychol, Institute of the State University of Utrecht,* 1962, No. 2.

Thorndike, E.L., *Elements of Psychology.* New York, 1919.

Thouless, R.H., The present position of experimental research into telepathy and related phenomena. *J. Parapsychol.,* 1943, 158—171.

Thouless, R.H., Experimental Research and the Study of Spontaneous Cases. *J. Parapsychol.,* 1952, **16,** 23—40.

Thouless, R.H., Psychical research past and present. *J. Parapsychol.,* 1953, 6—23.

Tocquet, R., *Tout l'occultisme dévoilé.* Paris, 1952.

Tokizane, I., Sleep mechanism' hypothalamic control of cortical activity. *Neurophysiologie des états de sommeil.* Paris, 1965, 151—184.

Trömner, E., Zur Biologie und Psychologie des Schlafes, Berlin. *Klin. Wschr.,*1910, **2,** 1301.

True, R.M., Experimental control in hypnotic age regression states. *Science,* 1949, 110 (2866), 583—584.

True, R.M. and Ch. W. Stephenson, Controlled experiments corelating EEG, pulse and plantar reflexes with hypnotic age regression and included emotional states. *Personality,* 1951, **1,** 252—263.

True, R.M. and Ch. W. Stephenson, *Brit. J. Med. Hypnt t.,* 1952, **4,** No. 1.

Tuckey, C.L., *Treatment by Hypnotism and Suggestion.* London, 1921.

Valatx, J.M., D. Jouvet and M. Jouvet, Evolution électroencephalographique des différents états de sommeil chez le chaton. *EEG & Clin. Neurophysiol.,* 1964, **17,** 218—233.

Van Blaaderen-Stock, C.L., Entwicklung von Gefühlen und Beziehungen in der analytischen Gruppenpsychotherapie (Abstracta). *Group Psychotherapy, 4th International Congress. Vienna*, 1968, 319.

Van E, de Boas, C. and C.L. Van Blaaderen-Stock, Einzelne Aspekte der Ko-Therapie in der analytischen Gruppentherapie (Abstracta). *Group Psychotherapy, 4th International Congress,* Vienna, 1968, 237.

Van Meter, W.G. and G.F. Ayala, EEG effect of intracarotid intravertebral arterial administration of d-amphetamine in rabbits with basilar artery ligation. *EEG & Clin. Neurophysiol.,* 1961, **13,** 382—384.

Vaschide, E., *Monstre Humain.* Paris, 1907.

Veronese, F., *Zur Physiologie des Schlafes,* 1910.

Verzeano, M., Neuronal interaction and synchronization of the EEG. (Excerpta Med., 5th Inter. Congr.), *EEG & Clin. Neurophysiol,* 1961, 49—54.

Vinacke, W.E., The discrimination of color and form at levels of illumination below conscious awareness. *Arch. Psychol.,* 1942, **38,** No. 267.

Vogt, O., Hypnotismus, *Ztschr. f. Hypn.,* 1895, Bd. 3.

Volavka, J., M. Matousek and J. Roubicek., Mental arithmetic and eye opening. *EEG & Clin. Neurophysiol.,* 1967, **19,** 2.

Wallerstein, H., An electromyographic study of attentive listening. *Canadian Journal of Psychology,* 1954, 8, No. 4.

Watkins, I.G. and B.I. Showalter, Unpublished paper on reading test given a hypnotized subject while regressed to various age levels.

Weiss, H.O., The treatment of performance neurosis in the psychodramatist (Abstracta). *Psychodramatis et communitatis therapeuticae. Congressus Internationalis tertius.* Praga, 1968, 73.

Weitzenhoffer, A.M., *Hypnotisme' An objective study in suggestibility.* New York, 1953, 808.

Welch, L., A behavioristic explanation of the mechanism of suggestion and hypnosis. *J. Abnorm, Soc. Psychol.,* 1947, **42,** 359—364.

Wertheimer, M., *Uber Gestalttheorie.* Erlangen, 1925.

White, R., G. Fox and W. Harris, Hypnotic hypermnesia for recently learned material. *J. Abn. Soc. Psychol.,* 1940, **35,** 88—104.

White, R.W., An analysis of motivation in hypnosis. *J. Gen. Psychol.,* 1941, **24,** 145—162.

Whitlow, J.E., *Experimental Hypnosis.* New York, 1948.

Williams, A.C., Perception of subliminal visual stimuli. *J. Psychol.,* 1938, **6,** 187—199.

Williams, G.W., Suggestibility in the normal and hypnotic states. *Archives of Psychology,* 1930, No. 122.

Wingfield, H.E., *An Introduction to the Study of Hypnotism.* London, Balliére, Tindall, and Cox. 1920.

Winter, E. de, L'entrainement psychotonique. *Atti del Simposio Internazionale di Medicina Psicosomatica Sportiva.* Roma, 1967, 23—32.

Wittkower, E., Uber den Einfluss der Affekte auf den Gallefluss. *Klin. Wchnschr.,* 1928, **7,** 2193.

Wittkower, E., Uber affektiv-somatische Veränderungen, Die Affektleucozytose. *Klin. Wchnschr.,* 29, **8,** 1082.

Wolberg, L.R., *Medical Hypnosis.* New York, V, 1948, No. 2.

Wundt, W., *Beiträge zur Theorie der Sinneswahroohmung.* Leipzig u. Heidelberg,

1862.

Wundt, W., *Hypnotismus und Suggestion.* Leipzig, 1892.

Yankov, G., I. Petrov, P. Petrov and D. Traikov, Application de l'hypnoanesthésie dans les tonselectomies. *Société française d'otorhinolaryngologie et de pathologie cervico-faciael, 62-ème Congrès Française.* Paris, Octobre, 1965-b, 29—34.

Yankov, G., I. Petrov, P. Petrov and D. Traikov, Application de la sofroanesthesia en les tonsilectomias, Reimpreso de la Revista Ibero Americana de sofrologia, Buenos Aires, Argentina, 1965-b.

Yates, A.J., Hypnotic age regression. *Psychol. Bull.,* 1961, **58,** 429—440.

Young, P.C., An experimental study of mental and physical function in normal and hypnotic states. *Amer. J. Psychol.,* 1925-a, 36, 214—232.

Young, P.C., An experimental study of mental and physical functions in the normal and hypnotic states. Additional results. *Amer. J. Psychol.,* 1926, **37,** 345—356.

Young, P.C., Hypnotic regression, fact or artifact. *J. Abnorm, Soc.* Psychol., 1940, 36, 273—278.

Young, P.C., Experimental hypnotism: a review. *Psychol. Bull.,* 1942, 38.

Zanchetti, A., Afferent regulation of waking and emotional behaviors in the decorticated cat. *Cortico-Subcortical relationship in sensory regulation.* Havana, 1965.

Zaslow, R.W., Rage reduction: a form of psychodrama on the couch. (Abstracta). *Psychodramatis et communitatis therapeuticae, Congressus Internationalis tertius.* Praga, 1968, 74.

# Bibliography - Bulgarian

1. Абашев-Константиновский А. Л., Проблемы сознания в свете клинической психопатологии, Вопр. психологии, 1958, 4, 30—41.
2. Аминеев Г. А., М. И. Ситкин, Влияние переменного магнитного поля низкой частоты на поведение мышей в Т-образном лабиринте, Вопр. гематологии, радиобиологии и биологического действия магнитных полей. Томск, 1965.
3. Амфитеатров, Л. Г., Гипноанестезия при искусстзенном аборте, Акушерство и гинекология, 1966, вып. 4—6.
4. Андреев М., За структурата на взаимоотношенията в колектива, Народна просвета, 1966, 64—76.
5. Андреев М., За разкриването на противоречията във възпитателните отношения, Народна просвета, 1967, 12, 24—30.
6. Анохин П. К., Рефлекс и функциональная система как факторы физиологической интеграции, Физиол. журн. СССР, 1949, 35, 5, 491—503.
7. Анохин П. К., Вопр. философии, 1957-а, 4.
8. Анохин П. К., Значение ретикулярной формации для различных форм высшей нервной деятельности, Физиол. журн. СССР, 1957-б, 43, 11, 1072—1085.
9. Анохин П. К., Внутреннее торможение как проблема физиологии, М., 1958.
10. Анохин П. К., Методологический анализ узловых проблем условного рефлекса, Ин-т философии АН СССР, М, 1962-а.
11. Анохин П. К., О специфическом действии ретикулярной формации на кору головного мозга, в кн. Электроэнцефалографическое исследование высшей нервной деятельности, М., 1962-б, 241—254.
12. Анохин П. К., Электроэнцефалографический анализ корко-подкорковых соотношений при положительных и отрицательных условных реакциях, в кн. Высшая нервная деятельность, М., 1963, 86—120.
13. Антропова М. В., В. Н. Иванов, Л. В. Михайлова, Г. И. Сальникова, Учебная нагрузка и отдых учащихся средней школы в режиме их дня, Изв. АПН, 1955.
14. Арнаудов М., Студии върху българските обреди и легенди, Унив. библ., С., 1924, 38.
15. Артемов В. А., Гипнопедия и обучение, в кн. «Научные и практические вопросы обучения с использованием естественного сна», М., 1967, 5—12.
16. Асатиани М. М., Метод репродуктивных переживаний в лечении психоневрозов, Клиническая медицина, 1926, т. I, 912.
17. Атанасов А. Г., Проучвания върху българските отреагиращи психолечебни методи репродукция и декапсулация, автореферат на дисертация, С., 1969.
18. Бакалска В., Г. Лозанов и И. Петров, За някои особености на двигателната и речевата функция при задръжни състояния на кората и главния мозък, БАН — Известия на института по експериментална медицина, 1957, II, 567.

19. Балевски П., Някои възрастови и типологични особености на висшата нервна дейност на децата и юношите, дисертация, 1962.
20. Балевски П., Б. Възвъзова, Б. Митева, П. Милев, Проучване натовареността и режима на студентите от II курс на ВИСИ, Трудове на НИХИ, 1966.
21. Балевски П., Б. Възвъзова, Б. Митева, П. Милев, Режим, натовареност и реактивност на студентите от III курс на ВМЕИ, Изв. на Научноизслед. хигиенен ин-т, 1968, I.
22. Балевски П., Работоспособността и здравословното състояние на изучаващите чужди езици по сугестопедичната методика, Народна просвета, 1968, 5, 100—103.
23. Балевски П., Р. Трашлиев, Медицински проучвания при сугестопедичното обучение, Здравен фронт, 7. XII. 1968, бр. 49, с. 5.
24. Балхашов Й., К вопросу о скоростном обучении иностранному языку прослушиванием уроков во сне, Вопросы психологии, 1965, 5, 130—132.
25. Бассин Ф. В., Фрейдизм в свете современных научных дискуссий, Сообщ. I, Вопр. психологии, 1958-а, 5, 133—145.
26. Бассин, Ф. В., Фрейдизм в свете современных научных дискуссий, Вопр. психологии, 1958-б, 6, 140—153.
27. Бассин, Ф. В., Сознание и «бессознательное», Философские вопр. физиологии высшей нервной деятельности и психологии, М., АН СССР, 1963, 425.
28. Бассин Ф. В., Проблема «бессознательного» (О неосознаваемых формах высшей нервной деятельности), М., 1968-а.
29. Бассин Ф. В., Проблемът за «безсъзнателното» в неговото отношение към теорията на установката, Философски въпроси на биологията и медицината, София, 1970, 47—55.
30. Бассин Ф. В., Э. С. Бейн, О применении электро-миографической методики в исследовании речи, материалы совещания по психологии, 1—6 июля 1955, М., АНП РСФСР, 1957.
31. Бахтиаров В. А., Гипнотическое внушение в хирургии, Уральский мед. журн., 1930, вып. 1.
32. Бахтиаров В. А., Случай верхней торакопластики под гипнозом, в сб. Борьба с туберкулезом, 1933, вып. 1.
33. Белицкий Г. Ю., в кн. «Труды научн. конф. посвящ. 40-й годовщине Октябрьской социалистической революции», Л., 1957.
34. Белицкий Г. Ю., Обратная связь в формировании основных уровней реактивности у человека, Методологические проблемы психоневрологии, Л., 1966.
35. Бернштейн Н. А., в кн.: Физиология человека, М., 1946.
36. Бернштейн Н. А., Новые линии развития физиологии и их соотношение с кибернетикой, И-т философии АН СССР, М., 1962.
37. Берон В., Естествена история, Болград, 1870.
38. Бессмертный Б. С., Математическая статистика в клинической, профилактической и экспериментальной медицине, М., 1967.
39. Бехтерев В. М., О лечении навязчивых идей гипнотическим внушением, Врач, 1892, т. XIII, вып. 1.
40. Бехтерев В. М., К вопросу о врачебном значении гипноза, Неврологический вестник, 1893, т. I, вып. 1.
41. Бехтерев В. М., Роль внушения в общественной жизни, Обозрение психиатрии, неврологии и экспериментальной психологии, 1898, 1.
42. Бехтерев В. М., Внушение и его роль в общественной жизни, СПб., 1908.
43. Бехтерев В. М., Гипноз, внушение и психотерапия и их лечебное значение, Вестник знания, 1911, вып. 4.
44. Бехтерев В. М., Об опытах над «мысленным» воздействием на поведение животных, Вопр. изучения и воспитания личности, Пг., 1920, т. 2, 270.

45. Бехтерев В. М., Внушение и воспитание, Пг., 1923.
46. Бехтерев В. М., В. М. Нарбут, Объективные признаки внушенных изменений чувствительности в гипнозе, Обозрения психиатрии, неврологии и экспериментальной психологии, 1902, № 1—2.
47. Бжалава И. Т., Психология установки и кибернетика, М., 1966.
48. Бикард В. А., О связи между высотой и устойчивостью цветовых барьеров, в кн. «Вопросы комплексного исследования кожнооптической чувствительности», Ученые записки, Свердловский государственный педагогический и-т, Свердловск, 1968, 52—64.
49. Бирман Б. Н., Экспериментальный сон, Л., 1925.
50. Бирюков Д. А., Физиология против религии и мистицизма, Л., 1965·
51. Близниченко Л. А., Ввод и закрепление информации в памяти человека во время естественного сна, Киев, 1966.
52. Богаченко Л. С., Опыт экспериментального исследования влияния школьного дня 1 и 2 смен на высшей нервной деятельности учащихся., Изв. АПН РСФСР, 1953, № 47.
53. Богаченко Л. С., Опыт изучения высшей нервной деятельности школьников в связи с некоторыми задачами гигиены нервной системы, Труды И-та высш. нерв. деятельности, М., 1956, т. II.
54. Богословский А. И., Опыт выработки сенсорных условных рефлексов у человека, Физиол. журн., 1936, т. XX.
55. Божинов С., Л. Гълъбов, К. Заимов, М. Йоцов, И. Темков, Х. Христозов, Практическо ръководство по психотерапия, Наука и изкуство, 1955.
56. Бойко Е. И., Основные положения высшей нейродинамики, в сб. «Пограничные проблемы психологии и физиологии», М., АПН РСФСР, 1957.
57. Бонгард М. М., М. С. Смирнов, «О кожном зрении» Р. Кулешовой, Биофизика, 1965, 10, 1, 148—154.
58. Боткин С. П., Общие основы клинической медицины, Физиология нервной системы, Избранные труды под ред. К. М. Быкова, М., 1952, вып. 3, кн. 2, 1003—1004.
59. Брезые М., Длительно сохраняющиеся электрические следы в головном мозге и их возможное отношение к высшей нервной деятельности, в сб. Электроэнцефалогр. иссл. высш. нервн. деят., М., 1962.
60. Бреус Е. Г., В. В. Плавинская, А. В. Безмен, Преимущества коллективной психотерапии в диспансерной практике, в сб. «Вопросы психотерапии в общей медицине и психоневрологии», Харьков, 1968, 71—72.
61. Буль П. И., Гипноз и внушение в клинике внутренних болезней, Л., Медгиз., 1953.
62. Буль П. И., Техника врачебного гипноза, Л., Медгиз, 1955.
63. Буль П. И., Гипноз и внушение в клинике внутренних болезней, Медгиз, Ленингр. отделение, 1958.
64. Бухарина Н., Т. П. Якимов, К вопросу оценки функционального состояния коры головного мозга по данным электроэнцефалографии, Журн. высш. нервн. деят., 1967, 3.
65. Быков К. М., Кора головного мозга и внутренние органы. Избр. произведения, М., 1954.
66. Быков К. М., И. Т. Курцин, Кортико-висцеральная патология, Л., 1960.
67. Васильев Л. Л., Таинственные явления человеческой психики, М., 1959.
68. Васильев Л. Л., Экспериментальные исследования мысленного внушения, Изд. Ленингр. у-тета, 1962.
69. Василиев Л. Л., Внушение от разстояние, Мед. и физкул., 1963.
70. Вашенюк В. А., Случай проведения аппендэктомии под гипнозом, Труды Душанбинского медицинского института, 1950, т. 5, Душанбе.

71. Вельвовский И. З., Психопрофилактика и психотерапия в акушерстве и гинекологии. В кн. «Вопросы психотерапии», М., Медгиз, 1958, 263—270.

72. Вельвовский И. З., Принципиальные основания к внедрению психотерапии в комплексе санаторно-курортной медицины, в сб. «Психотерапия в курортологии», Киев, 1966-а, 15—24.

73. Вельвовский И. З., Методические и организационные основы внедрения психотерапии в санаторно-курортную медицину, в сб. «Психотерапия в курортологии», Киев, 1966-б, 155—193.

74. Вельвовский И. З., Е. А. Шугом и В. А. Плотичер, Система психопрофилактичного и психотерапевтичного обезболивания родів. — Педіатрія, акушерство і гінекологія, 1950, № 1.

75. Вельвовский И. З., Г. Н. Балтпурвин-Безуглова, Принципы и предварительная схема построения психопрофилактического обслуживания беременных с первого дня обращения в консультацию, в сб. «Психопрофилактика в акушерстве и гинекологии», Киев, 1967-а, 250—254.

76. Вельвовский И. З., И. Д. Арист, И. И. Усоскин, О. И. Барсукова, Вопросы организации психопрофилактической и психотерапевтической помощи в акушерско-гинекологической сети, в сб. «Психопрофилактика в акушерстве и гинекологии», Киев, 1967-б, 273—278.

77. Виготски Л. С., Умственото развитие на децата в процеса на обучението, С., 1937.

78. Винер Н., Нелинейные задачи в теории случайных процессов, М., 1961.

79. Виш И. М., Хипнотичният сън и внушението като фактори, възстановяващи нервната дейност, Вопр. совр. психоневрологии, 1966, т. XXXVIII, 157—166.

80. Вольперт И. Е., Сновидения в обычном сне и гипнозе, Ленингр. отделение, изд. Медицина, 1966.

81. Вундт В., Лекции о душе человека и животных (перевод), СПб., 1894.

82. Възвъзова Б., Проучване натовареността на студентите по биохимия от I курс на Биологическия факултет, Трудове на НИХИ, 1966.

83. Выготский Л. С., Избранные психологические исследования, Москва, 1956.

84. Гарвалов Д., Социална психопатология, Н. Загора, 1936, т. I, 1937, т. II.

85. Генкин А. А., Е. Ф. Мордвинов, Электроэнцефалографические корреляты гипнотического состояния, Журн. высш. нервн. деят., 1969, вып. 3, 471—479.

86. Георгиев К., Д. Илиев и др., Наблюдения за влиянието на непроветрения въздух в класните стаи върху реактивността на учениците, Изв. И-та за физ. възп. и училищна хигиена, 1958, т. IV.

87. Георгиев К., П. Балевски, Пулсът и кръвното налягане на учениците и промените им в течение на учебния ден, Изв. на Педаг. и-т, С., 1961, кн. 7.

88. Герсамия Е. А., О некоторых особенностях фиксированной установки у детей олигофренов, Доклады АПН РСФС, 1960, № 5.

89. Гершуни Г. В., Изучение субсензорных реакций при деятельности органов чувства, Физиол. журн. СССР, 1947, 33, 4.

90. Гершуни Г. В., Журн. высш. нервн. деят., 1951, 1, 1.

91. Гилев Д. К., Характеристика тактильных и темистратурных признаков цвета, Проблемы кожно-оптической чувствительности. Ученые записки, Сборник 33, Свердловск, 1965.

92. Гиляровский В. А., Психиатрия, М., Медгиз, 1954.

93. Головина А., За спиритизма във връзка с душевните болести (между 1888 и 1900), Информационен бюлетин НИПИ, 1958, 2, кн. 1.

94. Гольдберг И. М., К вопросу об упражняемости тактильной чувствительности, Вопр. психологии, 1963, № 1.

95. Гольдберг И. М., Феномен Розы Кулешовой. Проблемы кожно-оптической чувствительности, Ученые записки, Сборник 33, Сэердловск, 1965, 23—51.

96. Гольдберг И. М., О распознавании признаков цвета через металлические покрытия, в кн. «Вопросы комплексного исследования кожнооптической чувствительности», Ученые записки, Свердловский государственный педаг. и-т, Свердловск, 1968, 104—114.

97. Гохблит И. И., К характеристике особенностей электрической активности коры мозга в различные возрастные периоды в связи с состоянием сна и бодрствования, III конференция по вопросам электрофизиологии нервн. системы, Киев, 1960, 134—135.

98. Гоцев, Т., А. Иванов., Психогенно повлияване на телесната температура у здрави хора, Годиш. мед. акад., С., 1949—1950.

99. Гращенков Н. И., Историко-философские представления и развитие современной физиологии мозга, Методологические проблемы психоневрологии, Л., 1966.

100. Гройсман А. Л., Схемы методики коллективно-групповой психотерапии в санаторно-курортных условиях, Психотерапия в курортологии, Киев, 1966.

101. Гуляев П. И., Электрическая активность коры больших полушарий головного мозга человека во время сна, Физиол. журн. СССР, 1955, 41, 2, 168—177.

102. Гуляев П. И., Электрические процессы коры головного мозга человека, Л., 1960.

103. Гуляев П. И., В. И. Заботин, Н. Я. Шлиппенбах, Электроаурограмма нерва, мышцы и сердца лягушки, сердца и мускулатуры человека, ДАН СССР, 1968-а, т. 180, № 6, 1504—1506.

104. Гуляев П. И., В. И. Заботин, Н. Я. Шлиппенбах, Электроаурограммы человека и животных, Нервная система, 1968-б, вып. 9, 159—171.

105. Данаджиев С., Принципите на психичната хигиена, С., 1935.

106. Данилевский В., Гипнотизм, Харьков, 1924.

107. Даскалов Д., Съвременно лечение на душевните болести, С., 1947.

108. Даскалов Д., Опит за изучаване на периодичните промени в реактивността на нервната система у хора през деня, Изв. и-та експер. мед., 1958.

109. Деменева А. Н., А. М. Кочигина, Дифференцирование цветовых раздражителей с помощью кожной чувствительности, в кн. «Вопр. комплексного исслед. кожно-оптич. чувствительности», Ученые записки, Свердловский госуд. пед. и-т, Свердловск, 1968, 95—103.

110. Дик В. Г., Гипноз как вспомогательное средство в гинекологической терапии, Врачебное дело, 1927 Б, № 21.

111. Димитров Х. Т., Психоанализата и нейните разновидности, 1965.

112. Димитриев А. С., Г. А. Жидкова, Влияние учебного дня на взаимоотношение первой и второй корковых сигнальных систем, Журн. высш. нерв. деят., 1956, 3.

113. Добронравов С. Н., Проблема кожного «зрения», Вестник высшей школы, 1963, 8.

114. Добронравов С. Н., Я. Р. Фишелев, Феноменальная чувствительность кожных рецепторов у человека, Сборник материалов научной сессии вузов Уральского экономического района, Свердловск, 1963.

115. Добронравов С. Н., И. Иванов, Н. Захаров, Выявление светочувствительности кожи путем выработки условных оборонительных рефлексов на световые раздражители, в кн. «Вопр. комплексного исследов. кожно-оптич. чувствительности», Ученые записки, Свердловский госуд. пед. и-т, Свердловск, 1968, 115—120.

116. Дубровский К. М., Методика директного группового внушения, Психотерапия в курортологии, Киев, 1966.

117. Е г о р о в А. С., Б. Н. Я к о в е ц, О зависимости уровня работоспособности и характера кривой утомления при мышечной работе от понимания задачи и отношения к ней испитуемых, Вопр. психологии, 1965, 1.
118. Ж е л т а к о в М. М., Показания к применению гипноза и условнорефлекторной терапии в дерматологии, в кн. «Вопр. психотерапии», под ред. М. С. Лебединского, М., Медгиз, 1958, 284.
119. Ж у к о в И. А., Гипнотерапия дерматозов в санитарно-курортных условиях, в кн. «Вопр. психотерапии», под ред. М. С. Лебединского, М., Медгиз, 1958, 305.
120. З а в а л о в а Н. Д., В. П. З у х а р ь, Ю. А. П е т р о в, К проблеме гипнопедии, Вопросы психологии, 1964, 2, 98—102.
121. З а и м о в К., Предчувствие и телепатия, Здраве, 1963, 6, 10—11.
122. З а х а р ы н Г. А., Клинические лекции и избранные статьи, М., 1909.
123. З д р а в о м ы с л о в В. И., Опыты применения гипноза в акушерстве и гинекологии, Медгиз, 1930.
124. З д р а в о м ы с л о в В. И., Значение психотерапии в акушерстве и гинекологии, в кн. «Вопр. психотерапии», М., Медгиз, 1958, 255—263.
125. З о т о в С., Сърце и кръвообращение при спорт и физически усилия, Физкултура, 1955.
126. З у х а р ь В. П., Актуальные вопросы нейрофизиологического изучения естественного сна человека в условиях направленного речевого воздействия, в кн. «Научные и практические вопросы обучения с использованием естественного сна», М., 1967, 61—70.
127. З у х а р ь В. П., Нейрофизиологические механизмы словесного воздействия, автореферат диссертации на соискание ученой степени доктора медицинских наук, М., 1968.
128. З у х а р ь В. П., Е. Я. К а п л а н, Ю. А. М а к с и м о в, И. П. П у шк и н а, Опыт проведения коллективной гипнопедии, Вопр. психологии, 1965, 1, 143—148.
129. И в а н о в Н. В., Основные вопросы методики коллективной психотерапии неврозов, в кн. «Вопр. психотерапии», М., 1958.
130. И в а н о в Н. В., О применении коллективной психотерапии в курортной практике, Психотерапия в курортологии, Киев, 1966.
131. И в а н о в а З., Динамика на работоспособността на учениците, Изв. пед. и-т, 1964, кн. XVII.
132. И в а н о в-С м о л е н с к и й А. Г., Опыты мысленного воздействия на животных, Вопр. изучения и воспитания личности, 1920, 2, 266—271.
133. И в а н о в-С м о л е н с к и й А. Г., Пути развития идей И. П. Павлова в области патофизиологии высшей нервной деятельности, в сб. «Научная сессия, посвященная проблемам физиологического учения академика И. П. Павлова», М., 1950.
134. И в а н о в-С м о л е н с к и й А. Г., Журн. высш. нервн. деят., 1951, т. I, вып. 1.
135. И в а н о в-С м о л е н с к и й А. Г., Очерки патофизиологии высшей нервной деятельности, М., 1952.
136. И с т о м и н П. П., П. Я. Г а л ь п е р и н, О влиянии внушенных состояний на колебания пищеварительного лейкоцитоза, Украинский вестник рефлексологии, 1925, 2.
137. И т к и н М. Г., О коллективном методе психотерапии в условиях амбулаторной обстановки, Врач. дело, 1936, 10, 885—887.
138. Й о н ч е в В., Върху лечебния механизъм на кортико-динамичната декапсулация, Съвр. мед., 1957, VIII, 5, 26—30.
139. Й о н ч е в В., Върху биоелектричната мозъчна активност по време на изпитното напрежение, Трудове на ВМИ И. П. Павлов, Пловдив, 1959/60, т. XIV.
140. Й о н ч е в В., Неврози в училищната възраст, Пловдив, 1962.
141. Й о н ч е в В., Лечебна хипноза, Пловдив, 1969.
142. К а ж и н с к и й Б. Б., Биологическая радиосвязь, Киев, 1962.
143. К а л и т к и н К. Н., Психотерапия в хирургии, Ташкент, 1965.

144. К а р т а м ы ш е в А. И., Возможности использования гипноза в дерматологии, Советская наука и техника, 1936, 5.
145. К а с а т к и н В. Н., Теория сновидения, Л., 1967.
146. К е ж е р а д з е Е. Д., Роль слова в запоминании и некоторые особенности памяти ребенка, Вопр. психологии, 1960, 1.
147. К е р б и к о в О. В., Лекции по психиатрии, М., Медгиз, 1955.
148. К и к о л о в А. И., Умственно-эмоциональное напряжение за пультом управления, М., 1967.
149. К и р я к о в К., Некоторые электроэнцефалографические критерии утомления при умственном труде, Журн. высш. нервн. деят., 1964, т. 14, 3.
150. К и т а й г о р о д с к и й А., Реникса, изд. Молодая гвардия, 1967.
151. К о в а л е в А. Г., В. Н. М я с и щ е в, Психические особенности человека, т. I, Характер. Л., 1957.
152. К о в а л е в А. Г., Психология личности, Л., 1963.
153. К о г а н И. М., Возможна ли телепатия? Радиотехника, 1966, 21, 8.
154. К о ж е в н и к о в М. М., Проблема кожно-оптической чувствительности, Ученые записки, Сборник 33, Свердловск, 1965.
155. К о ж е в н и к о в В. А., Р. М. М е щ е р с к и й, Современные методы анализа электроэнцефалограммы, М., Медгиз, 1963.
156. К о л е с н и к о в Н. И., Ю. М. Ф и л и м о н о в, В. Н. Б е л о у с о в, К вопросу о физической природе кожно-оптического чувства, Проблемы кожно-оптической чувствительности, Ученые записки, Сборник 33, Свердловск, 1965.
157. К о л о м и н с к и й Я. Л., Путь изучения и-формирования личных взаимоотношений между учениками класса, Вопр. психологии, 1963, 2, 101—**108.**
158. К о л о м и н с к и й Я. Л., Некоторые экспериментальные данные для критики социометрии, в сб. «Проблемы общественной психологии», М., 1965, 426—447.
159. К о л о м и н с к и й Я. Л., А. И. Р о з о в, Изучение взаимоотношений школьников социометрическими методами, Вопр. психологии, 1962, 6.
160. К о н И., Социология на личността, С., 1968.
161. К о н с т а н т и н о в В. Н., Гипноз в хирургии, Казанский медицинский журнал, 1937, т. 6.
162. К о п ы л о в А. Г., Метод ЭЭГ-кривых усвоения ритма, в сб. «Вопр. электрофизиологии», М.—Л., 1960.
163. К о р о т к и н И. И., Т. В. П л е ш к о в а, М. М. С у с л о в а, Изменение слуховых порогов в результате внушения в гипнозе, Журн. высш. нервн. деят., 1968, т. XVIII, вып. 1, 53—56.
164. К о р с а к о в С. С., Курс психиатрии, М., 1901.
165. К о р с а к о в С. С., Избранные произведения, М., 1954.
166. К о с т а н д о в Э. А., Влияние изменений функционального состояния коры и активирующей системы ствола мозга на обнаружение слабых звуковых сигналов, Журн. высш. нервн. деят. им. И. П. Павлова, 1967, вып. 4, 634—642.
167. К о с т а н д о в Э. А., Эффект неопознаваемых «эмоциональных» словесных раздражителей, Журн. высш. нервн. деят., им. И. П. Павлова, 1968, вып. 3, 371—380.
168. К о с т а н д о в Э. А., О возможностях и границах физиологического изучения «бессознательного», в сб. «Материалы пятого всесоюзного съезда невропатологов и психиатров», М., 1969, т. 3, 89—93.
169. К о т и к Н., Непосредственная передача мыслей, М., 1908.
170. К р а и н с к и й Н. В., Порча кликуши и бесноватые как явление русской народной жизни, Новгород, 1900.
171. К р а ф т-Э б и н г, Гипнотические опыты, Харьков, 1927.
172. К р е ч м е р Е., Медицинска психология, превод от 5-о изд. на А. Андреев, С., 1947.

173. К р у п н о в А. И., Индивидуальные особенности высоты цветовых барьеров у испытуемых с различными характеристиками силы возбудительного процесса, в кн. «Вопр. комплексного исследов. кожно-оптической чувствительности», Ученые записки, Свердловский государ. пед. и-т, Свердловск, 1968, 52—64.

174. К р у п н о в А. И., А. С. Н о в о м е й с к и й, В. А. Б и к а р д, О нахождении цветовых барьеров на основе остаточного излучения, в кн.: Вопр. комплексного исследов. кожно-оптической чувствительности», Ученые записки, Свердловский государ. пед. и-т, Свердловск, 1968, 121—136.

175. К р ы ж а н о в с к и й В. Г., Изменения частоты пульса при умственной работе, диссертация, М., 1957.

176. К у д и н о в а М. П., М. С. М ы с л о б о д с к и й, О зависимости параметров вызванного потенциала мозга человека от состояния внимания, Журн., высш. нервн. деят., 1968, 18, вып. 6.

177. К у л и к о в В. Н., К вопросу о гипнопедии, Вопр. психологии, 1964-а, 2, 87—97.

178. К у л и к о в В. Н., Обучение во сне, Сов. педагогика, 1964-б, 6, 51—58.

179. Л а н г е Дж., В. Н. С т р о м в а н Л ь о в е н, П. Ф. В е р р е, Корреляция между психологическими и энцефалографическими явлениями, в кн. «Электрофизиологическое исследование высшей нервной деятельности», М., АН СССР.

180. Л а т а ш Л. П., Гипоталамус, приспособительная активность и электроэнцефалограмма, М., 1968.

181. Л е б е д и н с к и й М. С., Психотерапия при нарушении речи, Невропатология и психиатрия, 1945, вып. 6.

182. Л е б е д и н с к и й М. С., Очерки психотерапии, М., 1959.

183. Л е б е д и н с к и й М. С., Некоторые соображения по вопросам психотерапии на курортах, Психотерапия в курортологии, Киев, 1966.

184. Л е б е д и н с к и й М. С., В. Н. М я с и щ е в, Введение в медицинскую психологию, Л., Медицина, 1966.

185. Л е й т е с Н. С., П. И. Р а з м ы с л о в, Юбилейная научная сессия и-та психологии, 1963, 2.

186. Л е н и н В. И., Соч., т. 14, изд. 1-е, стр. 116.

187. Л е о н Э. Л., Опыт организации обучения с использованием гипнопедии, в кн. «Научные и практические вопросы обучения с использованием естественного сна», М., 1967, 13—32.

188. Л е о н т и е в А. Н., Проблемы развития психики, АПН РСФСР, М., 1959.

189. Л и н е ц к и й М. Л., Новые материалы о нейродинамике реализации неадекватных внушений в гипнозе, Вопр. психологии, 1967, 1, 135—141.

190. Л и ф ш и ц С. Я., Гипноанализ инфантильных травм у истериков, Тверь, 1927.

191. Л о з а н о в Г., Въпроси на хипносугестията в светлината на учението на И. П. Павлов, Съвременна медицина, 1955, 9, 69—76.

192. Л о з а н о в Г., Диссоциированные движения глазных яблок в физиологическом и гипнотическом сне и теория сна, Журн. невропат. и психиатрии, М., IX, 1959, 4, 1095—1099.

193. Л о з а н о в Г. Внушението, в кн. «Ръководство по психотерапия», Ем. Шаранков, Г. Лозанов, Ив. Петров, Ат. Атанасов, С., 1963-а.

194. Л о з а н о в Г., О физиологических механизмах феномена Белла, Доклады Болгарской Академии Наук, 1963-б, т. 10, 7.

195. Л о з а н о в Г., О существовании в подкорье ассоциативных супрануклеарных центров движения глазных яблок, Доклады Болгарской Академии Наук, 1964, т. 17, 2.

196. Л о з а н о в Г., Сугестопедия — път към хипермнезия в учебния процес, Народна просвета, 1966, 6, 23—41.

197. Л о з а н о в Г., в кн. «За по-висока ефективност на учебния процес във висшите учебни заведения» (материали от семинара с преподаватели от висшите учебни заведения, състоял се на 15 март 1968 г. в ЦИУУ — Княжево, София), С., 1968, 49—53.
198. Л о з а н о в Г., А. А т а н а с о в, Психотерапията и културтерапията в психоневрологичните диспансери, Бюлетин на НИИНП, 1964, 1.
199. Л у б о ц к а я-Р о с с е л ь с Е. М., Профилактика невро-психических отклонений у учащихся, М., Медгиз, 1957.
200. Л ь о в е н ф е л д Л., Гипноз и его техника, Житомир, 1927 (перевод с немецкого).
201. М а й о р о в Ф. П., Физиологический журнал СССР им. Сеченова, 1950, XXXVI, вып. 6.
202. М а й о р о в Ф. П., М. М. С у с л о в а, Исследование экспериментальной регрессии речи в гипнозе, Журн. высш. нервн. деят., 1951, т. I, вып. 4, 479.
203. М а й о р о в Ф. П., М. М. С у с л о в а, Гипнотические опыты с внушенными возрастами, Труды и-та физиологии им. П. И. Павлова, 1952, I, 290.
204. М а к а р е н к о А. С., Лекции о воспитании детей, Учпедгиз, М., 1940.
205. М а к е д о н с к и В., Неврози, БАН, С., 1957.
206. М а к к е й Р., Возможности телеметрии при изучении физиологии животных и человека, в кн. «Биотелеметрия», М., 1965.
207. М а к с и м о в Ю. А., Электроэнцефалографическое исследование сна человека при действии звуковых и словесных раздражителей, в кн. «Научные и практические вопросы обучения с использованием естественного сна», М., 1967, 71—111.
208. М а л а х о в А. Н. и др., Электромагнитное поле СВЧ как сигнальный фактор в оборонительном условном рефлексе белых мышей, в кн. «Материалы к 3 поволжской конференции физиологов, биохимиков и фармакологов», Горький, 1963.
209. М а р е н и н а А. И., Электроэнцефалографическое исследование естественного и гипнотического сна у человека, в кн. «Проблема сна», хрестоматийный сборник, М., Медгиз, 1954, 264.
210. М а т в е е в В. С., Неосознаваемые формы психической деятельности в свете Ленинской теории отражения, Вопр. психологии. Материалы научной сессии, посвященной 50-летию Великой Октябрьской Социалистической Революции, Свердловск, 1967, 73—78.
211. М е г р а б я н А. А., Г. А. С а ф р я н, Терапия психогений барбамилкофеином в сочетании с вербальным внушением, Нервозы. Труды конференции, посвященной проблеме неврозов, Л., VI, 1955, 6—9.
212. М е р л и н В. С., Очерки психологии личности, Пермь, 1959.
213. М о г е н д о в и ч М. Р., А. Г. М а р к и н, О некоторых функциональных сдвигах в организме учащихся ремесленных училищ под влиянием рабочего дня, Труды второй науч. конференции по возрастной морфологии, физиологии и биохимии, М., 1955.
214. М о р д в и н о в Е. Ф., А. А. Г е н к и н, О возможностях прогнозирования внушаемости человека по данным спонтанной электроэнцефалограммы, Журн. высш. нервн. деят., 1969, вып. 6, 1027—1032.
215. М о р е н о Дж. Л., Социометрия, Экспериментальный метод и наука об обществе, М., 1958.
216. М у д р о в М. Я., Слово о способе учить и учиться медицине практической или деятельному врачебному искусству при постелях больных, М., 1820.
217. М у ш л о в и н а М. И., Метод коллективного внушения наяву при лечении токсикозов I половины беременности, в сб. «Вопросы психотерапии в общей медицине и психоневрологии», Харьков, 1968, 352—354.
218. М э г у н Г., Бодрствующий мозг, М., 1961.
219. М я с и щ е в В. Н., в сб. «Новое в рефлексологии и физиологии нервной системы», Л., 1926, 201—217.
220. М я с и щ е в В. Н., Вопр. изуч. и воспит. личности, 1930, 1—2, 24—32.
221. М я с и щ е в В. Н., Тр- и-та мозга, т. II, Л., 1939, 125—127.

222. М я с и щ е в В. Н., Некоторые вопросы теории психотерапии, Вопр. психотерапии, М., 1958.
223. М я с и щ е в В. Н., Личность и неврозы, Л., 1960.
224. М я с и щ е в В. Н., Понятие личности и его значение для мидицины. — Методологические проблемы психонаврологии, Труды Ленингр. науч. иссл. психоневрол. и-та им. В. М. Бехтерева, Л., 1966-а.
225. М я с и щ е в В. Н., Психотерапия на курорте, Психотерапия в курортологии, Киев, 1966-б.
226. М я с и щ е в В. Н., Медицинская психология и психопрофилактика, в сб. «Вопросы психотерапии в общей медицине и психоневрологии», Харьков, 1968.
227. Н а с т е в Г., Р. К о й н о в, Сьзнание и ретикуларна формация, С., 1961.
228. Н е в с к и й М. П., в кн. «Вопросы клинической невропатологии и психиатрии», Чельбинск, 1958, стр. 217.
229. Н и к о л а е в А. П., Гипноз в акушерстве и гинекологии, Врачебная газета, 1924, № 19—20.
230. Н и к о л а е в А. П., Гипноз при родах и операциях, Казанский мед. журн., 1930, № 1.
231. Н о в и к о в а Л. А., Электрофизиологическое исследование речевых кинестезий, Вопр. психологии, 1955, 5.
232. Н о в о м е й с к и й А. С., Кожно-оптическое чувство — свойство многих людей, Наука и жизнь, 1963-а, 2.
233. Н о в о м е й с к и й А. С., Цвет и свет на ощупь, Техника молодежи, 1963-б, 7.
234. Н о в о м е й с к и й А. С., Образная память и типы познавательной информации, Тезисы докладов на II съезде общества психологов, М., 1963-в, вып. 1.
235. Н о в о м е й с к и й А. С., Роль кожно-оптического чувства в познании, Вопр. философии, 1963-г, 5.
236. Н о в о м е й с к и й А. С., О природе кожно-оптического чувства у человека. Вопр. психологии, 1963-д, 5.
237. Н о в о м е й с к и й А. С., Из опыта формирования кожно-оптического чувства у незрячих людей, Проблемы кожно-оптической чувствительности, Ученые записки, Сборник 33, Свердловск, 1965.
238. Н о в о м е й с к и й А. С., Изменение кожно-оптической чувствительности в различных условиях освещенности, в кн. «Вопр. комплексного исследования кожно-оптической чувствительности», Ученые записки, Свердловский гссудар. пед. и-т, Свердловск, 1968, 8—51.
239. Н о в о м е й с к и й А. С., В. И. Я к о в л е в, О возможной сенсибилизации кожно-оптической чувствительности, Ученые записки, Свердловский государ. педагогический и-т, Свердловск, 1968, 74—94.
240. О п п е н г е й м Д. Г., Основы индивидуального режима, в кн. «Основы режима лечения и отдыха в санаториях и на курортах», М., 1954.
241. О р м а н д ж и е в С., И. М е з а н, Х. Й о р д а н о в, Д. В а ч о в, Автоматичен анализ на амплитудите и периодите в електроенцефалограмата, Невропатология, психиатрия и неврохирургия, 1967, 1.
242. П а в л о в Б. В., Ю. А. П о в о р и н с к и й, К вопросу о взаимодействии первой и второй сигнальных систем в сомнамбулической фазе гипноза, Журн. высш. нерв. деят., т. III. 1953, вып. 3, стр. 386.
243. П а в л о в И. П. Полное собрание сочинений, т. I — IV. М.—Л., 1951—1952.
244. Павловские среды, М.—Л., 1949.
245. Павловские клинические среды, М.—Л., 1954—1957.
246. П а в л о в Т. Теория на отражението, С., 1945.
247. П а в л о в Т. Теория на отражението, С., 1947.

248. П а в л о в Т. Теория на отражението, С., 1962.
249. П а л а м а р ч у к В. М., Характеристика этапов коллективно-групповой психотерапии при лечении хронического алкоголизма в амбулаторных условиях, в сб. «Вопросы психотерапии в общей медицине и психоневрологии», Харьков, 1968, 256—257.
250. П а н е в А., М. П о п о в, Лекари в средновековна България и равнището на медицинските им познания, Науч. тр. ВМИ, С., 1957.
251. П а н т е л е е в В. М., Опыт коллективной психотерапии в условиях местного санатория (Филипповский санаторий), Психотерапия в курортологии, Киев, 1966.
252. П а р и г и н Б. Д., Социалната психология като наука, С., 1968.
253. П е т р о в Й., Хипноза, Ръководство по психотерапия. Ем. Шаранков. Г. Лозанов, Ив. Петров, Ат. Атанасов, С., 1963.
254. П е т р о в П., Д. Т р а й к о в, Ц. К а л е н д ж и е в, Принос по въпросите на психообезболяването при някои стоматологични манипулации. Бюлетин Науч. изсл. и-т невролог. психолог., 1963-а, 4, 60—66.
255. П е т р о в П., Психоанестезията чрез хипноза при лечение на стоматологични заболявания, Стоматология, 1963-б, 6, 59—68.
256. П е т р о в П., Психотерапия при лечение на стоматологични заболявания, Стоматология, 1965, 5, 74—77.
257. П е т р о в П., Психостоматологична методика, Стоматология, 1966, 1. 35—42.
258. П е т р о в Ф. П., Действие электромагнитного поля на изолированные органы, в кн. «Физико-химические основы нервной деятельности», Труды института по изучению мозга им. В. М. Бехтерева, Ленинград, 1935, 97—104.
259. П е т р о в Ф. П., Действие электромагнитного поля низкой частоты на высшую нервную деятельность, Труды и-та им. И. П. Павлова, I, 1952. 369—375.
260. П л а т о н о в К. И., Психорефлексы и влияние на них гипнотического внушения, Харьковский медицинский журнал, 1915, № 6.
261. П л а т о н о в К. И., И. З. В е л ь в о в с к и й, К вопросу о применении гипноза в хирургии, акушерстве и гинекологии, Врачебное дело, 1924. № 7.
262. П л а т о н о в К. И., Внушение и гипноз в хирургии, Труды съезда хирургов левобережной Украины, Харьков, 1925-а, ч. II.
263. П л а т о н о в К. И., Гипноз и внушение в практической медицине, Науч ная мысль, 1925-б.
264. П л а т о н о в К. И., Врачи и гипноз, Врачебное дело, 1925-в, № 24—26.
265. П л а т о н о в К. И., К вопросу о лечении психоневроз гипнопсихотерапией, Совр. психоневрология, 1925-г, № 6—7.
266. П л а т о н о в К. И., О роли внушения в родообезболивании, Труды VIII Всесоюзного съезда акушеров, 1926-б.
267. П л а т о н о в К. И., К учению о природе гипноза в гипносуггестивной психотерапии, Совр. психоневрология, 1926-а, № 3.
268. П л а т о н о в К. И., О словесном гипносуггестивном методе исследования в области психофизиологии и психологии, Труды IV Всесоюзного съезда физиологов, 1930-а.
269. П л а т о н о в К. И., Гипноз и алкоголизированная нервная система. — Вопр. общей психоневрологии. Психотерапия, Труды украинского психоневролог. и-та, 1930-б, т. XV.
270. П л а т о н о в К. И., О своеобразном методе экспериментальной репродукции психоневрологических синдромов, Проблемы неврологии и психиатрии, Киев, 1939, 507—514.
271. П л а т о н о в К. И., Внушение и гипноз в свете учения И. П. Павлова, М., Медгиз, 1952-а.
272. П л а т о н о в К. И., К учению о значении сонного гипнотического торможения как терапевтическое средство при лечении некоторых патологических состояний человека, Журн. высш. нерв. деят., 1952-б, т. II, вып. 3.

273. П л а т о н о в  К.  И., Слово как физиологический и лечебный фактор,
     М., 1957.
274. П л а т о н о в  К.  И., От старейшего психотерапевта СССР — врачам
     курортологам, в сб. «Психотерапия в курортологии», Киев, 1966, 14—15.
275. П л а т о н о в  К. И.,  Е. Л.  П р и х о д и в н ы й,  К объективному дока-
     зательству изменения личности путем внушения (экспериментально-пси-
     хологическое исследование), в сб. «Психотерапия», Труды Украинского пси-
     хоневрологического института, т. XIV, 1930.
276. П л е х а н о в  Г.  Ф., Некоторые материалы по восприятию информации
     живыми системами, в кн. «Бионика», М., 1965.
277. П л е х а н о в  Г.  Ф.,  В.  В.  В е д ю ш к и н а, Выработка сосудистого
     условного рефлекса у человека на изменение напряженности электро-
     магнитного поля высокой частоты, Журн. высш. нервн. деят., 1966, 16, 34.
278. П о д ъ я п о л с к и й  П.  П., Пузырь от мнимого ожога, получены словес-
     ным внушением в состоянии искусственного сна, Труды Саратовского об-
     щества естествоиспытателей, Саратов, 1903—1904, т. 4, вып. 2.
279. П о д ъ я п о л с к и й  П.  П., О вазомоторных расстройствах, вызываемых
     гипнотическим внушением, Журн. им. Корсакова, 1909, вып. 1—2.
280. П о д ъ я п о л с к и й  П.  П., О применении гипнотического внушения при
     эпилепсии, Невролог. вестник, 1913, № 3.
281. П о д ъ я п о л с к и й  П.  П., Случаи применения гипнотического внуше-
     ния в лазаретной практике, Невропатология и психиатрия, 1915, вып. 2.
282. П о д ъ я п о л с к и й  П.  П., Гипнотическое внушение и его применение
     в хирургии, Природа, 1926, № 9—10.
283. П о д ъ я п о л с к и й  П.  П., Гипнология и применение гипнотического
     внушения в медицине, Труды II Поволжского съезда врачей, 1927-а,
     т. VI.
284. П о д ъ я п о л с к и й  П.  П., Гипнотическое внушение в гинекологии,
     Труды II Поволжского съезда врачей, 1927-б, т. VI.
285. П о д ъ я п о л с к и й  П.  П. Гипнотическое внушение, его значение при
     диференциальной диагностике, применение в терапии и хирургии, Кли-
     нический журнал Саратовского у-тета, 1929, т. VII. № 4—5.
286. П о з н а н с к а я  Н. Б.,  И. Н.  Н и к и т с к и й, Х.,Ю.  К о л о д н а я,
     Т. С.  Ш а х н а з а р я н, Кожная чувствительность к видимым и инфра-
     красным лучам, Сборник докладов VI Всесоюзного съезда физиологов,
     Тбилиси, 1937.
287. П о з н а н с к а я  Н. Б., Кожная чувствительность к видимому и инфра-
     красному обучению, Физиол. журн. СССР, 1938, т. 24, вып. 4.
288. П р а н г и ш в и л и  А.  С., Исследования по психологии установки,
     Тбилиси, 1967.
289. П р а т у с е в и ч  Ю.  М.,  Н. Н.  К о р ж, Изменение электрической реак-
     тивности головного мозга у детей после классных занятий, Гигиена и
     санит., 1961, кн. 1.
290. П р а т у с е в и ч  Ю.  М.,  П.  В. М е л ь н и ч у к, Л. А.  А л е к с е е в а,
     Н. Н.  К р о ж, Изучение состояния электрической активности головного
     мозга у школьников до и после учебных занятий, Педиатрия, 1959, вып. 6,
     Сообщение I.
291. П р а т у с е в и ч  Ю.  М., Умственное утомление школьника, М., 1964.
292. П р е с м а н  А.  С., Электромагнитные поля и процессы регулирования в
     биологии, в сб. «Вопросы бионики», М., 1967, 341—350.
293. П р е с м а н  А.  С., Электромагнитные поля и живая природа, М., 1968.
294. П у ш к и н а  И.  П., Психологические аспекты проблемы восприятия ин-
     формации в период естественного ночного сна, в кн. «Научные и прак-
     тические проблемы обучения с использованием естественного сна», Москва,
     1967, 112—142.
295. П у ш к и н а  И.  П.,  З у х а р ь  В.  П., Психофизиологические механизмы
     восприятия информации в естественном сне, в кн. «Научные и практи-
     ческие вопросы обучения с использованием естественного сна», М., 1967,
     143—155.

296. П ш о н и к А. Т., Кора головного мозга и рецепторная функция организма М., 1952.

297. Р а й к о в В. Л., О неоднородности сомнамбулической стадии гипноза, в сб. «Психоневрологические проблемы», I Мед. и-т, Москва, 1969-а.

298. Р а й к о в В., Влияние глубокого гипноза на резервные возможности памяти и регистрация уровня гипнотического состояния с помощью электроэнцефалограммы, в кн. «Психологические исследования в практике врачебно-трудовой экспертизе», М., 1969-б, 128—136.

299. Р а т а н о в а Т. А., К вопросу об условиях возникновения установки на восприятие, Вопр. психологии, 1962, № 4.

300. Р е й д е р Э. Г., С. С. Л и б и х., Запоминание языкового материала. в условиях мышечной релаксации и аутогенной тренировки, Вопр. психологии, 1967, 1, 106—114.

301. Р о ж н о в В. Е., Гипноз в медицине, М., 1954.

302. Р о ж н о в В. Е., К вопросу о физиологических особенностях гипнотического сна различных стадий глубины, Вопр. психотерапии, М., 1958.

303. Р о ж н о в а М. А., В. Е. Рожнов, Гипноз и «чудесные исцеления», М., 1965.

304. Р о й т б а к А. И., Анализ электрических явлений в коре больших полушарий при угасания ориентировочных и условных рефлексов, в кн. «Электроэнцефалографическое исследование высшей нервной деятельности», М., 1962, 87—95.

305. Р о й т б а к А. И., С. М. Б у т х у з и, О механизме реакции пробуждения при действия периферических раздражений, Гагрские беседы, Тбилиси, 1963, 237—248.

306. Р о с с и Д ж. Ф., А. Ц а н к е т т и, Ретикулярная формация ствола мозга, М., 1960.

307. Р у б и н ш т е й н С. Л., Основы общей психологии, М., 1940.

308. Р у б и н ш т е й н С. Л., Бытие и сознание, М., 1957.

0 9. Р у б и н ш т е й н С. Л., Принципы и пути развития психологии, М., 1959.

310. Р у т е н б у р г Э. С., О суточном ритме пульса, артериального давления и температура тела у рабочих подрастков, III. републ. конфер. по вопросам школьной гигиены. Тезисы докладов, М., 1959.

311. С а м с о н о в а В. Г., Журн. высш. нервн. деят., 1953, т. III, вып. 5.

312. С а м с о н о в а В. Г., Труды и-та высшей нервн. деят., серия физиологическая, М., 1955, т. 1, стр. 192.

313. С в я д о щ А. М., Нервозы и их лечение, М., 1959.

314. С в я д о щ А. М., К истории гипнопедии, Вопр. психологии, 1965, 3. 147—149.

315. С в я д о щ А. М., Восприятие и запоминание речи во время естественного сна, Вопр. психологии, 1962, 1, 65—80.

316. С е г а л А. С. Медицинское обследование лиц, обучавшихся гипнопедическим способом, в кн. «Научные и практические вопросы обучения с использованием естественного сна», М., 1967, 156—164.

317. С е г а л Б. М., Ю. С. С а в е н к о, В. М. К у ш н а р е в, Л. Н. С о б ч и к. Э. Л. М а к с у т о в а, Пути воздействия на личность при психотерапии, в сб. «Материалы пятого всесоюзного съезда невропатологов и психиатров», 30 июня—6 июля 1969, М., 1969. т. 3, 317—324.

318. С е п е т л и е в Д., Статистически методи за обработка на данни от медицинските научни проучвания, С., Медицина и физкултура, 1965.

319. С е р г е е в Г. А., Л. П. П а в л о в а, А. Ф. Р о м а н е н к о, Статистические методы исследования электроэнцефалограммы человека, Л., 1968.

320. С е р г е е в Г. А., Г. Д. Ш у ш к о в, Э. Г. Г р я з н у х и н, Методика регистрации и статистической обработки биоплазмограммы, в кн. «Вопросы биоэнергетики» (материалы научно-методического семинара), Алма-Ата, 1969-а, 46—49.

321. Сергеев Г. А., Г. Д. Шушков, Э. Г. Грязнухин, Новый тип датчиков для регистрации физиологических функций организма, в кн. «Вопросы биоэнергетики» (материалиы научно-методического семинара), Алма-Ата, 1969-б, 49—51.

322. Сергеев Г. А., В. В. Кулагин, Энергетические характеристики биоплазмограммы, в кн. «Вопросы биоэнергетики» (материалы научно-методического семинара), Алма-Ата, 1969-в, 51—53.

323. Сеченов И. М., Избранные философские и психологические сочинения, М., Госполитиздат, 1947.

324. Сеченов И. М., Рефлексы головного мозга, Изд. АМН СССР, М., 1952.

325. Сидис Б., Психология внушения, перевод, СПб, 1902.

326. Сикорский И. А., Психологическая эпидемия 1892 г. в Киевской губернии, Университ. известия, Киев, 1893, 33, 4.

327. Симсон Т. П., Неврозы у детей, их предупреждение и лечение, М., Медгиз, 1958.

328. Сировский Э. М., Результаты обучения иностранным языкам при помощи гипнопедии, в кн. «Научные и практические вопросы обучения с использованием естественного сна», М., 1967, 52—60.

329. Слободяник А. П., Писхотерапия, внушение, гипноз, Киев, 1966.

330. Соколов А. Н., Памет, в Психология, под ред. на А. А. Смирнов, А. Н. Леонтиев, С. Л. Рубинщайн, Б. М. Теплов, Народна просвета, 1967.

331. Соколов А. Н., Внутренняя речь и мышление, М., изд. Просвещение, 1963.

332. Соломонов О. С., А. А. Шишло, О снотворных рефлексах. Труды общества русских врачей, СПб, 1910. Препеч. в сб. «Проблема сна», М., 1954.

333. Сорохтин Г. Н., Атония нервного центра, М., 1961.

334. Срезневский В. В., Гипноз и внушение, Л., 1924.

335. Срезневский В. В., Гипноз и внушение, Л., 1927.

336. Старобинец М. Х., Постоянные поляризационные потенциалы головного мозга человека во время бодрствования, наркоза и сна, Журн. высш. нервн. деят., 1967, 17, 338.

337. Стоев С. Г., Фройдизмът и преодоляването му в България, С., 1969.

338. Стрельчук И. В., Опыт дифференцировочного гипнотерапевтического воздействия в свете учения И. П. Павлова. Журн. высш. нерв. деят., М., 1953, III. 3.

339. Суботта А. Г., О влиянии импульсного СВЧ электромагнитного поля на высшую нервную деятельность собак, Бюлл. экспер. биол. и мед., 1958, 10.

340. Судаков Н. И., О различении цветовых тонов с помощью пальцев. Проблемы кожно-оптической чувствительности, Ученые записки, Сборник 33, Свердловск, 1965.

341. Сумбаев И. С., К методике внушения в бодрственном состоянии, Вопр. психотерапии, М., Медгиз, 1958.

342. Суслова М. М., Труды института физиологии им. И. П. Павлова, 1952, I, 296.

343. Сухарева Г. Е., Клинические лекции по психиатрии детского возраста, М., Медгиз, 1959, II.

344. Танцюра М. Д., Опыт лечения больных навязчивым неврозам методом активного возбуждения паталогической инертности, Сов. медицина, 1956, 11, 80—84.

345. Тапильский А. А., Изменение количества лейкоцитов при внушении сытости или голода в состоянии условнорефлекторного сна, Медицинская мысль Узбекистана, 1928, № 2.

346. Тарханов И. Р., Гипнотизм, внушение и чтение мыслей, СПб., 1886.

347. Ташев Т., Върху психотерапевтическите методи, Сборник трудове ВМИ — Пловдив, 1957, т. X, с. 57.

348. Т е л е ш е в с к а я  М. Э., Патофизиологический анализ наркопсихотерапии зафиксированных истерических реакций, Неврозы, Труды Конференции, посвященной проблеме неврозов, Л., 1955, V, 6—9, Петрозаводск, 1956.

349. Т е л е ш е в с к а я  М. Э., Психотерапия неврозов в условиях курорта, в сб. «Психотерапия в курортологии», Киев, 1966, 64—67.

350. Т е о д о р о в  И., Ролята на душата при заболяване и лекуване, Варна, 1921.

351. Т е о д о р о в  И., Леко раждане. Бързо и почти безболезнено, С., 1931.

352. Т к а ч е н к о  В. Я., К вопросу о лечении больных неврастенией с расстройствами сна в условиях санатория, Психотерапия в курортологии, Киев, 1966.

353. Т о к а р с к и й  А. А., Гипнотизм и внушение, Архив психиатрии, 1887, т. XI, вып. 1 и 3.

354. Т о к а р с к и й  А. А., Терапевтическое применение хипнотизма, Доклад на IV съезде русских врачей, СПб, 1891.

355. Т о л с т о й  Л. Н., Полн. собр. соч., т. 46, Гослитиздат, М., 1934, 1937.

356. Т р а й к о в  Д.,  С.  П а ш о в с к и,  Приложение на хипноанестезията при извършване на Resectio Septinasisubmicosis Ото-рино-ларингология, 1967, 3, 119—121.

357. Т у г а р и н о в  В. П., О некоторых новых проблемах сознания, Вестник Ленинградского у-тета, 1964, № 11.

358. У е л с  Г., Павлов и Фрейд., Ню Йорк, перевод, изд. Иностр. лит., М., 1959.

359. У з н а д з е  Д. Н., Психологические исследования, М., 1966.

360. У о л т ъ р  Г., Живой мозг, М., 1966.

361. Ф е д о т о в  Д. Д., Проблемы исследования восприятия слабых сигналов, Материалы научной конференции: Проблемы исследования восприятии слабых сигналов, М., 1968, 22—23 мая.

362. Философская энциклопедия, М., Советская энциклопедия, 1967.

363. Ф и ш е л е в  Я. Р.,  С. Н.  Д о б р о н р а в о в, О «кожном зрении» у человека. Проблемы кожно-оптической чувствительности, Ученые записки. Сборник 33, Свердловск, 1965, 52—62.

364. Х а ч а п у р и д з е  Б. И., Об отражательной функции установки в связи с проблемой воздействия невоспринимаемых раздражителей, Труды Тбилисского государ. у-тета, Тбилиси, 1966, т. 124.

365. Х о в р и н  А. Н., Редкая форма гиперстезии высших органов чувств, Вопр. нервно-психической медицины, Киев, 1898, вып. 3—4.

366. Х о д ж а в а  З. И., Роль установки в интерференции навыков, Вопр. психологии, 1961, № 4.

367. Х о д ж а в а  З. И., Основной закон смены установки в теории установки Д. Н. Узнадзе, Тбилиси, 1964.

368. Х о л о д о в  Ю. А., Об образовании условных рефлексов на магнитное поле у рыб, в кн. «Труды совещания по физиологии рыб», АН СССР, М., 1958.

369. Х о л о д о в  Ю. А., Некоторые особенности физиологического действия электромагнитных полей по данным условнорефлекторной и электроэнцефалографической методики, XX совещание по проблемам высш. нерв. деятельности, Тезисы докладов. АН СССР, М.—Л., 1963-а.

370. Х о л о д о в  Ю. А., Влияние постоянного магнитного поля на ЭЭГ изолированного мозга кролика, в. кн. «Электрофизиология нервной системы», Ростов-на-Дону, 1963-б, 418.

371. Х о л о д о в  Ю. А., Влияние электромагнитного поля УВЧ на электрическую активность нейронально изолированной полоски коры головного мозга, Бюлл. эксп. биол. и мед. 1964, 57, № 2, 98.

372. Х о л о д о в  Ю. А., Человек в магнитной паутине, Знание—сила, 1965-а, 7, 13—16.

373. Холодов Ю. А., Магнитное поле как раздражитель, в кн. «Бионика», Наука, М., 1965-б.
374. Холодов Ю. А., Влияние электромагнитных и магнитных полей на центральную нервную систему, Наука, М., 1966-а.
375. Холодов Ю. А., Влияние постоянных магнитных полей на биологические обекты, Всесоюзный симпозиум по сильным магнитным полям, Красноярск, 1966-б, 38.
376. Холодов Ю. А., Особенности реакции головного мозга на постоянное магнитное поле, XVIII Международный психологический конгресс, М., 1966-в, т. 1, 322.
377. Холодов Ю. А., С. Н. Лукьянова, Р. А. Чиженкова, Электрофизиологический анализ реакций центральной нервной системы на электромагнитные поля, в сб. «Современные проблемы электрофизиологии центральной нервной системы», М., 1967, 273—280.
378. Христозов Хр., Върху етиопатогенезата и патофизиологията на неврозите, Научни трудове на ВМИ — София, 1959-а, т. XXXVIII, 3, 23—58.
379. Христозов Хр., Сравнителен клинико-статистичен анализ на неврозите, Научни трудове на ВМИ — София, 1959-б, т. XXXVIII, 3, 59—111.
380. Христозов Хр., Върху сравнителната патофизиологична характеристика на неврозите, Известия на и-та по физиология, БАН, 1960, кн. 4, 88—112.
381. Чакъров А., Д. Трайков, З. Ботев, З. Якимов, Применении гипноанестезии при некоторых брюшных операциях, Вестник хирургии им. И. И. Грекова, 1966, 12, 103—105
382. Четин Ф. Е., А. С. Новомейский, К вопросу о физической природе кожно-оптической чувствительности, в кн. «Вопр. комплексного исследования кожно-оптической чувствительности», Ученые записки, Свердловский государ. пед. и-т, Свердловск, 1968, 137—163.
383. Чистович А. С., Труды института физиологии им. И. П. Павлова, т. I, 1952, стр. 425.
384. Чолаков К., Психофизиологичната декапсулация като казуално лечение на психоневрозите, Русе, 1933.
385. Чолаков К., Основи на учението за неврозите, С., 1940.
386. Чолаков К., Психоанализата на Фройд в критично осветление, С., 1947.
387. Чуприкова Н. И., Слово как фактор управления в высш. нервн. деятельности человека, изд. Просвещение, М., 1967.
388. Шаранков Е., Нестинарството. Същност и прояви. Психофизиологичен и патопсихологичен поглед върху огнеходството, С., 1947.
389. Шаранков Е., Общи насоки и предпоставки за едно невропсихично изследване на децата, Доклад пред конференцията на училищните лекари, 20 април 1949.
390. Шаранков Е., Мястото и значението на хипермнезията при психолечението, Трудове на НИПИ, т. 2, С., 1956.
391. Шаранков Е., Неврозите, клиничен поглед, С., Медицина и физкултура; 1961.
392. Шаранков, Е., Психотерапията и нейната същност, в Ръководство по психотерапия — Ем. Шаранков, Г. Лозанов, Ив. Петров и Ат. Атанасов, С., Медицина и физкултура, 1963.
393. Шахнович М. И., Современная мистика в свете науки, М.—Л., 1965.
394. Шерман И. А., Опыт индивидуальной и групповой гипотерапии с последующим сном — отдыхом в комплексе лечения неврозов в санатории «1-е Мая», Психотерапия в курортологии, Киев, 1966.
395. Шеханова Е., Лечение на психоневрозите по метода на изкуствената репродукция, Медицинско списание, С., 1928, XII, 10.
396. Шеханова Е., Учението на Н. Кръстников в светлината на Павловското учение, Известия на мед. институти, БАН. С., 1954, т. IX—X.

397. Шипковенски Н., К. Гълъбов, И. Рачев, Медицинска терминология и клиничен речник, С., 1955.
398. Шипковенски Н., Клинична психиатрия, С., Наука и изкуство, 1956.
399. Шичко Г. А., К вопросу о выработке условных рефлексов через вторую сигнальную систему, Совещание по проблемам физиологии и патологии речевой деятельности, Л., 1955.
400. Шичко Г. А., О возрастных особенностях образования слюнных условных рефлексов через вторую сигнальную систему, Труды третьей науч. конфер. по возрастной морфологии, физиологии и биохимии, М., 1959.
401. Шпильберг П. И., Электроэнцефалограмма человека во время сна и гипноза, Физиол. журн. СССР, 1955, 41, 2, 178—186.
402. Штерн Л. С., К вопросу смены сна и бодрствования. — Невропатология и психиатрия, 1937, вып. 2, 189—200.
403. Юк А., К. Юс., Нейрофизиологические исследования «бессознательного». Журн. невропат. и психиатр. им. С. С. Корсакова, 1967. вып. 12, 1809—1815.
404. Якобсон П. М., Психологические проблемы мотивации поведения человека, М., 1969.
405. Янков Г., Ив. Петров, П. Петров, Д. Трайков, Приложение на хипноанестезията при тонзилектомия, Ото-рино-ларингология, 1965-а, 2, 71—75.
406. Яковенко В. С., Психические эпидемии на религиозной почве, М., 1911, т. III и IV.
407. Янев Б., З. Иванова, Влияние на политехническото обучение върху реактивността на учениците, Изв. И-та физ. възп. и уч. хигиена, 1959, т. V.